Sexual and Reproductive Health Promotion in Latino Populations

Parteras, Promotoras y Poetas
Case Studies across the Americas

M. Idalí Torres
George P. Cernada
Editors

Baywood Publishing Company, Inc.
AMITYVILLE, NEW YORK

Baywood Publishing Company, Inc.
26 Austin Avenue
Amityville, NY 11701
(800) 638-7819
E-mail: baywood@baywood.com
Web site: baywood.com

Library of Congress Catalog Number: 2002043988
ISBN: 0-89503-276-7 (cloth)

Library of Congress Cataloging-in-Publication Data

Sexual and reproductive health promotion in Latino populations =
Parteras, promotoras y poetas : case studies across the Americas / M.
Idalí Torres, George P. Cernada, editors.
    p. cm.
 title: Parteras, promotoras y poetas.
Includes bibliographical references and index.
 ISBN 0-89503-276-7 (cloth)
 1. Reproductive health- -United States. 2. Hispanic Americans- -Health
and hygiene. 3. Reproductive health- -Latin America. 4. Hygiene,
Sexual- -United States. 5. Hygiene, Sexual- -Latin America. 6. Birth
control- -United States. 7. Birth control- -Latin America. I. Title:
Parteras, promotoras y poetas. II. Torres, M. Idalí, 1954- III. Cernada,
George Peter.

RG136.S475 2003
362.1'9665'008968- -dc21

                                                                            2002043988

Table of Contents

SECTION THREE
Ensuring Participation of the Community
in Program Planning, Implementation, and Evaluation . . . 215

Foreword

This new book is a first in bringing together a rich, multidisciplinary multicultural collection of case studies of public health, sexual and reproductive health education with U.S. Latino and Latin American populations.

Its authors provide fresh insight into innovative, culturally sensitive health promotion approaches based on qualitative research at the community level. Moreover, the intercepts of politics, culture, community and health are clearly drawn in this exciting work.

This collection of innovative, often alternative to the mainstream, chapters is must reading for cultural anthropologists as well as public health professionals, community development specialists, policy makers and social behavioral scientists. It also is a highly specific case reader for adoption in community health courses at all levels.

William A. Darity, Ph.D.
Professor/Dean Emeritus
School of Public Health and Health Sciences
University of Massachusetts Amherst

Preface

Sexual and Reproductive Health Promotion in Latino Populations—Parteras, Promotoras y Poetas: Case studies across the Americas emerged out of the need to understand the cultural landscape of sexual and reproductive health in U.S. Latino communities and Spanish speaking countries in Latin America and the Caribbean. In seeking to meet our own need for a multidisciplinary collection of case studies that brings together scholarship focused on the Latino experience across the geographical borders of the Americas, we also attempt to understand the evolution of lay health promoters, educators, and other cultural brokers in the Latino experience with reproductive and sexual health.

This collection of case studies is a testimony to the increase in scholarship and research for the development and evaluation of heterosexual and reproductive health programming directed to Spanish-speaking Latin Americans who have migrated to the United States. Results from the 2000 Census rank the United States as the "fifth largest Hispanic country" in the Americas. Demographic predictions support even more dramatic increases for decades to come. This population increase in conjunction with changes in economic policies and migration has made the demand for transnational perspectives in public health more significant for both academic and public health practice settings. In response, the number of academic multidisciplinary programs focused on Latin America, Latino, and Caribbean studies has increased. Academic professional organizations such as the Latin American Studies Association and the Puerto Rican Studies Association are not only gaining more visibility in public health forums but also actively seeking to include Latino health scholarship on their agendas. In addition, Latino Caucuses in the American Public Health Association, American Anthropological Association, and American Psychological Association have experienced significant growth in membership, and become more representative scientific sections. As a sign of progress, the times when national Latino advocacy organizations such as the National Council La Raza and the National Congress for Puerto Rican Rights were the only Latino health voices in Washington have lapsed into history supported now by stronger advocacy efforts of U.S. professional organizations and labor unions. Most recently, professional academic programs in public health and nursing in the United States have begun training partnerships with universities in Spanish speaking countries from Central America and the Caribbean. Furthermore, there is a continuous exchange of public health professionals between the United States and Latin American countries beyond the traditional professional conferences and research exchanges. Needless to say, public health training across the geographical boundaries of the Americas requires an understanding of transnational perspectives.

While health promotion scholarship addressing transnational relationships is still scarce, we believe that it warrants our attention. We hope this book plants the seed for specific inquiry by examining a collection of case-studies published in the *International Quarterly of Community Health Education* and focused primarily on research and intervention projects conducted in U.S. Latino communities and Spanish-Speaking Latin American and Caribbean countries, including Mexico, Guatemala, Peru, and Puerto Rico. Of the 19 case-studies selected for this book, only one was published before 1990 and is still very much relevant to current trends in public health at the community level. Articles were selected based on three criteria: location of the work described, central topic, and contribution to current debates in the field. Among those addressing the United States, there are several from California, two from Massachusetts, and single articles from Connecticut, Louisiana, and North Carolina. These articles emphasize research methodologies that utilize qualitative research strategies to the study of what are generally very personal and private topics: sexual behaviors associated with HIV and other sexually transmitted infections, sexual assault, cervical and breast cancer, first sexual intercourse, birth control, pregnancy, and birth-related problems. In addition, we selected articles about the most effective strategies for dissemination of Spanish language health information and prevention messages: media, theater, and literature (i.e., poetry). Finally, our selection process considered the needs of both the academic and professional settings. We view this collection as course reading material for students in the fields of social science (e.g., anthropology) and public health as well as those specializing in Latin American and Latino studies, and as a tool for health practitioners working with Latino populations in the United States and elsewhere.

Our introductory piece is an overview of the entire collection. It highlights the cultural landscape in which sexual and reproductive health behavior occurs and the evolution of lay health promoters who have successfully served as brokers between the people and the systems, including culture. Succeeding chapters by our collaborators deal with specific themes and are organized into three sections. Each section is comprised of a number of chapters preceded by a short summary of salient themes.

Section One: Researching Cultural Constructions of Sexual and Reproductive Health contains eight chapters addressing research of cultural constructions significant to the promotion of sexual and reproductive health in Latin America and U.S. Latino communities.

Section Two: Promoting Sexual and Reproductive Health Through Popular Culture has four chapters. It is the smallest, but richest, collection of specific methodologies to promote sexual and reproductive health, provide information, and disseminate prevention messages.

Section Three: Ensuring Participation of the Community in Program Planning, Implementation, and Evaluation presents seven chapters of methodologies to build personal and community capacity for meaningful and active community participation in sustaining strategies for the promotion of sexual and reproductive health in Latin American and U.S. Latino communities.

In general, chapters are a reflection of the diversity of available published materials. At times we are reminded of our insidious tendency to ascribe general labels to what we cannot explain about the "other(s)." At other times we have faith in our own capacities to honor people's experiences from where we situate ourselves in the current state of knowledge in our fields and place our own cultural scripts and perceptions. It is our hope that in the process of reconciling contradictions entangled in this collection of case studies, the readers feel inspired to pursue their own analysis.

Contributing to the shortage of transnational perspective in community health promotion and education is the inadequate access to advanced training to produce a significant cohort of Latino/Hispanic researchers and writers who can document and evaluate the numerous innovative and successful health promotion and field programs that have been and continue to be implemented on both continents. We suggest that the new generation of Latino scholars is perhaps in a more privileged position to chart a fresh agenda for community health research and interventions across the borders of the Americas, because regardless of their place of birth, their personal experience and cultural scripts can help us correct the short-sightedness of the past.

M. Idalí Torres
George P. Cernada
Editors

Cultural Landscapes and Cultural Brokers of Sexual and Reproductive Health in U.S. Latino and Latin American Populations

M. Idalí Torres
George P. Cernada

This literature review is an attempt to meet the demand for Latin American transnational perspectives of sexual and reproductive health that has surfaced as a direct result of the continuous flow of Spanish-speaking people across the borders of the American Continents. In the absence of true transnational studies, we are examining case studies from both sides of the U.S. border published by the *International Quarterly of Community Health Education* over the past decade, and suggest a future direction to address this area of study in the field of sexual and reproductive health promotion and education at the community level.

As a starting point, in community health promotion and education we must consider the broader context of quality of life indicators for Latin Americans and Latinos. Below the U.S. border, Latin American countries experience the enormous disparity and inequity in distribution of economic resources typical of the "developing" world [1]. The extent to which the so-called "developed" countries, through their greed, contribute to this economic disparity is well documented elsewhere [2]. High rates of infant mortality, maternal mortality, disability, hunger, and premature deaths in many Latin American countries continue to prevent large populations from fulfilling their potential and asserting their basic rights as human beings [3], including access to health education and services. Governments frequently have neglected their fiduciary duties to provide adequate sanitation, potable water supplies, and access to basic education and health care. The result has been unconscionably high infant mortality, maternal mortality, and communicable disease prevalence, much of which could be eliminated by low technology, low cost community-based health care and preventive services, and adequate provision of resources [4].

In North America, the U.S. "Latino" population also continues to experience inadequate attention in social and health resource allocation despite growing numbers and increasing level of need. The tally of the Year 2000 national census shows a significant increase in the numbers of people in the United States who self-identified as "Hispanics" [5]. In spite of, and perhaps even because of, the rapidly growing numbers of Latino/Hispanic/Spanish-speaking peoples in the United States, access to health care and preventive services is profoundly weighted against a large proportion of the Latino population in the United States as well as the bulk of the population in most countries in Latin America.

A glance at the statistics on health outcomes of sexual behavior gives a panorama of vulnerability to death and disability at an early age. Latin American and Latino women are disproportionally affected by HIV/AIDS [6-8] and other sexually transmitted infections (STIs) [9, 10], cervical cancer [11, 12], and negative pregnancy outcomes [12]. This is attested to by the infant mortality rates in Central America of 28 per 1,000 and South America of 29 with a range of a high of 61 in Bolivia to a low of 12 in Chile [13]. In the case of HIV, although only slightly more than one of ten U.S. residents in 1998, Latinos accounted for nearly two of ten AIDS cases reported to the Centers for Disease Control and Prevention [14].

In light of this disturbing panorama, the dearth of collected readings on community health education program planning, implementation, and evaluation limits the training of a new generation of practitioners and researchers. Since the *International Quarterly of Community Health Education* is one of a handful of U.S. academic journals that have consistently published articles from Latin American countries and U.S. Latino communities, it seems natural that we undertake the task of synthesizing what we have learned over the past decades from the journal and share our thoughts about future directions.

This introductory piece represents an overview of 19 articles on research and interventions conducted in Mexico, Guatemala, Peru, and Puerto Rico and the states of California, Massachusetts, Connecticut, Louisiana, and North Carolina. The essay is organized in two parts. Part 1 is devoted to the spheres of social influence in heterosexual and reproductive health behaviors: male partners, family, and other community structures. Part 2 describes the role of lay health providers and promoters (*parteras, promotoras, poetas*) as cultural brokers in the transmission of information, renegotiation of social and cultural resources in the community, and influence of behavior. Recommendations for a new generation of sexual and reproductive health research and interventions at the community level are presented at the end.

PART 1: CULTURAL LANDSCAPES FOR SEXUAL AND REPRODUCTIVE HEALTH IN LATIN AMERICA AND U.S. LATINO COMMUNITIES

Conceptualizing Culture

Culture is one of the most cited constructs in the health promotion and education literature focused on Latin America and U.S. Latino populations. It is persistently used as a descriptor of individuals, groups, and communities; as an explanation of behavioral differences, negative health outcomes, and statistical variance; as a barrier to preventive health care measures and provider-consumer communication; as a reason for intervention specificity and segmented targeting, and as a justification for failure to meet program objectives or broader public health agenda such as reduction of preventable health conditions. Culture has also been identified as an abundant component of the human capital available in communities to support the promotion of health and well-being. All of these attributions of culture often contain no specifics beyond the surface, pay little heed to how ideas develop and evolve into behavioral performance, and assume that changes in values, norms, and meaning at the macro-level of society are produced by formal education rather than indigenous funds of knowledge acquired from natural observation and imitation in the exchange of relationships among individuals and groups.

Generalizations and oversimplifications of the complexity embedded in the notion of culture at this time when rapid change is forcing people to transcend boundaries of ideology, language, class, gender, ethnicity, nationality, and geography to construct new cultural templates are obfuscating our search for new knowledge to address health problems. Added to this cultural tapestry are layers of political and economic conditions that are not always shared by all Latin Americans in their native or foreign lands, as is the case of the colonial experience for Puerto Rico and indigenous groups in Latin America. Furthermore, when migrants enter into contact with U.S. pluralistic culture, existing templates to reach exponential levels of complexity that are not always captured by the existing tools of public health research.

The study of reproductive and sexual health for education, policy, and other health promotion targets of intervention requires an understanding of the plethora of cultural formulations involved in the development of idea systems and behavioral performance and how these two dimensions are linked up in people's explanatory models used to conceive of, act on, and represent their expressions of sexuality and reproduction. Key to our analysis of the cultural systems for sexual decision making is the lacuna opened during transcultural exchanges that is often filled with new formulations of ideas and behavioral strategies through ongoing negotiation with the intermediate structures of the environment. Because culture as a social process is both tenacious and tenuous, we often observe among Latin

Americans and U.S. Latinos the "old" and the "new" strategically combined in a third way that gives continuation of their history in the culture of origin by embracing cognitive symbols and language that affirm collective identity while meeting the current conditions of the immediate environments by negotiating other social standards [15, 16].

Under this fluidness in the culture of the mesosystem of the Latino experience, social power becomes a function of human agency and the capacity to penetrate community structures. Relevant to this discussion is the suggestion of Minkler and her coauthors that as health educators and health promoters we must depart from the hierarchical dominant models of power analysis to discover opportunities for influence and change in communities [17]. Two examples in this book representing different regions of the Americas suggest a reassessment of women's decision-making power. Co-authored by Bertrand, Ward, and Pauc, Chapter 1 reports on the differences between the descriptions of sexual pleasure obtained from Guatemalan Mayan women for their study and those provided by earlier ethnographic accounts [18]. The women's willingness to share their experiences of enjoyment and pleasure is testimony to the evolution of cultural construction that is not frequently covered in the literature. In the following chapter, Gil presents the differences in sexual negotiation power between women in Puerto Rico and women who have migrated to California from Mexico and Central America [19]. More attention to new constructions of power in gender relations significant to the lives of Latin Americans and Latinos will help test old assumptions about the distribution of social influence in dyads, families, and broader community structures. It is critical that we do not undermine our own efforts to promote sexual and reproductive health education by operating against the evolving cultural and social systems instead of seeking opportunities for influence within the natural flow of change to greater extends.

Cultural Data Gathering Techniques

Searching for the best opportunities for sexual and reproductive health promotion and education across the boundaries of Latin America and Latino communities in the United States entails research approaches with methodologies that achieve the level of comprehensiveness of the "complex whole." In our case, this Taylorian staple of the anthropology legacy refers to the socio-cultural landscape in which expressions of human sexuality are learned and shared through social relations. As Gil reminds us in Chapter 2, "for cogent health education, specifics are necessary" [19]. Specificity in human sexuality can only be found in the interactions between cultural systems (i.e., morality), psychological factors, and biological needs that influence gender and sexual behavioral performance in people's natural forms of social organization.

The collection of works in this book includes several in-depth studies conducted by anthropologists and other social scientists. Among the research methodologies utilized to gather cultural data are: 1) focus groups with Quiché-speaking male and female Mayas in Guatemala, with women who have migrated from Central America and Mexico to North Carolina and California; 2) life history interviews with female adolescents from second or third generation Central Americans and Mexicans residing across the border in the state of California and some of their male partners; and 3) in-depth focused thematic interviewing sessions with breastfeeding mothers in Lima and Peru and Puerto Rican women in Connecticut, Massachusetts, California, and in their native island of Puerto Rico. Together, these chapters suggest that methods of qualitative research are more successful than quantitative ones in capturing people's experience with sexual and repro-ductive decision making because of the abundance of data to decipher cultural meaning and the circumstances beneath variation in sexual behavior. As a body of literature, it highlights the interpersonal processes of social relations relevant to sexual and reproductive health promotion.

Reflecting the general literature on sexual and reproductive health promotion and community education, the collaborators of this book focused mainly on women's interpersonal relationships with: their sexual male partners; family members and other significant people in their lives; and community structures involved in the economy, education, religion, and other social influentials. Only two studies include adolescent male participants. One of these also includes adult males, and there is a sole chapter addressing the participation of gay men in sexual health promotion.

Women's Relationships with Male Partners

The role of men in women's sexual decision-making and negotiation receives considerable attention by the collaborators of this book. Writers of the Latin American experience found that gender interpersonal dynamics determined com-munication with male partners and others and the frequency and circumstances of sexual intercourse and perceptions about contraception technologies. Among Guatemalan Quiché Mayan participants in the study described in Chapter 1 by Bertrand, Ward, and Pauc, men influence the frequency and circumstances in which sex happens [18]. For example, women's refusal to accept men's request for sex when they are under the influence of alcohol results in sexual coercion and other forms of violence. However, the study from Puerto Rico presented by Gil in the second chapter shows a different experience in another part of Latin America [19]. Participants in his Puerto Rican research project characterized their sexual negotiation process as a reciprocal relationship in which both women and men shared decision-making related to the initiation and conditions in which the sexual encounter happened. Whether or not this new gender dynamics is associated with the higher education attainment, increased participation in the labor force and access to structures of political power that women in Puerto Rico have attained during the past 20 years, or the influence of the more fluid gender roles of the

United States, or both is a question for future research. Indeed, the high degrees of autonomy in negotiating sexual matters shown in Gil's study distinguished women in Puerto Rico from the experience of all other Latin American women described in this book.

Some other areas of reproductive health in which the role of Latin American men is prominent are discussed by Oliveros and her collaborators [20], and Rice [21] in Chapters 5 and 8 respectively. The team of researchers led by Oliveros found that Peruvian husbands represented one of the sources of influence in their wives' decision to continue lactation or not during pregnancy. Rice's literature summary reports that men in some Latin American and Caribbean countries oppose contraceptive technological barriers because they fear marital infidelity. Her assessment that limited sex education for adolescents stems from the belief that information becomes a motivator of "sexual promiscuity" is a common theme in all the chapters that include youth. In contrast to this belief are reports that adolescents are engaging in sexual relationships [18] (in Chapter 1, 3, and 8) and in some cases in selling sex for money as described by Burgos and her colleagues [10] in Chapter 7.

Similar patterns of gender dynamics involved in sexual negotiation were found in some of the studies conducted among Mexican and Central American women in the United States. The Gil [19] and Erickson [22] chapters reported a more significant role of the males in seeking, requesting, or initiating sex. There are two chapters addressing the utilization of preventive services, Chapter 4 authored by Wilcher and her research team [11] and Chapter 15 by Guendelman and Witt [23] which found that the attitudes of Mexican and Central American migrant men toward women's pelvic organs contributed to their female partners' underutilization of Pap screenings and prenatal care respectively. The reluctance of U.S. Latina women to expose their "private parts" during pelvic exams required for these preventive measures has been attributed to culture. (We will further comment on the cultural context of these findings below in the section devoted to religious structures.)

Most studies presented in this book agree about the significance of gendered cultural scripts in the perception and use of male condoms as a technology for sexual protection. Notwithstanding these similarities, Chapter 16 by Torres and her team suggests that gender roles are in transition in segments of young Puerto Rican women residing in Western Massachusetts, particularly among those who obtained the cooperation of their male partners to use the female condom during a trial period [24]. When considered in light of Gil's study in Puerto Rico [19] (which documents leadership roles of women in sexual decision making), these findings are suggestive of the need to research decision-making patterns of Puerto Rican women across the Atlantic Ocean. Recent HIV intervention research suggest that Latina women are making strides in their efforts to communicate about sex and sexual protection with their partners and other influentials [25].

As a body of literature, the articles and chapters reviewed above present a picture of a male dominance in sexual decision-making and negotiation that hinders women's ability for self-protection. While there is a small number of males educated about sexuality and sexual health, they engage in sex at a very early age, have more sexual partners during their life time and multiple partners simultaneously, are more likely to have unprotected sex with infected partners and be the carrier of infections to women, and make many decisions about the couple's sexual behaviors with very little information about potential negative health outcomes. At issue here is that the public health response assumes that progress in reducing the incidence and impact of sexual health problems depends on women's success in negotiating safe sex with their partners and places the emphasis on strengthening behavioral capacity of women at the individual level. It is not difficult to see that an unintended repercussion of the exclusion of male partners from health education and health promotion research and intervention projects [25] is the establishment of yet another layer of social support to sustain the cultural constructions that guide women to assume not only the primary responsibility for sexual health protection, but also the burden of negative consequences.

Women's Relationships with Family and Significant Others (Beyond Their Male Partners)

The family (*familia*) continues to be the most powerful social system in the communities described by the collaborators of this book. At the heart of the Latin American family are the values of motherhood and childbearing that preserve the continuation of the structure and its social functions. While women are venerated for their roles as mothers, they are expected to assume the main responsibility for the entire family, even during pregnancy. In Chapter 8 Rice asserts that Latin American women often experience malnutrition and high morbidity during pregnancy due to the multiple tasks they perform to maintain the quality of life of other members of the family, including eating after serving everybody else [21]. However, Chapter 5 by Oliveros and her coauthors shows that the influence of Peruvian mothers in decision-making can be situational and conditional to the type of relationship and the level of persuasion of the others around them [20]. While they were swayed by the attitudes and opinions of family and significant others about breastfeeding in their decision to continue breastfeeding or not during pregnancy, occasionally they gave more weight to their own beliefs and perceptions about health of their toddler, fetus, and pregnancy than to the recommendations (or expectations) of significant others.

Data presented in Chapter 1 by Bertrand and co-writers [18] about mating is consistent with other studies found in the literature and shows that in most Latin American countries there is a tradition of marriage in the adolescence stage for both females and males that is generally accompanied by high fertility rates. This, according to Erickson's chapter, presents a conflict with social expectation in the United States where teen pregnancy frequently happens out of wedlock and without the social and economic supports of the family that extend into the community as in Latin America [22]. Indeed, the U.S. Latino family structure has evolved from the traditional extended family to what Cordoza-Clayton calls in Chapter 18 a "nuclear and interdependent kinship structure with multiple and mobile networks," referring to the specific experience of California [28]. The diversity of constellations in the structure of the Latino family can also be seen in Puerto Rican communities in the eastern part of the United States as well as on the island of Puerto Rico where there is an emerging matrifocal structure according to recent anthropological work [16]. While there is vast evidence of family values as a strength of the culture, they also can represent a barrier to education efforts aimed at promoting sexual health in families with non-sexual adults and other non-traditional unions as in the case of gay men in Mexico described by Carrillo in Chapter 19 [26].

Regardless of the structural form, its social function of mutual support, reciprocity and loyalty of the *familia* is deeply ingrained into the identity of Latinos in the United States, and serves as the main context for the transmission of cultural ideology and preserver of the ties with the country of origin and associates elsewhere in the world. The significance of the family in U.S. Latino communities is noticeable in the names, orientation, and objectives of the projects described in this book. Chapter 17 by Buchanan and his coauthors [27] describe the decision of program participants to select a name resembling the Puerto Rican family tree of "cepa" (mother) and her "cepitas" (daughters) to give symbolic meaning to their HIV prevention work in the City of Holyoke, Massachusetts. Two other examples of successful models of community interventions built on the interception of culture, health, and social systems, *El Centro Familiar* and *Padres* and *Madres,* are presented in Chapter 18 by Cardoza-Clayton and coauthors [28]. An important consideration in the examination of this triology is that culture is rooted in social institutions beyond the family as we discuss below.

Women's Relationships with Macrostructures of the Economy, Education, Religion, and other Social Influential Sectors

Urban community structures for generation of income and other material resources required to meet basic human needs force adolescent and adult women who are unable to find employment into sex behaviors that place them at high risk for HIV/ STIs, sexual violence, as well as drug addiction and depression. Chapter 19 by Carrillo describes situations in which women in Mexico are coerced into sexual intercourse without a condom for more money or in exchange for drugs to sustain their addiction [26]. In Chapter 6, Romero-Gaza and her anthropologist colleagues [9] provide a vivid description of how women who migrate from Latin American countries, primarily Puerto Rico, become entangled in a progressive continuum pattern of drug selling, drug using, and sex trading as a means of economic survival in the city of Hartford. The narratives in the chapters mentioned above illustrate the role of government policies for welfare reform and job training in sustaining the contributing factors to women's health problems associated with sexual behavior and drug use. Like the Puerto Rican women in Hartford, the adolescent who sold sex for money in Puerto Rico described by Burgos and coauthors in Chapter 7 had limited access to the health education, STI screening procedures, primary care, and drug treatment services [10].

While discussing health behaviors among Latino adolescents in California, Erickson [22] (Chapter 3) and Chávez and Dorfman [29] (Chapter 12) identified unprotected sex and violence as adaptive responses to long-term economic scarcity in their communities. Inaccessibility to resources appears to be a contributing factor to unprotected sex among Latina adolescents who become mothers. Stress induced by social conditions associated with chronic economic poverty is expressed in violent behaviors at home and outside. In their chapter, Chávez and Dorfman assert that mortality and morbidity statistics show that Latina women experience the greatest impact of domestic violence in the form of physical and mental abuse in their communities. In this context, the authors are not surprised by the high numbers of female-headed families in Latino communities.

Education systems have different standards according to the social characteristics of the population. In the Guatemalan-Mayan context, schools provide more access to sexual health education to males. According to Bertrand and coauthors in Chapter 1, Mayan boys knew more, had more access to information, and spoke more about the body and sexuality at school than the girls of the same age that expressed more interest in these topics [18]. Sexual health education is also restricted by the state in many other ways. Carrillo's chapter [19] provides an example of the impact of the politics of state funding distribution for HIV prevention on community groups that were assuming the primary responsibility for the outreach work in most vulnerable communities in Mexico City [26].

Opinion leaders are key components of social influence for the adoption and preservation of behavior. In health promotion and education we need them on our side to encourage, model, persuade, and support change. Bertrand and coauthors found that social pressures of older men in the community who expected young men to act on their sexual desires contributed to sex initiation at an early age. However, some of the same older men who were community leaders rejected the idea of sex education or discussing sexuality in public forums because they believe that it "stimulates [youth] interest in sex" [18]. However, in the *Cuidaremos* project described by Lorig and Garcia Walters [30] in Chapter 14, opinion leaders were *Chicana* women with extensive social connections in the community, who served as planners and facilitators of a group-based breast health education program.

At an even broader sphere of the cultural landscape is the notion that "bad" sexual behaviors such as extramarital sex were influenced by the "dominant" culture *(Latino)* and not necessarily emerging from their own group (Quiché Mayan). Despite the interpretation that we give to this finding, it does raise a question about the influence of colonialism in gender scripts. While there is vast documentation of the effect of Spanish Colonialism on reproductive health related behaviors, attempts to understand the influence of other dominant cultures present in contemporary Latin America and their impact on gendered culture are few. Indeed, colonialism and its by-product dependency are identified as structural barriers to healthy communities. Coauthors of Chapter 17 present it as an important contributing factor to risk-taking behaviors that deserve attention from health promoters and educators working in HIV prevention programs in Puerto Rican communities [27]. The combination of colonialism with exclusion from structures of formal economy, gender inequity, and ethnic discrimination is a powerful template for vulnerability to sexual health problems among Latina women.

Various chapters in this book address religion's multiple functions in the development of the ideology that gives meaning to sexuality, reproduction, contraception, abortion, and birth. Religious systems shape beliefs and patterned behaviors associated with human sexuality. Perhaps the greatest effect of religion is in the cognitive frameworks of morality that guide sexual and reproductive behavior. Bertrand and coauthors tell us in Chapter 1 that Guatemalan Mayas believe that sexual desire and pleasure is part of the legacy that God transferred to their ancestors and in turn, to their generation [19]. But God's blessing is for married women because those unmarried feel "ashamed" of their sexual activities. Related to this dichotomy is Rice's observation in Chapter 8 that religion's framing of sexuality as a mechanism for human procreation raises moral dilemmas for women who do not want to become pregnant [21]. The psychological impact of violating religion-established moral premises results in feelings of *verguenza* associated with a combination of shame, guilt, and embarrassment described in the literature [11-12]. As mentioned earlier, and discussed in Chapters 4 and 15, it is believed that these feelings prevent Latinas from seeking preventive services that require health care providers, especially males, to observe and touch pelvic organs such as the vagina. In addition, they serve to sustain views of *fatalismo* or powerlessness associated with negative health outcomes and their own ability to adopt new behaviors to protect their own health. This example of the relationship of culture and behavior highlights the significance of powerful cultural brokers who often can simultaneously negotiate the cultural multi-layered template for the protection of sexual and reproductive health through social relationships and serve as provider and promoter of health in the community.

PART 2: LAY PROVIDERS AND PROMOTERS OF SEXUAL AND REPRODUCTIVE HEALTH AND THEIR INFLUENCE IN U.S. LATINO COMMUNITIES

In Latin America, the most powerful traditional cultural brokers in the promotion of sexual and reproductive health in Latin America are *parteras* and *comadronas* (midwives or Traditional Birth Attendants (TBAs)) and *promotoras de la salud* (health promoters). Less known in the United States are the contributions of the *trabajadores de la cultura* (cultural workers) to health promotion and health education in Latin America. Poets, musicians, actors, and others who promote health through cultural platforms have a long history of disseminating family planning information through performance in the streets as well as in mass media channels. The HIV epidemic in U.S. communities is reclaiming that legacy for public campaigns aimed at preventing HIV/STIs in Latino communities.

Parteras, Comadronas, and other Traditional Birth Attendants (TBAS)

Chapters 1 and 13 of this book highlight the survival of the continuing evolution of lay midwifery in Latin America, a health profession regarded as the oldest in womankind. While researching sexual practices among Quiché-speaking Mayan women, Bertrand, Ward, and Pauc found a predilection for midwives not only for delivery purposes but also during pregnancy for prenatal care services instead of trained medical doctors and nurses in hospitals. Women in the Mayan communities, they observed in Chapter 1, "prefer to use the [prenatal] services of a local midwife who is a well-known and trusted member of the community who, moreover, respects the traditions concerning the birth of a child" [18]. This finding is a testimony of contemporary views about TBAs. By all accounts, lay midwifery interventions are traditionally designed to ensure continuity of care—before, during, and after birth—and meet social, psychological, physical, and spiritual needs of the mother. This support is extended to the father, siblings, and even members of the extended family who are involved in what it is a family-centered social event. There seems to be no systematic, prescribed role for their interventions but rather a person-specific approach in a supportive and intimate environment in which women share decision making of their care. It is precisely this highly personal relationship that gives lay midwives access to the kind of information necessary for needs assessment and places them in a position of influencing health-related behavior in their communities, and, therefore, to impact public health outcomes.

As in other continents, in Latin America the indigenous training of midwives or TBAs happens through longer periods of apprenticeship with senior empirical practitioners who posses extensive expertise in natural methods of diagnosis and healing (i.e., body massage, binding of the abdomen, herbal remedies, aroma-therapy, and even how to prevent a breech birth) during parturition. However, not until they are considered older and in some cases have become grand-mothers, which in some countries can be in their 30s, do midwives assume their role and begin their solo practice [31, 32]. By then they are well-known and respected by others, a prerequisite for fulfilling their function as chain-linkers in the social support structures of their communities. Because they are indigenous to their communities and share many of the same lay theories and explanatory models for disease causation, risk management, and treatment as the rest of the women in their communities, they are viewed as partners rather than providers. While the embeddedness of their role into the cultural fabric of their communities facilitates their management of normal pregnancies, in some cases it jeopardizes their ability to incorporate biomedical skills and technologies into their practices, and thus lessens their potential impact on reproductive health outcomes.

Notwithstanding that TBAs generally come from segments of the population with low rates of literacy, economic resources, and access to primary care, formal training efforts in Latin America by international health organizations during the 1970s and 1980s succeeded in building the capacity of *parteras* to use basic biomedical technology that enabled them to serve as the first step in the primary health care system and link their communities with local clinics and regional hospitals. Chapter 13 of this book illustrates one example from Guatemala. O'Rouke's research shows that contemporary Guatemalan TBAs not only referred pregnant women at risk for negative pregnancy outcomes to the hospital but they were also trained to administer oxytocin, a synthetic labor inducer [32]. This example of biomedical interventions reflects a level of receptiveness to new knowledge and practices that is a characteristic of the evolution of the midwifery trade throughout the past centuries. Yet, in this same study, O'Rouke found that training midwives about the potential negative consequences of two common practices during early stages of labor—the traditional practice of coaching women to bear down to push and the biomedical practice of adminis-trating oxytocin—produced minimal change in these practices. Given the adaptive experience of lay midwives historically, one could theorize that the distinct cultural orientations in the development of these two practices may have produced the diminished effect of the training. Implicit here is the notion that no change happens without tensions between perceptions of biomedical domination and the local culture that have successfully sustained the role identity of TBAs as indigenous throughout our history. In addition, transferring new technology and practices from one culture to another not only requires an assessment of the negative impact on health outcomes [33], but also continuity of training and support that has not always been available in most Latin American countries [34].

Promotoras de la salud

While midwives, by virtue of their historical role in their communities, have played a significant role in providing health information, advice and in performing other key health promotion activities, most lay health *promotoras* of reproductive and sexual health in Latin America do not have either empirical or formal training in midwifery. Lay health promoters generally share the same socioeconomic characteristics as their collaborators, TBAs. Both are viewed as natural resources of social support in their communities, volunteer to receive formal training on first aid to diagnose and treat symptomatology for common illness, and function as community health educators supporting primary care systems in government and non-governmental organizations in their communities. Although in some countries *promotoras* receive a more broader training in public health sanitation and nutrition and work under much more supervision from professionals than *parteras*, they also are trained to provide women's reproductive and sexual health education to members of their communities. This trend appears to have continued in the 1990s at least in non-governmental organizations in Mexico that are training both *parteras* and *promotoras* to join other health workers in the implementation of HIV-related programming directed to women in their homes [35]. In addition to HIV and other sexually transmitted infections, *promotoras* are becoming involved in other areas of women's health promotion such as interfamilial violence and social issues affecting general quality of life in their own communities [36]. As Cardoza Clayson and her colleagues suggest in Chapter 18, the long history of *promotoras* sustaining the rural primary care systems in most Latin American countries is being recognized as a cost-effective method to reach underserved segments of the Latino population in the United States.

The role of *promotoras* as agents of social change in their communities is not new and can be traced to the sociopolitical activism generated by popular movements during the 1960s. The seeds sprouted during the 1970s literacy and land reform campaigns in Latin America with community health education components that promoted health as a human right and utilized Freirian methodologies. In what appears to be a reciprocal relationship, lay workers in the health sector extended their activities to the promotion of social change and economic development [37]. These endeavors produced the kind of social change orientation not found in previous generations of Latin American lay health workers. Since then *promotoras* have been key to the integrated development programs aimed at accomplishing the dual goal of public health and economic development in many parts of Latin America. Despite the efforts of the professional elite to minimize their natural role in promoting self-reliance and community strengths, *promotoras* have become a major force in health advocacy for the large number of rural Latin Americans who are disconnected from community structures of primary care help and support.

Approaching health and health care holistically, and relying on mutuality and collaborative relationships, *promotoras* frequently mobilize their community resources to meet people's health needs on a daily basis. For this reason, said Oliveros and her colleagues in their study of social influence in Peru presented in Chapter 5, these health workers are revered and highly influential in their communities [20].

Like many other constructions of Latin American culture brought by migrants to the United States, the traditional personal approach to pregnancy and other areas of reproductive and sexual health represented by *parteras* and *promotoras* became an unfulfilled expectation. Describing prenatal care utilization among Mexican and Central American women residing above the Mexican border in the state of California, Guendelman and Witt [23] (Chapter 15) reflected on how the medicalization of pregnancy and the professionalization of service providers are inconsistent with the experience of most Latin Americans in their countries of origin where pregnancy is viewed as a normal healthy state in the life of women which does not necessarily require special medical care but very personal interventions by trusted members of their community. Public health approaches are seeking to meet this need for social support among Latinas in the United States with community outreach and education workers, which include no birth attendant but a person attending to recreate the symbolism of the lost relationship with the *parteras*. One example found in the anthropological literature is *Proyecto Comadrona, a* community intervention to reduce negative pregnancy outcomes among Puerto Rican women living in the city of Hartford, Connecticut during the 1980s by utilizing indigenous outreach workers to promote prenatal care utilization in early stages of pregnancy [38]. Guendelman and Witt's chapter highlights the importance of reaching Latina pregnant women by health workers from their own community who help navigate the systems of prenatal care [23]. However, most medical institutions serving Latinos have intensified their efforts to reclaim the practice of midwifery for economic reasons, primarily as a cost-saving strategy for healthy pregnancies in birthing centers and obstetrical-gynecological services. These new generations of U.S. midwives are trained in universities with a medical curriculum, have a national organization for credentialing and professional certifications, are controlled by reimbursement policies of health insurance companies, and frequently have no cultural or linguistic capacity to communicate effectively with Latinas. Consequently, they are failing to take advantage of this cultural opportunity and recreate the kind of personal relationships that women develop with their *parteras* and *comadronas* below the U.S.-Mexican border. Instead, what is obvious to those observing the public health system of prenatal care provision in this country is that the only supportive relationships pregnant Latina women are more likely to establish in their encounters in the clinical settings is with the lay health workers who are indigenous to their community and share the same highly personal approach to social relationships.

Several chapters in this book present *personalismo* and *familismo* as requirements for successful provider-consumer relationships in Latino communities
and the basis for the potential contribution of *promotoras* to improving health
outcomes in the U.S. Latino population. Cardoza Clayson and her writing partners
in Chapter 18 noted that California-based *promotoras,* like their counterparts in
Latin American countries, work in communities to make health services accessible
to those unreachable by system structures because of cultural and class differences. An interesting insight from their description is the underlying belief of
the U.S. health care system that the *promotoras* model will adapt to the existing
bureaucratic structures and in some cases become part of the feeding or casefinding activities. This, of course will undermine their valuable natural role as
educators, advocates, and promoters of family-oriented approaches to health and
health care. Among the assumptions of the U.S. system that are not holding true, as
the authors so eloquently assert, is the expectation that *promotoras* will eliminate
all the access barriers presented by the existing structure of health and human
services. In addition, the perception of a cost-saving strategy to have Spanish
language capacity without having to hire professional staff to serve the needs
of Latinos also is not proving to be correct.

Reductionism in the role of the *promotoras* as community builders through
sustenance of social relationships is the result of biomedical models of health
promotion and community health education guided by organizational cultures
oriented toward individual behavior rather than social change. Consequently,
programs are naturally disconnected from the context of people's actions and
their collective experiences with the social, cultural, economic, and political
conditions. Addressing the limitations of biomedical approaches to health promotion, several chapters in this book present and/or suggest community development
interventions that nurture the development of critical consciousness as a human
capacity to take control over one's health and well-being. In the words of Minkler
and Wallerstein, this process "comes only through social analysis of conditions
and people's role in changing those conditions" [39] and it is aimed at building
personal and collective capacity. Some of our collaborators on this book believe
that the most appropriate theoretical framework and methodology to engage
people in their own course of action for capacity building are Freire's models for
popular education and popular culture interventions that have been tested since
the 1970s in Latin America and other developing regions of the world. A common
critique of these models is their inability to produce immediate results as often
expected by program evaluators and funders who have very little understanding
that the Freirian methodologies view behavior as a human response to environmental conditions developed over long periods of time and are aimed at long-term
results. It is in this context that we consider the skepticism about program
outcomes expressed by Gil in Chapter 2 [19] and the frustration with the super-
ficiality of some education interventions under the claim of Freirian guidance
that Carrillo [26] raises in Chapter 19.

Poetas and Other Promoters of Health through Culture

Supported by the ancient Latin American tradition of lyrical improvisations by street *trovadores* (troubadours), *cantores* (street singers), and *declamadores* (poetry reciters) to problematize social and economic conditions surrounding their lives and the writings of Paulo Freire on cultural action and conscientization [40], Latin American health promoters have been acting on the meaning of the common expression in Spanish, *la cultura cura* (the culture heals), a symbol of the therapeutic effects attributed to music, poetry, and drama throughout centuries. Sometimes called theater of the oppressed and aimed at promoting social change among the most disenfranchised segments of the population, improvizations take place in the street and other public spaces as dramatic representations of people's daily lives and are often interactive motivating spectators. Valente and his colleagues in Chapter 10 describe an example of how this type of street theater is used to address misinformation about family planning in a Peruvian community [41]. As in many other Latin American countries, Peru has a long history of street theater for popular education and recreation. These popular artistic productions reflect the sentiments and feelings of many individual members of a community in one single narrative, transforming personal cognitive maps into public expressions of the collective experience in which spectators can see themselves, their own drama, and the possibilities for change in the performance of the protagonists. Indeed, as Valente and coauthors assert, street theater is a valuable icebreaker to initiate public conversations about health-related topics and to promote new behavioral strategies while appealing to people's aesthetic values and desire for entertainment [41]. It is this kind of soul connectiveness that gives meaning to cultural identity that may have contributed to their finding in Peru that women were more likely to learn family planning information from street performance and act on the information than other members of the community.

The research teams led by Valente [41] and McDonald [42] suggest that street plays, poetry, and other art expressions of popular culture can effectively communicate information about very sensitive and very personal topics such as sexuality and sexual health in a context that is attuned to people's understanding of the human experience in their surrounding world. Other examples from Latin America and the Caribbean support the potential of popular culture for HIV-related work for community health education [43].

Expressions of Latin American people's art transcended the boundaries across the Americas. Indeed, manifestations of shared cultural, linguistic, and mystical histories of the community produce the kind of solidarity irreproducible by any other human interaction in Latin America. In Chapter 9, McDonald and her colleagues remind us of the long and rich history in U.S. Latino communities of the development of lyrics for music, poetry, and drama to promote social consciousness and advocacy for social action [42]. In Chapter 12, Chávez and

Dorfman list several plays (i.e., love and pain, *pesadilla familiar*) aimed at preventing domestic violence that were observed while examining Spanish television news in California [29]. Today it is not uncommon to see artistic expressions of health promotion that make it from the streets to the television and radio. Some examples are the Welfare poets in New York City and the *Pleneros de la Salud* in Chicago. Local poets, musicians, and actors use their cultural platforms to communicate messages about HIV prevention and sexual health protection in Spanish. Communicating information about sexuality, sexual health, and sexual health protection in a context that is attuned to people's understanding of the social experience in their surrounding world is a challenge that artistic expressions of popular culture can effectively address without the social stigma of other public forums.

Notwithstanding the cultural distinctions underlying the social function of mass media as a vehicle for popular but subordinate cultures in Latin America versus a vehicle for the popular dominant culture in the United States [44], most Spanish-speaking *locutores y reporteros* (radio and TV broadcasters) in the United States continue the legacy of media advocacy. According to Chávez and Dorfman in Chapter 12, their high sense of social responsibility make Latino broadcasters natural supporters of media campaigns designed to increase knowledge and awareness about health related topics and/or to mobilize residents for community health actions [29]. Within this context, it is not surprising that the authors observed that *reporteros* of Spanish language television news in California provide more in-depth coverage of the social implications of events than similar programming in English.

Two chapters in this book offer examples of media interventions linked to telephone help lines. Chapters 11 and 19 describe the combination of mass media and interactive telephone lines to promote health and provide information. In Chapter 19 Carrillo presents an HIV prevention government-sponsored media campaign linked to a hotline in Mexico City that included radio and TV commercials and printed materials (i.e., billboards, posters, and pamphlets) in public spaces to promote the use of condoms and sexual health protection behaviors [26]. The success of the campaign was evident in the 3,000 calls received by the hotline each month. Non-governmental organizations (NGOs) partnered with radio broadcasters to produce additional culturally specific messages in the form of *radio-novela* (radio broadcast soap opera) that was reinforced by community outreach workers who provided personal contact for direct information and counseling and access to condoms at the street level.

Spanish language radio interventions also have been conducted in Latino communities located on the east and west coasts of the United States. Anderson and Huerta in Chapter 11 describe a radio intervention tied to a telephone help line for interactive counseling and advice called *La Linea de la Salud* targeted at two metropolitan areas, Washington, DC-Baltimore, MD and San Francisco-Oakland, CA., where immigrants from El Salvador, Peru, Bolivia, and Mexico have settled [45]. The Spanish radio programming worked simultaneously with a telephone help line to provide information on the prevention, control, and treatment of cancer and other chronic conditions. For immigrants, particularly those undocumented, who are isolated from other structures of communication, radio health programming not only contributes to increase awareness, but also serve as a mechanism for persuading, modeling, and reinforcing behavioral changes. The film developed by the *Cuidaremos* Project described by Loring and Garcia-Walters [30] in Chapter 14 is an example of a media product that approaches breast health education within the context of Latino cultural norms and expectations by placing basic information about self-breast examination in women's daily personal experiences with their health and health care.

SUGGESTIONS FOR THE NEW GENERATION OF RESEARCH AND INTERVENTIONS

In closing this introduction, we propose that the new generation of sexual and reproductive health research addresses transnational factors affecting partnerships or couples rather than continue to examine the experience of a single partner in the dyad on each side of the U.S. border. Such an agenda must be conceptualized within the spheres of influence targeted by ecological models, aimed at addressing the culture of social relations in Latino communities across the borders of the Americas through popular education and popular culture methodologies and brokers such as *promotoras de la salud.*

Public health and social science's fixation with "machismo" as an explanation for cultural and behavioral expressions of sexuality by U.S. Latinos and Latin American men, albeit very little research, deserves a critical examination. The cultural construction of manliness in Latin America represents an amalgamation of cultural scripts, norms, skills, and behaviors that is far from static. Understanding it will be to the benefit of our goals in sexual and reproductive health. There was a time when it was important to focus on women only to address specific research questions and reexamine theoretical frameworks developed without the female experience and perspective. Today we have volumes of data and text on women's experience with sexual decision-making and negotiation and our greatest challenge is our limited understanding of a *couple's* relations with each other and the structures in the other spheres of social influence. Progress in reproductive and sexual health protection in U.S. Latino and Latin American populations depends on how well we can understand and influence change in cultural scripts for learning to perform gender-specific behaviors and for transmitting gender ideology. A circular multi-level social ecological model [46, 47] that places a woman at the center of spheres of primary social relationships with her male partner, the family, and other social structures and captures the multidimensional interaction of influence on individual and collective behavior is recommended as the best strategy to achieve the level of comprehensiveness of the "complex whole" in sexual and reproductive health in U.S. Latino and Latin American settings.

Similar to the arena of research, we need a new generation of comprehensive interventions aimed at engaging Latinas/os and Latin American women and men in a process of reflection on the acquisition and transmission of knowledge related to the human body and sexuality. In this type of intervention, examination of cultural constructions (ideology, symbols, codes, meaning, and context of power and social control) must be based on the premise that people are actors in their own education process. The goal is to build the capacity of *promotoras de la salud* and promoters of health through cultural manifestations to thin the layers of the cultural template sustaining values and symbols that prevent the adoption of protective sexual and reproductive health behaviors. The best example of this in this collection of case studies is the culture of pelvic organs as a barrier for preventive measures for negative pregnancy outcomes, STIs, and cervical cancer. Pelvic organs, especially the vagina, are one of the most powerful taboo symbols of the legacy left by the Spanish Catholic colonization process in Latin America that still nourishes patriarchal systems of human organization that we see reflected in some of the gender scripts presented in this book. In a culture of highly social connectiveness and tenuous delineations of personal privacy, the restriction of the pelvic organs to selected males serves to maintain gender differences when other distinctions of personal privacy are disappearing. Restrictions give privilege to female body parts involved in human reproduction and access to body organs that sexual prudery and modesty have traditionally restricted to a private relationship, and in turn elevate the social status of men in the community. This helps to explain why, since pre-colonial times, Latin American women involved in birth attendance (*parteras*) have been attributed sacred powers that facilitate fertility and procreation among human beings [48] and why their significant roles have survived to the present time as discussed earlier. That in this gendered cultural context, pregnancy and birth are outcomes of the function of the vagina may also help to explain Rice's finding that Latin American and Caribbean men determine the number of pregnancies a woman has despite the fact that she shoulders the primary responsibility for having and raising the children [21].

Popular education and popular culture interventions that bring together several theories aimed at human liberation, self-reliance, and self-determination can contribute to thinning the cultural symbolic value of the "private parts" for social control of women's health behaviors in the Latin American and U.S. Latino cultures. Freirian approaches are suggested because of their strong foundations in cultural deconstruction and cognitive decolonization in Latin American contexts and emphasis on building the capacity of community residents to assume leadership in actions directed to changing social and cultural landscapes. Building personal and community capacity for *promotoras de la salud* to facilitate education processes that digest information about the cultural landscapes of sexual behavior combined with opportunities for engagement in popular cultural activities must be the first step in any community health intervention aimed at changing interpersonal relationships in the dyad, family, and socio-cultural structures that place both women and men at risk for sexual and reproductive health problems.

It is important to remember that central to this agenda is our ability to increase people's understanding of the role of culture in the causality of health problems, as well as in the possibility for changing the conditions that affect health and well being, and of building capacity to take action at the personal and community levels. We believe that interventionists, by utilizing popular culture methodologies, will maximize their resources to reach those who have traditionally been isolated from, excluded by, or placed at the bottom of most economic, social, and political endeavors.

Manifestations of popular culture produce the kind of solidarity irreproducible by any other injection of hope in self and collective affirmation of the resilient human spirit and dignity found in this desire and aspiration. Expressions of Latin American people's tradition of lyrical improvisations transcend boundaries and are present in every U.S. Latino community. Crafters of poems, songs, and dramas touch on the cultural liminality lying in between the polarities of the human enterprise: the present and past, the imagined and the real, life and death, joy and tribulations. And it is in this open space of the lyrical narrative that health promoters and health educators can present new ideas, recreate new behaviors, and expand the scope of knowledge necessary to address sexual health in Latin America. This seems to be the one of the best hopes to answer the call for a new sexual health discourse with relevant gestural symbols for protection [49] advocated by Latin American women's organizations that is being echoed in the United States.

Furthermore, the long history of promoting social and cultural change in Latin America through mass communication [50] is yet another tool at the disposition of U.S. Latino health interventionists in sexual and reproductive health. Needless to say, radio *locutores* and TV *reporteros* are community assets that can contribute to develop audio and audiovisual productions for health promotion and education. Both Spanish television and radio provide a forum for bringing into the community view sexual and reproductive health issues affecting the U.S. Latino population: a channel for initiating public discussion as well as for influencing public health policy agendas in a manner that is consistent with people's cultural maps for making sense of their own realities. Linkages between visual portrayals and audio messages communicated through the broadcasting technology, combined with interactive modes of personal communication such as telephones help lines, are consistent with the highly interpersonal cognitive styles of Latinos who are not very likely to be passive recipients of information without reacting to it immediately.

Finally, we must echo the call for meaningful community participation in research and intervention suggested in some of the chapters of this book. Ecological models that require multiple spheres of intervention, combined cultural methodologies, and above all, the active collaboration of community residents will build capacity for the promotion of sexual and reproductive health for all. Researchers and interventionists will be more likely to increase their ability to obtain meaningful cultural data in the primary language and communication styles of the participants and base their intervention on the cultural constructions of people to be reached rather than on their own knowledge tradition and scripts. Local community residents and program participants will benefit from the development of skills and competences they can use for promoting sexual and reproductive health and transfer these to other areas of community life.

REFERENCES

1. *The World Bank Report,* Washington, D.C., 2001.
2. *Dying for Growth,* J. Y. Kim et al. (eds.), Common Courage Press, Monroe, Maine, 2000.
3. *PAHO Annual Report: 2000,* Pan American Health Organization, Washington, D.C., 2001.
4. *World Health Report: 1999,* World Health Organization, Washington, D.C., 2000.
5. First Glimpses from the 2000 U.S. Census, *Population Bulletin, 56*:2, Population Reference Bureau, June 2001.
6. *The AIDS Crisis among Latinos: A Report from the First Unidos Para La Vida Summit,* May 4, 1998, Harvard AIDS Institute, Cambridge, 1998.
7. T. Díaz et al., AIDS Trends among Hispanics in the United States, *American Journal of Public Health, 83*:4, pp. 504-509, 1993.
8. J. Lawrence and R. Crosby, HIV/AIDS in Puerto Rico and the Caribbean: Current Status and Future Directions, *Boletín de la Asociación Médica de Puerto Rico, 91*:1-6, pp. 22-28, 1999.
9. N. Romero, M. Weeks, and M. Singer, Much More than HIV: The Reality of Life on the Streets for Drug-Using Sex Workers in Inner City Hartford, *International Quarterly of Community Health Education, 18:*1, pp. 107-119, 1998-1999.
10. M. Burgos, B. Reininger, D. L. Richter, A. L. Coker, M. Alegría, M. Vera, and R. Saunders, Sexually Transmitted Infections among Street-Based Female Adolescent Sex Workers in Puerto Rico: Implications for Community Health, *International Quarterly of Community Health Education, 20*:3, pp. 253-264, 2000-2001.
11. R. Wilcher, L. Gilbert, C. Siano, and E. M. Arredondo, From Focus Groups to Workshops: Developing a Cultural Appropriate Cervical Cancer Intervention for Rural Latinas, *International Quarterly of Community Health Education, 19*:2, pp. 83-102, 1999-2000.
12. E. Acuña-Lillo, The Reproductive Health of Latinas in New York City: Making a Difference at the Individual Level, *Bulletin, Centro de Estudios Puertorriqueños,* 1998.
13. *2002 World Population Data Sheet,* Population Reference Bureau, Washington, D.C., 2002.

14. *The AIDS Crisis among Lations,* A Report from the First Unidos Para la Vida Summit, May 4, 1998, Harvard AIDS Institute, 1998.

15. R. R. Alvarez, Changing Patterns of Family and Ideology among Latino Cultures in the United States, T. Weaver (ed.), *Handbook of Hispanic Cultures in the United States,* Arte Publico Press, 1994.

16. A. Chaviro Prado, Latina Experience and Latina Identity, T. Weaver (ed.), *Handbook of Hispanic Cultures in the United States,* Arte Publico Press, 1994.

17. M. Minkler, *Community Organizing and Community Building for Health,* Rutgers University Press, New Brunswick, New Jersey, 1997.

18. J. Bertrand, V. Ward, and F. Pauc, Sexual Practices among the Quiche-speaking Mayan Population of Guatemala, *International Quarterly of Community Health Education, 12*:4, pp. 265-282, 1991-1992.

19. V. Gil, Empowerment Rhetoric, Sexual Negotiation and Latina's AIDS Risk: Research Implications for Prevention Health Education, *International Quarterly of Community Health Education, 18*:1, pp. 9-27, 1998-1999.

20. C. Oliveros, G. Marquis, R. Bartolini, G. Ormsby, and E. Rudatsikira, Maternal Lactation: A Qualitative Analysis of the Breastfeeding Habits and Beliefs of Pregnant Women Living in Lima, Peru, *International Quarterly of Community Health Education, 18*:4, pp. 415-432, 1998-1999.

21. M. Rice, Socio-Cultural Factors Affecting Reproductive Health, *International Quarterly of Community Health Education, 12*:1, pp. 69-80, 1991-1992.

22. P. Erickson, Cultural Factors Affecting the Negotiation of First Sexual Intercourse among Latina Adolescent Mothers, *International Quarterly of Community Health Education, 8*:1, pp. 121-137, 1998-1999.

23. S. Guendelman and S. Witt, Improving Access to Prenatal Care for Latina Immigrants in California: Outreach and In-Reach Strategies, *International Quarterly of Community Health Education, 12*:2, pp. 89-106, 1991-1992.

24. M. I. Torres, R. Tuthill, S. Lyon-Callo, C. M. Hernández, and P. Epkind, Focused Female Condom Education and Trial: Comparison of Young African American and Puerto Rican Assessments, *International Quarterly of Community Health Education, 18*:1, pp. 49-68, 1998-1999.

25. H. Amaro, A. Raj, E. Reed, and K. Cranston, Implementation and Long-Term Outcomes of Two HIV Intervention Programs for Latinas, *Health Promotion Practice, 3*:2, pp. 245-254, 2002.

26. H. Carrillo, Another Crack in the Mirror: The Politics of AIDS Prevention in Mexico, *International Quarterly of Community Health Education, 14*:2, pp. 129-152, 1993-1994.

27. D. Buchanan, E. Apostol, D. Balford, C. Claudio, J. Marinoff, N. O'Hare, M. Rodriguez, and C. Santiago, The CEPA Project: A New Model for Community Based Planning, *International Quarterly of Community Health Education, 14*:4, pp. 361-377, 1993-1994.

28. Z. Cardoza-Clayson, X. Castañeda, E. Sanchez, and C. Brindis, The Interception of Culture, Health and Systems in California, *International Quaraterly of Community Health Education, 19*:4, pp. 375-389, 1999-2000.

29. V. Chávez and L. Dorfman, Spanish Language TV News Portrayals of Youth and Violence in California, *International Quarterly of Community Health Education, 16*:2, pp. 121-138, 1996-1997.

30. K. Loring and E. Garcia Walters, Cuidaremos: The HECO Approach to Breast Self-Examination, *International Quarterly of Community Health Education, 1*:2, pp. 125-133, 1990-1991.

31. B. Faust, When is a Midwife a Witch?: A Case Study from Modernizing Maya Village, P. Whelehan (ed.), *Women and Health,* Bergin and Garvey Publishers, Granby, Massachusetts, 1988.

32. K. O'Rourke, Maternal Exhaustion as an Obstetric Complication: Implications for TBA Training, *International Quarterly of Community Health Education, 15*:4, pp. 395-404, 1994-1995.

33. I. Estrada-Portales, De Vuelta a los Origenes del Nacimiento, *Perpectivas: Revista de la Organización Panamericana de Salud, 6*(2), 2002.

34. L. Rendón, A. Langer, and B. Hernández, *Boletín de la Oficina Sanitaria Panamericana, 115*:6, 1993.

35. A. M. Hernández and E. Casanova, Las ONG que Trabajan sobre el SIDA y las Mujeres, S. González (ed.), *Las Organizaciones No Gubernamentales Mexicanas y la Salud Reproductiva,* Imprenta El Colegio de Mexico, pp. 97-123, 1999.

36. B. Reyes Nevares, Promotoras Sociales en el Centro de la Vida Comunitaria, *FEM 19*:150, p. 48, 1995.

37. M. Minkler and K. Cox, Creating Critical Consciousness in Health: Applications of Freire's Philosophy and Methods to the Health Care Setting, *International Journal of Health Services, 10*:2, pp. 311-322, 1980.

38. S. Schensul, Science, Theory and Application in Anthropology, *American Behavioral Scientist, 29*:2, pp. 164-185, 1985.

39. M. Minkler and N. Wallerstein, Improving Health Through Community Organization and Community Building (Chap. 12), K. Glanz, F. Lewis, and B. Rimer (eds.), *Health Behavior and Health Education: Theory, Research and Practice,* Jossey-Bass, San Francisco, 1997.

40. P. Freire, Cultural Action for Freedom, *Harvard Education Review, 40*:3, pp. 452-477, 1970.

41. T. Valente, P. Poppe, M. E. De Briceño, and D. Cases, Street Theater as a Tool to Reduce Family Planning Misinformation, *International Quarterly of Community Health Education, 15*:3, pp. 279-289, 1994-1995.

42. M. McDonald, G. Antunez, and M. Gottemoeller, Using the Arts and Literature in Health Education, *International Quarterly of Community Health Education, 18*:3, pp. 269-282, 1998-1999.

43. L. E. Santiago, Theater of Life: Theory, Method and Practice, *Puerto Rico Health Services Journal, 19*:1, pp. 77-82, 2000.

44. G. Yudice, The Globalization of Culture and the New Civil Society, S. Alvarez, E. Dagnino, and A. Escobar (eds.), *Cultures of Politics, Politics of Cultures: Re-visioning Latin American Social Movements,* Westview Press, 1998.

45. D. M. Anderson and E. Huerto, Developing and Evaluating Radio-Linked Telephone Helpline for Hispanics, *International Quarterly of Community Health Education, 19*:4, pp. 341-351, 1999-2000.

46. J. Sallis and N. Owen, Ecological Models (Chap. 19), K. Glanz, F. Lewis, and B. Rimer (eds.), *Health Behavior and Health Education: Theory, Research and Practice,* Jossey-Bass, San Francisco, 1999.

47. K. McLeroy, D. Bibeau, A. Steckler, and K. Glanz, An Ecological Perspective of Health Promotion Programs, *Health Education Quarterly, 15*:1, pp. 351-377, 1988.
48. I. Silverblatt, *Moon, Sun and Witches: Gender Ideologies and Class in Inca and Colonial Peru,* Princeton Press, pp. 29-31, 1987.
49. Irma Palma, *No Hay un Discurso que Facilite et Uso del Condón, Cuadernos Mujer y Salud,* Red de Salud de Mujeres LatinoAmericanas y del Caribe, 1998.
50. J. R. Finnegan and K. Viswanath, Communication Theory and Health Behavior Change: The Media Study Framework, K. Glanz, F. Marcus Lewis, and B. Rimer (eds.), *Health Behavior and Health Education: Theory, Research and Practice,* Jossey-Bass, 1997.

SECTION ONE

Researching Cultural Constructions of Sexual and Reproductive Health

The eight chapters in this section represent diverse examples of community-based research efforts undertaken by applied social scientists and public health practitioners to study cultural constructions that are influential in sexual and reproductive health behavior in Latin American and U.S. Latino communities. Reflecting current trends in health promotion and education, many of the chapters describe qualitative methodologies to research the local cultural landscapes of sexual behavior. The order of the chapters is arranged according to the central topic.

The first three chapters are focused on sexual decision-making and negotiation, are written by anthropologists, and highlight cultural representations of sexuality and sexual behavior. Chapter 1 presents focus group research with an impressive number of 13 sessions and a total of 226 women and men participants to describe sexual behavior and practices underlying resistance to family planning strategies among Quiché-speaking Mayas in Guatemala. Discussion of data centers on physical development and sexuality, courtship patterns, premarital and extra-marital relations, sexual decision-making within marriage and outside, coital frequency, abstinence, sexual pleasure for women, sex trade, and the relationship of alcohol and sex to male violent behavior against women. One key cultural theme in this chapter is the role of morality and religious ideology in knowledge, attitudes, and behavior associated with human sexuality.

Similar topics are addressed in Chapter 2. A combined ethnographic research approach produced data from 472 adult women in Puerto Rico and a Latino community in California. Findings are discussed in the context of the limitations attributed to some of the most frequently used theoretical frameworks in HIV prevention and education in the 1990s. Chapter 3 is specific to the negotiation of first sexual intercourse. Using portions of life histories with 40 Latina adolescent mothers residing in Los Angeles, California, the authors illustrate the cultural script of gender and heterosexual relationships that place young Latina women at risk for negative sexual health outcomes such as unplanned teen pregnancy and sexually transmitted infections (STIs).

The next two chapters examine cultural representations influential in women's behaviors aimed at preventing sexual and reproductive health problems. Chapter 4 is based on formative research with focus groups to inform a cervical cancer prevention intervention for Latin American women who were immigrants to rural settings in North Carolina. In addition to the typical structural and linguistic barriers to the utilization of screening services, the authors discuss the role of gendered culture as a powerful deterrent to pelvic exams for pap tests necessary for prevention and early detection of cervical cancer. Chapter 5 documents, with long, in-depth, qualitative interviews, Peruvian pregnant women's breastfeeding habits and beliefs and their influence on their decision to wean a child during a subsequent pregnancy.

The subsequent two chapters focus on sex trade behaviors in two different urban settings with two different research methodologies. In Chapter 6 on Latina women in Connecticut, the authors present findings from qualitative interviews describing the experience of women trading sex while facing the risk of HIV and other STIs, rape and other manifestations of violence in the streets, and the uncertainty about being remunerated with money or drugs. In contrast, the authors of Chapter 7 analyze sex trading behaviors of adolescents in Puerto Rico with a quantitative research approach to illustrate the interrelationships of sex trading, drug abuse, and depression and document the need for appropriate community interventions.

Finally, an overview of socio-cultural factors influencing reproductive health in Latin American countries appears in Chapter 8. The author discusses socio-economic factors that serve as the cultural context for the adoption of strategies to prevent unplanned and unwanted pregnancy, especially among adolescents. In addition, it describes the role of men in decision-making related to contraception and other protective measures against pregnancy.

All chapters included in this section provide recommendations for future community health education program planning and intervention research.

CHAPTER 1

Sexual Practices Among the Quiché-Speaking Mayan Population of Guatemala

Jane T. Bertrand
Victoria Ward
Francisco Pauc

This study was conducted as part of a larger effort to better understand the behaviors, beliefs, practices and values of the Mayan community of Guatemala with regard to family planning (FP). Numerically, it is estimated that the Mayans constitute from 37-42 percent of the total population of Guatemala (9.5 million inhabitants) [1, 2]. While the term "Maya" is used as a general description of this population, in fact it is made up of some twenty-three Mayan linguistic groups. The Mayan population is concentrated largely in the Western highlands of the country. While there is no standard definition of what constitutes a "Mayan," the operational definition usually includes speaking a Mayan dialect at home and/or using traditional rather than Western dress (especially in the case of women). The distinction between Ladino (the non-Mayan inhabitants of Guatemala) and Mayan is an ethnic/cultural rather than racial one. A Mayan who gives up traditional dress for Western clothes and uses Spanish as his primary language could over time be considered a Ladino.

Historically, this population has been subjugated economically and politically by the Ladino population. In the face of this, Mayans have maintained a strong sense of ethnic identity and many of the traditional values of their ancestors. Moreover, they have a healthy suspicion of outsiders, even from other Mayan groups. The language barrier has served to maintain these groups in isolation, although many Mayans, especially those who have completed primary school, speak Spanish as well as their own native language [3].

This economic and social subjugation has resulted in a far lower standard of living among Mayans as compared to Ladinos. These differences are reflected in social indicators across the board: lower educational attainment, higher infant mortality and morbidity, lower life expectancy, etc. [1]. While many programs have been introduced to improve specific aspects of quality of life among the Mayan population, these have met with mixed results, due in part to a protective distance which many Mayan populations have chosen to keep vis-à-vis outsiders.

In terms of reproductive health, maternal mortality is higher among Mayan than Ladino women [4]. They are less likely to seek prenatal care from clinically-trained personnel and are less likely to deliver in a hospital or clinic [1]. Rather, most prefer to use the services of a local midwife who is a well-known and trusted member of the community who moreover respects the traditions concerning the birth of a child. Similarly, Mayan women are far less likely to use contraceptive methods than their Ladino counterparts, as reflected in the results of the 1987 Demographic and Health Survey: only 5.5 percent of Mayan women of reproductive age, married or living in union, reported use of a method, compared to 34.0 percent among Ladino women [1].

There is a substantial body of research documenting the marked differences between the Ladinos and Mayans in terms of reproductive health, utilization of services, and acceptance of family planning [5-9]. However, much of this is based on large-scale surveys which provide quantitatively sound estimates of these phenomena but little insight into the beliefs and values which contribute to these differences. This prompted the current study which was based on focus groups and allowed for exploration into these previously reported differences.

This study was commissioned by and designed in conjunction with two Guatemalan institutions working in the area of reproductive health: AGES (the national sex education association) and APROFAM (the private family planning association of Guatemala). One objective of the study was to learn more about the resistance to family planning which has been widespread among the Mayan population. Results from this portion of the study have been reported elsewhere [10]. The second objective was to understand more about the ways in which this population learns about reproduction, enters into sexual unions, views sexual activity within and outside marriage, and related topics. Such information will help in developing more culturally-appropriate programs in sex education, family planning and other areas of reproductive health.

The importance of this study extends beyond programmatic implications for sex education and family planning programs in Guatemala. First, it demonstrates the utility of the focus group methodology in obtaining data on a population which is geographically dispersed, logistically isolated, and highly distrustful of outsiders.

Second, it illustrates the value of better understanding human sexuality as a factor in the acceptance of family planning. Family planning researchers have typically ignored such issues as who initiates sex, whether women experience pleasure in sexual relations, if and when women can say no to sexual relations, what periods of abstinence are respected, and so forth. Yet these may have an impact on the types of methods desired, ability to use barrier methods, counselling required and related issues.

METHODOLOGY

Selection of the Study Population

Of the twenty-three different linguistic groups, the four major ones are Quiché, Kekchi, Cakchiquel, and Mam. There are differences in social indicators between one language group and another (e.g., the Cakchiquel speakers have generally had more contact with the forces of modernization because of their proximity to the capital city). Moreover, certain differences are bound to exist within a given language group given variability within human populations. Thus, it is unwarranted to speak of the Mayans as if they were a single group. On the other hand, the differences found within a given linguistic group or between two different Mayan groups tend to be substantially less than those found between Mayans and Ladinos [11].

The current study was conducted among the Quiché, the largest of the Mayan language groups (constituting 27 percent of the total Mayan population in Guatemala) [11]. As such, the results cannot be generalized to the larger Mayan population or even to all Mayans who speak Quiché. Rather, it represents the pilot phase of a larger project which will obtain similar data from areas where Kekchi, Cakchiquel and Mam are spoken. Nonetheless, these findings provide insights into this population which would not be obtained from a quantitative survey.

The main site of data collection was Santa Cruz del Quiché in the northwestern highland area of Guatemala. Among possible Quiché areas, it was selected because it was relatively accessible to the capital city, had not been saturated with previous studies, and was considered relatively "safe" in terms of Guatemala's ongoing civil strife. The specific communities to be included were chosen based on the following criteria: predominantly Quiché speaking, within 25 km of the departmental capital, population size between 500 and 2500, and houses moderately dispersed. A community was considered "moderately dispersed" if the homes were in walking distance of each other (although sometimes they were separated by several kilometers).

Upon completion of the data collection as initially planned (nine focus groups, the details of which are presented below), the researchers felt that certain questions merited further investigation. The field team opined that the area around

Santa Cruz del Quiché had been saturated. Thus a second location was chosen for the remaining four groups: Sta. Lucia Utatlan in the *departamento* (province) of Sololá. The selection of specific communities was based on the same criteria as listed above.

Study Design

The data obtained herein were collected from a total of thirteen focus groups. This methodology consists of a series of guided group discussions among persons with specific characteristics. To facilitate communication, the eight to twelve participants for a given group are chosen to be as homogenous as possible; however, diversity is achieved by repeating groups with participants of different socio-demographic characteristics. In the current study, a total of nine groups were conducted in the initial phase of data collection, based on the following criteria:

Males:	Females:
(1) 15-20, single	(6) 15-20, single
(2) 15-20, married	(7) 15-20, married
(3) 25-30, married	(8) 25-30, married
(4) 35-40, married	(9) 35-40, married
(5) Community leaders	

To obtain further information on specific points, four additional groups were carried out; the composition of these groups included one each of categories 3, 4, 7, and 9 (directly above). In total, 226 persons participated in this study.

The age groups were selected so as to obtain information from participants who were at different stages of their reproductive life. Since most Mayans marry by age twenty-five, the older age groups included only respondents in union. The group of community leaders was limited to males, since most such leaders are males; also, it was important to avoid combining males and females in a focus group on the topic of sexual behavior, given that this might inhibit or otherwise bias the conversation.

The sessions were moderated by a Mayan of the same sex as the participants, who was assisted by an observer (also Mayan). The sessions were conducted in Quiché, according to a pre-established discussion guide. However, the moderators were free to digress from the guide to follow up on issues which seemed pertinent to the topic. The sessions were tape-recorded; subsequently each was transcribed in Spanish by the moderator and observer before they conducted the next session.

Data Analysis

The analysis was based on these transcriptions. Verbatim passages from the transcriptions were organized according to the main topics of the discussion guide; these were reviewed numerous times to determine the main ideas which emerged as well as important "minority" viewpoints. Since the moderators did not have training or experience in the analysis of focus group data, this phase of the work was conducted by the authors of this report. However, the moderators had the opportunity to review all of the results and offered suggestions regarding the interpretation of the findings.

RESULTS

Feasibility of Conducting Focus Groups on This Topic

It is widely recognized that sex is a highly taboo subject in most Mayan cultures. Thus, the researchers had some concern whether this would be a feasible means of collecting data on this topic. Indeed, the taboo on sex was repeatedly confirmed by participants in the groups, who were clearly not accustomed to discussing such topics, even among those close to them. One woman commented, "this is something we never discuss . . . perhaps the end of the world is coming, and that's why we are hearing these things."

One of the most important findings from this study was that the focus group methodology proved to be a useful vehicle for obtaining information on this highly personal, sensitive topic in a culture where sex is considered a taboo subject. It should be stressed that this would probably not have been possible without Mayan moderators who spoke the local language, used traditional dress, and were identified by participants as sharing a common cultural base. Especially among the women's groups, there was great embarrassment and reticence to speak openly at the beginning of the sessions. Yet due to the interpersonal skills of the moderators and the fact that they shared a common culture and language, participants in the vast majority of the groups overcame their initial shyness and contributed freely to the discussion.

The only group that was clearly offended by the subject matter and participated reluctantly was the group of community leaders. As the session progressed, part of the group left in protest. One leader commented that had he known the subject to be discussed, he never would have come, adding, "it is very much prohibited for us to talk about these silly matters to other people; this is talking like a woman . . . never, never since I was born have people talked about this."

In retrospect, it is possible that the leaders were particularly negative for one of two reasons. First, as "public figures" they may have felt more vulnerable in revealing information about their private lives. And second, several of those who objected to the discussion were lay religious leaders who felt they might be criticized for talking about sex or the related topic of FP. Although the information obtained from the community leaders was somewhat incomplete, we have included relevant portions from their session as well.

The Pervasive Influence of Moral/Religious Belief

Although not a topic in the discussion guide, moral/religious beliefs emerged as a main theme in many of the sessions. The respondents explained their attitudes and actions in line with the strongly held religious sentiments which were prevalent [12]. Whereas it is often said that Latin America is nominally Catholic, among this population religious beliefs (based on a mix of Christian and native religion) were a guiding principle which gave meaning and direction to their daily lives. The references to God and religious principles in the results presented below provide specific examples of the extent to which these shape the belief and behaviors of this group.

Sources of Information about Physical Development and Sexuality

It was very clear from all groups that there is little effort to educate young people on these topics. There was repeated mention that you don't have to teach young people about sex, it comes directly from God. "God is the One that has put this in every man and woman; you don't learn it, nor is there anyone that teaches it."

The adolescent girls confirmed that their parents had not taught them about physical development or sex. In general, mothers do not tell their daughters about menstruation until the girls see their first period (and are "startled"). When asked if they planned to tell their own daughters about menstruation before it occurred, most thought they probably would not.

The comments of the adolescent girls further indicated their lack of knowledge on this topic: "We don't know anything about sex . . . our parents don't tell us anything." Moreover, there was little mention of other sources from which one might get this information, such as at school or from friends. Only in the additional group of women twenty-five to twenty-nine did anyone mention getting information from other girlfriends or from television and movies. In contrast, adolescent boys had much more information about sex.

Many of the young men apparently had learned about physical development and sex at school, either in the classroom or among friends outside. One of the adolescents mentioned that "before, perhaps no one talked about sex, but today even the young boys at school talk about sex, and it's there that you can learn what sex is about."

The only information which young people receive with respect to marriage comes from traditional rules of Mayan religion. The couple kneels before their elders during the ceremony and the elders give them advice and ask if they are ready for marriage. However, the information obtained from the focus groups and other sources suggests that this event is primarily ceremonial and is not a source of practical information about marital relations.

In all groups, the moderator asked what they thought about sex education for young people, and who should provide it. The reaction was mixed. The community leaders were emphatic that one should not talk to young people about sex (or "sin" as they called it); men are born with sexual instincts and when they enter into a union (marry), they will experience sex naturally. One leader scoffed at the idea of saying "Look, son, this is what I do with your mother." To the contrary, this group would prohibit their children from talking about sex. Participants in the other adult groups were more open to the idea, but with some reservations. The major objection to sex education was the fear that this information would further stimulate their interest in sex.

The adolescent girls didn't hide their interest in learning more about the physical development of the human body and the nature of marital relations. In fact, they implored the moderator of the group to explain it all to them on the spot.

Courtship Patterns

"El noviazgo" (courtship) constitutes a stronger commitment among this population than is the case in Western societies where teens may have a number of boyfriends before choosing a lifetime partner. Among this group, it is common to marry one's first love. Although difficult to quantify in the context of focus groups, the usual/appropriate duration of courtship was judged by the participants to be eight to twelve months.

Because of this relatively short duration, the ideal age to begin courting versus the ideal age for marriage was somewhat blurred. The consensus in most groups was that the ideal age to begin courtship was sixteen to eighteen years for women and twenty or above for men. By this age, the girl would know how to do domestic tasks, the boy would be able to maintain his wife economically. Participants from various groups mentioned the advantage of not marrying too young, citing that the maturity of both partners would contribute to stability in the household.

There was consensus in the male groups that adolescent males begin to seek out a mate when they start to feel sexual desire. Only one participant cited pressure from older males to get interested in girls, lest he be thought "not to be a man."

It was striking that participants in both male and female groups of all ages concurred that parents have no right to get involved in these courtship activities, either in terms of the person selected or the age to marry ("assuming the girl wasn't twelve or thirteen"). One young woman summed up the position stated in most groups: "no one can tell me to do anything. If I find the person I love, then I'm going to get married." Another echoed the sentiment: "our parents can tell us what to do on anything else, except for marriage; this is the preference or desire of each person." The groups of parents supported this same idea, even in the case of a daughter who reached twenty and still wasn't married.

The possible explanation for this came from the comment made by one young woman: "no one can tell us what to do, we just follow God's will. God has planted this (desire) in each of us. No one can force us, God is the only One who knows when each of us will marry."

Premarital Relations

According to tradition, the young man should not have sexual contact with his girlfriend during courtship. Participants indicated that many years ago, a boy might be very fond of a girl, but be fearful of talking to her, much less taking her hand or embracing her. It was and is considered acceptable to go out in the afternoon to talk with one's girlfriend or write her notes. Signs of affection which may not be acceptable to all but appear to be widely practiced ("if no one is looking") are holding hands, kissing and embracing.

Based on the focus group discussions, one would conclude that these norms of chastity are in fact widely respected. One single girl reported that "if the two love each other, they talk, but nothing more." One comment seemed to sum up the experience of the group of single adolescent females: "here we are all very modest (timid), and we are ashamed to even talk about things having to do with sex with our boyfriends, much less do them."

The adolescent females who were already married related similar experiences. They recounted that during courtship their (future) husbands visited them frequently, telling them they loved them and wanted to marry them. They opined that if the boy is honorable, he will only talk with the girl. "Respectable people don't embrace." One young participant did cite the case that "if the boy wants to trick her, he may be more aggressive, bothering her, trying to hug and kiss her all the time."

The comments of various adolescent males seemed to confirm this lack of sexual contact. "The majority of couples don't embrace, they just talk. . . . A boy doesn't have the right to enjoy sex until he gets married. . . . Until you get married, you don't know about sex. . . . When we get married, we don't know how to make love or what to do in bed with a woman."

A few comments in the focus groups suggested that the situation may be changing. "Some young men have only heard about sex but haven't experienced it, but others are more aggressive." "Everyone has his own way of doing things; some (male teens) talk to their girlfriends using bad words, others have bad thoughts and have sex with them, whereas some just talk to their girlfriends at a distance."

Among those who commented on this change, they attributed it to the influence of the Ladino community. One respondent reported that the men involved in trade learned how to do "bad things" with women when they went into the big city, and then they brought this back home, causing the old ways to be lost. Several felt that this was an example of the negative influence of the Ladino community on the Mayan population.

Despite claims to the contrary, there is evidence of some premarital sexual contact, given that in almost all the groups, the participants cited cases of girls that had a child out of wedlock or gave birth less than nine months after the marriage. There were three distinct reactions to this situation. The most common was to criticize or punish the girl. The second response was to accept the situation, provided the couple gets married. A third reaction was not to intervene, but rather to stay out of other people's business.

The general conclusion from the series of focus groups was that pre-marital relations occur, but this is not the norm. One participant in the group of community leaders claimed that they couldn't tell what the reaction would be to a pregnant unmarried girl since this hadn't happened to anyone in the group. One woman in the thirty-five to forty age group summarized the general consensus that "this really doesn't happen much here; the cases are very few."

Sexual Decision-Making within Marriage

Among this group of participants, marriage was viewed as very sacred, and it was felt that sex was a God-given part of marriage. The union of the couple was described by one as "the heritage that God left to our ancestors." It was considered a mandate from God to love one's husband. As one woman commented, "this is the reason that my husband sought me out and for this reason I love him; if not, why did we get married?" In contrast to the "shame" that unmarried teenage girls felt, the married women viewed sex as an act blessed by God and as a basic human need.

Both men and women agreed that generally the man initiates sexual activity. Several participants concurred that "women don't need to think about sex until the man begins touching her." However, there was agreement that occasionally the woman takes the initiative. "If the man does heavy work, arrives home tired and thus doesn't think about sex, and if the woman is hot-blooded she can take the first step, leading the man to have sex." By contrast, the group of leaders insisted that the man always takes the initiative; the only woman that would ask a man for sex were prostitutes (and this for economic reasons).

Although it was agreed that the man generally makes the first move, the comments of the married women in the different age groups suggest that they are generally willing partners. "My husband starts touching me at night, we both like it, and we have relations." Another commented, "Maybe my husband doesn't know it . . . but he can have me any night he wants, because I like it, too."

A few participants alluded to the fact that either partner could take the initiative "because we both like it," while another cited that both partners should be in agreement before having sex.

There are situations in which the woman may refuse to have relations with her husband. Speaking of the post-partum period, one woman stated that "I tell him not to do it with me, I scold him and I tell him to go into the corn fields (i.e., masturbate) because I have to take care of myself." Another reason for refusing sex is if the husband asks for it at an inappropriate time, when she is doing other things. "Sometimes I'm behind in my work and he starts bothering me, he says he wants to have me ("use me"), and I tell him to wait until night when everyone's sleeping."

Apart from sexual desire, there may be other motives for having relations with one's husband. One is to avoid his becoming jealous. "If we don't accept, our husbands say we are saving ourselves for another man and that we are giving it to another man." A second is to avoid having one's husband go with other women (including prostitutes). And in some cases women accept sex against their will when their husbands have had too much to drink, to avoid being abused by them (a problem discussed in the paragraph titled "Alcohol, Sex and Violence against the Woman").

Coital Frequency

Men expressed the idea that *they* should make the decision about when to have sex, not only because they give the orders in their household, but also to be able to control the frequency of sexual relations. There were different reasons mentioned for the need to control coital frequency. Given the physical labor they do each day and the poor diets they have, a man who has sex every day would "kill himself" (figuratively speaking). (This was not seen as a problem for the woman, because she only "receives" during sex.) As one participant observed, "an understanding couple doesn't have sex everyday . . . they don't overdo it and destroy themselves."

A second reason to avoid sex everyday, put forward by a man in the thirty-five to forty age group, was to avoid letting the wife become accustomed to having sex daily. "I only have sex with my wife once a week, because if we do it daily and she gets used to it, the day may come when I can't respond to her and she could cheat on me."

Recently married couples have sex more often, according to the participants. Several commented that young men were capable of having sex every night of the week and possibly more than once a night. But thereafter, the frequency diminishes. One man in the twenty-five to thirty age group observed that "as time goes by, they get bored . . . just as happened to all of us."

In terms of coital frequency in general, many mentioned having sex two to three times a week, others only once a week. In general, participants gave the impression that they didn't have more than one relation per night on these occasions.

Periods of Abstinence

There are two periods when couples generally abstain from sexual relations: during menstruation and during the post-partum period. Apparently men respect these periods, unless they are very demanding (overbearing) or have had too much to drink.

With regard to menstruation, the woman communicates to husband that she is having her period and thus they abstain. The reasons women gave for abstaining during this period were to avoid getting their husbands dirty; and that the blood has an odor and they would feel ashamed for their husbands to smell it.

As for the post-partum period, participants in the focus groups defined it as lasting from one to three months. Both men and women acknowledged the need to avoid relations during this period. According to men, the woman needed to recuperate and also to avoid getting pregnant again. The women felt it was needed to recuperate ("since we don't have enough blood"), to avoid relations which would be painful before that time, and to avoid "swelling."

In general, abstinence during the post-partum period was considered a symbol of respect for the woman. A man that demanded sex during this period would be showing disrespect for his wife, according to both male and female participants.

Abstinence is not practiced in relation to religious or other holidays. To the contrary, special days could be a motive for having relations. As one man recounted, "If it is my wife's birthday, we ought to have relations so that she'll feel that she is alive, and if one manages to hit with a baby boy, then it is truly a gift for her, a reminder of her birthday."

Sexual Pleasure for the Woman

Anthropological research from the 1940s found that Mayan women submitted to sex only from duty, and that neither men nor women felt that the woman might feel pleasure [13]. Given the cultural norms still in existence that it is the woman's responsibility to serve the husband in all ways, the researchers had expected to find that women considered sex as a matter of duty. In fact, this was not the case.

The women who chose to talk about this subject during the sessions indicated that they do enjoy sexual relations. One said, "Yes, I'd say yes, because God has given this to us, and it's so we will feel good, not bad." One woman stated openly to the group that ". . . I want it and ask for it, I want to have relations with my husband, and it's certain that he wants me." Various respondents of both sexes stated that after relations, both the man and the woman feel satisfied, tranquil, or happy.

It was unclear from the first sets of focus groups whether experiencing pleasure was synonymous with achieving orgasm. This point was further explored in the second set of focus groups. The evidence suggests that in fact some Mayan women do achieve orgasm during sexual relations.

Extra-Marital Relations

Both men and women indicated that extra-marital relations are a great sin. While the majority spoke very negatively of this behavior, it was also clear that it does occur in these communities.

The women twenty-five to thirty years of age reported that extra-marital relations were rare in their community. Persons that would engage in such behavior were seen to be bad or deceitful. One woman cited the danger of the husband having children with another woman, who would then demand money from him and he wouldn't cover the expenses in his present house.

The other comments of women thirty-five to forty years of age were harder to interpret. Several women indicated that this practice does occur, and "just as the other woman sins, so does the man." However, two of the women in this age group participating in the discussions on family planning (part of this same study, reported elsewhere) claimed that in their community, they hadn't seen this and that it didn't happen.

The comments of men thirty-five to forty years old suggest that such cases do exist and that they may be more frequent than the women imagine. A number of men criticized this practice and indicated that it went against God's will. Others suggested directly or indirectly that one shouldn't be too harsh on those who had such relations; better to let them go unnoticed. One man recounted that he had been highly critical of such cases, but later realized he was wrong, because after harshly criticizing others, he fell into the same situation himself.

How strong is the influence of the Catholic Church on this practice? While a number of men acknowledged that this practice was a sin in the eyes of the church, others indicated that the church had little influence on their behavior in this area. One participant described in very graphic language that the Church was not going to curb the sexual desire of an aroused man. Another added that some men pay attention to the church regarding extra-marital relations when they no longer have much sexual potency.

The participants cited various motives that might cause a woman to seek out another man: because she 1) was immoral, 2) had economic reasons, or 3) had an impotent husband. The motives for a man to seek out another woman were 1) for physical reasons, especially if his wife didn't know the things that would please him, 2) to satisfy his sexual needs while the wife was in the post-partum period, and 3) because he wasn't brought up right.

The comments of participants suggest that this practice is more common among men than women. However, one participant commented that if a man seeks out another woman, "not only does it trouble his wife, but she waits or looks for the opportunity for another man to fall into her arms, to get even with her husband for betraying her."

A few participants associated the practice of extra-marital relations with the use of contraceptives, because "the woman wants to feel pleasure without getting pregnant."

Focus group methodology does not allow one to quantify the percentage of the population studied that have had extra-marital relations during a given period. A tentative conclusion, based on the transcriptions assembled for this study, is that extra-marital relations are not considered acceptable among this population; on the other hand, they do occur on a limited basis.

The Use of Prostitutes

Although use of prostitutes is one type of extra-marital relations, it was treated separately in the focus groups. Indeed, attitudes toward visiting a prostitute were much more negative than those toward extra-marital relations in general. The majority of participants viewed this as "pure stupidity," especially if the man had a wife.

The group of leaders opined that men in this population rarely visit prostitutes. One stated that men who visit prostitutes are those who "live only for sex." Another participant stated that it is traders that go to the cities who visit prostitutes. By contrast, another man was emphatic that (contrary to what was said by the others) "there are many men that tend to the needs of the family and their work."

The major objection to frequenting prostitutes, mentioned by both men and women, is that they have sexually transmitted diseases, and that the man could bring these back to his wife. They recognized that some of these diseases are not curable and that people can die. The conditions cited by the respondents included AIDS, lice, pus from the penis, chancres, and gonorrhea.

A second reason for avoiding prostitutes was the expense involved. Women feared that men who visited prostitutes would neglect the needs of their families. One male participant cited his own "lack of money" as a reason for not visiting a prostitute.

Third, the women simply did not see what motive a man would have for using a prostitute, given that he could have relations with his wife; as one said, "what good does it do him if he already has me?" Another echoed the same idea: "now that we've learned how to do it (have sex), there is no way that he should go with prostitutes."

The female participants considered that visiting a prostitute constituted a lack of respect for one's wife. The teenage girls mentioned that this not only was harmful physically (alluding to risk of disease), but also "wounded the sentiments." One man added that a man would feel very bad "in his heart" if his wife were to find out.

It is not uncommon in Latin America for boys to have their first sexual experience with a prostitute. In fact, in some societies the parents or other family members arrange for this, as a ritual to attaining manhood. However, this does not seem to be the norm among this population. The male teens recognized the danger of visiting prostitutes. Their comments suggested that because of this, they weren't much drawn to this idea. At least two made some indirect reference that it was better to relieve oneself with masturbation rather than running the risk (of disease) inherent in visiting a prostitute.

Alcohol, Sex, and Violence Against the Woman

As mentioned previously, women in these groups spoke in very positive terms about their relations with their husbands. However, their attitudes changed entirely regarding sex if/when the husband has had too much to drink. According to them and to other reports, it is common for men in this area to drink too much.

The comments of male participants tended to confirm this, for example: "The man begins to bother his wife and she doesn't want to be with him given his condition but the man will somehow force the wife to have sex with him." But he added: "This is bad." Apart from a lack of respect for the wife, several participants mentioned that if the woman got pregnant, the baby could be born with some defect.

Several women described their personal experiences with certain disgust: "When I'm in the kitchen doing my work, my husband comes in drunk to touch all of my body." "When our men come home drunk, it's when they most want our body, and we have to give it to them because otherwise they'll hit us." According to another, it is even worse if the wife doesn't have the meal ready and the man sees that she is mad.

Some felt that this physical aggression was the result of alcohol alone. However, alcohol was also felt to bring out jealousy in men. "They tell us we are saving our bodies for other men and that we are giving it to other men." Another woman explained that "if we are coquettish, they also get mad and then they hit us," but she added, "sometimes we provoke this." There was one woman who didn't even want to participate in the discussion on sexual pleasure for the woman (described above); "our husbands are jealous and if they hear us talking about such things, they will hit us and God save us from that."

There was mention that if in fact a wife had been unfaithful to her husband, then this would be a valid reason for him to beat her. One female respondent felt men were justified "in the case of some huge problem, that is if we have been with another man or if the man has been with another woman."

As this last comment suggests, the man may find motive in hitting his wife if *either* partner has been unfaithful. That is, the husband may hit the wife because *he* has been with another woman. One woman added that if men visit prostitutes, "they fall into vices, they begin to drink and they hit their wives."

In the male groups, the moderator asked whether alcohol increased sexual drive in men. The responses were mixed. Some felt that alcohol did increase sexual desire ("it is when men most get aroused"), whereas others denied this, especially if the man had had too much to drink.

Even the adolescent girls were aware of this problem. "It's not the same to talk with a boy who is drunk as with one who is sober." "When boys have too much to drink, we don't talk with them, because we're scared . . . maybe they'll hit us." The adolescent females who were married confirmed that their unmarried counterparts were right to avoid them. "When boys have too much to drink, they feel more manly and it's when they take advantage and embrace the girls." Another added, "the unmarried ones are the worst, they are the most abusive and most bothersome when they've had too much to drink; they are more brazen and say whatever they want to the girls."

The comments made by these various groups suggest that there exists a relation between alcohol, sex, and violence against the women and that it is fairly common in the population studied. As stated above, a qualitative study cannot yield data on the percentage practicing such behavior or the frequency of its occurrence. Based on the comments of one group of women, one would conclude that this set of behaviors is in fact common. By contrast, another group of women described the nature of alcohol/violence problem in detail, yet they concluded by defending the men in their community who "work very hard and don't have time to drink." In sum, it was noteworthy that in all the groups of women, there was widespread recognition of a relationship between alcohol and violence against the woman; all talked about men who hit their wives, especially if they'd had too much to drink. Moreover, the men themselves made comments which seemed to suggest this link between alcohol, sex, and violence against the woman.

DISCUSSION

This study yielded a great deal of information, yet skeptics might question the validity of the responses. With the upsurge of research on sexual behavior in response to the AIDS epidemic, there is a new awareness of the problems of reliability and validity of data on sexual practice [14]. In fact, this study was originally designed as a pilot study, the results of which were to be used to develop a questionnaire which could be administered to a representative sample of the population and thus measure the frequencies of the beliefs and practices reported herein. Curiously, having completed this phrase of the research, and having seen the depth of detail which was obtained from the focus group method, the researchers in fact questioned the value of conducting a conventional survey on this specific topic among a population known to be distrustful of outsiders. Even though Mayan interviewers could be used, a one-to-one survey may not encourage the type of openness which developed in the course of the focus groups reported herein.

The authors have had the opportunity to present these findings to researchers, family planning staff, and others (including a number of Mayans from this area) in Guatemala, in an attempt to test the results against the "everyday reality" described by focus group experts [15]. There are several areas in which the results reported herein diverge from the experiences and insights of those familiar with this population. The first involves premarital relations.

Anecdotal evidence suggests that in fact sexual contact before marriage is more common than the participants in the focus groups indicated. If true, it is surprising how consistent the responses of different groups were on this subject (especially for example among adolescent males who were already married, a group that one would expect to have good recall of their "premarital" experiences, and "little to hide" from a fellow Mayan male moderator.)

A second finding which merits comment involves extra-marital relations. Results of the focus groups would suggest that such relations occur but are relatively uncommon in this population. Individuals who have worked in different Mayan communities have questioned this result. This case illustrates the point made by Pickering that focus groups are an excellent means of defining community norms, but do not allow for quantification of actual behavior among members of the population [16].

A third finding which deserves cautious interpretation and further investigation regards sexual pleasure among women. The strongly positive attitudes toward sex as a healthy and sacred part of marriage directly contradicts the stereotypic norm that Mayan women must serve their husbands in all senses and that they submit to sex as part of this burden. Given the nature of focus groups in which participants are not required to answer every question or comment on every issue, it is possible that women who found sex pleasurable were more likely to talk about their experiences, whereas women who have sex out of duty may have been reticent to say as much. In short, the findings regarding women's sexual pleasure should be considered as preliminary rather than definitive.

The results of this study concur with earlier anthropological work on a number of points, including courtship patterns [17], a positive attitude of (at least some) women toward sex [18], the abuse of alcohol [19]. Not surprisingly, our results are not consistent with earlier work on all points, given the cultural differences among ethnic groups and changing behavioral patterns in response to outside influences. This chapter reopens the field of inquiry into practices which have been the subject of little research in the published literature and underscores the need for further validation of these findings.

ACKNOWLEDGMENTS

Two Guatemalan organizations sponsored and provided technical input to this study: the Asociación Guatemalteca de Educación Sexual, AGES (represented by Eugenia Monterroso, Carmen de Monterroso y Odilia Perén), and the Asociación Pro-Bienestar de la Familia, APROFAM (Dr. Roberto Santiso, Victor Hugo Fernández, María Antonieta Pineda, and Guillermo Nicholás).

REFERENCES

1. International Resource Development, Instituto Nutricional de Centroamerica y Panama (INCAP) and the Ministerio de Salud Pública de Guatemala. Encuesta Nacional de Salud-Materno-Infantil—Guatemala, 1987. (The Demographic and Health Survey of Guatemala.)
2. Instituto Nacional de Estadistica, Encuesta Nacional Sociodemografica, 1987.
3. B. Newman and B. Bezmalinovich, Relationship of Girls' Primary Education to Social and Development Indicators in Guatemala, Report prepared for USAID by DataPro, S.A., 1991.
4. T. Bossert and E. del Cid Peralta, *Guatemala Health Sector Assessment,* 1987 Update. USAID, Guatemala, 1987.
5. J. E. D. Glittenberg, *A Comparative Study of Fertility in Highland Guatemala: A Ladino and an Indian Town,* Doctoral dissertation, University of Colorado, Cultural Anthropology, 1976.
6. J. T. Bertrand, M. A. Pinea, and R. G. Santiso, Ethnic Differences in Family Planning Acceptance in Rural Guatemala, *Studies in Family Planning, 10*:8/9, pp. 238-245, 1979.
7. S. Annis, Physical Access and Utilization of Health Services in Rural Guatemala, *Social Science and Medicine, 15,* pp. 515-523, 1981.
8. C. Chen, R. Santiso, and L. Morris, Impact of Accessibility of Contraceptives on Contraceptive Prevalence in Guatemala, *Studies in Family Planning, 14*:11, pp. 275-283, 1983.
9. R. S. Monteith, J. E. Anderson, M. A. Pineda, R. G. Santiso, and M. Oberle, Fertility and Contraceptive Use in Guatemala, 1978-83, *Studies in Family Planning, 16*:5, pp. 279-288, 1985.
10. V. Ward, J. T. Bertrand, and F. Pauc, *Estudio sobre el Comportamiento Sexual y Actitudes hacia la Planificacion Familiar entre la Poblacion Mayense de Guatemala,* Final report presented to APROFAM and AGES, Guatemala City, Guatemala, 1990.
11. V. Ward and B. C. Newman, *The Mayan Population of Guatemala: A Further Analysis of the 1987 Demographic and Health Survey,* Final report presented to the Population Council, 1990.
12. D. Mondloch, *Guia Antropológica para Trabajar en Comunidades Indígenas,* Unpublished document, 1981.
13. L. Paul and B. D. Paul, Changing Marital Patterns in a Highland Guatemalan Community, *Southern Journal of Anthropology, 19*:2, pp. 131-148, 1963.
14. J. A. Catania, D. R. Gibson, D. D. Chitwood, and J. J. Coates, Methodological Problems in AIDS Behavioral Research: Influences on Measurement Error and

Participation Bias in Studies of Sexual Behavior, *Psychological Bulletin, 108,* pp. 339-362, 1990.

15. B. Calder, Focus Groups and the Nature of Quantitative Marketing Research, *Journal of Marketing Research, 14,* pp. 353-364, 1977.

16. H. Pickering, Asking Questions on Sexual Behavior . . . Testing Methods from the Social Sciences, *Health Policy Planning, 3*:3, pp. 237-244, 1988.

17. M. Gonzalez Fontaneda, *La Educación Sexual en un Grupo de Indígenas: Estudio de Conocimiento, Actitudes y Valores Sexuales en Sexto Grado de Magisterio,* B.A. thesis in Psychology, Universidad San Rafael, Guatemala, 1976.

18. E. A. Maynard, *The Women of Palín: A Comparative Study of Indian and Ladino Women in a Guatemala Village,* Ph.D. thesis, Cornell University, Ithaca, New York, 1963.

19. F. Termer, Los Indígenas de Guatemala en la Actualidad, Ethnología y Etnografía de Guatemala, Editorial del Ministerio de Educación Pública, Guatemala, C.A., 1957.

CHAPTER 2

Empowerment Rhetoric, Sexual Negotiation, and Latinas' AIDS Risk: Research Implications for Prevention Health Education

Vincent E. Gil

The face of AIDS has changed significantly in the last decade, becoming less a disease of dominant social groups and more reflective of the racial and ethnic fabric of the United States. The Centers for Disease Control continues to report the rapid spread of HIV among women of childbearing age, particularly among Blacks and Hispanics [1]. This upward trend among women underscores increases in the number of women who were principally infected with HIV through sexual contact, mainly by injection drug-using partners, and who are now progressing to AIDS [2]. Overall trends inadvertently mask diverse local sub-epidemics, which in the case of Latinas, also include infections due to male bisexuality, male serial monogamy, or outright male promiscuity [2-7].

Among Latinas, Puerto Rican, and Mexican/Central American-descent women are the largest infected subsets [1]. Puerto Rican women, particularly Island Puerto Rican women in environments of poverty and heavy drug use have been variously documented to be substantially at risk for HIV [4, 8-11]. Nationally, five states continue to account for over half the AIDS cases reported, California among them. In a statewide study of California minorities at risk, Hispanics composed a higher proportion of the high-risk minority category than any other ethnic group: Hispanics were 1.4 times significantly more likely than blacks to be high risk heterosexuals [12]. Latinas have the highest seroprevalence ratios and associated risk factors of all minority women according to the California State Office of AIDS [13, 14].

Programs of prevention and education which have arisen to meet the challenge of minimizing infection among Latinas have produced mixed results [15-20]. There have been few *longitudinal* follow-ups on their impact.[1] Moreover, only recently have prevention program assessments begun nation-wide [21, 22]. Most programs targeting the non-IDU Latina attempt a reorientation of her personal beliefs and attitudes. They have historically used some form of "empowerment education" as a means of generating more sexually assertive women, in the hope that these will negotiate safer sex more effectively with their male partners.

Despite the well-proven social paradox that knowledge and beliefs are not a good predictor of behavior, such programs have maintained popularity while missing fundamental understandings about Latinas, both idiosyncratic as well as subculture-specific, which are argued here as essential ingredients to cogent prevention education. The failure lies, in great part, on the models and theoretical assumptions these programs use to build behavior change methodologies. After critiquing such assumptions, I draw on two anthropological studies of distinct Latina subpopulations to explore just how diverse the sexual, attitudinal, and emotional universe of Latinas really is, and how distinct subcultural issues about *negotiating sex* often impede such women from obtaining safer sex via any present "empowerment" recipe.

EMPOWERMENT RHETORIC AND CULTURAL FUNDAMENTALS

Toward the end of the first decade of AIDS, when women, especially ethnic women, were beginning to show growing signs of infection, there was strong mobilization to enable a voice and procure funding for prevention programming [17, 23-29]. The growing recognition was that women "needed help" in demonstrating to both the medical community as well as the funding establishment that they, too, "had a problem" with HIV and merited attention [30-34]. Hispanic women, in particular, were assisted by the social realization that these were often partnered with IDU-males and consequently, at risk not solely because of male sexual infidelities, bisexuality, or multiple partnerships [1, 3, 4, 9, 12, 29, 35, 36].

By the late 1980s and early 90s a number of national Hispanic groups had turned their attention to the escalating AIDS crisis in their communities, and proferred a host of model programs, designed it seemed, to be culturally specific and attentive to issues unique to Latinos/as. HDI Projects (National Hispanic Education and Communications Projects) formed the Education Leadership

---

[1] As is often the case, many of these programs were funded through demonstration grants, or have been short-lived. For a longitudinal survey, see Catania et al. [44, 45].

Council in an effort to establish a Latina perspective in the development and implementation of AIDS education/prevention strategies [37]. This was a critical step, since then-Council members represented frontline service providers and professionals in the fields of health, education, media, and medicine. All were coming together to generate a strategy for effective Latina AIDS education, risk reduction, and treatment [37]. The Council developed guidelines for program development for Latinas and, while not probably the first to do so, did cement Latina AIDS prevention/intervention efforts in an emerging *empowerment* philosophy [38]:

> The Council believes that health programs and strategies [for Latinas] need to be guided by the principle of empowerment in program or policy development and in allocation of resources. The Council views empowerment as the involvement of women in the making of informed choices about their health and well-being, as well as those of their family and community [37].

COSSMHO (the National Coalition of Hispanic Health and Human Services Organizations) released a "cultural and empowerment approach" curriculum for HIV prevention among Latinas, also in 1990, modeled under the understandings of the HDI guidelines. It again affirmed,

> . . . [Latinas] are expected to follow varying levels of submissive and passive behaviors in front of others compared to men. Although this seems to be true in many cases, women control many situations and assume a high degree of power behind closed doors . . . They become skillful in identifying and using different kinds of resources available to them, very often taking advantage of the social network they belong to. ["Empowerment"] . . . is referring to the validation of this "hidden," sometimes unacknowledged power, facilitating a self-recognition of their power and providing external validation which can be transferred internally and then directed toward action [39].

This curriculum in particular began to establish a syncretic, often monolithic understanding of the Hispanic woman, with generalized statements about her role ("The Latina woman [sic] has always assumed responsibility and made decisions which affect her future and that of her family"), the importance of her social network ("Her culture makes accessible an informal network to provide her support, e.g., 'comadres' "), and family dynamics ("The family—nuclear and extended—is a major source of love, commitment, concern, information, sharing, pride, and consultation for decision making") [37].

Moreover, reviews of programs from that period forward [9, 19, 40-45], show a confusing acknowledgment of the need for specific differentiations between Latina subsets, but go on to talk generically about Hispanics, the Latina, her problems, ideology, lifestyle, needs, and even sexual habits in terms that approximate clichés (e.g., prudery, virginity, domesticity, etc.). Empowerment becomes entrenched in *her* becoming assertive, informed; in capturing *her* already existing power (presumed) and authority in other areas of life, and redirecting its energy to the pursuit of safer sex outcomes [46]. Empowerment rhetoric thus focuses exclusively on changing the Latina, while completely ignoring the intricacies of her structural, interpersonal, and intimate worlds. The very fact that she approaches the sexual moment with idiosyncratic, situation-bound, or subculturally mediated understandings is marginally addressed at best. In many instances the fact that she harbors a risk-taking bias which favors salvaging her relationship with a man, versus her health, is not understood [27, 47, 48].

Rather than correcting the limitations of an empowerment ideology, or situating the acquisition of such capacities within the matrix of the inter-personal and the intimate, health educators in the early '90s often sought methodological solutions to what was already "not working out" as easily as presumed: That Latinas, once guided into self-awareness and capacitated by rehearsing with like others their new-found power, could as easily translate its authority into sexual decision making in the bedroom. Pedagogical solutions to effecting changes in behavior and preventing the spread of HIV/AIDS seemed logical remedies, since early strategies of empowerment obviously did not teach women enough, or did not teach empowerment correctly [3, 16, 38, 42, 44].

"Problem-posing" methodologies, heavily influenced by the non-formal education philosophies of Paulo Freire [49] were touted to be more effective in modifying behavior than traditional methods of health education [3]. Here, dialogical processes work through the "problem" and bring the "subject" (i.e., the Latina at risk and being "taught") into the equal-status of co-learner with the educator, thereby "empowering" change through jointly developed solutions [50-52].

Problem-posing methods may work well with literacy campaigns, or in other arenas where the individual—not a significant other or a sexual dyad—has deter-mination or control over the major variables affecting decision making behavior. The methodology never translated well to health education campaigns for HIV/AIDS, because here, health risk is concomitantly tied to sexual partners who also influence sexual decisions along with a subject. The critical mistake repeated by these education methods—even if by default—was to again situate sexual decision making within the narrow confines of one individual's authority struc-ture. Sexual outcomes, as discussed below, are rarely determined by one indi-vidual—and men, in Hispanic culture at large, are usually more than joint arbiters [4, 5, 9, 14].

Also fueling empowerment rhetoric are those popular, but severely myopic psychosocial models of health behavior change now so inured in HIV/AIDS prevention schemas [53-55]. These often employ constructs from "rational choice" models of health-seeking. Such models, which include the Health Belief Model [56] and the Theory of Reasoned Action [57], view behavior as the outcome of a cognitive process in which the costs of performing a particular health action are weighed by individuals against the possible benefits. An individual's assessment of "costs vs. benefits" may be influenced by perceptions about the health threat, normative beliefs about a health-seeking action, or perceptions of self-efficacy in accomplishing the desired behavioral change. Aiming to consolidate, Catania, Kegeles, and Coates proposed the *AIDS Risk Reduction Model* (ARRM), integrating psychosocial and behavioral concepts from rational choice, health-seeking models into three central constructs deemed key in the behavioral change process: Assessing one's behavior; committing one's self to reduce risk; and, developing strategies for change [58].

Critiques of these models have been historically [31, 59, 60] and recently [61-63] aired by applied anthropologists at work in the health sector. Suffice it here to restate the limitations of such models as seen by the original theorists themselves, that "these models are limited to accounting for as much of the variance in individual's health-related behaviors as can be explained by [only] their attitudes and beliefs"; and that, "It is clear that other forces influence health actions as well" [56].

Precisely, it is the trivialization of just such "other forces" that results in reductionism. In the case of Latinas this omits, severely, the dynamics of interacting with their male sexual partners; an acknowledgment of just how sexualizing dynamics result in behavior; and, how behavioral outcomes are negotiated through the filters of culture and subculture, moment-bound circumstances, personal need or serendipity. This reductionism, again, fuels empowerment assumptions by presuming that the locus of sexual behavior outcomes can be situated solely within the purview of one partner, his or her ideology, attitudes, values, etc. [64]. Catania et al. [58] have themselves pointed out that sexual risk reduction is complicated by the "social nature" of sexual behavior and the need to obtain the cooperation of another person. "Individuals may correctly label their [own] behaviors as being problematic, make a genuine commitment to change—yet not achieve desired solutions if they are unable to obtain their partner's cooperation through effective communication and persuasion" [53]. To date, few studies have examined the applicability of existing models of health behavior change to at-risk for HIV populations, longitudinally, or how such models might be modified to reflect the specific issues, concerns, subcultural and life circumstances that motivate individuals to risks rather than protection [18, 48, 65].

In sum, the difficulties experienced with empowerment-based models of prevention among Latinas are reflective of the difficulties inherent in the paradigms that support health belief or "reasoned action" perspectives. These models fit best with middle-class Americans whose individualized authority structures and socioeconomic positions allow "reasoned action" [66], but not in the world of ethnic populations where "commonsense knowledge of the world takes on quite a different form" [61].

THE DIFFERENTIATED UNIVERSE OF LATINAS' SEXUAL NEGOTIATION DYNAMICS AND THEIR BEHAVIORAL OUTCOMES

To illustrate the variegation, and the need to document such distinctives in ethnic and Latina populations holistically as a critical first step in cogent prevention education planning, I draw from previous studies I conducted among Latinas of varying ethnic provenances [4, 8, 9, 14]. I use the *sexual negotiation dynamic* (defined below) as a foil for the ensuing discussion.

These studies collected ethnographic and empirical data on two distinct subgroups of Latinas at risk for HIV:[2] (Island) Puerto Rican women[3] ($n = 202$) [9], and predominantly Mexican- and Central American-born women residing in Los Angeles and Orange Counties, CA ($n = 270$) [14] (hereafter, Mexican/CA Latinas). These studies assessed a variety of Hispanic/cultural, subcultural/ provenance, personal-ideological, interpersonal, sexual/behavioral, and contraceptive attitudes and practices variables thought to condition risk for HIV. Mean ages for these convenience samples were 33.1 and 33.5 years, respectively, and represent Latinas in remarkably similar life stages and economic levels, regardless of provenance. All subjects reflected very low, or no acculturation (as measured), and were predominantly monogamous in partnership. (Readers should note all quoted data which follow are found in the author's studies, as cited above).

Sexual negotiation was identified as the discursive/behavioral arbitration between a sexualizing pair which determines sexual outcomes [4, 9, 14]. These dynamics occur prior to and during the sexual moment, and condition actual "practices" [65]. Formal operationalization included variables in the dynamic (e.g., verbal/non-verbal "come-ons," requests for sex, initiating certain behaviors) as well as those which surround the dynamic (e.g., role attitudes, scripts, etc.).

---

[2] As measured by an HIV risk index, a composite measure derived from twenty-four questions and specifically designed for these studies. See Gil [4, 9]. Convenience and random samples from high seroprevalence neighborhoods were obtained using community canvassing, outreach programs, and actual randomized lists obtained from housing authorities servicing these low-income neighborhoods. All women included in the studies were confirmed at risk using the risk index constructed.

[3] Puerto Ricans have been historically and culturally differentiated from Mexican and Central American Latino populations due to their distinctive ethno-histories. In the context of HIV/AIDS, this is especially important since these populations exhibit distinctive infection patterns, with Island Puerto Ricans especially having high rates of IDU-related infections, vs. Mexican/Central Americans having predominantly heterosexual transmissions. See Martinez-Maza [25]; Mays and Cochran [17], Peterson and Marín [68]; Ramos [69]; and Worth [27].

Twelve items assessed those discursive, attitudinal, and behavioral domains entertained by a sexualizing pair.[4]

Eventually, a summary measure of negotiation capacities was constructed using nine of the twelve items, all highly intercorrelated, as a "negotiation index" (expressed as a mean index score). *T*-test for significant differences between means of the two samples revealed that there were none ($F = 2.14$, $[t = 2.14, 470 \, df\,] \, p = .433$): Both groups showed similarly low means in negotiation potential based on this summary measure (Puerto Rican Latinas, 3.747, $SD = 1.815$; Mexican/CA Latinas, 3.637, $SD = 1.241$), a finding which presumes to speak of Latinas' overall low influence over her sexual moments, as measured.

But how does this statistical finding translate into actual elements of the negotiation dynamic, or behavioral outcomes in each population? In other words, does the face validity of this "low" level of overall negotiation potential sustain itself through further testing? Exactly how are the dynamics of sexual negotiations both perceived and actually carried out? Can deconstruction using empirically derived control measures *and* ethnographic information support the overall conclusion? For cogent prevention education, specifics are necessary.

In both samples, initiation of sexual activity was perceived by women as a "mutual affair," with 62 percent of Puerto Rican, and 64 percent of Mexican/CA Latinas reporting that sexual activity took place when *either* partner initiated. Clear requests for sexual liaisons (i.e., verbal come-ons for sex) were also stated by Puerto Rican women to be mutually shared (63 percent). However, Mexican/CA Latinas did not report mutuality here, but rather, that the majority of sex requests came from their partners (69.4 percent).

In the sexual moment, what again took place was described by Puerto Rican women as largely a mutual decision (48.3 percent). Nineteen percent of Puerto Rican women even claimed *they alone* decided what predominated in the sexual moment with a male. In this sample, males alone (33 percent) were not regarded as the principal decision makers of sexual activity. Puerto Rican women strongly disagreed (78 percent) with the notion that the female is mainly a passive partner in the sexual act. Over 47 percent also stated they could say "no" at will to their partner's sexual advances without generating negative repercussions from them. Puerto Rican women claimed that initiation of vaginal intercourse was mainly "mutual" (66 percent), as was almost all sex (50 percent). Sixteen percent also engaged in anal sex regularly, and of these ($n = 32$), over 80 percent confirmed it was they alone who controlled the timing of this event, not their partners. When these subjects did not have anal sex, it was

---

[4] These studies also controlled for the influence of mediating variables on the research variables, such as marital status and length of partnership; provenance differences; access to HIV/AIDS information; use of social support networks; resources available to a woman, including socioeconomic opportunities; life conditions like her level of acculturation; and, if an immigrant, time in the United States.

because they disliked the practice (70 percent). Similarly, Puerto Rican women also stated that when there was no oral sex ($n = 57$), it was mainly because she herself disliked it (49.7 percent).

Specific behaviors as measured in Mexican/CA Latinas differed markedly. Vaginal intercourse was most often initiated by male partners (56 percent), as was almost all sex (69.4 percent). Few Mexican/CA Latinas engaged in oral sex (21.1percent), but when it was engaged ($n = 30$), it was the male partner that initiated it most frequently (50.8 percent). Those who did not practice oral sex ($n = 169$) cited *personal dislike* (53.4 percent) or cultural taboos (22 percent) as reasons. Overwhelmingly, Mexican/CA Latinas avoided anal sex (91.5 percent). But again, when it was practiced (8.5 percent), it was the male partner who most often initiated it (58 percent of $n = 24$). Mexican/CA Latinas cited personal dislike (44.2 percent), cultural prohibitions against the practice (33.8 percent), and discomfort-pain with the practice (5.6 percent) as reasons for not having anal sex. Mexican/CA Latinas saw their male partners as overwhelmingly the more "active" partner (72 percent), but when he was not (27 percent), then subjects believed both of them were equally active (88 percent of $n = 75$).

These studies also tested for the effects of other "mediating" variables on the above perceptions and behaviors. Suffice it here to report, as example, the influence of one variable set which acted differentially on the subjective opinions and behavioral outcomes of both Latina groups being discussed: attitudes and experiences with male condoms. This is another illustration of how theoretical models must account for those cultural-perceptual nuances which differentially intervene in sexual negotiations and their outcomes. Condom use, and the female's own perceptions and attitudes toward male condoms, were employed as intervening variables with potential effects on the sexual negotiation dynamic.[5]

Puerto Rican women in relationships where the condom *was not used* were significantly more prone to communicating their sexual desires openly, and having greater say in what sexual activity was undertaken in the act ($\chi^2 = 29.58$, 4 *df*, $p = .000$), 4 *df*, $p = .001$). It was in this type of *unprotected* sexual relationship that Puerto Rican women tended to assert themselves most, and to enjoy a more mutually-oriented sexual role. However, Puerto Rican women who *disliked* male condoms, but were in relationships where males used them, also showed significant positive associations between their open communication of sexual desires and their capacity to make decisions about activities in the sexual act ($\chi^2 = 24.25$, 4 *df*, $p = .000$). These were also active in initiating sexual activities ($\chi^2 = 14.95$, 4 *df*, $p = .001$). Consequently, while condom use "freed" some Puerto Rican women to act and say more (and interview data show that

---

[5] Independent Chi-square tests of association controlling for condom use were performed on the variables discussed.

"freedom" related more to lowered worries about *pregnancy* than to *disease*), the absence or use of condoms—or for that matter the woman's own opinions about the condom—did not significantly alter the Puerto Rican female's more assertive role in sexual decision making. In this sense, the use or absence of condoms, the enculturated implications about their use which some women harbored, did not significantly reduce the overall trend toward mutuality these women reported.[6]

Distinct from these were Mexican/CA Latinas, who, when in relationships where the condom was *not* used, were less communicative of their sexual desires, and also less active in the sexual act ($\chi^2 = 8.14$, 4 *df*, *p* = .08). Even though these women claimed mutuality in sex, actual behaviors reported when controlling for condom use show, overall, that Mexican/CA Latinas guided their activity by the male's initiation of sexual behaviors; by his dictating occurrences for liaisons; as well as by his overall determination of what activities were likely to occur sexually. In other words, Mexican/CA Latinas' sexual behaviors were predominantly situated within the matrix of male initiations and behaviors in the sexual act, and his use or non-use of condoms.

Unlike Puerto Ricans, who showed a broader range of attitudes regarding condoms in general, Mexican/CA Latinas were substantially in agreement with male condom use (61.1 percent). It is therefore understandable why in relationships where their men used condoms, these Latinas tended to feel more assertive, and to perceive a more mutually-oriented sexual role for themselves. Here, protected sex seemed to afford Mexican/CA Latinas greater opportunity for self-expression, and a stronger positioning in their opinions and actions during sex ($\chi^2 = 25.74$, 4 *df*, *p* = .000).

Ethnographic comments explain: When their men used condoms there was little need for Mexican/CA Latinas to voice protection concerns. When men voluntarily used condoms, it spoke silently to both probabilities of pregnancy and to disease prevention, and these were emphatic points in ethnographic interview responses (e.g., "I don't have to worry, even about asking him, when he uses [condoms]"). Unlike Puerto Rican Latinas, Mexican/CA Latinas were very aware, and consequently concerned about disease protection—a fact underscored by the number of partners who worked seasonally away from home and potentially could have sex elsewhere [7, 70, 71].

Could Latinas suggest condom use? These samples again show similarities and differences. In both samples, a woman's personal attitude toward male condoms was correlated with her *suggesting* or *not suggesting* condom use to

---

[6] Burgos and Perez [81] explore themes of sexuality in Puerto Rican culture, and concluded early in 1986, before the HIV/AIDS epidemic had reached the proportions it had on the Island when the Gil [4, 9, 14] studies were conducted, that a Puerto Rican woman's assertiveness in sex among lower income groups had much to do with survival tactics, and the "manipulation of men." In the service of self-interests in this sense, Puerto Rican women "know how to handle their men," as the author was told directly many times.

her partner (Puerto Rican woman, $r = .0134$, $p = .000$; Mexican/CA Latinas, Mantel-Haenszel $= 1.526$, 1 df, $p = .21$). Among Puerto Rican women, a positive linear correlation reveals the greater her dislike of condoms, the greater her reluctance to suggest their use to her partner. Ethnographic interviews confirmed that the Puerto Rican Latina's own attitudes about male condoms, her experiences with male condoms, which are the greater influences on her suggesting or not suggesting use. Among Mexican/CA Latinas, the trend is not overtly linear, and the association does not support the notion of a low willingness to suggest their use. In this regard, 47 percent of Mexican/CA Latinas agreed, regardless of their own feelings about male condoms—and in ethnographic interviews often stated—that a woman should try to request condom use from her partner.

However, in both samples, if the partner was perceived as "faithful" (and the distinction is not a relative one in the minds of women interviewed),[7] she then should not request condom use. Ethnographic interviews were a rich source for revealing the rationale: Latinas overall are hesitant to introduce condom requests in their sexual moments with a "faithful partner" because of the perceived threat such a suggestion would introduce to a relationship they deemed trustworthy [27, 48]. Asking for condom use when there is "no apparent reason" is to virtually say to your partner "I don't trust you." This threat, combined with the oft-repeated by-lines women share about suggesting condom use—when and to whom—disable Latinas from evaluating *for themselves* the actual risk to self or relationship if such a suggestion were made to a "faithful" partner.

Both samples were also reflective of relational and partner concerns, and such concerns were shown to create hesitations and inabilities when these did, in fact, negotiate condom use [48]. Low condom usage is thus consistent with Puerto Rican women's overall low regard for the product. However, *there is a line of demarcation*, and a Puerto Rican woman will "only go so far in pushing her man" to use condoms when she feels them necessary. Certainly, that line is at best crossed with hesitation if she is with a perceived "faithful man." Loss of male partnership is a constant threat to the stability of a Puerto Rican woman's self perception and feminine role [4, 8, 9, 48].

In the case of Mexican/CA Latinas, the near opposite was true. It was protected sex which made her feel more mutually engaged; which lowered her worries, enabled communication; and which allowed her sometimes to initiate sex. While Puerto Rican women could worry about not having a male partner, here, the

---

[7]Ethnographic dialogues as well as focus groups define the notion of "faithful" as a partner who does not give a woman cause to worry about extramarital affairs (i.e., is trustworthy), who is "home at night and on weekends," and who is not prone to getting drunk. (In the minds of women from both samples, drinking was highly correlated with male infidelity.)

consistent absence of many men from the home due to seasonal work eased the social pressure. According to Mexican/CA Latinas interviewed, returning males often did not hesitate to use condoms, relieving women from having to ask. (This is not reported to be the case among *migrant* Latinos elsewhere, cf., Mishra, Conner, and Magaña [7].)

In sum, Latinas' sexual negotiation potential is sensitive to differential perceptions, emotions, experiences, and ideologies. Provenance and subculturally specific attitudes, as well as her own relational ties and condom predilections color her potential to express, decide, negotiate the sexual moment and thus, self-protect. It is not a simple matter of becoming informed, or more assertive with her partner: Sexually "negotiating" safer sex involves the interplay of all, and more, of the variables illustrated above. Added to these, and furthering the example of our need to be specific about distinctives between Latinas, is the well-documented set of *other differences among Latinas*, including those surrounding gendered notions; use, or lack of support networks; circumscribed worlds; issues of self-worth, of intrafamilial abuse, and the like. These also condition the nature and extent of a Latina's sexual prowess, or even her capacity to "empower" herself, no matter what she may decide unilaterally [2, 4, 9, 72-76].

It would thus be a grievous error to create generic narratives about Latinas, or to suggest uniform prevention strategies that did not reflect the distinctives evidenced in the examples above: as to the meaning of sexual negotiation; as to its interpersonal locus; as to how it is arbitrated; and, as to how elements like attitudes about and use of condoms enter the behavioral outcome equation. What does it mean for one Latina to be free to express herself sexually when her partner does not use condoms, while another Latina feels inhibited by the same circumstance? These differences need understanding before prevention efforts can truly work.

DISCUSSION

The failure of so many AIDS prevention activities in the United States and abroad—now prompting massive infusions of U.S. government money into "program evaluations" [21, 22]—should not make us hesitate in critiquing what does not work, or stating why. The HIV pandemic requires us to work toward constant evaluation and reorientation of our public health activities related to prevention, and hopefully, to a more solid anchoring of these in theoretical and practical knowledge about specific communities and cultures. Bibeau [63], in his recent critique of public health models, clearly states the limitations: "The insights of the behavioral models for predicting behavior discussed (health belief model and others) are most applicable to monolithic cultures. As the age of monolithic cultures disappears, and individuals refer constantly to cultural forms that are hybrid and creolized, the operational value of these models disappears."

To enable theoretical and model applications to such variegated populations, cultural, "grounded theory" components must be integrated as intervening variables. An anthropological and *holistic* paradigm which emphasizes ethnographic discovery of the linkages between cultural ideologies, values, and artifacts as substrates, and personal behavior as "reasoned outcome," can elevate such models to productive levels. It can do so by including such variables as, culturally mediated, gendered sexual scripts; cultural, subcultural, and processual models for the sexual act; analysis of culturally and personally constituted sexual negotiation dynamics; and a host of other necessary considerations suited to addressing populations that are differentiated or intraculturally diverse.

As is the case, the Latina universe illustrates that their "realities" (plural intended) are far more complex than rational choices or reasoned action would suggest. Behavior should be seen "as discourses and narratives acted out in specific contexts derived from personal histories" [63]. Personal mental constructions are not uniform from social member to member; each individual's beliefs, ideas, and representations of reality serve to produce and project the tremendous variety of actions and discourses that are made meaningful only within the specific contexts of individual lives. To suggest homogeneity by virtue of the educational curricula we construct to combat AIDS negatively flies in the face of such variety.

By placing the actions and practices of individuals once again into their culturally and interpersonally constructed spaces, anthropologists working in public health and HIV/AIDS *have* been able to document the "real world" of individuals (see Feldman [77], among myriad others)—meaningful, coherent understandings that usually fragment when measured only "empirically." Taken out of context and reconstructed *etically*, they are prone to simplification for the sake of program building. (Medical anthropologist Michael Clatts [78] has rightfully complained that "AIDS prevention has become an exercise in behavioral modification theory, an enterprise that has more to do with social control than with the prevention of a disease."

The failure of "empowerment" models is a consequence of the lack of acknowledging variegation and finding the educational means to include such in prevention research agendas. We uniformly try to teach Latinas to be assertive, how to put condoms on their partners, how to 'bargain' and 'negotiate', answer back, and fail to realize the limited utility of these practices in the context of their realities [18, 79]. Latinas' AIDS risks require a ferreting out of those nuances of text and context which make a difference depending on one's provenance, subculture, life history, personal experience, and partnership. To suggest that the prevention agenda cannot handle such diversity is at once to suggest we cannot treat individuals as such. In short, we are increasingly required to operate from a constructivist research paradigm, not one of logical empiricism, if we are to enable prevention education which meets needs in the "lived lives" of people [80].

CONCLUSION: IMPLICATIONS FOR AIDS
PREVENTION EDUCATION

It should be evident even from the cursory, contrastive set of illustrations presented above, that there exist sizeable distinctions between Latinas at risk for HIV. The differences, once known, can assist us in the design of cogent prevention education that does not isolate her from her relationships or presumes she can unilaterally change her world.

Simple enough. Unfortunately, present "models" which explain human behavior, as I have tried to show, are dimensionally and interpersonally flat and consequently, do not encourage us to "see the world" as others see it. If gaining an understanding of the relation between knowledge and prevention involves what Bourdieu (1977) called a "feel for the game" [61], then we must recognize that such knowledge cannot be obtained without extensive fieldwork.

In the "decades of AIDS" we have rushed, sometimes madly, to generate program solutions *without fieldwork* because of the press of the epidemic. At other times we have settled for steady-state understandings of social interaction dynamics to examine behavior change over time. Our penchant for empirical exactitude has often robbed us of the "thick descriptions" so necessary for bringing depth and life to our knowledge.

The strongest implication raised here for HIV prevention education is the necessity to rework the paradigms which orient our work, first to include those necessary avenues—theoretical and processual—that enable depth understanding of our subjects. From there, we can proceed to articulate, and build, those more individualized and specific programs of education and prevention tailored to *individuals* living in more specific, interpersonal contexts of understanding.

Latinas need to be understood as variously as they are: constructed from different awareness of self, relationships, community, experiences, and subculture. While Latinas share many of the cultural elements which define them as such—and consequently assist them in connecting in varied ways—they are as different as a mosaic. These differences are in need of study, analysis, interpretation. To be useful, these efforts need involve a description of the contexts in which individuals make decisions, as well as how those contexts—interpersonal and social—influence decisions. In this respect, any prevention education program for sexually active Latinas that does not, somehow and eventually, reach their partners concurrently, has limited utility.

We need to make visible the nuances that differentiate and define Latinas, and which, sadly, allow many to continue to be at risk for HIV.

ACKNOWLEDGMENTS

Research on which this chapter is based was variously funded by the American Foundation for AIDS Research (AmFAR) for Puerto Rican data; and by University-wide AIDS Research Programs, University of California Systems, for Mexican/Central American data.

REFERENCES

1. Centers for Disease Control, *HIV/AIDS Surveillance Report*, U.S. Government Printing Office, Atlanta, Georgia, *8*:1, 1996.
2. E. de la Vega, Considerations for Reading the Latino Population with Sexuality and HIV/AIDS Information and Education, *Siecus Report, 18*:3, pp. 1-8, 1990.
3. J. R. Magana and J. M. Carrier, Mexican and Mexican American Male Sexual Behavior and the Spread of AIDS in California, *Journal of Sex Research, 28*:3, pp. 425-441, 1991. *See also*, J. M. Carrier and R. Magna, Use of Ethnosexual Data on Men of Mexican Origin for HIV/AIDS Prevention Program, *The Journal of Sex Research, 28*:2, pp. 198-202, 1991.
4. V. E. Gil, *Dilemmas of Puerto Rican Women at Risk for AIDS: Information Access and Sexual Negotiation Issues*, paper presented at the 39th Annual Meeting of the Society for the Scientific Study of Sex, San Diego, California, November 1992.
5. V. E. Gil, *Entre amor y terror: Mexican Immigrant Women's Negotiation of Sex, AIDS Risk, and Partner Fidelity*, paper presented at the 39th Annual Meeting of the Society for the Scientific Study of Sexuality, Symposium Session "Race and Ethnicity," Houston, Texas, November 1996.
6. J. M. Carrier, *Des Los Otros, Intimacy and Homosexuality among Mexican Men*, Columbia University Press, New York, 1996.
7. S. I. Mishra, R. Conner, and R. Magana (eds.), *AIDS Crossing Borders, The Spread of HIV among Migrant Latinos*, Westview Press, Boulder, Colorado, 1996.
8. V. E. Gil, *Dilemmas of Access to HIV Information and Sexual Negotiation among Puerto Rican Low-Income Women*, paper presented at the Joint Conference of Anthropologists and the Center for Disease Control, Atlanta, Georgia, October 1991.
9. V. E. Gil, *Sources of HIV/AIDS Information and the Negotiation of Sexual Risk by Low-Income Puerto Rican Women*, Published Final Research Report, (American Foundation for AIDS Research [AmFAR]), Southern California College (ms.), Costa Mesa, California, 1992.
10. V. E. Gil, AIDS: The Cultural Factors. Puerto Rico and the Caribbean, *AIDS and Society Bulletin, 1*:3, pp. 1-8.
11. V. E. Gil, *Latinos and AIDS: Low Income Puerto Rican Womens' Isolation, AIDS Risk, and Sexual Negotiation,* paper presented at the 1993 Annual Meeting of the Society for Applied Anthropology, San Antonio, Texas, 1993.
12. L. A. Araba-Owoyele, M. J. Hughes, and G. W. Rutherford, HIV Infection in Women, *Western Journal of Medicine, 160*:6(June), pp. 581-582,1994. *See also*, L. A. Araba-Owoyele and R. A. Littaua, AIDS-Related Knowledge, Attitudes, Beliefs and Behaviors among Blacks and Latinos in California, *California Department of Health Services*, March 1992.
13. California State Office of AIDS, California Department of Health Services, *California and the HIV/AIDS Epidemic, A State of the State Report*, California State Office of AIDS, Sacramento, California, 1995.

14. V. E. Gil, *Latinas and HIV/AIDS: A Comprehensive Study of Factors Associated with Their Risk and Sexual Negotiation Capacities*, Final Report, Southern California College, Costa Mesa, California, 1996.
15. C. Amezcua, A. Ramirez, A. McAllister, R. McCuan, C. Galavotti, and C. Reed, *Effects of a Spanish-Language Community Intervention in Southwest Texas on Reported HIV Infection Knowledge, Attitudes, and Behavior*, paper presented at the Vth International Conference on AIDS, Montreal, Canada, 1989.
16. L. Arguelles and A. M. Rivero, HIV Infection/AIDS and Latinas in Los Angeles County: Considerations for Prevention Treatment and Research Practice, *California Sociologist, 11*:12, pp. 68-89, 1989.
17. V. Mays and S. D. Cochran, Issues in the Perception of AIDS Risk and Risk Reduction Activities by Black and Hispanic/Latina Women, *American Psychologist, 43*:11, pp. 949-957, 1988.
18. D. Worth, Women at High Risk of HIV Infection: Behavioral, Prevention, and Intervention Aspects, in *Behavioral Aspects of AIDS*, D. L. Ostrow (ed.), Plenum Press, New York, pp. 101-119, 1990.
19. S. L. Coyle, R. F. Boruch, and C. F. Turner (eds.), *Evaluating AIDS Prevention Programs* (Expanded Edition), National Research Council, National Academy Press, Washington, DC, 1991. *See also*, A. M. Nyamathi, J. Flaskerud, C. Bennett, and W. DeJong, Evaluation of Two AIDS Education Programs for Impoverished Latina Women, *AIDS Education and Prevention, 4*, pp. 296-309, 1994.
20. L. O'Donnell, A. San Doval, R. Vornefett, and W. DeJong, Reducing AIDS and Other STDs among Inner-City Hispanics: The Use of Qualitative Research in the Development of Video-Based Patient Education, *AIDS Education and Prevention, 6*:2, pp. 140-153, 1994.
21. M. Renaud and E. Kresse, *HIV Prevention Community Planning Profiles: Assessing the Year One*, U.S. Conference of Mayors, Washington, D.C., 1995.
22. M. Renaud and E. Kresse, *HIV Prevention Community Planning Profiles: Assessing the Impact*, U.S. Conference of Mayors, Washington, D.C., 1996.
23. H. Amaro, Considerations for Prevention of HIV Infection among Hispanic Women, *Psychology of Women Quarterly, 12*, pp. 429-443, 1988.
24. H. Amaro, Women in the Mexican-American Community: Religion, Culture, and Reproductive Attitudes and Experience, *Journal of Community Psychology, 16*:1, pp. 6-20, 1988.
25. O. Martinez-Maza, *Latinos and AIDS: A National Symposium, Proceedings*, Los Angeles: Center for Interdisciplinary Research in Immunology and Disease (CIRID) at UCLA, 1988.
26. R. M. Selik, K. G. Castro, and M. Pappaioanou, Racial/Ethnic Differences in Risk of AIDS in the United States, *American Journal of Public Health, 78*:2, pp. 1539-1545, 1988.
27. D. Worth, Sexual Decision-Making and AIDS: Why Condom Promotion among Vulnerable Women is Likely to Fail, *Studies in Family Planning, 20*:6, pp. 297-307, 1989.
28. K. K. Holmes, J. M. Karon, and J. Kreiss, The Increasing Frequency of Heterosexually Acquired AIDS in the United States 1983-88, *American Journal of Public Health, 80*:7, pp. 853-863, 1990.

29. S. Kane, AIDS, Addiction, and Condom Use: Sources of Sexual Risk for Heterosexual Women, *Journal of Sex Research, 27*:3, pp. 427-444, 1990.
30. E. Carrillo, AIDS and the Latino Community, Boletín, *Centro de Estudios Puertorriquenos, 4*, pp. 7-14, 1988.
31. M. Singer, AIDS and the U.S. Ethnic Minorities: The Crisis and Alternative Anthropology Responses, *Human Organization, 51*:1, pp. 89-95, 1992.
32. P. B. Holman, W. C. Jenkins, and J. A. Gayle, Increasing the Involvement of National and Regional and Ethnic Minority Organizations in HIV Information and Education, *Public Health Reports, 106*, pp. 687-694, 1991.
33. J. E. Osborn, Women and HIV/AIDS: The Silent Epidemic? *Siecus Report, 19*:2, (December 90/January 91), 1991.
34. D. Quadagno, D. Harrison, K. Wambach, P. Levine, A. Imersheim, J. Byers, and K. Maddox, Women at Risk for Human Immunodeficiency Virus, *Journal of Psychology and Human Sexuality, 4*:3, pp. 97-110, 1991.
35. S. Kane, HIV, Heroin, and Heterosexual Relations, *Social Science & Medicine, 32*:9, pp. 1037-1050, 1991.
36. J. M. Carrier, Mexican Male Bisexuality, in *Bisexualities: Theory and Research*, F. Flein and T. J. Wolf (eds.), Haworth Press, New York, pp. 75-85, 1985.
37. HDI (National Hispanic Education and Communication Projects), *Latina AIDS Action Plan and Resource Guide*, Washington, D.C., HDI Projects, 1990.
38. E. H. Barnett, *The Development of Personal Power for Women: An Exploration of the Process of Empowerment*, Ph.D. Dissertation, Boston University, University Microfilms, Ann Arbor, Michigan, 1981.
39. COSSMHO (National Coalition of Hispanic Health and Human Services Organizations), *A Cultural and Empowerment Approach to HIV Prevention among Hispanic/ Latino Women: A Curriculum*, COSSMHO, Washington, D.C., 1990.
40. J. H. Flaskerund and A. M. Nyamathi, Effects of an AIDS Education Program on the Knowledge, Attitudes and Practices of Low Income Black and Latina Women, *Journal of Community Health, 15*:6, pp. 343-355, 1990.
41. B. V. Marin, AIDS Prevention for Non-Puerto Rican Hispanics, in *AIDS and Intravenous Drug Use: Future Directions for Community Based Prevention Research*, C. G. Leukefeld, R. J. Battles, and Z. Amsel (eds.), USDHS Public Health Services NIDA Research Monograph 93, Rockville, Maryland, 1990.
42. J. Cook, A. M. Boxer, and M. H. Cohen, *Education for Inner-City Women at Risk for AIDS/HIV: Effectiveness and Cultural Relevance*, paper presented at the 1992 Annual Meeting of the American Sociological Association, Session 59, Pittsburgh, Pennsylvania, August 1992.
43. J. Catania, T. J. Coates, E. Golden, M. Dolcini, J. Peterson, S. Kegeles, D. Siegel, and M. T. Fullilove, Correlates of Condom Use among Black, Hispanic, and White Heterosexuals in San Francisco: The AMEN Longitudinal Survey, AIDS in Multi-Ethnic Neighborhoods Survey, *AIDS Education and Prevention, 6*:1, pp. 12-26, 1994.
44. J. Catania, D. Binson, M. Dolcini, R. Stall, C. Kyung-Hee, L. Pollack, S. E. Hudes, J. Canchola, K. Phillips, J. T. Moskowitz, and J. T. Coates, Risk Factors for HIV and Other Sexually Transmitted Diseases and Prevention Practices among US Heterosexual Adults: Changes from 1990 to 1992, *American Journal of Public Health, 85*:11, pp. 1492-1499, November 1995a.

45. Coreq, G. *The Invisible Epidemic. The Story of Women and AIDS,* HarperCollins, New York, 1992.

46. R. Robles, H. M. Colon, A. Gonzalez, and T. Mateos, Social Relations and Empowerment of Sexual Partners of IV Drug Users, *Puerto Rican Health Sciences Journal, 9*:1, pp. 99-104, 1990.

47. B. V. Marin, Hispanic Culture: Implications for AIDS Prevention, in *Sexuality and Disease: Metaphors, Perceptions, and Behavior in the AIDS Era,* J. Boswell, R. Hexter, and J. Reinisch (eds.), Oxford Press, New York, 1990.

48. E. J. Sobo, *Choosing Unsafe Sex: AIDS-Risk Denial Among Disadvantaged Women,* University of Pennsylvania Press, Philadelphia, Pennsylvania, 1995.

49. P. Freire, *Education for Critical Consequences,* Continuum Press, New York, 1983. *See also,* P. Freire, *Pedagogy of the Oppressed,* Seabury Press, New York, 1970.

50. T. Sanders, The Paulo Freire Method: Literacy Training and Conscientization, *Dialogue, 7*:1, pp. 1-17, 1973.

51. J. Murphy, Paulo Freire's Program for Adult Literacy, *The Forum for Education, 36*:3, pp. 107-119, 1977.

52. J. McFadden, *Consciousness and Social Change: The Padagogy of Paulo Freire,* Ph.D. Dissertation, School of Education, California State University Sacramento, University Microfilms, Inc., Ann Arbor, Michigan, 1975.

53. A. Kline and M. VanLandingham, HIV-Infected Women and Sexual Risk Reduction: The Relevance of Existing Models of Behavior Change, *AIDS Education and Prevention, 6*:5, pp. 390-402, 1994.

54. A. Fishbein and S. Middlestadt, Using the Theory of Reasoned Action as a Framework for Understanding and Changing AIDS-Related Behaviors, in *Primary Prevention of AIDS,* V. Mays, G. Albee, and S. Schneider (eds.), Sage Publications, Newbury Park, California, pp. 93-110, 1989.

55. A. Bandura, Perceived Self-Efficacy in the Exercise of Control Over AIDS, in *Primary Prevention of AIDS: Psychological Approaches,* V. Mays, G. Albee, and S. Schneider (eds.), Sage Publications, Newbury Park, California, pp. 128-141, 1989.

56. N. Janz and M. Becker, The Health Belief Model: A Decade Later, *Health Education Quarterly, 11,* pp. 1-47, 1984.

57. I. Ajzen and M. Fishbein, *Understanding Attitudes and Prejudices and Predicting Behavior,* Prentice-Hall, Englewood Cliffs, New Jersey, 1980.

58. J. Catania, S. M. Kegeles, and T. J. Coate, Towards an Understanding of Risk Behavior: An AIDS Risk Reduction Model (ARRM), *Health Education Quarterly, 17,* pp. 53-72, 1990.

59. J. Catania, V. Stone, D. Binson, and M. Dolcini, Changes in Condom Use among Heterosexuals in Wave 3 of the AMEN Survey, *The Journal of Sex Research, 32*:3, pp. 193-200, 1995.

60. N. G. Schiller, What's Wrong with this Picture? The Hegemonic Construction of Culture in AIDS Research in the United States, *Medical Anthropology Quarterly, 6*:3, pp. 237-254, 1992.

61. P. Bourdieu, *Outline of a Theory of Practice,* Cambridge University Press, Cambridge, Massachusetts, p. 27, 1977.

62. P. S. Yoder, Negotiating Relevance: Belief, Knowledge, and Practice in International Health Projects, *Medical Anthropology Quarterly, 11*:2, pp. 131-146, 1997.

63. G. Bibeau, At Work in the Fields of Public Health: The Abuse of Rationality, *Medical Anthropology Quarterly, 11*:2, pp. 246-255, 1997.

64. P. J. Pelto and G. H. Pelto, Studying Knowledge, Culture, and Behavior in Applied Medical Anthropology, *Medical Anthropology Quarterly, 11*:2, pp. 147-163, 1997.

65. B. E. Schneider and N. E. Stoller, *Women Resisting AIDS: Feminist Strategies of Empowerment*, Temple University Press, Philadelphia, 1994.

66. A. P. M. Coxon, P. M. Davies, A. J. Hunt, and P. Weatherburn, The Structure of Sexual Behavior, *Journal of Sex Research, 29*:1, pp. 61-83, 1992.

67. B. J. Good, *Medicine, Rationality, and Experience*, Cambridge University Press, Cambridge, Massachusetts, 1994.

68. J. L. Peterson and G. Marin, Issues in the Prevention on AIDS among Black and Hispanic Men, *American Psychologist, 43*:11, pp. 871-877, 1988.

69. L. Ramos, *Perspectives on AIDS in a Group of Latinas at the South Central Family Health Center*, unpublished Master's thesis, University of California, School of Public Health, Los Angeles, California, 1987.

70. B. V. Marin, C. Gomez, and J. M. Tschann, Condom Use among Hispanic Men with Secondary Female Sexual Partners, *Public Health Reports, 24*, pp. 742-750, 1993.

71. B. V. Marin, C. Gomez, and N. Hearst, Multiple Heterosexual Partners and Condom Use among Hispanics and Non-Hispanic Whites, *Family Planning Perspectives, 24*, pp. 170-174, 1993.

72. E. Acosta-Belen (ed.), *The Puerto Rican Woman: Perspectives on Culture, History, and Society*, Praeger, New York, 1986.

73. O. M. Espin, Cultural and Historical Influences on Sexuality in Hispanic/Latin Women, in *All American Women. Lines that Divide, Ties that Bind*, J. B. Cole (ed.), The Free Press, New York, 1986.

74. E. Pavich, A Chicana Perspective on Mexican Culture and Sexuality, *Sexuality, Ethnoculture, and Social Work*, The Haworth Press, New York, 1986.

75. C. T. Garcia-Coll and M. de L. Mattei, *The Psychosocial Development of the Puerto Rican Women*, Praeger, New York, 1989.

76. K. A. Elder-Tabrizy, R. J. Wolitski, F. Rhodes, and J. G. Baker, AIDS and Competing Health Concerns of Blacks, Hispanics, and Whites, *Journal of Community Health, 16*:1, pp. 11-21, 1991.

77. D. A. Feldman (ed.), *Culture and AIDS*, Praeger, New York, 1990.

78. M. Clatts, All the King's Horses and All the King's Men: Some Personal Reflections on Ten Years of AIDS Ethnography, *Human Organization, 53*, pp. 93-95, 1994.

79. J. D. Fisher, Possible Effects of Reference Group-Based Social Influence on AIDS-Risk Behavior and AIDS Prevention, *American Psychologist, 43*:11, pp. 914-920, 1988.

80. J. Coreil, More Thoughts on Negotiating Relevance, *Medical Anthropology Quarterly, 11*:2, pp. 252-255, 1997.

81. N. M. Burgos and Y. I. Diaz Perez, An Exploration of Human Sexuality in the Puerto Rican Culture, *Journal of Social Work and Human Sexuality, 4*, pp. 135-151, 1986.

CHAPTER 3

Cultural Factors Affecting the Negotiation of First Sexual Intercourse Among Latina Adolescent Mothers

Pamela I. Erickson

In the United States today, adolescent pregnancy and childbearing are perceived as serious health, social, and economic problems [1, 2]. Despite a substantial research literature and numerous intervention programs, teenage childbearing rates have remained high for two decades [3, 4]. The most recent statistics on adolescent birth rates indicate that those of Latina adolescents have now surpassed those of African Americans for the first time, and among Latina teens, birth rates are highest for those of Mexican descent [5]. This chapter explores the social and cultural context of romantic relationships in which Latina teen pregnancy occurs using narratives from young mothers and their partners to illustrate experiences surrounding initiation of sexual intercourse and pregnancy.

The literature on teenage motherhood clearly demonstrates that adolescent childbearing is largely a socioeconomic class phenomenon intertwined with issues of race and ethnicity [3, 4, 6, 7]. Although it is commonly believed that teenage childbearing is disadvantageous for both mother and child [1, 2, 8, 9], recent research suggests that adolescent childbearing may be an adaptive response to severe, generational, socioeconomic constraints experienced most acutely by adolescents of color [7, 10, 11].

Although political economy is an important factor in race and ethnic differences in adolescent childbearing, cultural expectations may also influence reproductive behavior [12]. In fact, Latina adolescents have distinct sexual behavior patterns. Compared to African-American and White adolescents, Latina adolescents have the lowest proportion of sexually active females, and they exhibit low use of family planning clinics, low use of contraceptive methods before becoming pregnant, and low use of abortion [13-25]. Latina adolescents may also be more likely to plan their pregnancies. Two surveys of primarily Mexican origin teen mothers delivering at a large public hospital in Los Angeles found that the proportion of young mothers who had planned to have a baby had increased from 34 percent in the 1986-87 survey to 58 percent in 1992-94 survey [7]. In contrast, national data indicate that only 18 percent of pregnancies to adolescents of all races are planned [8]. In addition, greater acculturation has been associated with higher levels of sexual risk taking behavior and higher birth rates among Latina adolescents [13, 26-30].

Religious values are thought to buttress traditional gender role patterns through opposition to contraception and abortion [31]. In fact, however, Latinos are more similar to other Americans regarding both contraceptive use and attitudes about abortion [15, 31-35]. The use of abortion by Latinas actually exceeds that of Whites, although it may be used less often by Latina adolescents [15, 17, 36].

Research and prevention efforts dealing with teenage pregnancy and childbearing have tended to assume three things: 1) that teenage motherhood is socially, economically, and often medically disadvantageous and should be prevented [1, 2, 9]; 2) that all pregnancies should be consciously planned and young women should prevent unintended pregnancy through abstinence or contraception [8]; and 3) that young women have a choice about whether or not to engage in sex and they make decisions about sex and birth control after weighing the opportunity costs [37]. Yet, such a "rational decision-making" model of sex and reproduction seems to be a construct imposed by researchers, health practitioners, and other professionals dealing with adolescent pregnancy and childbearing issues. It is at odds with the emotional, highly intimate context in which sex is initiated by adolescents [38]. In the real world, sexual initiation is affected by a wide range of factors including emotions, sexual desire, coercion, and social, cultural, and moral norms [37, 38].

In order to understand high rates of Latina adolescent childbearing it is important to understand how the social and cultural aspects of young Latinas' lives may put them at risk for early pregnancy. Latino culture places high value on family and motherhood, and childbearing occurs at younger ages than is normative in the broader American culture [39-44]. Latino cultural norms also tend to value premarital virginity and non-aggressive, modest, sexually ignorant, and sexually passive young women [40, 45-47].[1] American cultural norms make young women the sexual gate-keepers in heterosexual relationships [38] and

---

[1] Although these stereotyped versions of gender behavior are still influential, changes in socio-economic realities necessitating female labor participation, lower fertility, the emergence of an educated Latino middle class, and exposure to more egalitarian gender norms in the United States, result in great variation in actual gender behavior among Latinos.

place high value on consciously chosen, responsible, planned motherhood [1, 8]. This non-traditional, essentially middle class, American gender role pattern may be one for which many Latina teens are not prepared.

If we are to lower Latina teen childbearing rates to allow Latinas to benefit from the social and economic rewards of delayed childbearing, we must understand the social and cultural context of sexual initiation. We need to find out how and why Latina adolescent mothers enter into sexual relationships and how social, cultural, and personal factors shape their sexual experiences. This chapter explores Latina adolescent mothers' narratives about the context of their first sexual experience and pregnancy.

METHODS

The interviews are from a study of the social and cultural context of Latina adolescent childbearing in East Los Angeles.[2] Forty Latina teen mothers under age eighteen at the time they gave birth were recruited from a public hospital providing care to a low income, Latino population. Participants were purposively chosen to represent the dominant Latino sub-groups in Los Angeles, those of Mexican and Central American origin, and to represent varying levels of acculturation based on the country of birth, length of residence in the United States, and language preference. The partners of the young mothers were also invited to participate subject to her permission. Fourteen male partners agreed to participate.[3]

Life histories of participants were collected during one to five informal interviews of one and two hours in length. Participants were paid $25 per interview. The interviews were conducted by bilingual, bicultural female interviewers and in a private room in the outpatient building of the hospital. Participants were simply asked to tell the story of their lives. Topics probed included neighborhood, school, and family, sex and romantic relationships, pregnancy and delivery, being a parent, school and work, migration history, acculturation, health care, and future life plans and goals. Interviews were taped and transcribed in the language of the interview.

RESULTS

Narratives are presented for five cases which illustrate the range of experiences surrounding sexual debut for young mothers. The interviews suggest that for these young mothers, it was not really sex that was being negotiated, but the couple's

[2] The research is funded by the National Institute of Child Health and Development (HD32351).

[3] About half of the young women had no partner at the time of recruitment or did not want us to contact him. Many men who were contacted declined due to time constraints of employment.

entire relationship.[4] "Rational" decision making regarding sex, contraception, and STD prevention could only become the norm for these young couples after they had been having intercourse for some time.

EVA AND RUDY[5]

At age sixteen, Eva moved out of her mother's house because they fought and she thought her mother drank too much, had too many boyfriends, and made her take care of her younger siblings all the time. Eva moved into a small apartment with her sister and another couple, but the situation was strained. Since the lease was in the couple's names, Eva left so her sister could stay:

Eva: That's why I ended up living with Rudy.

Interviewer: When you were living with your sister, and you and Rudy were just *novios* (boyfriend/girlfriend)—you weren't really involved sexually yet. Did it happen after you moved in with Rudy?

Eva: After we moved to his house. He would like ask me, you know, if we could be together like. "No, no, no—I don't want it." Like, I didn't wanna go that far, you know: I was, like, scared. So he—well, he respected me. But we had tried for (having intercourse) sometimes, but it was like—oh! I wouldn't even know what to do. So, just forget it, you know. I was scared, so, I was like, no.

After six months of resistance, Eva gave in to Rudy's urging for sex and got pregnant in the first month.

Eva: The first time (we had sex), I was living with him, he just came outside, but I still got pregnant. (Sex) scared me at first because I was never introduced to my body or even a male's body. I didn't even know how my body worked, you know? To me, in my head it (premarital sex) was wrong.

Interviewer: Were you willing to *entregar* (give yourself up, surrender) yourself to him?

Eva: Yeah, because, see like, I really did love him a lot and I really did care for him, but it was just the fact that I was gonna lose my virginity. I mean, for a Hispanic girl, you know, that's like, God, that's a big thing! That's like something precious. And, you know, like, you just have to wait 'til you're married and stuff, you know? I did love him a lot, but I just didn't want to go that far. I didn't even know why. I just didn't want to do it . . . maybe because of what I had been taught. But I did. I didn't like being at home, and maybe it was a better way to stay away from home. So, being with him was better, and

---

[4] All of the participants were in consensual relationships, and 90 percent had had only one sexual partner in their lifetime. However, about one-third revealed a history of sexual abuse in the past.

[5] Names and details that would identify respondents have been changed to protect confidentiality.

eventually I just gave up to it. But I was just looking for comfort, because I wasn't getting it at home.

Interviewer: Was it ever talked about, planned?

Eva: He would always ask me and I would say "No, no, no, no, no, no."

Eva and Rudy never talked about sex or contraception, but they had talked about a baby.

Eva: He had told me before that he wanted a baby, but I told him "I don't. I don't want a baby."

Eva was surprised that she got pregnant because they had only had sex that one time. By the time she realized she was pregnant she was about twelve to thirteen weeks and would not consider an abortion. After her daughter was born, Eva went back to high school and she is now in college. She and Rudy have a rocky relationship. They don't live together now, but he is very involved as a father and takes Sara frequently.

Rudy was born in Los Angeles and dropped out of school in ninth grade about the time his parents separated. He began working construction and met Eva when he was sixteen.

Rudy: . . . I used to mess around with a lot of girls. But not in, you know . . . to put it this way, I was a virgin. *But yo me la hacía creer que yo* (I let her think that I)—I was a big time player with the girls. And, uh, she was my first one.

Interviewer: So, how did you decide to have sex?

Rudy: Well, to me it wasn't really hard, but you know, *para* (for) Eva it was. 'cause . . . you know guys always *se dejan ir siempre* (*they always leave them*), you know. But the girl, like Eva, she was scared.

Interviewer: Was she scared about getting pregnant? Did you guys ever talk about that?

Rudy: She never did talk to me about that.

Interviewer: And were you trying to get her pregnant?

Rudy: Yeah, in a way, I was like . . . how does it feel to have a kid?

Interviewer: Were you in love with Eva?

Rudy: Well, see, I never loved someone, like really loved 'em (sic). You know? I don't know why. I'm just like that. I do like Eva and everything, but like, I miss her, but I don't like, love her, you know. *Todavía no.* (Not yet). I don't know, we share a lot of things together, you know, but, I don't know how to love someone.

JULIA AND JUAN

Juan met Julia in Mexico. He was born and raised in Los Angeles but was visiting his grandparents in Mexico. Julia's family lived in the same neighborhood and they were family friends of his grandparents. She was twelve years old when they first met, but told him she was fifteen. He was sixteen. For two years, he visited whenever he could. He was in love. He wrote her poems and called her on the phone. He moped around the house and neglected his studies.

Juan: I wasn't doing good (in school) 'cause all the time I was thinking about Julia—all the time . . . from one period to the next. I just couldn't stop. I couldn't help it. I tried not to think of her but I just couldn't stop.

Interviewer: You were really in love with her.

Juan: Yeah, but not—it was more, uh, spiritual, you know than just wanting to kiss her. No, it was true love. So I didn't want to have sex with her. I got tempted sometimes—when we were kissing so passionately—but I respected her. She was the first girl I respected.

Juan eventually found out that Julia had lied about her age and he agonized over how young she was. He wanted to wait until she was older before going out, to ask permission from her parents to date her, and then to have a long courtship. But when Julia was fourteen and Juan eighteen, her parents sent her to relatives in Los Angeles. She and Juan arranged to meet, and he took her to live with him at his mother's house.

Juan: I decided to steal her with her permission. She was having troubles with her brothers and with her parents. And everybody was trying to talk me out of it because I was too young, but I was really in love with her and didn't want her to go through any more pain. So, when she was here, I stole her. That's when I got on the bad side of her parents. And they really got upset with me and I understood, 'cause that made me feel like less of a man. So, I decided to go ahead and live with her. I didn't want to 'cause I wanted to get married first instead of taking her, because I knew that once she was there, where was she was gonna sleep? So, I just thought I might as well sleep with her, but I swear I wasn't thinking about the physical—the sexual part didn't hit me until a day before (she moved in).

Interviewer: So, did you and Julia talk about it (having sex)?

Juan: No, we just felt so free that it just happened. When you're in love, it's like a sense of freedom—like you could do anything. You feel real positive about things. I couldn't believe it that she was there with me. I mean one time she's in Mexico and the next she's in my room. She was so beautiful. And I was thinking, well, if I'm gonna marry her it might be OK. So, then, it just happened and it was like—we didn't—it wasn't even planned.

Julia was also in love with Juan.

Julia: *El me respectaba mucho a mí—pues, ese día que ya me vine yo sen . . . yo sentí que ya tenía que estar con él.* He respected me a lot, and that day that I came (to live in his house)—I felt that I had to be with him.

Interviewer: *Entonces, tu no sentiste que te puso presión?* Then, you didn't feel like he was pressuring you?

Julia: *No . . . yo sabía lo que estaba haciendo. Él me lo da todo, pues. Él me da calor, me da felicidad. Éso es al amor que es bonito.* No, I knew what I was doing. He gives me everything. He excites me, makes me happy. This is a love that is beautiful.

Interviewer: *Tus intenciones sería ser mujer para él y tener familia para él?* You intended to be his wife and have his children?

Julia: *Sí.* Yes.

Julia got pregnant about six months after they began having intercourse. They weren't using birth control because Julia had had an ovarian cyst in Mexico and she thought the doctor had told her she would never be able to have children. Juan and Julia wanted children someday, and they were hoping that Julia had been misdiagnosed, but they had not pursued medical follow-up in the United States. Thus, when she became pregnant, they were both surprised, but also very happy. They thought it was a little early and that they were a little young, but they were happy. Juan and Julia now have two children and they were married shortly after Julia's eighteenth birthday.

SYLVIA

Sylvia, twenty years old at the time she was interviewed, was born in a small town in El Salvador. She came to the United States with her partner, Luís, when she was seventeen years old and three months pregnant with their daughter. Sylvia met and fell in love with Luís in El Salvador when she was fifteen. He was thirty. He had already moved to the United States, but had come back to visit relatives. Two years later when he returned to her village, she was still in love with him.

Luís began coming to her house and walking her to work. One day her stepfather caught them kissing, and her family tried to put an end to the relationship because he was so much older than she was. They threatened to call the police and have him put in jail, but Sylvia and Luís kept seeing each other secretly for about three months and one day:

Sylvia: *Y ya, ahí empesó todo. Ya él me iba a traer a mi trabajo escondidas de mi mamá. Me iba a traer a mi trabajo y de ahí nos fuimos (laughter). Y el condenado me llevó a un motel (laughter). Yo no, um, no sabía que se iba a hacer ahí. Yo pensé que (laughter), que a comer a un restaurant. Y cuando llegué y entró y llegué a la puerta y veo la cama . . . ay, yo me quize ir y me agarró y no me dejo ir. Bueno, ya de ahí quizá me gustó porque allá seguido ibamos (laughter). Ya, de ahí, salí embarazada. Yo no conocía nada sobre preservativos—nada, nada, nada. Entonces, no me cuidé. Cuando salí embarasada el me dijó: ¿Por qué no te cuidabas?* That's where it all started. He was going to take me to work, hidden from my mom. He was going to take me to work, and from there we left. And the condemned man took me to a motel. I thought to eat at a restaurant. And when I got there and he went in and I got to the door and I see the bed. Ay, I wanted to go but he grabbed me and wouldn't let me go. Well, maybe I wanted to, because then, we went together. I didn't know anything about condoms—nothing. And, I didn't protect myself. When I got pregnant he said: why didn't you take care of yourself (use contraception)?

In a later interview Sylvia continues with this theme:

Sylvia: A mí, nadie me educó, nadie me enseñó (sobre el sexo). Yo creo por éso caí en un embarazo tan joven. No voy a ocultar nada, para que ella (la hija) sepa. Tiene que saber todo que ella elija lo que quiere . . . Porque a mí nunca me dijeron nada. Yo nunca supé nada y por éso, yo creo, pasan las cosas. Nobody educated me, nobody taught me (about sex). I think that's why I got pregnant so young. I'm not going to hide anything so that she (her daughter) can know. She has to know everything so she can choose what she wants to do. Because for me, they never told me anything. I never knew anything and because of that, I think, things happen.

Luís was surprised to find out that Sylvia was pregnant, and for awhile it was not clear what they would do. They finally decided that she would accompany him to the United States, but they have not married and Sylvia feels that their relationship is changing, or, perhaps that she thinks about things differently now.

Sylvia: Cuando yo me viné y salí embarazada yo estaba super enamorada de él. Ahora yo no sé. Sería por los problemas que tuvimos cuando llegamos aquí. Que él mucho tomaba. Quizá yo le perdí un poco de todo lo que yo sentía por él. Ahora lo quiero y todo, pero no como cuando habíamos (antes). When I gave in and got pregnant I was head over heels in love with him. Now I don't know. It could be due to the problems we had when we got here. He drank a lot. Maybe I lost a little of all that I felt for him. Now I love him and all, but not like we were before.

Luís would like another child, but Sylvia does not—not yet anyway. Until things get better financially and emotionally she is using the oral contraceptive pill, despite Luís not wanting her to contracept.

ERIKA

Erika is a U.S.-born Latina who grew up in the housing projects. She was thirteen when she met junior who was twenty at the time. She had her first baby at fourteen.

Erika: I met him in Halloween. I was just a playboy bunny (her Halloween costume), so I didn't look my age. I was wearing heels and makeup—all of that. In the beginning I didn't really care for him, to tell you the truth. When I first started seeing him, I was like, ay, go away, you know, go somewhere else. He kept coming and coming, so I guess that is what made me like him because he kept on coming.

Erika and Junior dated for about seven months before they had sex for the first time. Erika did not plan to have sex with Junior, but she was clear that he did not force her into it. She said that she didn't want to do it, but at the same time she wanted to do it. They never talked about having sex or about using birth control. She got pregnant within the first month.

Interviewer: Were you trying to get pregnant, Erika?
Erika: In a way I was, but in a way I was like no, no. It was in between.
Interviewer: So, why did you want to get pregnant?
Erika: The truth, the truth because I didn't want to be older.
Interviewer: You didn't want to be a mother at an old age?
Erika: Uhuh. My friend, she got a baby too, she got pregnant at thirteen. I had her (first baby) at fourteen. But her sister got pregnant at fifteen, had her (child) at sixteen. Everybody I know had a man, you know? Everybody I know has kids. I only know two people that don't have kids from everyone I know.

Erika and Junior are still together and they now have two children.

CORI

Cori came to the United States from Mexico with her mother after her parents' divorce when she was a small child. When Cori was ten, her mother sent her to live with her father in Mexico because she had a new partner and was beginning another family. When Cori turned thirteen she began having problems with her stepmother and came back to East L.A. where she lived with her mother and stepfather until she was sixteen. They lived in a rough neighborhood with a lot of gang problems, but now Cori lives in an upscale beach community with her new partner. Cori thinks that the old neighborhood is part of the problem.

Cori: My old friends there, a lot of them want to get out. They don't want to live in the neighborhood and they try to get out and it's too hard. They end up like me getting pregnant, but then they just get on welfare and they just say: "Oh well, I get on welfare I won't have to work." They like those little gangsters, little *cholo*[6] guys. They get all those girls pregnant and they just leave, and they don't think of their kids . . . when they need to give them money, to the girl, to take care of the kid, they are not there.

Cori met Carlos, her baby's father, through friends when she was fifteen. He was already eighteen and out of school, and she would ditch school to be with him. Her mother didn't know they were dating. They went out for about a year before they had sex for the first time.

Cori: I mean it (sex) just happened. (laughs) We didn't talk about sex. He did once and got—I slapped him really hard. (laughter) He told me, we are shits, because we were six months together and all his friends were having sex and he wanted a girlfriend and a girlfriend was somebody he could sleep with and be with, and you know. I didn't let him, and he tried grabbing my butt, and I punched him so hard, (laughs) and he didn't like that, and he got mad for a while but then we went back together again, and it happened after a year. Then, we kind of broke off for a while and went back together. But he goes "you need to think about that (his needs) too." He goes, (laughter) "and you don't think we (guys) have needs? If you want me to go with someone else?" (And I said) "So if you want to go with someone else go ahead. I am not going to stop you."

Interviewer: So then, you guys went back together . . .

Cori: . . . for like six more months and then we did (had sex).

Interviewer: And how did that happen? Were you ready for it? Did you want to?

Cori: I don't know. I didn't really want to. It just happened, because I left my house. My mom threw me out. I didn't have anywhere to go, and so I stayed (at his house). I felt like I was trapped, and I am not going to say that he forced me but I was trapped. . . . I don't know, we did it for the wrong reasons. I felt like I was so desperate, I had nothing else to live for. (I thought) "I don't care about anything else, you know? Forget it, it's just you (him, Carlos) now." It would get to a point that I really didn't care. Then I let him. I let him but I didn't feel like it. I don't know, afterwards I felt like oh! What did I do? I just, we did it twice, then after that I didn't want to. I thought I was too young for that.

(Then) I went to my friend's, I didn't feel comfortable staying there (with Carlos), because he wanted me to sleep with him again, and I just didn't want to, so I left. And then I went to my other friend's house and I was just there

---

[6] *Cholo* is a slang term that refers to youth who identify with the Latino gang culture by dress, behavior, and action [48].

with her. She has a baby and she is on welfare. She has been on welfare forever, since I know her. So then I said "I don't want to see myself like that—I don't," and I thought about it and I go "God! I could be pregnant." You know, it could happen. And I never, never let him touch me again.

We did it twice or whatever, and he gave me something and got me pregnant. . . . I found out after, when I found out I was pregnant five months later, I had chlamydia . . . and when I found out, I was so mad I wanted to kill him. I was so mad. Afterwards, I found out that he was sleeping with my best friend. All my friends were sleeping with him. He was really cute. He was a gorgeous little thing. He was a *cholo*, but you know how girls like *cholos*.

DISCUSSION

These case studies reveal the complexity of negotiating sexual behavior within a romantic relationship. Having sex was an act that, in the words of so many of these young people, "just happened." It was not negotiated verbally. The couple did not discuss or plan it. Rather, sexual involvement was negotiated physically through a gradual escalation in the level of intimate sexual contact allowed by the young woman during the times they were together. Verbal negotiation that occurred in the context of sexual passion consisted of little else but "please" and "no, not yet." One young man, Cori's boyfriend, who tried to discuss sexual involvement outside the context of hugging and kissing, was slapped for his efforts. That slap was a signal that conscious discussion about sexual involvement was not appropriate or appreciated.

In all cases the young man was the initiator of sexual involvement, and the young woman was the resistor and controller of passion. This is a familiar sexual "script" in contemporary *American culture* [38]. Most of the young women were able to resist having intercourse for a considerable length of time (several months to a year) before giving in to their partner's urging and, although muted in these excerpts, in many cases their own desire as well. This period of waiting was called *respecto* (respect). The respect the young men had for their girlfriends (pressuring for sex, but not too hard, and allowing her to make the decision about the timing of their first sexual intercourse) is interpreted by the young women as an indication of their partner's emotional involvement in the relationship. It is a sign of the young man's good intentions, a test period during which he proves that he cares for her, is not just after sex, and will stay with her in a committed relationship.

In some cases, as with Julia and Juan, sexual intercourse became a spontaneous symbol of commitment and love within the context of the development of their relationship. As the relationship evolved and they became emotionally closer, they naturally wanted to express this closeness physically. As they fell in love, sex became a natural part of the union of their two selves into one, the much sought after goal of passionate, romantic love [49]. For Cori and Eva, allowing

intercourse to occur seemed to be a bid for greater commitment in the relationship, a strategy that ultimately failed for both of them. Erika and Sylvia both
had much older partners, and intercourse took them by surprise, but was not
unwelcome. Perhaps the powerful feelings inherent in passionate love in combination with cultural expectations about the importance of female virginity and
naiveté about sex preclude these young women from planning for sex, the circumstances under which it should occur (the timing of the event) and the prevention of
pregnancy and STDs (use of contraception and condoms).

One of the more unfortunate precipitators of sexual debut for three of the
cases presented here was conflict within the young women's home. Eva and
Cori both felt pressure to leave their mothers' homes and said they had nowhere
else to go. Julia, too, was having difficulties at home, and was sent to her aunt in
the United States. All three of these young women eventually chose to live with
their boyfriends. Julia clearly loved Juan and was ready to become his "wife."
Eva and Cori both recognized that they were seeking a safe haven and comfort
from their partners. Neither was ready to initiate intercourse. Eva thought it was
morally wrong, and Cori thought she was too young. Both were also unsure of the
depth of their own feelings for their partners—and their partner's feelings for
them. Eva eventually came to love Rudy, but she was not in love with him when
she moved in with him. She liked Rudy and was sexually attracted to him, but
she needed a place to stay. Cori said she was not in love with Carlos. She gave
in to sex because she needed a place to stay, because she thought he was cute,
and because he was comforting.

An alternative reading of Cori's and Eva's stories, however, suggests that they
only used the excuse of having nowhere else to go to justify the initiation of a
sexual relationship with their boyfriends. Cori, it turns out, did have somewhere
else to go, and Eva had a close school friend to whose family she probably could
have turned had she wanted to do so. Instead, both arranged a scenario in which
they could be blameless for engaging in sexual relations they felt were taboo.

Another striking chord in these narratives is the extent to which the young
women were ignorant about the biology and physiology of human reproduction.
Eva and Sylvia, in particular, thought this was a major reason for their unintended
pregnancies fear and ignorance of the mechanics of sex and contraception. For
all except Julia, pregnancy was the consequence most feared by these young
women. Although Erika wanted to get pregnant, she was somewhat ambivalent
and considered abortion at the urging of her mother and Junior's mother, but all
her friends had a man and kids, and she wanted to be like them. Junior was
amenable to being a father and is still with her. Eva, Sylvia, and Cori had
unintended pregnancies that changed their lives. Rudy wanted to see what being
a father was like. He tried using withdrawal, but the method did not work well for
him and Eva. Luís seemed to think pregnancy prevention was Sylvia's responsibility, but took on responsibility for her and their daughter. Carlos seemed to fit
the *cholo* pattern described by Cori in which young men take no responsibility

for their sexual behavior at all. Cori contracted chlamydia and became pregnant. She was the only young mother who expressed any anger at her boyfriend's irresponsible behavior and at her own "stupidity." Interestingly, none of young women talked about fear of STDs as a deterrent to having sex.

The role of older men dating teenage women and fathering children is just beginning to be addressed in the literature on adolescent pregnancy [50]. In the cases presented here, only Eva and Rudy were within two years in age. For the other four cases, age differences were three, four, six, and fifteen years. Certainly there can be knowledge and power differentials in such relationships, especially when the girl is a young teen (e.g., 12 to 15 years old) and the partner is an adult man. Sylvia's and Erika's families expressed concern about their dating much older men, and Juan also recognized it was problematic. In a later interview he said that he often felt more like Julia's father or her teacher than her husband and worried that perhaps he had stolen her girlhood. Despite their own and their families' concerns, they all persisted in their relationships.

Although none of these young women said they were forced into having sex, all, save Julia, did feel pressured by their partners. Cori came closest to describing a forced situation. She said she felt trapped, but it was a trap partly of her own making. The contradictions in some of these narratives both wanting and not wanting sex at the same time suggest the conflict in these young women's minds. For others, like Erika and Sylvia, sex was not unwelcome, but the timing was unexpected. Julia was the only one who seemed to embrace her sexual relationship with Juan, and her narrative stands in stark contrast to the other four which depict conflicting desires, lack of preparation for sex, and uncertainty about their own or their partner's feelings.

Adult, middle class health professionals working with adolescents tend to assume that anyone in a romantic relationship can be reasonably sure he or she might have sex and should be prepared to prevent unintended pregnancy and STDs. All of these respondents, however, indicated that their first intercourse experience together was neither expected nor planned. Moreover, almost all respondents, when asked how couples decide to have sex or use birth control, responded like Eva: "How do they decide? (long pause) They don't decide. they don't think about it." When adolescents say that they were not expecting or planning to have sex, even though they were involved in a romantic relationship that could reasonably be expected to include sexual involvement, we must take them at their word. As these cases indicate, both parties might have been thinking about sex, wanting to have sex, wondering when they would have sex, or trying to delay sex, but they were not consciously planning to have sex.

The implications of these findings for the prevention of pregnancy and STDs among young Latinas are not optimistic. The cultural scripting of gender roles in romantic relationships makes it almost certain that sex will be unplanned and unprotected. The young man pressures for sex, but allows his girlfriend to control the timing of the evolution of sexual intimacy within the relationship in order to prove his love and commitment. The young woman resists sex until she is sure of her partner's emotional commitment to her or wants to put it to the test, but she must remain unprepared for sex to be perceived as virtuous. Although this period of *respecto* (respect) lasted six months to a year for these couples, abstinence eventually gave way to intercourse. These months were full of sexual uncertainty and emotional risk during which each person tested the other, and frank discussions about having sex, using birth control, or preventing STDs were culturally inappropriate and too emotionally risky for both parties. If either member of the couple violated these rules, he or she ran the risk of losing the partner.

Ironically, the initiation of sexual intercourse seemed to move the couple into another phase of their relationship in which they either broke up or developed mutual trust and affection that allowed for a more "*rational*" *approach* to sexual behavior and concern with its consequences. By this time, however, the young women were all pregnant and other decisions had to be made.

Cultural and social norms and values about appropriate sexual behavior, appropriate sexual partners, the importance of virginity, and contraception shape our experience of love and restrict what can be talked about at different stages of involvement in a romantic relationship. A script for romantic love that portrays spontaneous, unplanned, and unprotected sex after a protracted period of resistance by the female allows young women to retain their purity and relinquish their virginity at the same time. This script when enacted in the contemporary world of incurable STDs and the social and economic burdens of teenage motherhood places young women at enormous risk. Young couples will not behave as "rational decision-makers" in their sexual behavior until their society and community expect them to. Currently, as a society, we expect young people in love to behave "irrationally," to value spontaneous, unplanned (and therefore unprotected) sexual initiation. How, then, can we be surprised when they say, despite months of thinking about having sex, that they did not plan or expect to have sex. But, love can also accommodate prevention. Love, after all, is a valuing of the partner above the self. Surely, protection of the partner's health is part of love. We must teach our youth new scripts for falling in love, scripts that include this message.

REFERENCES

1. R. A. Hatcher, J. Trussell, F. Stewat, et al., *Contraceptive Technology*, Irvington Publishers, Inc., New York, 1994.
2. C. Hayes, *Risking the Future: Adolescent Sexuality, Pregnancy, and Childbearing*, National Academy Press, Washington, D.C., 1987.
3. K. Luker, *Dubious Conceptions. The Politics of Teenage Pregnancy*, Harvard University Press, Cambridge, Massachusetts, 1996.

4. C. A. Nathanson, *Dangerous Passage, The Social Control of Sexuality in Women's Adolescence*, Temple University Press, Philadelphia, Pennsylvania, 1991.
5. T. J. Mathews, S. J. Ventura, S. C. Curtin, and J. A. Martin, Births of Hispanic Origin, 1989-95, *Monthly Vital Statistics Report, 46*:(6 Supplement), pp. 1-28, 1998.
6. J. G. Dryfoos, *Adolescents at Risk: Prevalence and Prevention*, Oxford University Press, New York, 1990.
7. P. I. Erickson, *Latina Adolescent Childbearing in East Los Angeles*, University of Texas Press, Austin, 1998.
8. S. S. Brown and L. Eisenberg, *The Best Intentions. Unintended Pregnancy and the Well-Being of Children and Families*, National Academy Press, Washington, D.C., 1995.
9. L. S. Zabin and S. C. Hayward, *Adolescent Sexual Behavior and Childbearing*, Sage Publications, Newbury Park, California, 1993.
10. L. M. Burton, Teenage Childbearing as an Alternative Life Course Strategy in Multi-generational Black Families, *Human Nature, 1*:2, pp. 123-143, 1990.
11. A. T. Geronimus, Teenage Childbearing and Social and Reproductive Disadvantage: The Evolution of Complex Questions and the Demise of Simple Answers, *Family Relations, 40*, pp. 463-471, 1991.
12. J. B. Lancaster and B. A. Hamburg, *School-Age Pregnancy and Parenthood. Biosocial Dimensions*, Aldine, DeGruyter, New York, 1986.
13. C. S. Aneshensel, E. Fielder, and R. M. Becerra, Fertility and Fertility-Related Behavior among Mexican-American and Non-Hispanic White Female Adolescents, *Journal of Health and Social Behavior, 30*, pp. 56-76, March 1989.
14. R. M. Becerra and D. de Anda, Pregnancy and Motherhood among Mexican American Adolescents, *Health and Social Work, 9*:2, pp. 106-123, 1984.
15. P. I. Erickson and C. P. Kaplan, Latinas and Abortion, in *The New Civil War: The Psychology, Culture and Politics of Abortion* (Chapter 6), L. J. Beckman and S. M. Harvey (eds.), American Psychological Association, Washington, D.C., pp. 133-155, 1998.
16. S. K. Henshaw, Teenage Abortion and Pregnancy Statistics by State, 1992, *Family Planning Perspectives, 29*:3, pp. 115-122, 1997.
17. S. K. Henshaw and J. Silverman, The Characteristic and Prior Contraceptive Use of U.S. Abortion Patients, *Family Planning Perspectives, 20*:4, pp. 158-168, 1988.
18. T. Joyce, The Social and Economic Correlates of Pregnancy Resolution among Adolescents in New York City, by Race and Ethnicity: A Multivariate Analysis, *American Journal of Public Health, 78*:6, pp. 626-631, 1988.
19. A. Leibowitz, M. Eisen, and W. K. Chow, An Economic Model of Teenage Pregnancy Decision Making, *Demography, 23*, pp. 67-79, 1986.
20. W. D. Mosher and C. A. Bachrach, First Premarital Contraceptive Use: United States 1960-1982, *Studies in Family Planning, 18*:2, pp. 83-95, 1987.
21. W. D. Mosher and J. W. McNally, Contraceptive Use at First Premarital Intercourse, United States, 1965-1988, *Family Planning Perspectives, 23*:3, pp. 165-172, 1991.
22. P. Namerow and J. E. Jones, Ethnic Variation in Adolescent Use of a Contraceptive Service, *Journal of Adolescent Health Care, 3*:3, pp. 165-172, 1982.
23. A. Torres and S. Singh, Contraceptive Practice among Hispanic Adolescents, *Family Planning Perspectives, 18*:4, pp. 193-194, 1986.

24. P. I. Erickson and C. P. Kaplan, *Abortion among Hispanic Women in the U.S.: Data from the H-HANES*, American Public Health Association, Washington, D.C., 1992.
25. J. D. Forrest and S. Singh, The Sexual and Reproductive Behavior of American Women, 1982-1988, *Family Planning Perspectives, 22*:6, pp. 206-214, 1990.
26. T. Reynoso, M. E. Felice, and P. Shragg, Does American Acculturation Affect Outcome of Mexican-American Teenage Pregnancy? *Journal of Adolescent Health, 14*:4, pp. 257-261, 1993.
27. A. J. Rapkin and P. I. Erickson, Acquired Immunodeficiency Syndrome: Ethnic Differences in Knowledge and Risk Factors among Women in an Urban Family Planning Clinic, *AIDS, 4*:9, pp. 889-899, 1990.
28. P. I. Erickson, Cultural Factors Affecting the Negotiation of First Sexual Intercourse among Latina Adolescent Parents, *International Quarterly of Community Health Education, 18*:1, pp. 119-135, 1998-1999.
29. R. H. DuRant, R. Pendergast, and C. Seymore, Sexual Behavior among Hispanic Females Adolescents in the United States, *Pediatrics, 85*:6, pp. 1051-1058, 1990.
30. K. F. Darabi and V. Ortiz, Childbearing among Young Latino Women in the United States, *American Journal of Public Health, 77*:1, pp. 25-28, 1987.
31. H. Amaro, Women in the Mexican American Community: Religion, Culture, and Reproductive Attitudes and Experiences, *Journal of Community Psychology, 16*:1, pp. 6-20, 1988.
32. H. Aviaro, Latina Attitudes towards Abortion, *Nuestro, 5*:6, pp. 43-44, 1981.
33. K. F. Darabi, P. B. Namerow, and S. G. Philliber, *The Fertility Related Attitudes of Mexican-Americans*, Population Association of America, Pittsburgh, Pennsylvania, 1983.
34. P. B. Namerow and S. G. Philliber, Attitudes toward Sex Education among Black, Hispanic, and White Inner-City Residents, *International Quarterly of Community Health Education, 3*:3, pp. 291-299, 1983.
35. A. S. Rossi and B. Sitaraman, Abortion in Context: Historical Trends and Future Changes, *Family Planning Perspectives, 20*:6, pp. 273-282, 1988.
36. L. M. Koonin, J. C. Smith, and M. Ramick, Abortion Surveillance—United States, 1991, *Morbidity and Mortality Weekly Report, 44*:SS-2, pp. 23-53, 1995.
37. J. Abma, A. Driscoll, and K. Moore, Young Women's Degree of Control over First Intercourse: An Exploratory Analysis, *Family Planning Perspectives, 30*:1, pp. 12-18, 1998.
38. S. Thompson, *Going All the Way. Teenage Girl's Tales of Sex, Romance, and Pregnancy*, Hill and Wang, New York, 1995.
39. F. D. Bean and M. Tienda, *The Hispanic Population of the United States*, Russell Sage Foundation, New York, 1987.
40. B. R. Flores, *Chiquita's Cocoon. A "Cinderella Complex" for the Latina Woman*, Pepper Vine Press, Inc., Granite Bay, California, 1990.
41. B. V. Marin, G. Marin, and A. M. Padilla, Attitudes and Practices of Low Income Hispanic Contraceptors, *Spanish Speaking Mental Health Research Center, Occasional Paper, 13*, 1981.
42. C. W. Molina and M. Aguirre-Molina, *Latino Health in the U.S.: A Growing Challenge*, American Public Health Association, Washington, D.C., 1994.

43. K. Fennely, Sexual Activity and Childbearing among Hispanic Adolescents in the United States, in *Early Adolescence: Perspectives on Research, Policy, and Intervention*, R. M. Lerner (ed.), Lawrence Erlbaum Associates, Hillsdale, New Jersey, pp. 335-352, 1993.
44. K. D. Forrest, Timing of Reproductive Life Stages, *Obstetrics and Gynecology, 82*:1, pp. 105-111, 1993.
45. S. C. M. Scrimshaw, Stages in Women's Lives and Reproductive Decision Making in Latin America, *Medical Anthropology, 2*:3, pp. 41-58, 1978.
46. N. Williams, *The Mexican-American Family: Tradition and Change*, General Hall, Inc., New York, 1990.
47. E. G. Pavich, A Chicana Perspective on Mexican Culture and Sexuality, *Journal of Social Work and Human Sexuality, 4*:3, pp. 47-65, 1986.
48. M. G. Harris, Cholas, *Latino Girls and Gangs*, AMS Press, New York, 1988.
49. E. S. Person, M.D., *Dreams of Love and Fateful Encounters. The Power of Romantic Passion*, Penguin Books, New York, 1988.
50. D. J. Landry and J. D. Forrest, How Old are U.S. Fathers? *Family Planning Perspectives, 27*:4, pp. 159-161, 1995.

CHAPTER 4

From Focus Groups to Workshops: Developing a Culturally Appropriate Cervical Cancer Prevention Intervention for Rural Latinas

Rose A. Wilcher
Lisa K. Gilbert
Cara S. Siano
Elva M. Arredondo

National statistics indicate that U.S. Latinas are disproportionately affected by cervical cancer, a disease that can be prevented, detected, and treated; the incidence of cervical cancer (per 100,000 population) among Latinas is nearly double that of White women, 16.2 versus 8.7, respectively [1]. Moreover, Latinas are one-third more likely to die from cervical cancer than are White women [1]. Latinos currently account for approximately 11.6 percent of the population in the United States, however, they are predicted to be the largest ethnic minority group by the year 2005 [2, 3]. The disproportionate impact of cervical cancer among Latinas coupled with the dramatic increased representation of Latinos in the United States illuminates the need for effective, culturally appropriate programmatic efforts aimed at preventing cervical cancer among this population.

It has been established that cervical cancer is causally related to infection with Human Papillomavirus (HPV), a sexually transmitted disease [4]. Research indicates that HPV DNA is present in more than 93 percent of cervical cancer cases [5]. Because HPV is sexually transmitted, risk factors for cervical cancer in all women involve sexual behavior, with multiple sex partners being the most important determinant for HPV infection [6, 7]. Studies have indicated that while most Latinas practice monogamy and refrain from risky sexual behaviors, they are still at particularly high risk for STDs due to low rates of condom use and high rates of multiple partners by their male counterparts [8, 9].

Pap screening is the most common way to detect cell changes caused by HPV that may lead to cervical cancer. Since its introduction in the United States in 1941, the mortality rate for cervical cancer has declined by 70 percent, making Pap screening one of the most effective cancer screening tests [10]. Studies have shown, however, that the prevalence of adequate Pap screening is low among Latinas, particularly those who speak only or mostly Spanish, compared to White women [11, 12]. Further, similar to self-reports of screening among Black and White women, self-reports of Pap screenings among Latinas are inaccurate and greatly overestimate the prevalence of Pap screening among this population [13].

Just as the Latino population has increased rapidly at the national level in the last few years, a comparable trend has been observed in the state of North Carolina (NC). From 1990 to 1998, the NC Latino population increased 110 percent compared to 14 percent among Blacks and 13 percent among Whites [2]. Moreover, Latinos in NC are increasingly settling out of the migrant streams or arriving directly from abroad for permanent, as opposed to seasonal, jobs [14]. Data on cervical cancer in NC Latinas is limited; however, two studies on the sexual behavior of Mexican immigrants living in NC provide insight regarding Latinas' risk for cervical cancer. A study of married immigrant Latinos living alone in NC, "unaccompanied" men, and married Latinos residing in NC with their wives, "accompanied" immigrants, found that both groups of men engaged in extramarital sexual behavior, but the unaccompanied men had more lifetime sexual partners, more extramarital partners, and more contact with prostitutes [15]. The men and women in the study perceived STDs as only minimally relevant to their lives and revealed limited accurate knowledge of STDs. The women in the study held low perceived risk of STDs. Another study of newly immigrated Mexicans to NC found that Latino men and women often practiced after-exposure behaviors to prevent STDs, such as going to get a check-up, and believed that cleanliness was an effective STD prevention strategy [16]. In both studies, males reported high rates of condom use with prostitutes and other extramarital partners, but rarely used them with their wives. These studies indicate that inaccurate knowledge of STDs, ineffective prevention practices, inconsistent condom use, and the extramarital sexual behavior of the NC male Latino population may place NC Latinas at increased risk for cervical cancer due to increased risk for STDs.

Research indicates that high mortality rates for cervical cancer among Latinas are associated with complex cultural and environmental factors as well as aspects of the health care delivery system that impact Pap screening and follow-up practices. Studies have shown that many Latinas subscribe to misconceptions about the cause and risk factors for cervical cancer and that low levels of accurate knowledge about cervical cancer screening are related to lower screening rates [17, 18]. Cultural beliefs such as *fatalismo,* fatalistic attitudes about cancer, and *verguenza,* feelings of shame or embarrassment around sexual issues, also predict lower Pap screening behavior [19-22]. Environmental factors such as social support networks also have been shown to be important determinants of Pap screening and follow-up practices among low-income Latinas [23, 24].

In addition to cultural and environmental variables, socioeconomic factors and the health care delivery system impact Pap screening behavior among Latinas. With 26 percent of Latinos compared to 11 percent of Whites living in poverty, economic factors such as cost of the procedure, insurance status, and lack of transportation and child care can be barriers to regular screening among this population [25-27]. It also has been shown that low levels of English language skills can be a barrier to accessing health services and that English language proficiency is associated with increased cancer screening [28-30]. However, these studies also have shown that language preference and use are proxies for socioeconomic status indicating that factors such as income, education, and access to care may be stronger determinants of screening behavior. In NC, the language barrier and provider's lack of cultural knowledge make health care inaccessible or unacceptable to many recent immigrants [16].

In 1997, the CDC-funded Cervical Cancer Prevention Project (CCPP) was initiated to create a national model to increase timely Pap screening and follow-up practices among low-income Latina and African American women in rural and urban areas, respectively. A community-based demonstration project, CCPP was developed and piloted with Latinas in a rural NC county and African American women in an urban NC county. CCPP is a public education campaign consisting of written educational materials, local and national media campaigns, provider education trainings, a toll-free recorded information line, and community-based educational workshops, the primary intervention activity, for women of the priority communities.

CCPP's workshop intervention aims to improve knowledge, attitudes, skills, and practices for the prevention of cervical cancer among Latinas and African American women in the pilot counties. To ensure the workshops were relevant and culturally appropriate for each audience, the curriculum was informed by community-based research collected with members of the priority populations in the pilot counties. This chapter will present the findings from the formative data collection in the Latina community and describe how the data were used to tailor the intervention workshop curriculum to meet the cervical cancer prevention needs of this community.

METHODS

Focus group methodology was selected as the primary means to collect the priority population's range of perceptions, opinions, and spontaneous reactions to themes regarding cervical cancer and Pap screening. Focus groups produce data of a qualitative nature by soliciting the ideas and opinions of a limited number of people regarding a defined topic in a comfortable, non-threatening environment

[31]. Focus groups allow for data collection in a manner that respects the culture, language, and literacy levels of various audiences and is a methodology that has proven effective for ethnic minorities [31].

Three focus groups were held with Latina women ($N = 27$) in a rural NC county in August of 1998. The scope of the focus group discussions was limited to the following: barriers and facilitating factors to accessing health care services; knowledge, attitudes, and health seeking behaviors related to cervical cancer and Pap screening; communication and other critical aspects of women's relationships with partners and health care providers; and suggested health promotion strategies. All communication occurred in Spanish including the focus groups, consent forms, and data collection questionnaires. Consent forms for both participation and permission to record the discussion were read aloud. Each participant signed and returned one copy of the consent form and kept another.

Two instruments were designed for the focus group data collection. The first consisted of a questionnaire to collect demographic information such as age, income, education level, and amount of time in the United States and to assess current health seeking behaviors including Pap screening behavior. Prior to the focus group discussions, the moderators completed the questionnaire for each participant in a five-minute face-to-face interview. The second instrument was a focus group moderator's guide to assure consistency across three focus groups. The focus group questions were open-ended to elicit a broad range of opinions and issues related to each topic. The focus groups were facilitated by two bilingual co-moderators. One of the moderators was White and the other was Latina. The two-hour long focus groups were held at a local non-profit organization during the week. Free transportation, childcare, and snacks were provided. A $15 gift certificate to a local discount store was given as an incentive.

The first focus group consisted of ten women who were recruited from the community by a Latina staff interpreter at a rural NC county health department. The second focus group was conducted with ten women recruited by a Latina AmeriCorps volunteer from the community. Both recruiters invited participants by contacting Latinas in their community, not necessarily Latinas accessing their services. Whether or not the participants were users of the health department or AmeriCorps services was not known. The third focus group consisted of seven women recruited by the two focus group moderators during a Saturday evening local Spanish Mass. While several of the women knew each other, this familiarity did not appear to affect the focus group discussions.

The quantitative data collected from the interviews were translated into English and analyzed using SAS [32]. The tapes from the focus groups were transcribed and translated into English; however, all qualitative data analysis used the original Spanish transcripts to summarize the conversations more accurately. Ethnograph software was used for the qualitative data analysis [33]. The qualitative data were analyzed by two researchers, then compared for accuracy and consistency.

An outline of a five-session workshop series followed by a graduation ceremony was developed concurrently with the formative data collection. The outline described the major content areas to be covered including female anatomy, risk factors for cervical cancer, details of the Pap screening procedure, interpreting Pap smear results, the importance of follow-up care, STD prevention, and communication with providers. The curriculum structure was also outlined with each session consisting of a review of the last session and preview of the current session, an ice breaker activity, empowerment learning activities, a homework assignment for the next session, and an evaluation activity. However, the information and activities outlined lacked a cultural and environmental context. Based on the analysis of the focus group data, recommendations were made on how to tailor the workshops to the needs of Latinas in rural NC.

RESULTS

The sociodemographic characteristics and descriptive data obtained from the face-to-face interviews are summarized in Table 1. Although the total number of focus group participants was twenty-seven, one of the participants was not included in the demographic calculations because she was visiting from Central America and did not represent the local Latina population. Her opinions were compiled in the qualitative focus group data, however, because the anonymous nature of the protocol prevented identification and exclusion.

The mean age of focus group participants was thirty-one with a range of sixteen to fifty-three. The mean number of years participants had been living in the United States was 4.2 with a range of one month to fifteen years. Seventy percent (18) of the women had less than a ninth grade education and 60 percent (15) reported not having health insurance. Thirty-nine percent (10) reported a monthly gross household income of less than $800, 39 percent (10) reported an income between $800 and $1,600 per month, and 19 percent (5) reported a monthly income of $1,600 or more. Of the participants who reported they visited a provider for female care, in the last five years, 50 percent (9) reported getting a Pap smear every two to three years, 17 percent (3) reported getting a Pap smear every year, and 28 percent (5) reported never getting a Pap smear.

The qualitative data analysis revealed that preventive Pap screening practices among low-income, rural Latinas were impacted by three main factors: 1) cognitive and affective factors, 2) psychosocial factors, and 3) institutional factors. Cognitive and affective factors are the awareness, knowledge, and attitudes held by Latinas regarding Pap screening and cervical cancer. Psychosocial factors include the emotional, cultural and environmental influences on Latinas' willingness and ability get Pap screenings. Institutional factors are those aspects of the health care delivery system that facilitate or inhibit Latinas' willingness and ability to get Pap screenings.

Table 1. Sociodemographic and Behavioral Characteristics of
Focus Group Participants ($N = 26$)

Variable	Respondents (%)
Age	<25 years (38.5) 25-38 years (34.6) >40 years (26.9) *Median 31 years*
Education	<9 years (69.2) 9-12 years (15.4) >12 years (15.4)
Monthly gross family income	<$800 (38.5) $800 - $1,600 (38.4) ≥$1,600 (19.2)
Relationship status	In stable relationship (84.6) Not in stable relationship (15.4)
Number of children	≤2 (57.1) 3-5 (33.4) 6-7 (9.5) *Median 2.8*
Number of dependents	≤2 (19.2) 3-5 (73.1) 6-7 (7.7) Median 3.4
Employment status	Full time (19.2) Part time (3.9) Unemployed (76.9)
Country of origin	Mexico (73.1) Honduras (15.4) Guatemala (11.5)
Years in the United States	≤1 year (36) 2-4 years (32) ≥5 years (32) *Median 4.2 years*
Language spoken at home	Spanish (88.5) English (3.8) Both (7.7)
Health insurance	No (60) Yes (40)
Frequency of Pap screenings in past 5 years	Screened more than once a year (5.6) Screened once a year (16.7) Screened 2-3 times (50) Never screened (27.8)
Previously received an abnormal Pap screening result	No (71.4) Yes (28.6)
Previously diagnosed with an STD	No (96.2) Yes (3.8)

Cognitive and Affective Factors

Several participants in all three focus groups exhibited an accurate under-standing of the purpose and benefits of Pap screenings. An understanding of the need for preventive clinical services to determine if one was healthy was reflected in one woman's comment: "The truth is, when you haven't gone for it [Pap], you are always thinking, especially when you feel some pain, 'Now do I have cancer? Because I didn't get my test'."[1] Benefits of Pap screenings mentioned by participants included the ability of Pap smears to "find things you don't feel" and, if an abnormality is detected, "they can tell you to get a timely treatment." Other women stated that going to the doctor and getting check-ups were necessary to prevent cervical cancer, thus acknowledging the outcome efficacy of practicing preventive Pap screening. A few misconceptions regarding the purpose of a Pap smear were evident when several women described the procedures as being able to detect uterine cancer, to check the condition of the uterus, and to detect inflammation of the uterus or cysts. Knowledge regarding who should get Pap screenings and recommended screening frequency was incon-sistent among focus group participants.

While several focus group participants expressed an accurate understand-ing of the importance of Pap screenings and seeking preventive services, most demonstrated limited knowledge about cervical cancer. The general lack of under-standing of cervical cancer was reflected in one woman's series of questions: "I want to know what is cancer due to. What risks does a woman have for getting cancer? And what are the symptoms of cancer?" The lack of informa-tion about cervical cancer was further described by another woman who said, "Actually, we hear very little about it [cancer]. You only hear about somebody who got uterine cancer and that they took it [uterus] out. . . . but nothing else." In all three focus groups, participants demonstrated a poor understanding of the lack of symptoms common to cervical cancer. Several women asked about symptoms, while others did not understand how cancer could develop without causing pain. Misconceptions regarding the prevention of cervical cancer were evident in beliefs that it could be prevented through exercising, main-taining good hygiene, and eating nutritious foods. Women asked other questions that reflected inaccurate knowledge of cervical cancer including whether or not it is contagious and whether pain during sexual intercourse is indicative of cervical cancer.

Two participants stated that the cervical cancer can develop from a sexually transmitted disease, indicating a more accurate understanding of the cause of cervical cancer. Another woman stated that young people with risky sexual behavior are at highest risk for diseases and in greatest need of Pap screenings,

---

[1] All quotes were taken directly from focus group transcripts and translated into English by the researchers.

acknowledging the relationship between cervical cancer and sexual behavior. Several woman spoke of STDs from first-hand experience or second-hand knowledge; however, none of the participants stated a specific link between cervical cancer and HPV. As a result, many women discussed their perceived susceptibility to STDs, but not to cervical cancer. Many women felt particularly vulnerable to STDs as a result of immigration patterns and gender norms. One woman described how men immigrate to the United States before the rest of their family and, in their partner's absence, have sexual relations with other women. As a result, she stated, "we get infected." Another woman confirmed that partners' infidelity can cause women to become infected with an STD: "We get infected without them (male partners) telling us. They are not going to say that they had relations with another person. They are not going to protect themselves nor are they going to use protection with us."

On the other hand, two women seemed to exhibit an exaggerated perception of their susceptibility to cervical cancer. This high perceived susceptibility is reflected in one woman's statement: "I have always been afraid of it (cancer). In Mexico I went to the gynecologist a lot because I was afraid."

Participants demonstrated varying degrees of knowledge regarding treatment opportunities and the sequelae of cervical cancer, which seemed to impact their perception of the severity of the disease. A total of five women in two focus groups mentioned death in relationship to cervical cancer and one woman referred to a case in which a woman died because her husband would not let her get a Pap screening. A great sense of fear of an abnormal result was expressed by several women in one focus group, also indicating a high perceived severity of cervical cancer. One woman described her experience waiting for results to be returned: "Each time I get my exam, I am praying to heaven, praying to God." A lack of knowledge regarding the effectiveness of early detection and treatment may lead women to have an exaggerated perception of the severity of cervical cancer.

Psychosocial Factors

In addition to expressing limited and often inaccurate knowledge regarding cervical cancer and Pap screening, the Latina focus group participants discussed cultural, emotional, and environmental variables that impacted their cervical cancer screening behavior. Such variables included relationships with health care providers, emotions associated with previous Pap screening experiences, communication efficacy, the influence of male partners, and one's social support network.

Patient-Provider Interaction

It was clear that deeply rooted cultural norms for interpersonal interactions, *personalismo* (rapport) and *confianza* (trust), were important components of a health care visit for Latinas and a determinant of their desire to return for care.

Participants expected an interpersonal bond, or level of trust, to be established between the patient and provider by informally chatting and building rapport before delving into the patient's personal health concerns. If these expectations were not met, the visit was likely to be perceived as a negative experience and posed psychosocial barriers to accessing future care.

In general, *confianza* was established between the patient and provider after *personalismo* had been exhibited. One woman said, "First we talk about everything . . . the economic crisis, the politicians here," and then she described time spent chatting and building rapport as a crucial step in gaining the trust of the provider so that the visit "is like dealing with my husband, with someone of my family." However, prior to any sort of communication with the patient, the provider could destroy any opportunity for establishing trust simply by the look on his or her face. "As soon as you see their face and see that it is unpleasant, you no longer want to talk. You arrive expecting to talk about how you feel, but you just take one look at the doctor, and there is no longer that trust . . . and that is where the visit ends." Another woman reiterated the need for trust in order for Latinas to communicate with their providers by saying that, without trust, "you will see this brings about a fear and you will never open up with your doctor to talk about what you feel or what you have." Furthermore, a lack of trust with the provider led women to doubt the truth of what providers told them.

Fear, Pain, and Shame

While women expressed the need for trust with their provider in relation to health care services in general, the trust component was of particular importance with regard to Pap screening. Focus group participants mentioned pain, shame, and fear when describing previous Pap screening experiences. However, focus group data indicated that improving the patient-provider interaction by building levels of trust could alleviate the feelings of discomfort Latinas experience and improve their likelihood to return for future screenings or follow-up care. One woman described the pain of a Pap smear as a result of fear and other anxieties around the procedure: "Well, yes, it makes me afraid . . . but it depends on your state of mind. If you are nervous, then you will feel pain." Women also said getting a Pap smear is an embarrassing experience, which contributed to nervousness during the Pap smear as well. Recognizing that feelings of anxiety contribute to the pain, women said they are encouraged by providers to relax. However, simply being told they need to relax does not improve their discomfort: "They only tell you, 'get comfortable' and that's it, or 'relax,' but still it hurts." Relaxation during a Pap smear, though, is likely to be facilitated if trust exists between the patient and provider. One woman who had a trusting relationship with her doctor said that because of this trust, "I am completely relaxed . . . he only tells me to breathe deeply and I forget about the shame."

Another woman stated that the fear of an abnormal result may also serve as a barrier for some woman obtaining a Pap screening: "Because people don't go regularly to the clinic, whether it's because the doctor didn't warn them, or they have no symptoms. I also wonder if it's because of this fear that people aren't interested in going." Thus, fear of the procedure and of abnormal results, as well as feelings of shame or embarrassment, were emotional variables that negatively impacted participants' Pap screening behavior. The existence of trust between the patient and provider, however, appeared to facilitate overcoming those barriers.

Communication

Several comments made by women indicated their need for greater ability to communicate effectively with health care providers. A woman's real or perceived inability to communicate in English impacted negatively on her belief in her ability to negotiate in the clinic setting and, therefore, her willingness to seek health care services. Women felt that not speaking English prevented them from asking questions or speaking their mind, and put them at the mercy of interpreters: "Now, when you can express yourself, then you can say what you feel to the doctor. But if you depend on the interpreter who works there for them, that is the thing, that is where the problem is."

While some women described interpreters as an important source of trust and of feeling welcome in the clinic, others expressed feelings of discomfort involved in using an interpreter, especially when discussing sensitive issues such as sexual health: "So, like, it can be more embarrassing with the interpreter than with the doctor because she is somebody who knows you." ". . . in the health center . . . there should be . . . at least a doctor who can speak one's language at least for, for the test (Pap), you know, to deal with intimate things like sexually transmitted diseases, cancer, right? Because as a woman, you are not going to open up about these topics with just anybody." Thus, the inability to communicate effectively with providers, even with the presence of an interpreter, was a barrier for many Latinas to seeking Pap screenings.

Knowledge of Actual Cases of Cervical Cancer

It appeared that for some women, knowing other women who have had cervical cancer personalizes the issue for them, and may lead to preventive action. One woman demonstrated how not knowing anyone with cancer led her to not consider it as a risk: "I have heard that cancer exists, but I have never known of any actual case of cancer." In contrast, some participants told stories of women they had known who had died from cancer. The participants who told the stories attributed their deaths to these women not getting regular gynecological exams. "Recently a friend of mine died, a woman of only thirty-eight years. It seems she no longer regularly practiced her cytology (Pap screening)." For these participants it was clear how knowledge of particular people with cervical cancer reinforced the importance of regular Pap screenings.

Role of Male Partners

It was also clear that male partners played a strong role in Latinas' willingness to seek Pap screening services. Several statements indicated that a lack of support from male partners caused women to downplay their perceived susceptibility to cervical cancer: "My husband thinks I am too young to get sick, too young to get cancer." "I think many times they (partners) think it's not necessary to get a check-up . . . They say, 'How do you feel?' and you say 'well' and then they think it's not necessary . . . 'Why do you need them to bother you?'."

On the other hand, some women felt that male partners bolstered women's trust and confidence in their provider by expressing support and approval of going to doctor: "If I am feeling well, I say to him, 'if I go, they are going to tell me I am sick, I may return sad,' . . . and he says, 'go, get checked, go' . . . and I say, 'but, how do I do it?' and he says, 'That (interpreter) is there, ask her to make you an appointment and from here you can walk, it's close' . . . .and he is concerned." Because of the vital role of sexual partner's attitudes in women's decision making, several women mentioned the need to include male partners in the workshop intervention. They felt men would learn to take women's health more seriously if they heard messages about the need for prevention from trained health professionals.

Mental Health and Social Support

Depression and other mental health concerns appeared to impact women's ability and desire to seek health care services. Mental health concerns were expressed in two of the focus groups and appeared to stem from a lack of social support. Several women talked about feeling depressed and lonely as a result of immigrating to the United States. One woman said the loneliness that results from having to adapt to a new culture can lead to "a depression crisis." Another woman, referring to her disillusionment with life in the United States, said that "life in the United States is sad." One woman's isolation and loneliness made her feel as if she was "locked up at home," and described her situation as, "here I am dead." This feeling was echoed by another participant who said that one can die of sadness when one is so isolated. One woman described the emotional impact of learning about an illness: "But sometimes you say to yourself, 'I feel fine' . . . and you don't think about going to the doctor, because you feel fine; and you go to the doctor and he tells you the sicknesses you have and you return feeling more worried." Depression and mental health concerns as a result of a lack of social support seemed to impact a woman's self-efficacy in seeking preventive health care services and to compound the emotional impact of receiving negative results. Latina immigrants, in particular, may lack sufficient encouragement or comfort form a social support network to seek Pap screenings.

However, the role of a Latina within her immediate family may serve as a cue to action for Latinas to get Pap screenings. Many women commented on their responsibility to maintain one's health for the good of the family. Thus, while recent immigrants may lack an extended social support network, the perceived importance being healthy in order to support the immediate family may be a motivating factor for Latinas to seek health care.

Peace of Mind

Finally, women's need for peace of mind about their health appeared to serve as reinforcement for regular Pap seeking behaviors. Several women mentioned the relief associated in knowing they are healthy as a result of their Pap screening results: "The truth is, each time you get that exam (Pap), you are waiting to find out (the results) and when they give you the results, you say, 'Good.'" you feel good. They did (the Pap screening) to me, and it feels good to know it turned out OK." The benefit of peace of mind served to motivate women to get timely screenings.

Locus-of-Control

While women expressed several emotional barriers to seeking preventive Pap screening services, they also exhibited an internal health locus-of-control. Many health problems were often referred to as "mysterious" or unknown; however, many women expressed a desire to become better educated in order to understand the origins of their problems and take steps to prevent illness. In addition, one woman said there is a need to talk about taboo subjects such as those related to sexuality and sexually transmitted diseases, thus encouraging a proactive approach to preventing health problems.

Institutional Factors

Aside from cognitive/affective and psychosocial factors, focus group participants discussed aspects of the health care delivery system that affected their Pap screening behavior. Such institutional factors included physical accessibility of clinics, clinic policies related to cost and payment, clinic climate related to discrimination, and interpreter services.

Physical Accessibility

Women believed there were more clinics in Mexico and therefore greater accessibility of health care services than in the United States. Furthermore, many participants felt they had limited knowledge about the availability of low-cost Pap screening services in their area. Finally, women felt that transportation was a barrier to accessing health care services for many Latinas. Two women mentioned that although they had been getting regular Pap screenings in Mexico, lack of access had stopped them from getting regular check-ups in the United States. Thus, lack of physical accessibility to clinics appeared to be a major reason why women were not accessing preventive services as regularly as they did in their native countries.

Clinic Policies: Cost and Payment

Cost was a barrier mentioned by fourteen women across all focus groups. Several women noted that charges for medical visits, especially preventive care, were much more expensive than they were in their home country, particularly without insurance: "But here is not like in Mexico. In Mexico you go for a check-up and they charge you something reasonable. Here the cost is sky high." "The truth is yes, here it seems very expensive . . . it's very difficult to go because the consultations are costly." "I have a saying here, right, that people without insurance can't get sick, because to get sick in this country is only for the rich." "Yes, it's a luxury to get sick." Another woman felt that women did not know about Pap screening but did not get it due to high cost: "If you have a very low salary, even if you wish to, even if you feel the need to go (to the clinic) . . . you can't go." The high cost of health care often meant that seeking health care services was of lesser priority than other needs such as sending money to one's home country, or other family needs. Women preferred to tolerate pain to see whether it would pass rather than undergo expensive procedures. The following statement exemplifies the complex nature of decision-making when financial resources are limited: "It's that . . . you fret because you are not in your country . . . you feel all alone and even more so depending on what you do with your money . . . Like, if you don't have money, the best thing is to endure and better to use it for other things rather than health care. Even though (health) is important, for the day's work and everything . . . it's just, as a woman you are better off not going."

Climate of Discrimination: Language, Race, and Insurance Status

Several participants in one focus group perceived discrimination in various clinics as a result of not speaking English, being Latina, and not having insurance. One woman felt that clinic staff became angry and lost patience with Latinas because they didn't speak English: ". . . maybe because you don't speak English, they get like disgusted. I think they should have patience with you, because sometimes you don't come with an interpreter . . . they get mad . . . that is what I have seen." One woman said that when you only speak Spanish, the staff in the room laugh and talk about you in English. Another participant felt that clinic staff look at them differently as if to say "Ay, a weird insect!" Some women attributed behaviors such as these directly to racism against Latinas.

As a result of not having health insurance, women described experiences in which they were not accepted at the hospital and were not paid the same standard of attention and respect as patients who did have insurance. "You feel you are not given the same respect as when you say, 'here is my insurance,' and they respond to you. So, sometimes this is why many women fear going to the doctor because they don't treat you the same once you say 'I don't have insurance.'" "It's the first thing they look at, is to see if you have insurance, right? Yeah, and if not, you aren't attended to."

Interpreter Issues: Availability, Confidentiality, and Inherent Limitations

Participants mentioned aspects of interpreter services and professionalism that were barriers imposed on the part of the health care delivery system. For example, one woman said she does not believe an interpreter will translate a patient's dissatisfaction to the doctor because the interpreter's job might be jeopardized: "For example, OK, in the clinics where there is an interpreter, if you tell the interpreter, 'tell the doctor that I don't agree,' the interpreter is not going to, because her position will be called into question." Others echoed this belief that interpreters might not translate what women said if they say something negative about the services. Furthermore, several participants believed clinic interpreters did not uphold the confidentiality of the patient: ". . . in the clinics . . . the interpreter should, well, make you feel confident . . . that you feel confident that she is not going to divulge what she is translating (to others)."

One woman provided a suggestion on how interpreter services and professionalism of interpreters could be improved: "I think the solution is that they (clinic staff) are conscious of the position which they are carrying out and know that not all of the people who are going to arrive speak English. And that the interpreter is aware of his/her mission and interprets even the most minor detail of what the client expresses."

DISCUSSION

The findings from focus groups with rural NC Latinas add to and confirm existing data regarding the factors that impact the Pap screening behavior of Latinas. Consistent with other studies, Latinas in rural NC held several misconceptions about the cause and risk factors for cervical cancer [17, 18]; however, they did demonstrate an accurate understanding of the importance of Pap screening. Participants alluded to male sexual behaviors, such as extramarital relationships, that were consistent with findings from other studies [8, 9, 15, 16]. The women's perception of their risk for STDs as a result of their partners' behavior, however, was more accurate than previously found. Still, despite concern over getting infected with an STD from their partners, they were unaware of the link between cervical cancer and HPV and did not express an accurate perception of their risk for cervical cancer. Also similar to other studies, participants associated feelings of shame or embarrassment with previous Pap screening experiences [20]. This has been described as a result of *verguenza*, or Latinas' modesty around sex and sexual issues [22]. Such modesty may make Latinas uncomfortable to have such an intimate procedure performed. Specific to the focus group findings, however, is the role that *personalismo* and *confianza* can have in alleviating discomfort during a Pap screening. While *personalismo* and *confianza* have been described as important cultural codes of conduct for interpersonal relationships [34], focus group participants described more specifically how respect for those values between the patient and provider can help Latinas relax during a Pap screening. Also contrary to other studies was rural NC Latinas' expression of internal locus of control. Several studies have found fatalism to be an important factor in inadequate Pap screening practices among Latinas [19-21]; however, participants in the NC focus groups expressed proactive attitudes toward preventing health problems. A discussion about depression and mental health concerns as a result of a lack of social support appeared to impact Latinas belief in their ability to get Pap screenings and to cope with fears of a negative result. This confirms other studies' findings that social networks are an important predictor of cancer-screening behaviors [23, 24]. While language has been described as an important institutional barrier to health seeking behaviors among Latinas, focus group participants were more concerned about the psychosocial disadvantages of needing to use an interpreter, particularly for discussing sexual health issues [28, 29]. Finally, economic factors such as cost of the Pap screening procedure and lack of health insurance were barriers consistent with other studies, despite the availability of low-cost services in the area [26-30].

In addition to providing insight into how perceptions of Latinas in rural NC regarding cervical cancer compare with those of other groups of Latinas cited in previous studies, the focus group data were used to inform the curriculum of CCPP's community-based workshops. An analysis of the knowledge, attitudes, barriers, and facilitating factors to cervical cancer prevention expressed by focus group participants led to recommendations on how to frame the key messages and design learning activities so they would be meaningful to, respectful of, and culturally appropriate for the priority population.

The original curriculum outline identified the main content areas to be covered. However, after the analysis it was possible to frame the educational messages in a way that would be meaningful to workshop participants. For example, CCPP wanted participants to understand that cervical cancer can be prevented and that Pap screenings are the most common way to detect cervical cancer early. In order to communicate these concepts, it was recommended that the following message be established in the first workshop session and reinforced in every session thereafter: *Cervical cancer is almost always curable if detected in early stages and regular Pap screening provides opportunities for early detection.* Framing the message in this way allowed for the creation of a positive association between regular Pap screening and cervical cancer prevention. In turn, this message established the idea that cancer does not mean death when preventive measures are taken, helped defuse fears of abnormal results, and lessened the perceived severity of cervical cancer. It was also recommended that the concept that women should not wait for symptoms to get a Pap screening be incorporated into the workshops. This would address Latinas' poor understanding of the lack of symptoms associated with cervical cancer and challenge the commonly held belief among Latinos that health services need to be accessed only in the presence of symptoms. Since most focus group participants felt susceptible to STDs, but did not make the connection between HPV and cervical cancer, it was recommended that the link between the two be emphasized throughout the workshop series. The researchers suggested that this message be woven into an activity in which risky behaviors for contracting STDs were identified so that participants would recognize not only their susceptibility to STDs, but also to cervical cancer. Finally, an important message to incorporate into the workshops was that there are low-cost Pap screening services available in the area? Given Latinas' concern over the high cost of health care, the researchers recommended identifying services in the pilot community that were free or based on a sliding fee scale to facilitate Pap screening among this population. It was recommended that this be accomplished by giving participants a homework assignment in which they identified local resources such as low-cost Pap screenings, interpreter services, transportation, and child care. This information would then be shared and discussed in the following session in order to make all workshop participants aware of the services available.

Suggestions for culturally and environmentally appropriate learning activities were also made based on the focus group findings. To address Pap screening barriers faced by rural Latinas, the researchers recommended that quotes representing both psychosocial and institutional barriers taken directly from the focus groups be presented in the workshops for participants to react to and develop solutions. This activity would not only address the specific needs of Latinas in the pilot community, but would also build social support and empower participants by having them practice decision-making skills and develop realistic solutions based on their own knowledge and experiences.

It was clear from the focus group results that many Latinas felt susceptible to STDs because of their partners' sexual behavior. Furthermore, participants expressed that male partners influenced their health seeking behavior. To address these aspects, it was suggested that the curriculum incorporate activities for building communication skills with partners around sexual health and sexuality. It was clear that Latinas needed to be able to communicate the risk they perceived for contracting STDs as well as the importance of Pap screening to their partners in order to decrease their risk for cervical cancer and enlist the support of their partners for regular Pap screening.

The researchers believed the fifth and final workshop session should be revised to include a panel of health care providers and the workshop participants' partners. By inviting local health care providers to a workshop session, it would be possible to initiate a dialogue between community members and the providers who serve them and begin to break down some of the psychosocial and institutional barriers to accessing Pap screenings. Participants could express their concerns about Pap screenings and the health care delivery system and address their questions to medical authorities. In turn, the providers could reinforce information about Pap screening and cervical cancer presented in the workshop thus far. Inviting partners to this session would provide an opportunity for men to learn about women's health needs from respected "authority figures," whose opinions are often highly regarded in Latino culture. This recommendation would address Latinas' desire that their partners know more about women's health and potentially increase male support of women seeking regular Pap screenings.

It was recommended that the final session conclude with an activity in which the female participants develop a follow-up strategy or action plan. This activity would ask participants to think about how they would use their new information and skills beyond the workshops. Ideally the action plan would help promote sustainability of the project and encourage participants to apply their newly acquired knowledge and skills.

Implications for Public Health Educators

Because the findings presented in this chapter represent data collected from a small sample of a specific Latino population in rural NC, the findings may not be generalizable to other Latino communities. For example, levels of acculturation and social support networks may vary in different geographic areas, therefore, the environmental factors predicting Pap screening behavior may also vary. However, the findings illuminate the importance of assessing the current beliefs and knowledge base of the priority population regarding a specific health topic and using that information to develop health education messages. Although some of our findings are consistent with findings from similar studies, other findings were unique. Therefore, formative research should be conducted with any community prior to designing and implementing an intervention for that community.

Summary

The use of focus groups to elicit the priority population's perspectives and experiences related to cervical cancer, Pap screening, and the health care delivery system was an essential step prior to developing a community-based intervention to address the disproportionate impact of cervical cancer among Latinas. The formative research identified the cognitive/affective, psychosocial, and institutional factors that impact Latinas' utilization of timely Pap screening services. Based on the focus group findings, CCPP's workshop intervention could be tailored to address the cervical cancer prevention needs of Latinas in a rural North Carolina community in a culturally appropriate manner. This study serves as a model for public health educators to design and conduct focus group research with their priority populations in order to plan and implement successful and culturally appropriate community-based initiatives.

ACKNOWLEDGMENTS

This study was part of the Cervical Cancer Prevention Project, which is conducted by the American Social Health Association and funded by the Centers for Disease Control and Prevention, cooperative agreement U57/CCU415013-03.

REFERENCES

1. National Cancer Institute, *Racial/ethnic patterns of cancer in the United States, 1988-1992,* NIH Pub. No. 96-4104, 1996.
2. U.S. Census Bureau, *Population Estimates Program,* Population Division, 1999.
3. U.S. Census Bureau, *Population Projections Program,* Population Division, 1999.
4. National Institutes of Health, *Cervical Cancer. NIH Consensus Statement, 14,* 1996.
5. F. X. Bosch, M. M. Manos, N. Muñoz, M. Sherman, A. M. Jansen, J. Peto, M. H. Schiffman, V. Moreno, R. Kurman, and K. Shah, Prevalence of Human Papillomavirus in Cervical Cancer: A Worldwide Perspective, *Journal of the National Cancer Institute, 87*:11, pp. 796-802, 1995.
6. L. Koutsky, Epidemiologiy of Genital Human Papillomavirus Infection, *American Journal of Medicine, 102*:5A, pp. 3-8, 1997.
7. V. Kataja, S. Syrjanen, M. Yliskoski, M. Hippelinen, M. Vayrynen, S. Saarikoski, R. Mantyjarvi, V. Jokela, J. T. Salonen, and K. Syrjanen, Risk Factors Associated with Cervical Human Papillomavirus Infections: A Case-Control Study, *American Journal of Epidemiology, 138*:9, pp. 735-743, 1993.
8. G. Romero, G. E. Wyatt, D. Chin, and C. Rodriguez, HIV-Related Behaviors among Recently Immigrated and Undocumented Latinas, *International Quarterly of Community Health Education, 18*:1, pp. 89-105, 1998-99.
9. B. V. Marin, J. M. Tschann, C. A. Gómez, and S. M. Kegeles, Acculturation and Gender Differences in Sexual Attitudes and Behaviors: Hispanic vs. Non-Hispanic White Unmarried Adults, *American Journal of Public Health, 83*:12, pp. 1759-1761, 1993.
10. Centers for Disease Control, Regulatory Closure of Cervical Cytology Laboratories: Recommendations for a Public Health Response, *Mortality and Morbidity Weekly Report, 46,* pp. 1-3, 1997.
11. L. C. Harlan, A. B. Bernstein, and L. G. Kessler, Cervical Cancer Screening: Who is Not Screened and Why? *American Journal of Public Health, 81*:7, pp. 885-890, 1991.
12. J. P. Elder, F. G. Castro, C. de Moor, J. Mayer, J. I. Candelaria, N. Campbell, G. Talavera, and L. M. Ware, Differences in Cancer-Risk Behaviors in Latino and Anglo Adults, *Preventive Medicine, 20*:6, pp. 751-763, 1991.

13. L. Suarez, D. A. Goldman, and N. S. Weiss, Validity of Pap Smear and Mammogram Self-Reports in a Low-Income Hispanic Population, *American Journal of Preventive Medicine, 11*:2, pp. 94-98. 1995.

14. K. D. Johnson-Webb and J. H. Johnson, North Carolina Communities in Transition: An Overview of Hispanic In-Migration, *The North Carolina Geographer, 5,* 1996.

15. C. I. Viadro and J. A. Earp, The Sexual Behavior of Married Mexican Immigrant Men in North Carolina, *Social Science and Medicine, 50*:5, pp. 723-735, 2000.

16. C. McQuiston, L. B. Doerfer, K. I Parra, and A. Gordon, After-the-Fact Strategies Mexican Americans Use to Prevent HIV and STDs, *Clinical Nursing Research, 7*:4, pp. 406-422, 1998.

17. F. A. Hubbell, L. R. Chavez, S. I. Mishra, and R. B. Valdez, Beliefs about Sexual Behavior and Other Predictors of Papanicolaou Smear Screening among Latinas and Anglo Women, *Archives of Internal Medicine, 156*:20, pp. 2353-2358, 1996.

18. C. Morgan, E. Park, and D. E. Cortes, Beliefs, Knowledge, and Behavior about Cancer among Urban Hispanic Women, *Journal of the National Cancer Institute Monographs, 18,* pp. 57-63, 1995.

19. L. R. Chavez, F. A. Hubbell, S. I. Mishra, and R. B. Valdez, The Influence of Fatalism on Self-Reported Use of Papanicolaou Smears, *American Journal of Preventive Medicine, 13*:6, pp. 418-424, 1997.

20. K. M. Jennings, Getting a Pap Smear: Focus Group Responses of African American and Latina Women, *Oncology Nursing Forum, 24*:5, pp. 827-835, 1997.

21. B. M. Fishman, L. Bobo, K. Kosub, and R. J. Womeodu, Cultural Issues in Serving Minority Populations: Emphasis on Mexican American and African Americans, *American Journal of the Medical Sciences, 306:*3, pp. 160-166, 1993.

22. B. V. Marín, *AIDS Prevention in Non-Puerto Rican Hispanics,* unpublished paper prepared for the National Institute of Drug Abuse Technical Review, 1988.

23. L. Suarez, L. Lloyd, N. Weiss, T. Rainbolt, and L. Pulley, Effect of Social Networks on Cancer-Screening Behavior of Older Mexican-American Women, *Journal of the National Cancer Institute, 86*:10, pp. 775-779, 1994.

24. L. A. Crane, Social Support and Adherence Behavior among Women with Abnormal Pap Smears, *Journal of Cancer Education, 11*:3, pp. 164-173, 1996.

25. U. S. Census Bureau, *Current Population Survey, 1999.*

26. E. J. Perez-Stable, F. Sabogal, and R. Otero-Sabogal, Use of Cancer-Screening Tests in the San Francisco Bay Area: Comparison of Latinos and Anglos, *Journal of the National Cancer Institute Monograph, 18,* pp. 147-153, 1995.

27. Z. E. Suarez and K. Siefert, Latinas and Sexually Transmitted Diseases: Implications of Recent Research for Prevention, *Social Work and Health care, 28*:1, pp. 1-19, 1998.

28. C. L. Schur and L. A. Albers, Language, Sociodemographics, and Health Care Use of Hispanic Adults, *Journal of Health Care for the Poor and Underserved, 7*:2, pp. 140-158, 1996.

29. L. Suarez, Pap Smear and Mammogram Screening in Mexican-American Women: The Effects of Acculturation, *American Journal of Public Health, 84*:5, pp. 742-746, 1994.

30. G. Marks, J. Solis, J. L. Richardson, L. M. Collins, L. Birba, and J. C. Hisserich, Health Behavior and Elderly Hispanic Women: Does Cultural Assimilation Make a Difference? *American Journal of Public Health, 77*:10, pp. 1315-1319, 1987.
31. R. A. Kreuger, *Focus Groups: A Practical Guide for Applied Research,* Sage, Thousand Oaks, California, 1994.
32. *Applied Statistics and the SAS Programming Language,* R. P. Cody and J. K. Smith (eds.), Prentice-Hall, Inc., Englewood Cliffs, 1991.
33. *The Ethnograph v5.0: A User's Guide,* Qualis Research Associates, 1998.
34. D. L. Morris, G. T. Lusero, E. V. Joyce, E. V. Hannigan, and E. R. Tucker, Cervical Cancer, A Major Killer of Hispanic Women: Implications for Health Education, *Health Education, 20*:5, pp. 23-28, 1989.

CHAPTER 5

Maternal Lactation: A Qualitative Analysis of the Breastfeeding Habits and Beliefs of Pregnant Women Living in Lima, Peru

Catherine Oliveros
Grace Marquis
Rosario Bartolini
Gail Ormsby
Emmanuel Rudatsikira

Breastfeeding is seen as a positive feeding behavior throughout the world because most mothers perceive their milk as having qualities that protect their baby from sickness while helping children grow healthy. As an added benefit, breastfeeding encourages bonding between the mother and her child, it is easier on finances, and it is convenient [1-2]. In developing countries where infants are at higher risk of suffering from malnutrition, the World Health Organization (WHO) and other public health entities recognize the benefits of breastfeeding [3], and recommend breastfeeding to continue for at least two years, with adequate complementary food. It is imperative to effectively educate the public on the benefits of breast-feeding. Therefore, health professionals themselves need to be educated on the complicated "ins" and "outs" of a behavior that appears to be simple and natural, but in reality is complex [4-6].

A decline in the duration of breastfeeding due to misconceptions about its importance, according to Fernandez and Guthrie, puts infants at risk of mal-nutrition, infections, and death [7], especially for families with limited income and resources to provide their children with proper and safe nutritional supplements. To effectively encourage and maintain breastfeeding among populations at risk of premature weaning, the health community must consider the various factors that influence a mother's decision. Beliefs held by a community should always be considered in any community-based work. If their beliefs are not given proper attention, those who hold the beliefs will continue to stop breastfeeding for reasons that in their minds are legitimate, because of what they have been taught culturally. These actions can lack a scientific basis and could in fact be contradictory to medical opinion [4, 7, 8].

METHODOLOGY

Definitions of Criteria Used in Study

1. A woman who breastfed during pregnancy (BDP) is a mother, at least eighteen years old, who has breastfed an older child, less than four years old, throughout pregnancy.

2. A woman who did not breastfeed during pregnancy (NBDP) is a mother, at least eighteen years of age, with an older child less than four years old, who did not breastfeed at all during pregnancy.

3. A woman who breastfed some during pregnancy (SBDP) is a mother, at least eighteen years old, who did breastfeed an older child, less than four years old, during the first two trimesters, and then stopped for any reason.

4. Breastfeeding will be defined as at least one nutritive breastfeed in a twenty-four-hour period. Nutritive feed is defined as a feed during which the child is noted to suckle and swallow milk.

5. Weaned is defined in this study as the complete cessation of breastfeeding with no reintroduction of human milk to the child's diet at a latter date.

6. "Weaning period is a prolonged period during which infants are gradually introduced to a variety of non-milk goods . . ." [9, p. 45].

Study Site

The study was conducted in the San Juan Lurigancho district, a poor peri-urban district of Lima, Peru. The area is served by several maternal and child health centers funded by the Ministry of Health, and has a growing population of about 500,000. San Juan Lurigancho has an obvious social class division with those having better economic resources living in homes with cement walls and floors, latrines, and electrical appliances. Those on the bottom social stratus scale live in cardboard or straw-mat homes with dirt floors, no electricity, or adequate water storage. The National Institute of Statistics and Information found that 25 percent of the urban population in San Juan Lurigancho live with at least one basic necessity (i.e., access to clean water) unsatisfied [10].

Data Collection and Analysis

Forty women were selected, based upon the criteria described earlier, and interviewed individually in their homes. The interviews took place in the latter part of 1998 and were meant to be informal; however, interviewers did use a guide that was field tested during pilot studies. The average interview duration was twenty-five minutes to one and one-half hours.

Each interview was coded into eight identified themes described later. The aim was to determine how each theme influenced a mother's decision to breastfeed or wean when faced with simultaneous pregnancy and lactation. The themes were critically analyzed and main ideas extracted relevant to the understanding of a mother's circumstances, the connection between the themes, and how these factors lead a mother through a decision-making process. Relationships between and within the various themes were investigated and dissected to understand the underlined framework for each woman, for each group of women, and for the population in general.

A limiting factor in the gathering of data was that the majority of mothers could not be revisited to clarify missing information. However, this did not hinder the main analysis process.

DEMOGRAPHIC CHARACTERISTICS OF SAMPLE

The study families were from the lower SES, with the main income earned by the husband/partner. The women's age ranged from eighteen to forty years old, with the mean age being twenty-five years ($\pm$ SD). Twenty-two respondents were from the coast (primarily Lima), seventeen were from the mountain regions, and one woman was from the jungle. Women from outside of Lima spent an average of 11.9 years ($\pm$ SD) living in Lima, with the range of residency from two to twenty-five years. Only thirteen women had completed high school and seventeen had some high school education. At the time of the interview, the women had an average of 2.5 ($\pm$ SD) children.

QUALITATIVE FINDINGS ACCORDING TO THEMES

Mother's responses were coded according to the following themes: the pregnancy experience, beliefs, the role of milk and its importance to child health, the fetus and the older child, outside influences, and the beliefs and experiences of lactation during pregnancy and tandem lactation. Mother's opinions describe the diversity of this population, and the discussion shows how influential a concept was on maternal decisions about breastfeeding.

General Beliefs About Breastfeeding During Pregnancy

We found the beliefs shared by the mothers dealt with the idea of what type of things could affect the baby before and after birth. Most were general, ranging from what could happen if a mother washed clothes and then lactated, to how the fetus could be born depressed if the mother passed on these feelings to the child during pregnancy.

Only two mothers were able to identify a specific belief relating to pregnancy and lactation and both were lactating during pregnancy. In these cases the belief, regardless of where they acquired it, was not important enough to lead them to cease breastfeeding. One mother was told that if she breastfed her toddler while pregnant, she would delay him developmentally.

> They fall behind in their studies, they will be a little dumb . . . the milk has gone bad, it is not good—that is why they get sick.

This mother, however, knew of other women who had breastfed during pregnancy and their children were normal. She placed more importance on what she knew to be true versus what others told her was true. Another mother was also told that breastfeeding during pregnancy would delay the breastfeeding child, because the milk was bad. However, she also continued to breastfeed, suggesting that the belief was not a dominant factor influencing her decision to breastfeed.

These mothers held a variety of beliefs on how their actions could have negative effects on the fetus, the newborn, and the older child. Many identified the beliefs, unsure of whether or not they believed them. Some seriously believed and some did not. However, for the majority of these women, the role of their beliefs in terms of lactation during pregnancy was minimal.

Outside Influence

According to Lawrence, the attitudes taken on by a husband, close family, and friends have a strong influence on the mother's own attitude toward breastfeeding [11]. These outside influences, which may include health care workers, are therefore key in how a woman makes her decision [4]. The data from this study shows the prevalent attitude held by this influential population to be negative in terms of the continuation of breastfeeding during pregnancy.

Most of the outside influences centered on a belief that the milk produced during pregnancy was bad and therefore harmful. Milk for the toddler was different (more like water), and the milk's consumption resulted in the child becoming emotionally irritable, mentally delayed, and/or weak (malnourished). The child could get chronic diarrhea and vomiting from drinking the milk, and become so critically ill as to die. Forty-eight percent of the women were told by "someone" that breastfeeding during pregnancy would affect the toddler in some way—from loose stool to death.

Some say that the milk is bad for the toddler and that is why she has diarrhea.

Others say that breastfeeding the older child while pregnant will cause the older child to be mentally delayed—they fall behind in their studies, they become a little dumb.

Twenty-eight percent of the mothers were warned that there would be negative effects on her own health because of her nursing during pregnancy. Health issues used to influence the mother included the possibility of her getting sick with anemia or TB—as a result of getting too thin, her increased risk of losing calcium thereby debilitating her, and the possibility of her suffering a miscarriage. In addition, others expressed criticism, because of the mother's inability to avoid a new pregnancy, causing her to lose face to her and her family.

A common admonishment about the health of the newborn was the possibility of the child being born premature or sickly because of a loss of nutrients to the fetus in the womb. Twenty percent of the women were told by someone that there would be negative repercussions for the fetus.

It is going to be bad for the toddler's brain because the milk is not vitamin (for toddler), what toddler is drinking is the vitamin that belongs to the baby (fetus) and the toddler is taking the milk away from the baby so the baby will be born weak.

Eleven out of twenty women did not have support from their family, friends, or health professionals for their decision to breastfeed during pregnancy. Despite all the warnings of what could happen to the older child and the fetus, the mothers went against what others said and placed more importance on their own experience. For example, if a mother saw that her child was fat (a sign of health), and she was warned that that child would be malnourished and not grow, the mother was more likely to place more importance on the actual state of health of the child. If a mother was told that her child would become mentally delayed and she knew of a woman who had breastfed during pregnancy and her children were normal, then she would place more credibility on the woman.

Some women made the decision to breastfeed because of the health of their child—so that they would continue to be healthy or, if they were sickly, so that they could get better. They did not believe the milk had negative qualities and instead placed greater importance on the role the milk could play in the health of the child. One of the mothers who continued to breastfeed her toddler did so because she became pregnant when the toddler was only three months old, suggesting that the age of the toddler was a factor leading to her decision.

Nine of the twenty women who breastfed did find support for their decisions in their family and their doctors. For these women support from their family was more important in terms of their decision than any possible negative effects on the older child.

People told me that it is harmful and I should not give anymore. But no, the doctor when I went, told me—no, continue. He will stop on his own.

It is interesting to note that all women were primarily given advice on the negative outcomes of breastfeeding during pregnancy. Although the warnings emphasized the negative consequences, there was an understanding that the results were immediate but temporary. For example, a newborn could be born thin but with time could gain weight and develop normally. A mother could also become thin and anemic because of the stress on her body, but again this would be something from which she would recover. This thought process could be explained by the fact that often these communities live in the present, since families in situations of hardship and poverty live day-by-day. This disposition can function as a means to negate the perceived seriousness of the advice received by the women regardless of who it came from.

Outside influences provided a plethora of beliefs and advice on the positive and negative consequences of breastfeeding an older child. These informants were an unavoidable part of a society that is family- and community-oriented. We found, however, that uniformly the role that "others" played in the decision of the women depended on who the main influences were in a woman's life and the woman's own personality in terms of how easily she could be influenced.

Pregnancy

One of pregnancy's roles in the decision-making process was found in the knowledge of the development of a normal pregnancy. This knowledge base and how the women relate it to the fetus in terms of how it develops and what things during pregnancy affect this development influenced a mother.

Most of the mothers interviewed understood the necessity of a pregnant woman taking special care during pregnancy. Many were even able to name at least one important thing she could do to help insure that she and her baby would be healthy; the most important and most frequently stated was proper nutrition.

Others have bad pregnancies because "moms are lacking 'suero' and vitamins because they don't eat well."

When questioned, these mothers easily rattled off how little or bad nutrition, eating certain foods, having unsatisfied cravings, taking medicines, alcohol, smoking, and having emotional problems could all impact the pregnancy and the fetus.

Mother told me that alcohol, beer, and cigarettes should be avoided. I can eat all kinds of food, but I avoid grease because it is bad for the baby and me.

All these things could also affect the mother's organism, making her weak and capable of aborting her fetus or delivering a mentally delayed baby. According to the respondents, even normal pregnancy complications like nausea could be harmful to the pregnancy because of a mother's inability to eat or hold anything down. She would then become weak and anemic, which would continue while she lactated, resulting in poor milk quality. Small quantities of milk and a baby's weak stomach would affect the child who would become mentally delayed because of the lack of proper nutrition.

Even though most of the mothers were aware of what they should do to have a good pregnancy, very few of them actually followed it seriously. Many mothers did not change their eating habits or workload during their pregnancy even though they knew this was necessary to have a good pregnancy. The mothers knew what they should do, but like people everywhere, they did not do them.

An impressive underlined connection between pregnancy and a mother's decision to breastfeed was in the issue of child spacing. Studies have shown that short birth intervals increase mortality risk of the index child because of premature or involuntary weaning [6, 12,13]. Among the women in group BDP ($n = 18$), nine mothers became pregnant when their toddler was younger than twelve months, with a range of three to eleven months. According to the women it was shocking news to find out they were pregnant again. Many did not plan to have another child, and some sought methods to get rid of the new pregnancy.

> Mom was very surprised when she discovered she was pregnant—"surprised and I got desperate. I did not want to have it, so I desperately asked the young lady (nurse) to give me a shot so that my period would come."

Seven of the women became pregnant when their toddler was between thirteen and twenty-four months, and two were still lactating a toddler over twenty-four months when they became pregnant. The mothers with really young toddlers (below 12 months), where the child's age probably influenced them to continue breastfeeding, made up 50 percent of the group identifying an important public health issue in terms of family planning. The other nine women continued to nurse for a variety of other reasons other than the age of the toddler.

Among the women in group NBDP ($n = 12$) there was a wider inter-birth interval. Only one mother became pregnant while her infant was still less than one year old. The majority of the toddlers ($n = 7$) were between thirteen and twenty-four months and four were between twenty-five and thirty-three months. Three of these mothers stopped lactating only a few months before the new pregnancy. However, for most there was a considerable span between the end of lactation and the new pregnancy—the average time was 8.6 months ($\pm$ SD). The average birth spacing among group BDP was 19.4 months while for group NBDP it was 25.9 months ($\pm$ SD). Among the women in group SBDP, the majority of the toddlers fell in the middle age range (13-24 months) at the time of pregnancy. There was an average birth spacing of twenty-seven months ($\pm$ SD) among these women.

The Fetus

Breastfeeding a toddler during pregnancy was not identified as a behavior with a profound impact on the fetus or its development. Most mothers did not believe that lactating a toddler could affect the fetus in any way. According to the women, a fetus would be the first to "pull" any nutrients ingested by the mother thereby protecting the child, making breastfeeding harmless to a fetus. Some women expressed the idea that a fetus would not be nourished by milk but rather by blood, and therefore would not be affected by lactation during pregnancy.

Lactating during pregnancy does not affect the fetus because the fetus is nourished with blood from the umbilical cord.

One possible explanation to why mothers do not believe there could be negative effects on a fetus could lie in the fact that commonly mothers did not identify with their unborn children until they were actually born. Morgan, in her article *Imagining the Unborn in the Ecuadorian Andes,* found that adults are slow to assign individual identity and person-hood to the not-yet-born [12]. We found that mothers often did not plan their pregnancy, were surprised when they found out, and at first had feelings of rejection. If a mother did not bond with her child until after she gave birth or until late in pregnancy, it would clearly be easier for her to believe that nothing could affect the fetus during her pregnancy (Table 1). Mothers interviewed routinely expressed that if there was something that caused the fetus harm, it was usually late in pregnancy when the fetus was already formed, meaning that only at that point was the fetus attributed some person-hood and given some importance (Table 2). This was also reflected in the thinking shared by some women that, during the first trimester, a mother's attempt to bring on menstruation was acceptable because at this stage there is only blood, not a person or a baby. Therefore, a woman's attempt to bring down this "blood" using foods, pills, or shots was perceived as permissible.

Those who did identify an effect to the fetus noted the most likely consequence to be a low birth weight because of the toddler taking away the fetus' nutrients. This effect, however, was commonly believed to be reversible with time, meaning that the baby could recuperate anything that was not obtained in utero.

Breastfeeding is bad for the fetus because the toddler takes away (food) and the fetus does not get nutrition.

Breastfeeding a toddler during pregnancy was more generally seen harmful to the older child and/or to the mother. There was a uniform response among the two groups of women where about half had the belief that there could be some effect to the fetus. However, perceptions of the fetus did not play a big role in the actual decision a woman made about continuing to lactate during pregnancy.

Table 1. Summary of Mothers' Attitudes and Beliefs by Month of Pregnancy

IDENTITY GIVEN FETUS

- - - - - - - - - - - 3 mths - - - - - - - - - - - 5 mths -

ball of blood	movement	person that feels
coagulated blood	begins	is already formed
little piece of meat		is growing

does not "feel"		it exists—
it does not exist—		"ya es"
"no es"		

at this stage it is permitted		older child takes away
"botar lo—bajar la sangre"		nutrition fetus needs
the milk does not affect		to grow because it is
		already formed.

Table 2. Summary of How External and Internal Influences Impact
Developing Fetus According to Mothers

Conception - - - - - - - - - - - 4 mths - Delivery

External and internal	External and internal
influences will not	influences will "weaken"
affect fetus	the fetus

Milk

Mothers tended to view milk as nutritious. When asked what properties they attributed to mother's milk and milk during pregnancy, seven out of twenty women in group BDP and four out of thirteen women in group NBDP responded that milk was always good. One particular mother did not believe that milk during any time was bad, instead she believed milk was always the same (never changing) and always good.

The milk is always nutritious—it never changes in any way.

Mothers understood how important their milk was for their children in terms of the benefits it offered. They saw the milk as necessary for the child's health development, especially during the first six months of the child's life. However, not all mothers understood the concept of colostrum, and few were able to provide details about it. The few who did understand the importance of colostrum, understood it well. One mother described her colostrum in this manner: "at first the milk is more charged—the first milk comes more protected with more vitamins."

Another perception ascribed to the milk was that of a harmful or dangerous substance. Seven out of twenty women in group BDP, regardless of the fact that they breastfed during pregnancy, identified the milk during pregnancy as abnormal and a possible source of harm to their toddler. Five out of thirteen women in group NBDP also viewed this milk as non-nutritious and harmful to the toddler. The strongest advocates to this perspective were the women in group SBDP, where four out of five of them resoundingly saw milk during pregnancy as harmful, not milk, and not normal.

> I don't think it is nutrition . . . like drinking tea. I give them watered milk—it is clear and a little white.

Several of the women believed that milk changed during pregnancy. For many, this change was only compositional, not in it's nutrition, but still for others it was this change in composition that they believe led to the milk becoming harmful. This change was not limited only to pregnancy. Some women saw that with time came a change in milk, making it less pure and nutritious for an infant. This period was often quoted to be after six to eight months.

> The first 6 months of pregnancy the milk is thick and a cream color, after 6 months the milk turns a clear white and is less thick—it changes because the baby is growing.

> (After 8 months) the breast is pure water, already. So if only drink breast, it won't grow. It won't grow because it only absorbs water, already. They don't grow because the milk has no vitamins.

Consistently we found two prevalent views about milk—a negative view and a positive view. Women who held a negative view of milk believed that if the pregnancy occurred late in the toddler's life (i.e., past 18 months), the milk already had less nutritious qualities and was physically harmful to the toddler. The toddler would become ill, not because the milk was bad but rather due to the lack of nutrition the child received, because by drinking primarily breast milk it did not acquire other sources of nutrition. As pregnancy progressed, the milk would become even more harmful because it would affect the toddler both physically and psychologically. Older toddlers who breastfeed were considered to be at risk of regressing and/or becoming spoiled or delayed in some manner. This impact on the toddler, according to the women, made it necessary to wean; however, the toddler's age makes the attempt harder (Figure 1).

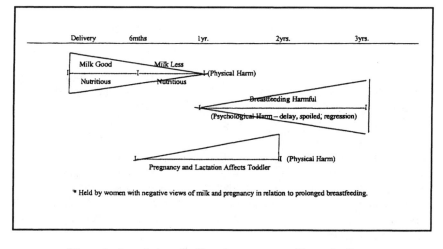

Figure 1. Association of milk and pregnancy and breastfeeding to
effects contributed to toddler.

According to the views of those women that held a positive view of milk and
pregnancy, there was no impact on milk caused by pregnancy because of maternal
milk's inability to change in quality—it is "always nutritious and good."

Mothers' view of milk do, to some extent, influence their decision to lactate
during pregnancy, depending on their circumstance. Mothers with a positive view
were more likely to decide to continue breastfeeding, while those with a negative
view were swayed to wean or at least attempt to wean.

The Older Child

The study suggests that the role of the toddler and the relationship and even
"control" the child has over the mother was an impressive factor contributing to
the decision a woman made in terms of breastfeeding during pregnancy. For
example, a passive mother may have been more influenced by a domineering
child, compared to a mother more capable of taking control in the relationship.

> He did not want to leave the breast, he would start to cry and I would feel bad
> so I kept on giving him breast.

The reason most stated to explain why mothers continued to breastfeed among
this population was that the toddler did not want to stop—"porque no le deja
todavia."

Because you feel bad it is hard to stop breastfeeding . . . the baby cries . . . doesn't want to stop. The baby feels the warmth of a mother, it feels protected, it feels more love.

Among the women nursing during pregnancy (BDP), for many of these mothers the toddler was the central figure in their decision-making process. A number of mothers did not try to wean because of their anxiety about the child's reaction to the process. They feared the child would act out psychologically, become depressed, withdrawn, cry often, and even refrain from accepting other food. Such a change in the child's eating habits could then result in weakness and vulnerability to illness. The mothers' believed that the psychological trauma of being cut from the breast would evolve into physical manifestations. However, many mothers did make at least one previous attempt to wean the toddler, but they failed and, because of it, they decided to continue breastfeeding until the toddler self-weaned.

Toddler did not want to stop and mom was afraid that while she was trying to wean him "he gets sick, it affects him—and he not eat until I give him breast milk." Because parents are afraid of toddler possibly getting sick— "they better just keep giving it to him."

Sometimes you cannot force them off, they have to leave it.

The role the mothers themselves played was key in continued breastfeeding. Feeling of guilt on the mothers' part reinforced the power the child had and thwarted any attempt to wean. These circumstances then lead her to decide to continue breastfeeding, at least until the new baby was born or when the child reached a certain age. Any negative effects on the fetus or toddler were overshadowed or ignored in light of the fact that the toddler could not be weaned.

I felt bad because I was taking away his nutrition, his communication.

For the women in groups NBDP and SBDP, weaning was not an issue. These women attempted and succeeded in weaning, or the child self-weaned. Because of this, these mothers did not have to face the decision of continuing to breastfeed while they were pregnant.

Jealousy turned out to be an important influential factor for the mothers, primarily in their decision to wean or make the attempt. Many mothers characterized their children as being jealous of the pregnancy and the newborn. Mothers found that their children were demanding more attention, crying more often, becoming shy or rebellious, and in some cases becoming sick. These mothers concerned with jealousy strongly believed the emotion had the potential of making the child sick, primarily in psychological terms (making them sad and depressed), but having the potential of affecting them physically (Figure 2).

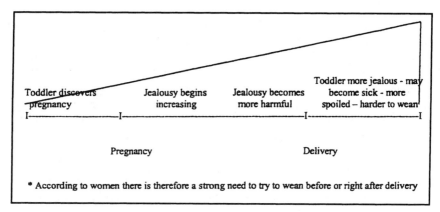

Figure 2. The relationship between toddler's jealousy, pregnancy, and newborn.

According to some mothers' accounts, children refused or decreased the amount of food they consumed, which resulted in them becoming weak and physically ill. To prevent this, mothers identified the need to have their children experience as little jealousy as possible. For some mothers this meant weaning the child before pregnancy (group NBDP) or weaning because of pregnancy (group SBDP). However, for others, allowing the child to continue breastfeeding until the toddler wanted to stop so that she/he would not feel differentiated when the newborn started breastfeeding was the only option (group BDP).

> He is affected psychologically because of jealousy—he thinks that you love the other more. The older child understands that there is another baby and it is going to affect him . . . if I was not pregnant I would continue to breastfeed until he turns seven.

Lactating Two Children

Out of twenty women in group BDP, thirteen of the mothers had given birth at the time of interview and eight of these mothers continued to lactate their toddler after the birth—tandem lactation. The reason most stated by these mothers for continuing to breastfeed the toddler after the birth of the new child was that they could not wean the older child. Six women specifically stated they could not wean, and continued breastfeeding regardless of any possible effects on mother, toddler, or newborn. One mother stated her reason for continuing to nurse both children was because she wanted to continue; another stated that if she were to stop, the toddler would become sick from jealousy. Seven of the women were still pregnant at the time of the interview and three were still lactating because they could not wean their toddlers. The others weaned their toddler right after birth or the toddlers weaned themselves.

Of the women in group BDP, among those that intended to wean or did wean the toddler because of the birth of the new child, what changed in the minds of the mothers was the idea of the ownership of the milk. Some mothers believed that the milk during pregnancy belonged to the toddler, and this was very common thinking among women who continued to lactate during pregnancy. However, once the newborn arrived, the milk belonged to the newborn and if the toddler continued to lactate it would not only be taking quantity of milk from the newborn, but also vitamins and nutrition.

> The milk belongs to the one in the stomach. When the baby is born, if it is sharing its milk that is not good, it is preferable only the newborn, for the older child that milk is no longer good, for the baby it is the only nutrition—its vitamin.

Most women identified effects on all involved parties directly resulting from nursing two children. The person most affected was identified as the woman herself. A mother who lactates two becomes weak, anemic, suffers from headaches and dizziness, she loses weight, or is always tired and irritable. However, not all the mothers agree. One mother's response to the possible negative effects on her health was "the organism is already prepared (for the pregnancy and lactation) so you don't have to ration things (food and nutrition), it has already separated enough for each one."

INTERPRETATION OF FACTORS LEADING TO LACTATION DURING PREGNANCY

Several factors have been considered in trying to answer the question of why mothers continue to lactate during pregnancy (Table 3). The most influential appear to be: the role of the older child and the experience of weaning along with how mother's identify the quality of their milk and whom they believe the milk belongs to during pregnancy. Lastly, any negative effects the women believe can be caused by lactating during pregnancy were also found to be influential in the decisions mothers made.

In assessing the role of an older child and the experience of weaning we found obvious differences between the three groups of women. However, looking specifically at those women who did lactate during pregnancy (BDP), it is apparent that the toddlers are central to the decisions made by the women.

Some of the women saw the weaning process as dangerous to the toddler [8], even more so than lactating during pregnancy. These women may have made a previous attempt to wean, but because of the child's reaction to being weaned—especially in physical terms (becoming ill)—they continued to nurse and came to fear more the negative effects to the child caused by weaning. Still some of the women who lactated during pregnancy just could not succeed in

Table 3. Contentions Given by Mothers as to Why Someone
May Continue Breastfeeding

- toddler "bajo de peso"—underweight due to difficult eating habits, will not eat other foods
- "porque no deja todavia"—toddler does not want to stop
- toddler is sleeping with mom
- toddler cries a lot and asks for teta
- "por pena"—mom feels bad
- "siente el calor de mama—se siente mas protegido"—toddler bonding
- toddler too young
- mother does not want to break up communication
- mother feels guilt
- child becomes irritable—pulls at breast
- "esta acostumbrada y encariñada"—mom is accustomed and endeared
- "los tienen engreidos"—mom has them spoiled
- milk is entertainment for toddler
- milk is "vicio"—habit for toddler

---

weaning their toddler. Many made attempts but failed because of a variety of reasons, such as own feelings of guilt and lack of sleeping accommodations (making it necessary for toddler to sleep in the same bed with mother). With the prolonged breastfeeding of the toddlers, mothers began to identify their breast as entertainment or a calming agent for the toddler—a habit that continues until mother can wean or child self-weans.

In Forste's study on the effects of breastfeeding and birth spacing on infant and child mortality in Bolivia, he found that one-third of infants that stopped breastfeeding before their first birthday did so because the mother had become pregnant [3]. Birth spacing [13, 14] was an issue for several mothers, but they continued to breastfeed because they felt they might cause more harm to the child by prematurely weaning.

> If toddler is still young then "for a young child it is an obligation continue nursing."

Most mothers believed that breastfeeding was a habit for the toddler, not really serving any nutritional importance. Even though the milk was not seen as nutritious, it was not seen by all as physically harmful to the toddler—an explanation as to why women in group BDP continued to nurse during pregnancy. In fact, no harm could result because for most of the women in group BDP the milk was seen as the toddler's property during pregnancy, only after the birth did the milk become the newborns.

The milk during pregnancy is the older child's and once the baby is born it belongs to the newborn.

The women from all three groups were swayed in their decisions by outside influences, their beliefs, and their perceptions of milk, pregnancy, fetus, and toddler (Figure 3). Any one or a combination of these factors influenced most mothers to take their first step—attempt to wean their child (before, during, or after pregnancy).

Groups NBDP and SBDP were able to successfully wean their toddlers. These mothers believed it necessary to wean their children because of their pronounced perceptions of the effects on the various parties involved. These women had longer time intervals between pregnancies, more family and outside support, and possibly stronger characters. The women in group SBDP were influenced to wean clearly by two main factors: their beliefs that nursing during pregnancy would make the toddler sick and possibly lead to the child's death and the outside influence they received about weaning the child. For the women lactating during pregnancy (BDP), the effects brought on by lactating during pregnancy were important but overshadowed by an inability to wean. However, they were one of the main influences for those women to continue making attempts at weaning.

APPLICATIONS OF FINDINGS

Findings show that providing further research, culturally appropriate health education, and family planning programs may greatly contribute to the decrease in premature weaning—in this instance before the minimum two years recommended by WHO in developing countries [15]. The majority of the women in this study did not really know what to believe in terms of whether lactation during pregnancy was harmful or not. Health professionals themselves provided these women with inconsistent and conflicting messages. This tells the health community that more research needs to be done so that definite answers can be reached and given to the community. Messages need to be clear whether breastfeeding during pregnancy is harmful or not harmful to a toddler, a fetus, or a mother, and only through research in this area can we then convey one message to communities.

Family planning and education services are recommendations that would take time, acceptance by the community, and dedication along with money by the health entities involved. These can be considered long-term goals for this community. However, the findings do reflect a strong need for these programs. Most of the women in this study believed that lactation was indeed harmful during pregnancy. Our study demonstrates that many of the women in groups SBDP and BDP were forced to wean or to attempt to wean because of a new pregnancy. Furthermore, many of the women in group NBDP prematurely weaned

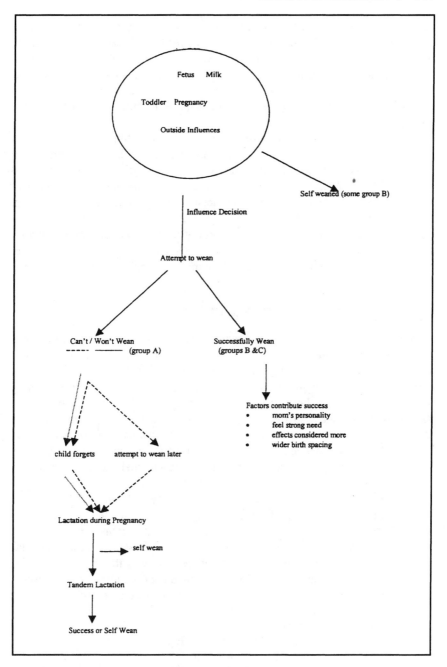

Figure 3. Interpretation of factors leading to lactation during pregnancy.

their children and several did significantly before the recommended two years because of lack of education on proper breastfeeding. Those women in group BDP, even though unable to wean, attempted to wean the child before the WHO recommendation because of a new pregnancy. Family planning programs may have prevented this situation altogether by allowing women the opportunity to have adequate birth spacing between pregnancies to ensure the health of the fetus, the toddler, and herself.

Short-term applications can also be made from this study. An emphasis on the clarity of messages given to the communities by health organizations and professionals is a priority. Health professionals at all levels, but especially field workers (FWs), should be trained to educate the mothers they come in contact with [5, 6] with a clear message about lactation during pregnancy and to some extent the mechanisms of breastfeeding [16]. For mothers, the FWs are sometimes the only access they have to any form of medical care and so they highly revere the opinion of these members of the health community [6]. FWs can then be used as an important and vital part of the information flow on breastfeeding.

CONCLUSIONS

A mother's new pregnancy is regarded as one of the major reasons outweighing what a mother, under normal conditions, would consider optimal for her child—breastfeeding [8]. Pregnancy is therefore a clear risk factor for a short breastfeeding period if perceived by women and some health professionals as harmful. Studies have shown that weaning before a child's first birthday is often associated with illness to the child or a new pregnancy. With this in mind the health community must come to the conclusion of whether a pregnancy does in fact need to result in premature weaning. Once this question is answered, health professionals looking to address the issues with educational and family planning interventions must have a good understanding of the importance of the underlined concepts that lead women to make the decisions they make in their lives. If we have a better understanding of the barriers, influences, and steps that dictate a woman's decision making, we can then better create and implement programs that will impact and be effective in a community. It is not enough to have a superficial understanding of why people act or to assume we know why they do what they do. By creating intervention programs with a thorough understanding of these issues, we will be more successful in bettering the health of the community.

ACKNOWLEDGMENTS

The authors carried out this research as discussed in the chapter with the support of the University of Alabama at Birmingham and with funding from the National Institute of Health. The Institutional Review Board of the University of

Alabama and the Ethical Committee of the Instituto de Investigacion Nutricional (IIN) approved this study.

REFERENCES

1. S. C. Weller and C. I. Dungy, Personal Preferences and Ethnic Variations among Anglo and Hispanic Breast and Bottle Feeders, *Social Science Medicine, 23*:6, pp. 539-548, 1986.
2. A. De La Torre and L. Rush, The Determinants of Breastfeeding for Mexican Migrant Women, *Migration and Health: International Migration Review, 11*:3, pp. 729-739.
3. R. Forste, The Effects of Breastfeeding and Birth Spacing on Infant and Child Mortality in Bolivia, *Population Studies, 48,* pp. 497-511, 1994.
4. M. Stegeman and M. H. Bottona, Breastfeeding Practices in Northeastern Brazil, *Ecology of Food and Nutrition, 36,* pp. 443-461, 1998.
5. S. L. Huffman, E. Rasmussan, V. Newman, and C. O'Gara, Breastfeeding: A Natural Resource for Food Security, *Wellstart: Expanded Promotion of Breastfeeding,* Washington, D.C., pp. 1-31, 1992.
6. J. Bradley and J. Meme, Breastfeeding Promotion in Kenya: Changes in Health Worker Knowledge, Attitudes and Practices, *Journal of Tropical Pediatrics, 38,* pp. 228-234, 1992.
7. E. L. Fernandez and G. M. Guthrie, Belief Systems and Breastfeeding among Filipino Urban Poor, *Social Science Medicine, 19*:9, pp. 991-995, 1984.
8. M. S. Jakobsen, M. Sademann, K. Molbak, and P. Abbey, Reason for Termination of Breastfeeding and the Length of Breastfeeding, *International Journal of Epidemiology, 25*:1, pp. 115-121, 1996.
9. E. M. E. Poskitt, Energy Needs in the Weaning Period, *Weaning: Why, What and When?* A. Ballabriga and J. Rey (eds.), Nestle Nutrition-Vevey/Raven Press, New York, pp. 45-61, 1987.
10. Instituto Nacional De Estadistica E Imformativa—UN Population Fund, *Peru: Mapa De Necesidades Basicas Insatisfechas En Los Lugares A Nivel Distrital—Toma III,* Lima-Peru, Agosto, 1994.
11. R. A. Lawrence (MD), Psychologic Bonding, *Breastfeeding: A Guide for the Medical Professional—Third Edition,* C. V. Mosby Company, St. Louis, pp. 148-255, 1989.
12. L. M. Morgan, Imagining the Unborn in the Ecuadorian Andes, *Feminist Studies, 23*:2, pp. 323-350, 1997.
13. Y. Oheneba-Sakyl and B. K. Takui, Sociodemographic Correlates of Breastfeeding in Ghana, *Human Biology, 63*:3, pp. 389-402, 1991.
14. M. M. Abdel Kader, R. Bahgat, M. T. Aziz, F. Hefnawi, M. H. H. Badradui, N. Younis, and F. Hassib, Lactation Patterns in Egyptian Women, *Journal Biosocial Science, 4,* pp. 403-409, 1972.
15. World Health Organization, Breast Milk Quantity and Composition: A Review, *The Quality and Quantity of Breast Milk: Report on the WHO Collaborative Study on Breastfeeding,* Geneva, Switzerland, 1985.
16. R. A. Lawrence (MD), Biochemistry of Human Milk, *Breastfeeding: A Guide for the Medical Professional—Third Edition,* C. V. Mosby Company, St. Louis, pp. 73-113, 1989.

CHAPTER 6

Much More Than HIV!
The Reality of Life on the Streets
for Drug-Using Sex Workers in
Inner City Hartford

Nancy Romero-Daza
Margaret Weeks
Merrill Singer

Women who exchange sex for money or drugs are exposed to a myriad of risks including physical and emotional abuse, rape, and even murder [1-4]. The actual incidence of violence against street women is hard to determine due to under-reporting. For example, less than 4 percent of rape cases among sex workers are reported to the police, and only about 7 percent of these individuals seek professional counseling to deal with their attack [1]. In addition to street violence, sex workers are especially at risk of sexually transmitted diseases (STDs) including HIV/AIDS. The risk of HIV infection for commercial sex workers is further exacerbated when they or their sex partners are involved in the use of injection drugs [5-8]. Moreover, studies demonstrate an association between the use of non-injection drugs, especially crack cocaine, with increased risky sexual activity and a concomitant increase in HIV infection [9-12]. As drug addiction increases, so does women's reliance on exchanges of sex for money or drugs. This in turn, augments the sex workers' vulnerability to violence and abuse, which further results in increasing exposure to HIV. Thus, a vicious cycle of drug use, prostitution, violence, and HIV risk is set in motion, from which disenfranchised drug-using minority women in the inner city find it difficult to escape.

The purpose of this chapter is to present a qualitative description of the daily risks encountered by minority street sex workers in inner-city Hartford, Connecticut, and the mechanisms they use to minimize the adverse effects of such risks. These data are presented in an attempt to illustrate the multiplicity of factors that increase a sex worker's susceptibility to HIV risks, and that may prevent her from adopting protective measures against the infection.

METHODOLOGY

Information was collected from a total of sixteen women who had previously participated in Project COPE (Community Outreach Prevention Effort), an HIV/AIDS prevention program for injection drug users and crack cocaine users, funded by the National Institute on Drug Abuse. The women were selected from the pool of female COPE participants who had reported involvement in commercial sex. The participants were re-contacted and recruited into the study by Project COPE community outreach workers in neighborhoods characterized by high levels of drug activity and prostitution. The interviews were conducted in private offices at the Hispanic Health Council, which is easily accessible from the major points of recruitment. Participants received tokens for transportation as well as a monetary incentive for their participation in the project. In addition, participants received educational material about HIV/AIDS, and those who expressed the need for social or health services, received the necessary referrals.

Data were collected through an open-ended interview instrument that covered topics such as participants' drug use history, their experience with selling sex for money or drugs, their perceptions of the risks to which they are exposed while working on the streets, and the behavioral mechanisms they develop to protect themselves against those risks. In order to increase participant's level of comfort, the interviews were conducted in the language of their choice by bilingual personnel. Seven of the nine Latino participants chose Spanish. All the interviews were tape-recorded with the participants' consent. The tapes were transcribed and the Spanish ones were translated into English. Content analysis of the interviews was done by the first author. This process included the careful review of the transcripts in order to identify major categories of information in each one of the interviews (e.g., history of drug use, participation in sex for money exchanges, risks identified while working the streets). Based on this review, a summary outline was produced for each interview, highlighting the major themes found in the interview. Finally, the sixteen outlines were compared against each other to identify recurrent patterns, similarities, and differences in the experiences described by the participants.

RESULTS

Respondents ranged in age from twenty-three to thirty-nine years; and were almost equally divided between African Americans and Latinas (see Table 1 for

Table 1. Sample Characteristics

	African American (n = 7)	Latino (n = 9)
Injection drug users	4	5
Crack users	5	6
HIV positive	3	2
Average number of years as sex worker	4.5	7
Homeless at the time of the interview	3	2
History of incarceration	4	7
Living with children under 18 years of age	4	5
Drug-using husband/live-in boyfriend	3	5

sample demographics). Most of the women interviewed reported initiating drug use during their teenage years, and all considered themselves heavily addicted to drugs. Nine of the women had used injection drugs during the previous six months. In this group four reported using only heroin, while the remaining listed "speedballs," a mixture of heroin and cocaine, as their drug of choice. Four of the injection drug users also reported the use of crack and powder cocaine. Among the seven women who reported never injecting, it was common to find a pattern of multiple-drug use, especially of crack cocaine combined with the use of marijuana and alcohol. Four of the respondents also reported using these drugs in combination with tranquilizers such as Valium, Trilafon, and Xanax.

All of the women interviewed were actively involved in prostitution, and reported having sold sex from as few as twenty times to as many as 1,800 times over the six months prior to the interview. As reported by all of the respondents, the need to support their drug habit was the major factor leading them to involvement in sex for money transactions. This was clearly expressed by Gloria[1] a thirty-three-year-old African American when trying to describe the frequency with which she exchanges sex for money or drugs:

> It's unimaginable . . . every single day, as many times a day as possible. Behind the buildings and hallways, in bed, everywhere, everything everywhere, every how to make your money to get your drugs . . . Jesus Christ, I just assume (I do it) a good ten times a day . . . every day! You don't want to stop 'cause you don't want to not have your drugs, so it's continuous. It could be three or four days continuous. You might get one day sleep but when you get up and start you go days and days and days again.

[1] All the names used in this chapter are pseudonyms.

In addition to the demands of a drug habit, women also mentioned the need for money to pay rent, and to get food and clothing not only for themselves but also for their children or other dependents. All the women interviewed were unemployed, six of them were on public assistance, and all had little or no economic support from their permanent partners. In fact, as the women reported, being in a permanent relationship may impose further economic burden on them, since they often have to secure money to support not only their own habit but that of their partners as well. This was the case with eight of the women interviewed whose partners were heavily dependent on drugs and did not have any work or any other reliable source of income. As Clara, a young Latino woman explained:

> If (my boyfriend) would try and go out there and get a job and help me out, I wouldn't have to do these things. It's hard trying to take care of my kids and then he's there and he's eating the food and getting on my nerves and wanting to use the drugs just as much as me. I can't afford to take care of him and the kids too, you know. And then I got the bills and all that stuff.

The women reported that their drug addiction usually prevents them from getting or keeping a job in a market where employment opportunities for ethnic minorities are limited. As the following comment by Laura illustrates, these difficulties may be further exacerbated when the women are HIV positive, as was the case for five of the respondents in this study:

> People like myself who have AIDS or the virus, we may be unable to get a job . . . they're testing. Even a McDonald job is asking to test you even to clean the floors, you understand what I'm saying? So what jobs can we get? Who's going to really give us a job? It ain't like I don't want to work, give me a job, I will work. But I have this problem where if I get cut or anything, you cannot touch me, you understand? And once they find that out Phm! I lost my job.

As several of the participants stated, those women who do find jobs quickly realize that they cannot derive enough income to meet their needs when working at or below minimal wages. In an environment of limited economic opportunities, prostitution offers an alternative to other illegal activities such as stealing, mugging, shoplifting, or selling drugs, activities in which most of the respondents had participated before starting to sell sex. In fact, participation in illegal activities had led most of the respondents to have extensive police records. In addition, eleven of them reported having spent time in jail, with an average prison time of seven months.

Although most of the women interviewed had a permanent residence, five of them were living on the streets or in homeless shelters. One of these participants specifically mentioned engaging in prostitution as a means of securing a place to spend the night. Further, the need for companionship also was mentioned by two women as one of the reasons for their involvement in sex for money transactions.

As Isabel, a thirty-three-year-old African American explained, however distant and cold their relationships with clients, they often provide at least some of the emotional comfort so desperately needed by women who, like herself, have very little or no social support from other sources:

> First of all, I (sell sex) because of my habit. Second of all, I feel lonely. Sometimes I feel lonely and that's the only way I can find somebody to talk to. I hate to admit it, but what can I say? It's sad, but it's true.

THE PRICE OF SEX

Women in the sample reported varying incomes depending on the number of partners they see and the prices they set for their services. In general they reported charging between twenty and forty dollars for intercourse, between ten and twenty dollars for oral sex, and between forty and one hundred dollars for spending the night with a client. Although most of the respondents stated that they set their price from the beginning and refused lower offers, they admitted that quite often they must settle for less when the threat of suffering withdrawal symptoms is too strong. Twenty-four-year-old Darleen explained the situation in the following way:

> I like charge $40, but sometimes they don't got it and I need the money for drugs and they offer me like $20, $10, whatever they got I take. I gotta do it, if I don't, I never know when I'm gonna get the next trick and by then I may be too sick.

Interestingly, although maintaining a drug habit was the major reason for the respondents's involvement in prostitution, the actual exchange of sex for drugs was rarely reported by the women in this sample. As the respondents explained, women usually insist on getting cash, even as partial payment. This pattern of "sex for money for drugs"[2] is especially convenient for women who have children to support. Sonia, a twenty-six-year-old Puerto Rican woman, explained why she prefers to get at least some cash in exchange for her sexual services:

> I (go) half and half, I want money and I want cocaine 'cause I got kids at home. That drug ain't gonna feed them, y'know? If I get no cash but I get only 'caine, and I go down the street and sell it, it ain't gonna be enough for me. That's a bad deal, man, real bad.

Women reported that they are selective in the types of sexual activities in which they engage. Although two of the participants reported having had sex with other women while clients watched and participating in anal sex and

---

[2] We are grateful to an anonymous reviewer who suggested this term to describe the exchange pattern found in this sample.

sadomasochism, most of the women limited themselves to oral or vaginal sex. In fact, the majority of the respondents expressed a preference for oral sex, and often devised ways of avoiding vaginal intercourse with their clients. Reportedly, this was done as a way to minimize the risk of HIV infection, but mainly because oral sex is quicker and, in their perception, much less intimate. As expressed by the women, not all the encounters with clients involved physical contact. Some men, especially those who are considered regular clients, often provide women with money and support in times of need, without asking for sexual services. Daniah, a thirty-two-year-old African American, explained her special relation with a much older man whom she had known for a period of over six years:

> When I be in jail (my client) sends me money, he look out for me. Even if I don't have sex with this guy, I could go over there and he'll give me money . . . He's like, y'know, the family that I never had. I could count on this guy for anything, anytime.

THE RISKS OF SELLING SEX

Physical Violence

The women interviewed identified several dangers involved in the sale of sex, including the risk of losing their money or drugs at the hands of either clients or strangers on the streets, and the risk of arrest and imprisonment and the resulting loss of custody over their children. However, by far the most salient risk identified by the respondents was that of physical violence, of which all but two of them had been victims. In addition, all of the respondents identified murder as a very clear danger to which they are exposed on a daily basis. Maureen, a thirty-six-year-old African-American woman explained the serious risks taken every single time a street sex worker goes out with a strange man:

> It's a gamble, y'know? You're taking a chance with your life, and the life of the person you're with . . . You don't know who's gonna come out. You don't know if you'd come out . . . (you worry) about getting killed, 'cause there is a lot of maniacs out there.

Physical violence against sex workers often results in rape and thus in an increase in the risk of HIV infection. In fact, seven of the women interviewed reported that they had been raped while working on the streets. One of them, twenty-three-year-old Clara, recalled her experience with gang rape:

> I was with this guy, and we were almost done, and I asked him to give me my money, right? So he says sure, let me just get money from my friend who's back there. So I follow him 'cause I don't want him to rip me off or nothing, and we go behind a building and there was like three guys over there, and this guy smiles at them, and they all come to me and start grabbing me. And I

know something's gonna happen, so I try to tell them to leave me alone and that I just wanted my money, right? But then two of them corner me and start touchin' me and stuff, and then the one I was with came over and all of them started forcing me to do things and I just wanted to die, y'know?

As the respondents reported, in order to protect themselves against rape and other forms of physical violence, they often carry weapons such as knives, metal clubs, and mace. However, for some of the respondents who must decide between buying a weapon and getting the drugs that will prevent the pain of drug withdrawal, the immediate need for drugs often overrides safety concerns. Ironically, as one of the respondents described, even for those who can afford protection, carrying a weapon may sometimes be a danger in and of itself, and may increase the risk of being seriously hurt:

I travel with a knife, sometimes you use it just to scare people off, but sometimes (men) are strong and . . . you might be afraid that they'd take it and kill you with it, so you might as well not even pull it out. You gotta know how to judge each situation and then decide if you wanna pull it out or not, it's up to you.

A very common tactic used by women to prevent being physically abused is the careful selection of clients. Most women reported that they prefer to go out with regular clients whom they have known for a while rather than with complete strangers. However, since this is not always possible, women usually rely on their intuition in judging a potential client. As thirty-five-year-old Samantha claimed:

You can always tell when a person is gonna be nice to you and you can tell when a person is gonna be nasty. You gotta trust your gut feelings. A nice looking guy may come to you, but if you got a bad feeling, you better stay away from him, if you have a chance, y'know?

An additional protective measure adopted by most of the women interviewed was avoiding the use of drugs while in the company of clients. As Gloria explained, being under the influence of drugs may decrease the degree of control women have over the sexual encounter, and may therefore increase their chances of being victimized at the hands of their clients:

I might do it for drugs but I don't stick with my dates and do drugs with them . . . I might really lose my head, I might not know what I'm doing . . . I might offer to give up more sex when I'm high or something, I might not get paid . . . maybe hurt.

While all of the women interviewed worked independently, a few of them reported the benefits of having clients believe they are working for a pimp.

According to respondents, this offers a sense of added security and may also increase the amount of money received for sex. As Jean explained:

> You always tell them (you have a pimp) 'cause that way they think they're being watched. They believe that that guy is there watching you, and so it gives you a little less (to worry about) . . . and they figure you got a pimp that you gotta give money to, so they throw you extra money.

While acts of violence against sex workers are usually perpetrated by clients, women also face additional dangers of rape and assault while walking or buying drugs on the streets. Participants reported that working in pairs with other women reduces their risk of being victimized. However, because of economic reasons all of the respondents preferred not to do so, since this may make it more difficult for both women to find clients and may require them to share their drugs with their companions.

AIDS and Other Sexually Transmitted Diseases

The women also identified health issues as a major risk involved in prostitution. All of the respondents reported AIDS and other sexually transmitted diseases such as syphilis, gonorrhea, and genital warts as major risks to which they are exposed on a daily basis. The majority of the women reported the practice of examining their clients for signs of sexually transmitted diseases, and all of them claimed to refuse to have sex when signs of infection are apparent or to demand the use of two condoms rather than only one as a measure of added protection. Lisa, who had been working on the streets for over twelve years, described the way in which she checks for the presence of STDs:

> You have to look at their privates . . . and see if it's leaking or dripping or something's coming out wet, and you ask them questions . . . And I always say ah ah, something ain't right, and I say no, that's OK I don't wanna (have sex) . . . I say 'wanna put two (condoms) on? Then I'll be safe.

Most of the women interviewed claimed to be highly successful in their attempts to make their clients use condoms. They further stated that they usually refuse to have sex with men who do not agree to their use. Maria's explanation of her interaction with clients illustrates a point of view shared by most of the women interviewed:

> You have to lay out the rules right there . . . you tell them "a condom or no go," and a few have said "No I want it without a condom, and that's it or you're not getting no money" and I say, "screw you," and I get out. I won't do it without a condom.

In addition, women reported that to ensure protection against diseases they pay close attention to the way in which their clients put the condoms on. A few of the women complained that their clients do not leave the necessary space at the tip of the condom, thus increasing the chance of rupture. In such cases women take it upon themselves to teach clients how to use condoms correctly, as explained by Linda, a twenty-eight-year-old African American who had been selling sex for seven years:

> Some men don't even know how to put rubbers on, and that's what I've found out. They put it all the way onto the thing, and one dude that I be with was arguing. I said "you don't put it on like that" He said "yes you do." And I said "let me show you. I know how to do it" I said "I ain't got another rubber, this is the last one I got, so let me show you." He said okay. So, I showed him. "You have to pull it up some, then roll it." He says "all the damn time I been doing it wrong."

This observation, combined with the respondents' report that they often instruct other sex workers on the correct use of condoms and, when they have extra condoms, provide them to their friends, indicates that sex workers play an active and very important role in the dissemination of information about HIV prevention measures.

In spite of their awareness about this health risk and of their efforts to avoid infection, women are sometimes unable to protect themselves against sexually transmitted diseases. As Laura explained, the price of condoms can be a major obstacle, especially when the need for drugs is overpowering:

> I use condoms, but there have been a few times that I haven't 'cause I didn't have them . . . I was taking money out of what I was getting from clients, buying condoms, and then I didn't have enough for my (drugs). I paid between 3.29 and 4.79 and that's a lot. I just didn't have extra money to buy them, that's too much.

In addition, as reported by participants, it is not unusual for men to increase their payment if women agree to have sex without condoms. A few of the women reported that on such occasions they are able to put a condom on a man without him noticing that she is doing so. Nelly, a thirty-nine-year-old African American who had been on the streets for close to nine years, explained the way in which she puts a condom on her partner while performing oral sex:

> If they refuse (to wear a condom) I just trick them. I put it in my mouth and pretend that I'm starting sucking them, and I put it on them. And I take it out with my mouth. They don't even notice, they think they're coming in my mouth but they're not.

However, in many cases when the need for money is extreme, women may settle for unprotected sex. This happens in spite of women's awareness about the possible risk for HIV or STD infection. As Linda explained:

> If you're desperate enough you're not gonna turn down no money because the guy don't want to use no rubbers . . . you think about the matter at hand, you're gonna get your money, you're gonna get your drugs. You might not think about it till days later. Crazy but true.

For the women interviewed, the risk of infection with HIV comes not only from their clients but also from their regular partners. This is especially so in light of the fact that, despite their insistence on the use of condoms with clients, thirteen out of the sixteen women reported not using condoms with their husbands or live-in-boyfriends. Women explained this behavior by citing the special bond and emotional closeness that usually exist between partners and that are absent in most exchanges of sex for money [13-15]. The perception of condoms as a sign of emotional distance between sex partners is clearly illustrated in the case of a thirty-two-year-old Latino woman who claimed to use condoms with her boyfriend of fifteen years only in those occasions in which she is mad at him. In most instances the use of condoms with regular partners is minimal even when women know their partners are involved in bisexual or homosexual relations or share intravenous needles with other drug users. One of the women noted:

> I know he be getting high and I know he had to share needles, and I know his brother is HIV positive, and I have seen him and his brother get off . . . (but) I don't feel like asking him to use condoms. We've lived together for sixteen years and I love him. I couldn't even dream of asking him.

CONCLUSION

As it is generally the case among commercial sex workers [16, 17], for the sixteen women interviewed in this project, engaging in the sale of sex is *not* a personal choice but rather a condition into which they are forced by their drug addiction and poverty. Participating in prostitution usually takes a major emotional toll on women. As feelings of low self-esteem become more and more entrenched, economic conditions deteriorate, and social and emotional support decrease, the need for drugs increases as a means to cope with an ever-threatening reality. As illustrated by the following comment made by Sonia, a vicious cycle is created from which women find it very difficult to break free:

> I don't want to have to go out and keep selling my body like this anymore. It's degrading . . . I'm afraid if I keep doing this that I'm going to get to

a point so low that I won't want to bring myself back . . . It's very degrading. It makes you feel like you're nothing and you get more higher and more higher just to not feel that, to get your body numb.

As the results of this exploratory study show, the need for drugs often overrides women's attempts to minimize the dangers involved in prostitution, including that of HIV infection. In order to curb the spread of AIDS among women who sell sex for money, the structural factors that force them into risky situations must be addressed. First and foremost, significant attempts must be made to increase women's access to drug treatment programs. An increase in the number of treatments slots must be combined with specific services such as childcare and transportation to facilitate the enrollment and completion of the program for women with small children. Equally important is the provision of services to prevent relapse to drug abuse. Once initial treatment is completed women usually find themselves back in a highly stressful environment that offers very few opportunities for survival, and limited social support to remain off drugs. Faced with poverty, sexism, and discrimination women are often forced again into the cycle of drug abuse and prostitution. Therefore, services such as support groups and individual case management that include health education are of paramount importance to ensure successful recovery from drug addiction. At the same time, access to biomedical services needs to be facilitated for the early detection and treatment of other sexually transmitted diseases that may increase women's chances of infection with HIV. Programs specifically directed toward commercial sex workers must incorporate sex and general health education, and should emphasize strategies that empower women in their efforts to avoid STDs, such as the inspection of clients' genital area for signs of infection and the practice of putting on a condom with the mouth while performing oral sex. At the same time, dangerous misconceptions such as the benefits of using two condoms at once, need to be clarified through sexual health education. Of special importance is the need to increase women's power to negotiate condom use with permanent partners, especially with those at high risk of HIV infection. Finally, job training programs and employment opportunities must be expanded to provide low income women with economic alternatives that allow them to lessen their dependence on the sale of sex for survival.

The implementation of these recommendations is, to a great extent, dependent on the social and political climate found in different settings throughout the United States. Specifically, changes brought about by welfare reform and the allocation of funds for HIV prevention in each state, play a decisive role in the viability of efforts to curb the spread of AIDS among populations such as the one described in this chapter. Now more than ever we are faced with a critical need to strengthen our health promotion, advocacy, and education efforts to bring about changes in the economic and social conditions that place disenfranchised ethnic minorities at a high risk for HIV infection. Until such changes take place it will be impossible for women to break free from the vicious cycle of drugs, prostitution, and AIDS, that presents a great challenge for sexual health protection at the individual and community levels.

ACKNOWLEDGMENT

Support for this study was provided by the National Institute on Drug Abuse (Grant #U01 DA 07284).

REFERENCES

1. M. Silbert, *Sexual Assault of Prostitutes*, Delancy Street Foundation, San Francisco, California, 1981.
2. M. Singer, N. Romero-Daza, and M. Weeks, *The SAVA Epidemic: Substance Abuse, Violence, and AIDS in the Puerto Rican Community*, Presented at the 96th Annual Meetings of the American Anthropological Association, Washington, D.C., November 19-23, 1997.
3. N. Romero-Daza, K. Radda, M. Weeks, and M. Singer, *Violence Victimization among Drug Addicted Sex Workers in Hartford, Connecticut*, presented at the Annual Meetings of the Society for Applied Anthropology, Seattle, Washington, March 1997.
4. N. Romero-Daza and M. Singer, *Another Type of Victim: The Effect of Witnessing Violence on Drug Use among Puerto Rican Women in Hartford*, presented at the 96th Annual Meetings of the American Anthropological Association, Washington, D.C., November 19-23, 1997.
5. R. J. Batjes, R. W. Pickens, Z. Amsel, and L. S. Brown, Jr., Heterosexual Transmission of Human Immunodeficiency Virus among Intravenous Drug Users, *Journal of Infectious Disease, 162*, pp. 1007-1011, 1990.
6. D. J. Bell, Reduction of AIDS Risk among 41 Heroin Addicted Female Street Prostitutes: Effects of Free Methadone Maintenance, *Journal of Addictive Diseases, 12*, pp. 7-23, 1993.
7. J. B. Cohen, Why Women Partners of Drug Users Will Continue to be at High Risk for HIV I Infection, *Journal of Addictive Diseases, 10*, pp. 99-110, 1991.
8. S. Kane, AIDS, Addiction, and Condom Use: Sources of Sexual Risk for Heterosexual Women, *The Journal of Sex Research, 27*, pp. 427-444, 1990.
9. R. E. Fullilove, M. T. Fullilove, B. Bowser, and S. Gross, Crack Users: The New AIDS Risk Group? *Cancer Detection and Prevention, 14*, pp. 363-368, 1990.
10. M. T. Fullilove, E. A. Lown, and R. E. Fullilove, Crack'hos and Skeezers: Traumatic Experiences of Women Crack Users, *The Journal of Sex Research, 29*, pp. 275-287, 1992.
11. J. A. Inciardi, D. Lockwood, and A. E. Pottieger, *Women and Crack Cocaine*, Macmillan Publishing Company, New York, 1993.
12. N. L. Weatherby, J. M. Schulz, D. D. Chitwood, H. V. McCoy, C. B. McCoy, D. D. Ludwig, and B. R. Edlin, Crack Cocaine Use and Sexual Activity in Miami, Florida, *Journal of Psychoactive Drugs, 24*, pp. 373-380, 1992.

13. K. Carovano, More than Mothers and Whores: Redefining the AIDS Prevention Needs of Women, *International Journal of Health Services, 21*, pp. 131-142, 1991.

14. J. Catania, T. J. Coates, E. Golden, M. M. Dolcini, J. Peterson, S. Kegeles, D. Siegel, and T. M. Fullilove, Correlates of Condom Use among Black, Hispanic, and White Heterosexuals in San Francisco: The AMEN Longitudinal Survey, *AIDS Education and Prevention, 6*, pp. 12-26, 1994.

15. L. E. Dorfman, P. A. Derish, and J. B. Cohen, Hey Girlfriend: An Evaluation of AIDS Prevention among Women in the Sex Industry, *Health Education Quarterly, 19*, pp. 25-40, 1992.

16. J. James, *Prostitutes and Prostitution: Deviants in a Hostile World*, General Learning Press, Morristown, New Jersey, 1977.

17. M. R. Weeks, M. Grier, M. J. Puglisi, M. Singer, and Z. Jia, Streets, Drugs, and the Economy of Sex in the Age of AIDS, *Women and Health, 27*, pp. 203-228, 1998.

CHAPTER 7

Assessing the Interrelationships of STIs, Substance Abuse, and Depression among Street-Based Female Adolescent Sex Workers in Puerto Rico: Implications for Community Health

Margarita Burgos
Belinda Reininger
Donna L. Richter
Ann L. Coker
Margarita Alegría
Mildred Vera
Ruth Saunders

Even at a time when public health initiatives are initially listening to the needs of priority populations and assessing assets from which to build programs, ongoing implementation efforts tend to remain centralized and habitual. Providing prevention and treatment-oriented community-based health services over time tends to remain based on staff's perceptions of need, and their own convenience regarding when and how services are provided. Real change in programming around bringing clients into the system, taking services to them, and modifying service delivery for the comfort of the client is happening sporadically. Often our current attempts at prevention and treatment programming places clients, particularly youth, in situations where they are not in contact with services until they require treatment. This chapter provides information on a youth population who is missed by traditional prevention health services, their health issues, and some implications of intervention strategies that must be modified to meet the needs of the priority population and linked to community services more effectively.

In addition to the problem of traditional health services not reaching adolescents, research shows that many teenagers initiate sexual activity and drug use activities that place them at greater need for prevention and treatment services [1]. Moreover, a correlation between risky sexual behavior and use of illicit drugs among adolescents has been established [2]. Baker et al. suggested substance use as an important antecedent of sexual risk-taking [3]. Research by Szalay, Canino, and Vilov identified drug use as a problem that particularly affects minorities and youth [4]. These behaviors together can lead to several unwanted outcomes, including sexually transmitted infections (STI).

Several risk factors contribute to STI among adolescents. At increased risk are those adolescents who have: multiple sex partners; sexual contact with individuals with a documented STI/HIV infection or with injecting drug users; a past history of STI; traded sex for money, drugs, or other goods; used drugs (particularly if injected) or alcohol; and/or been pregnant and continue to be sexually active [2-7]. Richter and collaborators have demonstrated that the tendency for adolescents to engage in risky behaviors is enhanced when they are under the influence of drugs or alcohol [2]. Also, Alegría, et al. found an association between depressive symptoms and STI [7]. Research conducted by Amaro showed that depressive mood and depression are related to illicit drug use among females [8]. The Centers for Disease Control and Prevention (CDC) reports that adolescents have a high risk of contracting STI [9]. Chlamydia and gonorrhea are the most prevalent [10]. One group of adolescents who are at increased risk for STI are adolescent sex workers who exchange sex for money, drugs, or other goods.

Depression has been correlated with the use of illegal drugs among Hispanic females [8]. An association has also been established between depressive symptoms and negative health outcomes, including HIV infection, among Puerto Rican women [9]. Family relationships consistently have been shown to be important in the development of risk practices within Hispanic communities, where family ties and obligations are highly valued [11-14]. Social context factors are particularly relevant for the participants in the present study because Puerto Rican women sustain a high level of interaction with their family of origin [15]. Unreasonably high expectations of Hispanic females and their concurrent multiple family roles (wife, mother, daughter) can lead to stress and depression [16].

This study focused on the prevalence and correlates of STI among street-based female adolescent sex workers in Puerto Rico. Information from this study can help generate prevention and intervention strategies needed to curb STI in this population. Additionally, this study highlights the importance of modifying and effectively linking intervention strategies in community settings.

METHODS

This study is based on data collected through personal interviews of street-based female adolescent sex workers in Puerto Rico. To identify sex workers, six recruitment sites in diverse areas of Puerto Rico were established. These sites were usually within or adjacent to public housing or areas where drugs were sold. Public health outreach workers from the Department of Health in Puerto Rico established initial contacts and obtained the participants' informed consent to participate in the study. Participants received a financial incentive as compensation for their time and effort. While not selected at random, this sample provides preliminary information about female adolescent sex workers in Puerto Rico. The final sample consisted of 78 female adolescents aged 13 to 18 years of age who traded sex for money, drugs, or other goods. Approximately 5 percent of those asked to participate in the study refused. All participants were offered a financial incentive.

All personal interviews with the respondents were conducted in Spanish; these lasted 45 minutes to an hour. Following the interview, the women attended counseling sessions in Spanish in which information about protection against STI was provided. Condoms were distributed and treatment for STI was administered when needed.

During the interview, sociodemographic and health-risk behavioral information was collected. Specifically, questions about marital status, number of children, frequency of and reasons for visiting a doctor/hospital, and educational status were asked to obtain information about sociodemographics. Several dimensions of health and health risk behaviors were measured including STI, depression, drug use, and sexual practices.

Biologic samples were collected from participants to determine whether the respondent currently had a sexually transmitted infection. Medical personnel were responsible for the collection of blood and cultures for STI tests. Blood samples were tested for antibodies against HIV and syphilis. Cultures were tested for gonorrhea and chlamydia. Specimens from the lower genital tract, a vaginal swab for *C. trachomatis*, and an endocervical swab for *N. gonorrhea* were collected. Plastic stemmed applicators were used for these purposes. Specimens for *C. trachomatis* were processed using the DNA-Probe technique. *N. gonorrhea* was isolated by culture on modified Thayer-Martin agar plates that were incubated at 35°C in a sealed plastic bag with CO_2-generating tablets. Blood specimens were screened for syphilis using the Venereal Disease Laboratory Test (VDRL) confirmed by Microhemoagglutination test for *T. pallidum* (MHA-TP). Also, blood specimens were tested for the presence of HIV. HIV testing included the Enzyme-Linked Immunosorbent Assay (ELISA) and Western-Blot to confirm the results. Test results represented current STI status. The outcome or dependent variable is a combination of all STI tests. Participants were classified according to their STI status. Those participants having a positive test result were assigned to one category. Those testing negative to all STI tests were assigned to another category.

The *Center for Epidemiological Studies Depression Scale*, the CES-D, was used to assess the current level of depression of each participant [11]. This scale, used previously with Puerto Ricans [12] corresponds to depressive symptoms experienced by the participant during a period of a week previous to its administration. We developed cut points for the scale to indicate those experiencing high levels of depression relative to those experiencing lower levels of depression.

Participants were also asked to indicate their drug use behaviors and identify which drugs including alcohol were used. Drug use was analyzed according to two categories. Those participants who reported using no drugs or consuming only alcohol belonged to one category. The category labeled *other drugs* corresponded to use of illegal drugs, such as marijuana, cocaine, crack, heroin, combination of these, or other illegal drugs. Respondents within this category might have or might not have used alcohol in combination with other drugs.

One final set of questions asked participants about their sexual practices. Included in these questions were items on condom use with paying and non-paying partners.

STATISTICAL ANALYSIS

The Statistical Analysis System (SAS) was used to perform the analyses for this study [19]. Table 1 presents the number of sex-workers found to have a given STI and the point prevalence of syphilis, chlamydia, gonorrhea, HIV, and having any sexually transmitted infection. To explore correlates of having an STI, where syphilis, chlamydia, gonorrhea, and HIV were combined, we calculated the distribution of the selected factors among those who did ($N = 15$) and did not have an STI ($N = 630$; unadjusted prevalence odds ratios were calculated for the association between correlates and having an STI (Table 2). Individual correlates for STI that showed statistical significance in the univariate analysis were included in a multiple logistic regression analysis (Table 3). The logistic regression analysis

Table 1. Frequency and Percent Distribution of Positive STI
Test Results among Street-Based Female Adolescent
Puerto Rican Sex Workers ($N = 78$)

Current sexually transmitted infection	n	Percent
Syphilis	5	7.7
Gonorrhea	0	—
Chlamydia	10	12.8
HIV	2	2.6
Any STI	15*	19.2

*Value represents the number of participants reporting one or more STIs.

was conducted to determine which variables were significantly associated with currently having an STI after adjusting for correlates. Included in the full model are all the factors that were either statistically significant ($p = .05$) or borderline significant ($p = .10$) in the simple models. Since the sample was restricted to inner-city, low income, female adolescent sex workers, differences in socio-economic status, age, and gender could not confound these associations and these demographic factors were not included in models.

RESULTS

Sociodemographic Characteristics

The majority of participants (87.2 percent) were born in Puerto Rico. Fifty-two percent were single (52.6 percent), 19.2 percent lived with a partner, and 19.2 percent were separated. Sixteen years was the mean age of participants, and approximately half had one or more children (48.7 percent). The mean number of years in school was 8.3 with a standard deviation of 1.8 years. Sixty-three percent of the participants were high school drop-outs. Approximately 60 percent of the participants reported living with their parents; while 23 percent were living with someone else without paying rent; 16.7 percent rented or owned their own home; and one lived on the streets.

STI Status

Approximately 8 percent of the participants had a positive test result for syphilis (Table 1). Cases were confirmed with the microhemoagglutination test (MHA-TP) so that only active cases were considered for the analysis. None of the participants were found to have gonorrhea but 12.8 percent of the participants had positive results for chlamydia. Two participants had a positive test result for HIV anti-bodies (2.6 percent). Of the 78 participants in the study, 15 (19.2 percent) tested positive for currently having syphilis, chlamydia, HIV, or any combination thereof.

Correlates of STI

Current depression was associated with having a current STI. Among those who currently had an STI, 86.7 percent were current depressed compared with 58.7 percent of those without an STI. The prevalence odds ratio for the asso-ciation was 4.6 and the association was statistically significant ($p < .05$). Almost half the participants who had an STI (53 percent) had seen a physician during the last year and those wh had been hospitalized during childbirth were sig-nificantly less likely to have a positive test result for an STI ($p \leq 0.5$). Those participants who currently had an STI were 4.5 times more likely to have used illegal drugs than those without an STI. Participants with an STI were more likely to have more clients and not to use condoms as compared to the referent

Table 2. Demographic, Behavioral, and Health Correlates of
Currently Having a Sexually Transmitted Infection among
Street-Based Puerto Rican Female Adolescent Sex Workers ($N = 78$):
Frequency and Crude Odds Ratios

| | STI | | No STI | | OR |
Variable	n	%	n	%	95% C.I.
Marital status					
Unmarried	13	86.7	49	77.8	0.5
Married	2	13.3	14	22.2	0.1–2.7
Number of children					
One or more	6	40.0	32	60.8	0.7
None	9	60.0	31	49.2	0.2–2.0
Educational status					
Drop-out	11	73.3	38	60.3	1.8
Studying	4	26.7	25	39.7	0.5–6.3
Level of depressive symptoms[a]					
High	13	86.7	37	58.7	4.6*
Low	2	13.3	26	41.3	1.0–20.2
Medical service used					
Seen a doctor[b]					
Yes	8	53.3	38	60.3	0.8
No	7	46.7	25	39.7	0.2–2.4
Been hospitalized[b]					
Live birth	—		15	23.8	0.1*
					0.0–1.0
Other reason	1	6.7	6	9.5	0.7
					0.1–6.1
Not hospitalized	14	93.3	42	66.7	
Illegal drug use[c]					
Yes	11	73.4	24	38.1	4.5*
No	4	26.6	39	61.9	1.4–14.8
Sexual practices					
Among non-paying partners					
Non-paying sexual partner					
(last six months)					
Yes	8	53.3	46	73.0	0.4
No	7	46.7	17	27.0	0.1–1.6

Table 2. (Cont'd.)

Variable	STI		No STI		OR
	n	%	n	%	95% C.I.
Condom use with non-paying sexual partner					
Not always	6	40.0	35	55.6	0.5
Always	9	60.0	28	44.4	0.2–1.7
Among paying clients Number of clients (per day)/condom use					
2+ and not always	3	20.0	18	28.6	2.0 0.3–3.4
2+ and always	6	40.0	19	30.2	3.8 0.4–32.6
1 and not always	5	33.3	14	22.2	4.3 0.–38.2
1 and always	1	6.7	12	19.0	1.00 REF

[a]Level of depressive symptoms during a week before being surveyed. [b]Time frame corresponds to a year prior to the survey. [c]Indicates illegal drug use, such as marijuana, cocaine, crack, and heroin.
*Indicates statistical significance at $\alpha \leq 0.05$.

Table 3. Logistic Regression Analysis of Correlates of Currently
Having a Sexually Transmitted Infection among Street-Based Female
Adolescent Puerto Rican Sex Workers ($N = 78$)

Variable	Adjusted odds ratio (95% C.I.) for currently having an STI		p-Value
Depressive symptoms	3.37	0.66–17.22	0.14
Hospitalizations	0.21	0.02–1.78	0.15
Drug use	3.11	0.84–11.57	0.09

group of those with one client a day who reported always using condoms. The odds-ratio suggests an increase in risk of currently having an STI with high risk behaviors with clients (O.R. range from 2.0-4.3). However, these associations were not statistically significant.

Further analyses were conducted to examine the associations between the independent variables: depression, hospitalization and drug use. Results show that participants who report current levels of drug use are 2.3 times more likely to be depressed ($p = 0.09$), and to have given birth in a hospital ($p \leq 0.01$). Further analysis of hospitalization shows participants who had been hospitalized were five times more likely to be drop-outs (95 percent C.I.: 1.01-23.44) and eight times more likely to have a non-paying sexual partner (95 percent C.I.: 1.29-50.09). Depression was not statistically associated with hospitalization for live birth.

After adjusting for the correlates, no factor was statistically significantly associated with having a prevalent STI in the logistic regression model at $\alpha = 0.05$. Illegal drug use was, however, associated with currently having an STI (OR = 3.11) with a p value of 0.09.

DISCUSSION

This study examined STI prevalence among street-based female adolescent sex workers in Puerto Rico. Approximately 19 percent of the participants tested positive for currently having one or more STI. These findings suggest the need for aggressive treatment of STI in this population and the need for innovative prevention strategies to be implemented. Correlates of STI were examined in the current study to explore possible intervention strategies and understand the risk behaviors of adolescent sex workers more fully. The results indicated that illegal drug use was found to be of borderline statistical significance in multivariate logistic regression model with an STI included as the dependent variable. Drug use, hospitalization for live birth, and depression were found to be significantly related to this population.

Drug use was found to be the strongest correlate of having an STI among female adolescent sex workers in this study. Although drugs such as alcohol, marijuana, or cocaine do not expose one to organisms that cause STI, their use often decreases one's ability or willingness to use preventive measures. These findings imply the need to address STI and substance abuse jointly in the delivery of interventions to treat and prevent these health problems among adolescent sex workers. However, if treatment is hard to access, has unreasonable expectations for admission, provides inappropriate modalities for the treatment of adolescents, and does not allow women to have their children with them, the rates of adolescents receiving effective treatment will remain low. Therefore, in order to effectively address STI and substance abuse jointly, creative and appealing strategies for adolescent sex workers need to be developed, implemented, and evaluated.

Some researchers have attempted to establish the sequence of events that lead to drug use among sex workers [7]. Since this is a cross-sectional study, it is not possible to determine whether adolescents were using drugs to deal with feelings of depression or if they were depressed because of drug use. This study only focused on the co-occurrence of current depression symptoms (experience during last week) and current drug use (over last six months) and found that these health issues do co-occur. Overall, the results show that although these adolescent sex workers tend to have multiple health issues affecting them, they tend not to seek preventative health services and show no clear pattern of seeking treatment services. Health care seeking is a central issue in control of STI and females delay health care seeking longer than men do [20]. There are multiple factors that contribute to their delay of health care seeking. Barriers to accessing the system as well as the stigma associated with STI are some of the factors mentioned by these adolescents. Locating health services in high-risk neighborhoods has been suggested as a strategy to overcome these barriers [1]. Additionally, the provision of child care removes a barrier especially for women. The results of this study point to the importance of prevention and treatment services concurrently addressing a broad spectrum of health issues for a given population. Research by Torres and Weeks [21] suggests the need to address human sexuality within the cultural context of communities since this is part of the reality of adolescents' daily experiences.

The recruitment of participants was basically dependent on the availability of subjects. Given the illegal nature of prostitution, the age of the subjects, and their fear of participating in research projects, this kind of sampling technique was the most appropriate for recruitment. Though not a probabilistic sample, this study provides representation of adolescent sex workers throughout the Island.

IMPLICATIONS FOR COMMUNITY INTERVENTIONS

Controlling STI among adolescents is an enormous challenge given they are typically in a stage of experimentation and risk taking. Therefore, youth service programming needs to be comprehensive and pro-active in nature and the style and content of these interventions should be particularly adapted for adolescents [22]. Some key results from this study indicate options for changing traditional preventative health services. This study found that 20 percent of the participants had an STI, 45 percent were using illegal drugs, and 64 percent had a high level of depressive symptoms, all indicators of a poor health level. Additionally, it found that many of these adolescents cannot be reached through school settings because they do not attend school and many did not regularly access health services. Therefore, intensive, comprehensive non-traditional services taken into the community for this population of adolescents may be a better alternative for youth programming. Also, outreach strategies must include youth-friendly health workers; people with whom adolescents can relate and feel comfortable discussing their risks and concerns during counseling sessions improve the chances of these efforts being effective. Finally, the development of strong communication skills that enable adolescents to act on decisions they make about their sexual behavior is recommended [2]. While prevention will play an important role, treatment services will remain essential for addressing STI in the adolescent sex worker population. Complimentary services, such as walk-in counseling, may need to be delivered to this population with a reasonable waiting time. Overall, it is clear that health issues present in the adolescent sex worker population need to be addressed holistically including their cultural context [15, 23].

SUMMARY

This research provides insight into the need for comprehensive prevention and treatment services for high risk youth. Adolescents who perform sex work should be considered a priority for preventive interventions as they have a variety of synergistically related health issues such as drug use, depression and sexually transmitted infections. Health workers are challenged to provide services to help adolescents go through this stage with the least harm possible. Aggressive outreach services, streamlining clinical services and ensuring the services are youth friendly and comprehensive are some implications of this research. Overall, health professionals who work with adolescents must be aware of the behavioral, cultural, and environmental risk factors affecting youth, particularly those not reached by traditional services. Furthermore, our data supports previous studies that point out the need for qualitative research on cultural context and its relationship with sexual health protective behaviors [15, 23].

ACKNOWLEDGMENT

This research was supported by Grant No. G12-RR-03051 to the Center for Evaluation and Sociomedical Research from the National Institutes of Health through the Research Center for Minority Institutions.

REFERENCES

1. W. L. Yarber and A. V. Parrillo, Adolescents and Sexually Transmitted Diseases, *Journal of School Health, 62*:7, pp. 331-338, 1992.
2. D. L. Richter, R. F. Valois, R. E. McKeown, and M. L. Vincent, Correlates of Condom Use and Number of Sexual Partners among High School Adolescents, *Journal of School Health, 63*:2, pp. 91-96, 1993.
3. S. A. Baker, D. M. Morrison, M. R. Gillmore, and M. D. Schock, Sexual Behaviors, Substance Use, and Condom Use in a Sexually Transmitted Disease Clinic, *The Journal of Sex Research, 32*:1, pp. 37-44, 1995.
4. L. Szalay, G. Canino, and S. Vilov, Vulnerabilities and Cultural Change: Drug Use among Puerto Rican Adolescents in the United States, *The International Journal of the Addictions, 28*:4, pp. 327-354, 1993.

5. U.S. Preventive Services Task Force, Counseling to Prevent Human Immuno-deficiency Virus Infection and Other Sexually Transmitted Diseases, in *Guide to Clinical Preventive Services* (2nd Edition), U.S. Department of Health and Human Services, Office of Disease Prevention and Health Promotion, Washington, DC, 1996.

6. A. Coker, D. Richter, R. Valois, R. McKeown, C. Garrison, and M. Vincent, Correlates and Consequences of Early Initiation of Sexual Intercourse, *Journal of School Health, 64*:9, pp. 372-377, 1994.

7. M. Alegría, M. Vera, D. Freeman, R. Robles, M. Santos, and C. Rivera, HIV Infection, Risk Behaviors, and Depressive Symptoms among Puerto Rican Sex Workers, *American Journal of Public Health, 84:*12, pp. 2000-2002, 1994.

8. H. Amaro, L. Fried, H. Cabral, and B. Zuckerman, Violence During Pregnancy and Substance Abuse, *American Journal of Public Health, 80*:5, pp. 575-579, 1990.

9. Centers for Disease Control, report by Division of Reproductive Health and Division of Adolescent and School Health, National Center for Chronic Disease Prevention and Health Promotion. Sexual Behavior Among High School Students—United States 1990, *MMWR, 40*, pp. 885-888, 1992.

10. P. B. Smith, M. Weinman, and D. M. Mumford, Knowledge, Beliefs, and Behavioral Risk Factors for Human Immunodeficiency Virus Infection in Inner City Adolescent Females, *Sexually Transmitted Diseases, 19*:1, pp. 19-24, 1992.

11. J. S. Brock, Personality, Family and Ecological Influences on Adolescent Drug Use: A Developmental Analysis, *Journal of Chemical Dependency Treatment, 22*, pp. 123-162, 1988.

12. J. S. Brock, D. W. Brook, A. J. Gordow, M. Whiteman, and P. Cohen, The Psychological Etiology of Adolescent Drug Use: A Family Interactional Approach, *Genetic Psychology Monolog, 90*:116, p. 2.

13. I. A. Canino, B. F. Earley, and R. M. Rogler, *The Puerto Rican Child in New York City: Stress and Mental Health*, Monograph 4. Hispanic Research Center, Fordham University, New York, 1980.

14. K. Cushner, Culturally Specific Approaches to Knowing, Thinking, Perceiving and Understanding, in *Advance Methodological Issues in Culturally Competent Evaluation for Substance Abuse Prevention*, CSAP Cultural Competence Series, Vol. 6, 1996.

15. M. Burgos, D. Richter, B. Reininger et al., Street Based Female Adolescent Sex Workers: Contextual Issues and Health Needs, *Family and Community Health, 22*:2, pp. 59-71, 1999.

16. L. I. Pearlin, The Sociological Study of Stress, *Journal of Health and Social Behavior, 30*(3), pp. 241-256, 1989.

17. L. Radloff, The CES-D Scale: A Self-Report Depression Scale for Research in the General Population, *Applied Psychological Measurement, 1:*3, pp. 385-401, 1978.

18. M. Vera, M. Alegría, and D. Freeman, Depressive Symptoms among Puerto Ricans: Island Poor Compared with Residents of the New York City Area, *American Journal of Epidemiology, 134*, pp. 502-510, 1991.

19. SAS Institute, Inc., *SAS User's Guide: Basics* (Version 5 Edition), SAS Institute, Inc., Cary, North Carolina, 1985.

20. J. Fortenberry, Health Care Seeking Behaviors Related to Sexually Transmitted Diseases among Adolescents, *American Journal of Public Health, 87*:3, pp. 417-420, 1997.
21. M. I. Torres and M. Weeks, Sexual Health Protection, Culture and Community: Contributions of Anthropology to Community Health Education Approaches: An Introduction, *International Quarterly of Community Health Education, 18*:1, pp. 3-7, 1999-2000.
22. Centers for Disease Control and Prevention, *STD Surveillance Report,* Atlanta, Georgia, 1993.
23. M. I. Torres, R. Tuthill, R. S. Lyon-Callo, and P. Epkind, Focused Female Condom Education and Trial: Comparison of Young African American and Puerto Rican Women's Assessments, *International Quarterly of Community Health Education, 18*:1, pp. 49-68, 1999-2000.

CHAPTER 8

Sociocultural Factors Affecting Reproductive Health in Latin America and the Caribbean

Marilyn Rice

This chapter begins by providing an overview of the socio-economic, health, and fertility conditions in the countries of the Americas, then discusses barriers for women and men to using contraception. Finally, it proposes some alternative actions to improve options for contraceptive choices in the populations of Latin America and the Caribbean.

SOCIO-ECONOMIC, HEALTH AND FERTILITY CONDITIONS AND TRENDS IN THE AMERICAS

Socio-Economic Factors

There are some major differences among the countries of the Americas in respect to socio-economic factors. The gross national product (GNP) per capita of twenty-one countries of the region ranges from US$300 in Haiti to US$6,000 in Trinidad and Tobago. Of these twenty-one countries, eight have a GNP of less than US$1,000 and nine have a GNP of less that US$2,000. In contrast, the United States has a GNP of almost US$7,000.

In these same countries, five have a negative annual growth rate and five others have annual growth rates of less than 1 percent [1]. Within the Americas the official annual inflation rate ranges from 5.9 percent in Chile to rates as high as 696.7 percent in Brazil and even higher. In the United States the figure is 5.3 percent [2].

Fertility Rates

The fertility rates in the region range from 1.97 percent in Cuba to 5.50 percent in Honduras. In the United States the fertility rate is 1.71 percent. These figures represent the years 1980 to 1985. The rates have been declining and it is estimated that by the year 2000 these declines will be sustained in all of the countries.

According to the latest United Nations Report of Population Projections, Latin America was the second most rapidly growing area of the world [3]. In 1987, the population growth was estimated at 2.3 percent, which means that the population should double within 30 years.

The Population Crisis Committee has developed an "International Human Suffering Index" which rates living conditions in 130 countries around the world [4]. Each country index is compiled by adding the following measures: 1) income, 2) inflation, 3) demand for new jobs, 4) urban population pressures, 5) infant mortality, 6) nutrition, 7) clean water, 8) energy use, 9) adult literacy and 10) personal freedom. Every country with extreme levels of human suffering has serious population problems. There is a direct relationship between the annual rate of population growth and the country's Human Suffering Index rating. Findings are consistent with other studies indicating that rapid population increases restrict economic and social progress.

Increasing Urbanization

This is the most important demographic factor in Latin America in the current decade, and it is expected that the percentage of urbanization will grow between now and the year 2000. By that year it is expected that 76 percent of the Latin American population and 72 percent of the regional population will be living in urban areas. This has clear health consequences and social implications, such as:

- individual and family conflict and breakdown,
- increased crime,
- increased population sizes with decreased amounts of available land,
- more and more people living without services and infrastructure, especially in the areas of health and education,
- increased demand for jobs, especially among young people (4 to 5 million young people will enter the labor market annually), and
- increased numbers of abandoned children living in the streets.

Life Expectancy at Birth

In 1985, the life expectancy at birth ranged from age fifty-three in Bolivia to seventy-four in Costa Rica and 76.3 in the United States. By the year 1990 the overall life expectancy for Latin America and the Caribbean should be sixty-four years of age [11].

Infant and Child Mortality

The child mortality rate per 1,000 live births ranged in 1980 from 81.2 in Guatemala to 11.1 in Martinique, and in the United States it was 12.6. In 1985 it ranged from 73.7 in Uruguay to 9.2 in Jamaica, and in the United States it was 10.6 [1].

A child's chances of being born healthy, surviving the first few years of life and growing well are reduced if children in a family are born very close together in time, if there are already more than three children in the family and if the mother is younger than twenty years old or older than thirty-five when the child is born.

During the first five years of the 1980s the child mortality rate in Latin America and the Caribbean decreased in many countries. However, the crisis continues, especially for the very poor. Of eight countries throughout the world shown to have increases in child mortality, five are in Latin America, and of twenty-eight countries with reported malnutrition, ten are in the region. There is a direct correlation between child mortality and socio-economic conditions.

When a woman has pregnancies close together, the likelihood increases that the pregnancy will end in miscarriage or that the infant born alive will die. Large family size and short birth spacing intervals interact with poor nutrition to create a group of children at very high risk of illness and death. The decline in intelligence scores as the family size increases has been vividly documented.

Maternal Mortality

Complications from pregnancy and childbirth are still a major cause of death among women in developing countries. Women's chances of having complications and therefore of death are increased when they already have greater than three children and when they are younger than twenty, or older than thirty-five years of age. Although this situation holds true for all social strata, it is the case predominantly in the lower educational and socio-economic levels.

Abortions and their complications cause approximately 30 percent of maternal deaths. Risk of women dying from causes associated with maternity is estimated at:

1 in 73 for South America
1 in 140 for the Caribbean
1 in 6,366 for the United States and Canada and
1 in 10,000 for Northern Europe [5].

For a few affluent women in urban centers, having an illegal abortion may be relatively safe, because they can personally pay for high quality medical attention. However, for the majority of women in developing countries, having an illegal abortion means pain, fear and a substantial risk of infections, hemorrhage and death. In the El Salvador Maternity Hospital, one fourth of the obstetric deaths were due to illegal abortions. In Bolivia, 60 percent of the cost of running the obstetric and gynecological service is devoted to treating women who come to the hospital with complications from illegal abortions.

In a survey of ninety-five developing countries of the world (97 percent of the developing world), the correlation between reduced family size and family planning program efforts is visible in government-sponsored services, especially those providing birth control *options*. In countries without government efforts, reduction in fertility is explained by:

- the existence of strong private programs
- high levels of internal strife and dislocation; and
- high per capita income, which enables people to obtain contraceptives from private sources [6].

FACTORS AFFECTING THE POPULATION IN LATIN AMERICA AND THE CARIBBEAN RELATED TO FERTILITY PRACTICES

Ethical and Moral Considerations

1. Is family planning a contradiction of nature and of God?
In many countries the Catholic Church promotes this perception and tries to instill in its members the belief that sexual intercourse should be strictly for the purpose of procreation. Therefore, the only acceptable way of controlling the number of pregnancies and births is through abstinence or the rhythm method. For many families this is not a practical or acceptable approach, thus many women live with the moral dilemma of either refusing their mates or living with repeated pregnancies.

2. Should not the outcome of sexual intercourse be left to God's will?
This belief opposes abortion and pits its followers, who believe that the right of the fetus is paramount, against those who believe that the woman has a right to control her own body and what happens to it. The former group tends not to be concerned with the child's welfare after birth, whereas the latter group tends to focus on the individual and social consequences of bringing children into the world who are not wanted or for whom the parents cannot adequately provide.

3. Are not the multinational corporations and national and foreign governments trying to reduce birth rates?
The followers of this belief feel that instead of improving socio-economic development in the developing countries, the above-mentioned groups are using family planning as "genocide" in disguise. In order to reduce or eliminate certain ethnic, religious, national or economic groups, more resources are made available for family planning than for other types of health and development programs.

4. Are fertility regulation devices really being made available to everyone, or is there some discrimination at play?

In the Caribbean, where there are government-sponsored family planning clinics, adolescent women who come to get contraceptive information and devices instead receive moral lectures about "promiscuity" [7]. There is a great concern over the equity and openness with which contraceptives are dispersed.

5. Are there choices in the types of contraceptive methods offered?

In many cases the contraceptive devices are provided by the government or by multinational corporations or agencies, and the devices are unilaterally distributed irrespective of the characteristics of the individual woman and what would be best for her.

6. Are the available contraceptive methods safe?

Although there may be many problems associated with the particular devices provided to third world women (many of which are outlawed in the United States), the argument is that the use of these methods is less threatening to the woman's health then is pregnancy or childbirth.

7. Are women given all the available information about the contraceptive methods available on the market?

Most women in developing countries are not given any choices, nor are they informed about the side effects or contraindications of the contraceptive devices they are given [5].

Barriers to Women and Men Using Contraception

1. There is no easy access to information and supplies.

The question of access is very complex, and there are innumerable factors that affect the availability and accessibility of contraceptive information and supplies. Although there are many women who want no more children, they still do not know how to prevent pregnancy, and the information is not readily available to them. Even when they are aware of the existence of family planning clinics, very often the time and expense involved in traveling to and from the clinic make it very difficult for them to make the journey. Additionally, for most women who have to carry the threefold responsibility of child care, maintenance of the household, and in addition work for pay outside the home, the hours that family planning services are available make it nearly impossible for them to utilize the services.

2. Throughout Latin America and some parts of the Caribbean, women have much lower status than men.

The incidence of maternal deaths has been linked directly to three key factors: unregulated fertility, poor quality of health services and low educational levels. In one study of fertility practices in Puerto Rico a direct relationship was demonstrated to exist between women's education level and the types of contraception they used (8). This same study indicated an inverse relationship between the number of deliveries a woman experienced and the frequency of her contraceptive use. It seems clear from this study that a woman's understanding of her contraceptive choices is directly related to her accessibility to them.

Women in general have much fewer educational opportunities than men. As a result, they have fewer opportunities for earning money, they have less of an understanding of their options in life and in employment, and as a result they are highly economically and physically dependent on men. This dependency makes them highly subject to submission to the will of their male partners in many respects, including that of contraceptive utilization and fertility regulation. Additionally, many women marry at a very young age in order to leave their biological families. In order to ensure that the man, who is their main or only source of economic survival, does not leave them, they will subject themselves to repeated pregnancies.

One result of women taking on the major responsibility for their families is that they are the last to eat in the household. The consequences of this situation for women include increased malnutrition, more frequent and more serious illnesses and higher risks during pregnancy. Additionally, since women have to shoulder the burden for so many family tasks, such as carrying and storing water, washing clothes and dishes, cooking and cleaning, child care and obtaining fuel, there is very little time left to utilize health services even if they were easily accessible.

Women's inferior status is also reflected in the fact that men make the major decisions that affect the community, the family and even the woman herself. A good example of this is seen in many water and sanitation projects, where men are consulted about the types of wells and pumps that should be installed, but it is the women who fetch and carry the water. An unfortunate consequence of this situation is that all too often the type of technology that is selected and installed might be very appropriate for men, but it is very difficult for women to use. Since manliness in many cultures is associated with the number of children a man sires; the man in his position of authority decides to have many children, whether or not the woman is really interested in having and caring for more children. Along these same lines, since men assume that all other men have the same "macho" approach to relationships with women, they are very concerned that if women use contraception they will then be in a situation that easily enables them to be unfaithful. In spite of these conditions, in very few cases are men ever educated about family planning and contraception.

3. The interface women have with the health services sends many of them away.

In an evaluation conducted by the Pan American Health Organization of the efficiency and distribution of health services in Latin America (1985-87), more than 75 percent of all types of health facilities were rated as unsatisfactory. When combined with those in critical situations almost 85 percent were rated as unacceptable [1].

Women indicated that they were treated by health personnel with a lack of respect, as if they were objects and not human beings. This brusque treatment inhibited them from continuing to utilize health services.

There was a noticeable lack of information given to women about their health conditions, what medication they were being given and what were the possible side effects, what caused their conditions and how they could prevent this situation in the future. Often, women were given the same prescription on different occasions, in different packages, without any explanation of why there was a difference. The basic attitude of health personnel appeared to be that the women were incapable of handling the information, therefore it was better not to bother to tell them anything.

Women were able to spend very little time with the medical staff. After waiting many hours to be seen, the medical staff pushed the patients through quickly in order to more rapidly attend to the many other people waiting and to leave as quickly as possible to attend to personal matters or personal medical practices. This situation was certainly not conductive to asking questions or stating that the information given was not clear.

In many situations the medical staff was basically unprepared when it came to family planning practices. Although the physician and nursing staff might have knowledge about the diseases most frequently seen in a given area, they tended to not have any specific training or information about the different contraceptives available, their contraindications and side effects, or the information that women needed to know.

Poor women tended to be treated as "low class" and inferior by the health personnel. Most people working in health centers seemed to have a "superior" attitude and they looked down on the poorer women [9].

Often, when young women came to health centers for family planning advice or services they were given moral lectures instead of being treated with the respect and understanding they deserved. The case cited earlier of a Caribbean family planning clinic is a good example of this [7]. This type of treatment did not engender confidence or a wish to return to the health center for future services.

Many people working in health centers see the information they possess as their source of power and influence. They fear that if they give away valuable information they are giving away all of their power. This attitude stems from the old "patron" system of governing plantations, as well as from the attitude of the Colonizers who came from Europe to subjugate the peasants for their own benefit. Additionally, all these cultures had a pedagogical tradition of "learning" by repeating what was heard or read. Through one-way and top-down communication, without any consideration or interest given to understanding and application in reality. Thus, the information that gets passed on to the population is in turn given in the form of lecture, without opportunity to question or clarify; or written material is distributed that illiterate populations do not understand; or information is passed on through the use of sophisticated language that the common person cannot understand.

Additionally, the medical education in all these countries has taught physicians that they are superior, that they possess the ultimate information about health, life and death, and that this is what empowers them to make the decisions they must make related to medical treatment. If they facilitated people taking responsibility and care of themselves, in terms of health promotion and illness prevention, many physicians fear that they just might be out of a job.

The medical orientation to health is based upon what is convenient for the medical staff. Some examples of this are:

Deliveries of babies are done with the woman in a horizontal position (easier for the medical staff) rather than the vertical position (which is natural and enables the woman to utilize gravity to facilitate the birth).

Physicians arrive at public health clinics late and leave early in order to adequately attend to their private patients, irrespective of how long people have been waiting in the public clinics.

Services are provided at times, days and locations that are convenient for the physicians, but not necessarily for the population they are supposed to serve.

Inadequate space is provided to wait in the public health clinics, so women often end up waiting hours standing up, sometimes in the hot sun, with their children constrained with no where to play.

In spite of the distance she may have travelled and the time a woman waits to be attended, if she does not get to see the physician before a certain hour of the day, she may be turned away and told to come another time.

All too often the hours of the public health clinic are established at the convenience of the medical staff and not when it is most feasible for the patients themselves to come.

The cultural values and beliefs of many women are frequently not known, understood or respected by the medical staff (this is particularly true of indigenous populations and their view of their own bodies and the causes of diseases and illnesses) [9].

Health professionals often do not have the correct information about the issues, concerns and health problems of the population; information is collected based upon the people that walk in the door of the health center, and the focus is on illness or physical status, without considering the role of other contributing factors such as housing, water, type of employment, if any, nutrition and eating behaviors, and environmental conditions.

All of these factors serve to alienate the women who may start out very much desiring and being open to the services and information they hope to receive in public health clinics. The final result of this type of treatment is disbelief in what they are told, rejection of the medications and treatments they are prescribed and ultimately refusal to return to the clinics.

4. Although a major proportion of pregnancies occur in the adolescent population, no special provisions are made to provide education or services to this population.

Adolescent pregnancy has reached crisis proportions in all the countries of the Americas. A study by the National Statistics Institute in Chile disclosed that 31.3 percent of children born in 1983 were born to young, single mothers. One study of pregnant girls in Chile between the ages of thirteen and seventeen indicated that 70 percent had sexual relations before the age of fifteen [10]. Additionally, adolescent pregnancy appeared to be a second-generation phenomenon. This same study revealed that 52 percent of the girls came from one-parent families and 76 percent had mothers who had become pregnant before marriage. In the English-speaking Caribbean, many adolescent girls see pregnancy as a way to "capture" a man, and marriage does not even have to come into the picture.

Part of the severity of the problem is due to the lack of awareness and understanding of the physical, psychological and social issues and needs of adolescents. Additionally, many parents, health personnel, and members of the society at large are afraid that if adolescents are given information about sexuality and contraception, then this will motivate sexually promiscuous behavior. As a result, adolescents are intentionally or inadvertently denied the information and services they so desperately need. The World Health Organization attributes the high rate of adolescent pregnancies to a lack of information about human sexuality, contraception and family planning methods [10]. Unfortunately, all too often, adolescents are simply not given any choices.

WHAT CAN BE DONE?

It must be recognized that there have been many improvements in the health sector's delivery of services. Most countries of the Americas have established, within their Ministries of Health, infrastructures which provide free medical services to the entire population, such as Maternal and Child Health Units, with programs of illness prevention and health promotion. There is an increased use of the "risk approach" to planning and delivering health services, whereby the population at greatest risk of incurring specific health problems is identified and sought out for preventive and promotive services.

Countries have expanded their efforts to cooperate and share experts, training opportunities, materials, technologies, and experiences in innovative ways of delivering the essential health services. An example of this is the use of the simplified perinatal clinical history to monitor perinatal health. Almost all the Latin American countries are using a similar approach to identify and provide follow-up to high risk women and families during the perinatal period. Child growth monitoring programs in most countries currently cover 65 percent of the population five years of age and under.

Greater emphasis can still be placed upon certain approaches that will improve the factors affecting reproductive health of the population in Latin America and the Caribbean.

Collaboration can be improved between governmental and nongovernmental organizations, in such a way that they coordinate and not co-opt each other. It will be necessary to find out what other agencies are doing in relation to health issues, and cooperate with them in supporting development at the community level.

Risks can be reduced by working with many different sectors, as well as with families, adolescents, and men as well as women.

Adolescent health services can be more uniformly incorporated into available medical services, including extra services such as counselling and prevention techniques. This will require the training of health personnel in the special physical, psychological and social characteristics of adolescents.

Intersectoral and intrasectoral actions must be developed with parents, teachers, and others from the community to help adolescents develop healthy life-styles and avoid risk-associated behavior that leads to drug abuse, accidents, sexually transmitted diseases and unwanted pregnancies.

Schools can include prevention activities related to family life education that will reach children at an early age, before their sexually-related attitudes and behaviors are completely formed.

New approaches should be used appropriately. Techniques such as informed consent, whereby the patient must attest to the fact that he or she has completely understood the information or procedure being discussed, have gone a long way to ensuring the patient's participation in the appropriate delivery of services. Again, the training of health personnel will be necessary to help incorporate new approaches.

Systems can be developed to identify and educate high risk women and their families, so that problems can be prevented, or at least ameliorated.

Activities should be increased with grass roots organizations that are already reaching men and women in the community, to disseminate information to the population and to feed information back to the health system about local conditions, needs and impacts of health activities.

Educational opportunities must be expanded for women. As women become more educated, their opportunities for social mobility increase, which in turn gives them greater access to and integration into the social structure. As this occurs, women will have additional options for deciding about fertility and child rearing practices.

Educational opportunities must also be provided to men related to contraceptive options, as well as to the need for them to cooperate with and respect women as equal partners in society.

National policies and efforts should be expanded in appropriate ways that will decrease maternal mortality, decrease unwanted adolescent pregnancies, and increase the mobilization and participation of women and men in their own decisions and social development.

Analysis of the local health and population factors must be kept current, so that the services can adequately respond. Essential elements to include in this assessment are poverty and high risk situations.

Effective means of interpersonal communication should be identified and utilized, to ensure that messages are generally understood. Within communities there are always indigenous ways that people communicate with each other. Some creativity will be necessary to reach the "hard to reach" populations; but these are the people most in need of the services.

CONCLUSION

As outlined above, fertility rates in Latin America both affect and are affected by a complex set of economic and social factors including income, infant mortality, literacy, levels of nutrition and traditional sex roles. Many of these factors which interact to affect reproductive health are difficult to change. Economic factors are primarily influenced at the macro level. Many infrastructure elements can be modified only with the infusion of great amounts of capital. Deeply ingrained social structures and sex roles are also difficult to influence in significant ways, and to do so takes more time and patience than most political leaders and health workers are willing to invest.

However, there are effective interventions for improving reproductive health which include increasing both men and women's access to contraceptive supplies, information, and education; reorienting health services to make them more "user friendly"; and designing targeted actions to respond to the special need of adolescents and other high risk populations. These initiatives need to be carried out with support and participation from as many sectors of the community as possible, and they should be designed to be relevant to specific local conditions. There is still great potential for improving reproductive health conditions in the Americas, and each year more countries are developing efforts that bring us closer to this goal.

ACKNOWLEDGMENT

This project was supported by USAID cooperative agreement # DPE-3052-A-00-0014 Johns Hopkins University, Population Communication Services.

REFERENCES

1. Report of the Director to the 101st Meeting of the Executive Committee of the Directing Council of the Pan American Health Organization, Annex 1, Maternal and Child Health and Family Planning Programs, Washington, DC, 21 pp., 18, May 1988.
2. The World Bank, *Trends in Developing Economies 1989*, Washington, D.C., September 1989.
3. United Nations, *World Population Prospects: Estimates and Projections as Assessed in 1984*, New York, 1986.
4. Population Crisis Committee, *Human Suffering Index*, Washington, DC, 1 p., 1987.
5. Population Information Program, *Population Reports*, Series L, No. 7. Population Information Program, Johns Hopkins University, Baltimore, 31 pp., September 1988.
6. J. Gay, *A Literature of the Client-Provider Interface in Maternal and Child Health and Family Planning Clinics in Latin America*, Pan American Health Organization, Washington, D.C. 79 pp., October 1980.
7. M. F. Fathalla, The Ethics of Family Planning, *World Health*, 3 pp., June 1984.
8. D. Maine, *Family Planning: Its Impact on the Health of Women and Children*, The Center for Population and Family Health, Columbia University, New York, 56 pp., 1981.
9. R. R. Robles, E. Martinez, M. Vera, and M. Alegria, Factores Socioculturales Asociados con el Uso de Contraceptivos en Puerto Rico, *Boletin de la Oficina Sanitaria Panamericana*, *104*:1, 12 pp. 1988.
10. Adolescent Mothers in Chile, *Women's Health Journal*, 6-7, p. 1 , March-June 1988.

SECTION TWO

Promoting Sexual and Reproductive Health Through Popular Culture

Four chapters comprise this section focused on popular culture and mass media methodologies for health promotion and education in Latin America and U.S. Latino communities. The first two chapters (9 and 10) capture the significance of popular cultural expressions embodied in the arts and literature for community health education. Chapter 9 provides an historical overview of the use of arts and literature in promoting health as part of a broader agenda for social change. Specific examples of art and literature interventions with health education goals in Latin America and other developing countries as well as U.S., Latino, and African American communities are presented. The use of the arts to assess community needs in a New Orleans Latino community is described. Chapter 10 presents a description of an evaluation of a street theater intervention in Peru. Popular theater dramas in the streets were found to be a useful education strategy to reduce misinformation about contraception and contraceptive methods.

The remaining two chapters in this section address some of the concerns raised in Chapter 10 about the limitations of mass media to induce behavioral change in Latino audiences. Chapter 11 adds *interactivity* to what is typically a passive intervention by linking a simultaneous telephone helpline with Spanish-speaking staff. The audience is encouraged to call with follow-up questions and requests for more specific information about the health topic being discussed by the broadcasters in Spanish in two metropolitan areas with large concentration of Latin American immigrants. Chapter 12 provides the readers with an overview of the role of broadcasters and other journalists in Latin America as social advocates. It goes on to examine the way in which Spanish language TV News in California frames social and health issues in contrast to the local English language news. Findings show differences in level of depth of socio-cultural context framing violence and other public health problems that are relevant to the advocacy and public policy goals of health promotion and education in U.S. Latino communities. Together, these four chapters makes a case for the use of the Spanish language and interactive popular culture (e.g., street theater) and media-related communication strategies (i.e., radio and telephone) to review mass media framing of issues of concern to health educators to disseminate health information and promote healthier behaviors.

CHAPTER 9

Using the Arts and Literature in Health Education

Marian McDonald
Giovanni Antunez
Megan Gottemoeller

This chapter is designed to begin a discussion of the usefulness of the arts and literature for health education theory and practice. Specifically, this chapter examines the potential and use of visual arts, music, textile arts, performing arts, and literature in health education practice today.

In doing so, the authors hope to promote the use of the arts and literature as health education strategies. By acknowledging both the effectiveness and appropriateness of creative forms of expression in health education, we hope to deepen the profession's understanding of such forms and heighten the legitimacy with which they are viewed.

The chapter will also comment on the particular relevance of the arts and literature for health education in urban settings, extracting insights about why they have become a central element of urban cultures and indispensable for health education. The chapter concludes with a discussion of experiences in a children's art program developed to begin community health organizing in a predominantly Latino community in metropolitan New Orleans.

The Arts as a Vehicle for Social Change

Throughout history, the arts and literature have played a role in the process of social change. That role has often been seen as incidental or secondary, with little intrinsic social value. Poet and educator Audre Lorde challenged this view in her essay on the importance of poetry in people's lives, especially the lives of women [1, p. 37]:

> For women . . . poetry is not a luxury. It is a vital necessity of our existence. It forms the quality of the light with which we predicate our hopes and dreams toward survival and change, first made into language, then into idea, then into more tangible action.

Lorde sees poetry and other forms of creativity and expression as necessary precursors to action. She shares this view with many artists, educators, and advocates throughout history and across the globe. These figures include African-American jazz singer Billy Holiday, whose rendition of a song about Southern lynchings shocked audiences; Chilean songwriter Victor Jara, whose courage stood and sang against the murder of the 1973 *coup d'etat;* and Maya Ying Lin, the Chinese-American architect whose design of the Vietnam War Memorial helped to create the conditions for national healing.

Legacy of the Arts in Social Movements in the United States

Within the United States, the arts and literature have played an important role in social movements in this century. Woody Guthrie's melodic tributes to the working people ("This Land is Your Land") and his biting criticisms of injustice ("Deportees") won him audiences in the strife-torn thirties and a permanent place in U.S. culture [2]. Legendary African-American singer Paul Robeson resisted bigotry and repression with his masterful voice in the fifties, helping set the stage for the civil rights movement.

The forceful refrain of the civil rights song "We Shall Overcome" became an anthem of the fight against segregation and for civil rights, and later was embraced by the peace and women's movements. "We Shall Overcome" was sung at rallies and in churches, on marches and in vigils. The power and longevity of "We Shall Overcome" comes from its collective affirmation of determination, hope, and courage.

A Global View: Nicaragua

In countries where democratic forces have challenged domination and foreign interference, the battle for control over cultural expression has long been a key arena. In Nicaragua, the effort to defeat the rule and legacy of dictator Anastasio Somoza created new and popular forms of expression, from a grass-roots literacy campaign to a new song movement and the flourishing of murals and poetry workshops [3-12]. With the change of government in 1990 and a determined "rollback" of *Sandinista* influence, one of the first tactics of

Managua's conservative mayor Arnoldo Aleman was to paint over some of the city's most impressive pro-*Sandinista* murals.

The Use of the Arts in Educational and Clinical Settings

Besides playing a role in work explicitly oriented to social change, the arts and literature have been acknowledged as essential to different forms of education. Increasingly, arts and literature are used as a vehicle for learning non-arts-specific fields in public schools [13].

The positive potential of the arts and literature in medical education has been well articulated [14, 15]. The arts and literature in medical education can affect both practitioner efficacy and the physician's ability to withstand the pressures of care-giving [14].

The restorative powers of the arts have long been acknowledged. Using arts in the healing process is a practice many clinicians have found very effective. Hospital programs that encourage patients to paint have been found to speed healing and improve patients' quality of life [15-17]. The healing aspect of art is among its fundamental features.

The arts and literature have been a catalyst for change and growth in wide-ranging circumstances, providing a rich legacy for health education to draw upon. It is against this backdrop that the use of arts and literature in health education can be understood.

USING THE ARTS AND LITERATURE IN HEALTH EDUCATION

The field of health education is constantly changing, seeking new and more effective ways to address the increasingly complex challenges of promoting health [18]. To meet these challenges, health education must be open to new approaches and new strategies for intervention. A careful consideration of the potential of the arts and literature for advancing health education is needed. To undertake this discussion it is helpful to examine the theoretical bases for using the arts and literature in health education.

Theoretical Bases for Using the Arts and Literature in Health Education

Health education, to be effective, needs to begin with a people's reality. Central to that reality is the culture which embodies the people's history and aspirations [19]. As Amilcar Cabral, an African leader who fought for the independence of Guinea-Bissau, noted [20, p. 210]:

> Culture is the dynamic synthesis, at the level of individual or community consciousness, of the material and spiritual historical reality of a society or a human group, of the relations existing between [people] and nature as well as among social classes or sectors. Cultural manifestations are the various forms in which this synthesis is expressed, individually, or collectively, at each stage in the evolution of the society or group.

More recently, the international women's movement has demonstrated, through a wide array of forms of art and literature, the indispensable role of culture in the development of consciousness and identity [21-26]. Specifically, the concept of the development of *the voice* has been advanced as a key element of the process of transforming women's lives [21, 27-29].

The creation of a voice to break the silence is a central idea in the work of the late Paulo Freire, whose writings have transformed the world's views of education and popular culture [30-34]. Freire's philosophy and practice stem from the view that change in human communities involves an interactive process between individuals and society, in which awareness begins in a person's own thinking and develops from that person's reflected-upon experience in a collective context.

Freire's views have proven an invaluable guide for health education practice today. His concept of empowerment rooted in critical consciousness and developed through practice has been applied in health education programs throughout the world [35-42].

The empowering potential of the arts and literature in the Freirian context is clear. The arts and literature give people a voice, and through this voice their dreams can be articulated. Most recently, Wang and Burris have added to this theoretical framework with the concept of *photovoice*, in which people can "identify, represent, and enhance their community through a specific photographic technique" [43, p. 369]. Developed in Yunnan, China with rural women, photovoice was designed to be a means of empowering women, promoting dialogue, and reaching policymakers [40]. Photovoice links photography with community assessment and empowerment, making it a leading example of both the theory and practice of using the arts and literature to advance health education.

Other theoretical frameworks and approaches to health education can draw on the use of arts and literature as well. The health belief model, for example, posits that the individual's perceptions of a health issue is key to whether and how that person will act [44]. One of the ways that the arts and literature affect society is in their ability to open eyes anew, to change perceptions.

Similarly, social learning theory links an individual's likelihood of change to the person's belief in her/his ability to change [45]. The arts and literature affect "self-efficacy" in two ways. First of all, a positive identity of self and community expressed and reinforced through culture can give communities and individuals strength. For example, the "Black is beautiful" slogan from the sixties reflected and reinforced pride and emerging power in the African-American community.

Secondly, the individual and personal process of creation can be empowering and exhilarating, opening up new vistas of self-confidence [28-29, 40].

Another way that arts and literature promote health is in the development and expansion of social support [46]. While art and literature are often solitary activities in the creation stage, the act of *sharing* art and literature is profoundly social and collective. By creating common reference points through culture, communities begin to break down isolation, share their common experience, and build collective vision.

The Arts and Literature in Health Education Practice

Dorothy Nyswander's watchword "start where the people are" is as appropriate applied to arts and literature in health education as it is in health education work generally [47, p. 270]. It suggests that health educators need to familiarize themselves with a people's cultural expressions as a part of working with the community. As Freire asks, "How is it possible for us to work in a community without feeling the *spirit* of the culture that has been there for many years, without trying to understand the soul of the culture?" [38, p. 131].

In the community, the arts and literature can work in the service of health education in the following ways, often simultaneously:

1. To Get People Involved

The use of art forms or activities involves people who might otherwise be disinterested or intimidated by more explicitly health-oriented activities. Simply put, the arts and literature can make health education fun. For example, rap contests have been conducted by the San Francisco Bay Area AIDS movement to involve youth in building AIDS awareness. The New Orleans Children's Advocacy Program (NOCAP) sponsored a poster contest for school-aged youth focused on violence prevention, adding children's poignant voices to the city's fight against crime [48].

2. To Find Out About a Community

The arts and literature can be a valuable strategy for conducting community needs assessments and mapping community assets [49]. Poetry workshops and arts workshops, offered to the community at low or no-cost, can provide valuable insights into the community, its leaders, and its history, as in the Louisiana experience discussed below.

3. To Change Awareness and Relay Health Education Messages

The arts and literature are powerful messengers. Because they reach into people's feelings, they have the potential to shape consciousness. Positive messages can be developed and promoted in popular culture. An example is a song gaining air time in Spanish-speaking communities throughout the Americas. *Ponte El Sombrero* (*Put on Your Hat*) encourages condom use in a playful, non-threatening way.

This form of bringing the message has been called *edu-tainment*, or *enter-education*, where education and entertainment are combined [50]. In this approach, the message is relayed through an already-established medium of popular culture, such as a television show, film, or song. Examples are the coming-out episode of television's *Ellen*, films like *Philadelphia*, and songs like Fiona Apple's *Sullen Girl*.

While potentially very effective, this approach to relaying a message can be challenging for health educators for a number of reasons. First of all, health educators do not always have access to screenwriters, songwriters, and producers. As a result, the content of the message may not always be what we would like, and the solutions posed not exactly what we would propose. Second, it can be very difficult to evaluate the effectiveness of these efforts [50]. Third, it can be argued that these vehicles are external to community, and encourage a passive, consumer approach.

When the message is relayed by one who *becomes* the singer, the actor, or the artist and is transformed through that process, change can take place both in the messenger and the audience [34]. An example of this is Teatro Campesino, the popular theater that arose alongside the United Farm Workers during the long strike in the grape fields in the seventies. When farmworkers took on the role of the boss in skits, it was initially difficult for them. Once they had assumed that role of power and strength on the makeshift stage, however, it carried over to their work to win the strike [51].

The transformative nature of participation in the creative process can be invaluable for community health education. Health educators need to determine both the message and the messenger in the context of the goals they are trying to attain, realizing that different choices will be made in situations with different objectives and resources.

4. To Attract Attention to a Health Issue

A cultural manifestation of an issue will often catch people's attention, changing their perceptions, as in the AIDS Quilt discussed below. Another example is the Clothesline Project, begun by women in Massachusetts in 1992 to promote awareness of violence against women. The Clothesline Project urges victims and survivors of violence against women to create a tee-shirt that expresses their feelings about their experiences. A white tee-shirt is in memory of a murdered woman, a blue tee-shirt is for survivors of childhood sexual abuse, and so on. When a series of these tee-shirts are made, they are displayed in a public place on a clothesline, a graphic and moving statement about the realities and impact of violence against women [52, 53].

5. To Promote Community-Building

The community building framework has brought dynamic new ideas into community health education and has helped to revitalize health education practice [49, 54]. By emphasizing health education as a process of establishing and strengthening relationships, the community building framework allows for unfettered forms of community expression to which the arts and literature are particularly well suited. Cultural forms of expression rooted in the community help not only to give voice to concerns, but to establish the collective life, whether it is through celebration, ritual, or grief.

6. To Promote Healing

Arts and literature are perhaps most effective as a source of healing. The creative process is both restorative and transformative, healing the one who undertakes it [16]. At the same time, the fruits of the creative process offers insights to others with similar experiences, and helps to promote *their* healing. Thus, an interactive healing process is made possible by the arts and literature. Among the most outstanding examples of this is the Vietnam War Memorial in Washington, D.C. The simple, stark wall where the names of the dead are etched has become a mecca for millions who need to reflect on, cry about, or exorcise the war. It has served to promote the healing, understanding, and forgiveness so elusive to the country in the years following the war [21].

Hand-Made Health Education: The NAMES Project AIDS Memorial Quilt

The most eminent example of using the arts and literature in health promotion is the Names Project AIDS Memorial Quilt, which has been successful in achieving all six of the above-mentioned purposes. The Names Project AIDS Memorial Quilt is the largest on-going community arts project in the world [55]. Its October 1996 display in Washington, D.C., constituted both the largest AIDS event and the largest community art event in history.

The AIDS Quilt began in 1987, when gay activist and Names Project founder Cleve Jones organized a community meeting in San Francisco to come up with a way to commemorate those who had died in the AIDS epidemic. He began by making a quilt for a friend. The quilt project grew quickly and on October 11, 1987 the first display of the Quilt was part of the national march for lesbian and gay rights. The quilt covered a space larger than a football field. Today the Quilt is made up of over 50,000 panels, and covers an area over the size of over twenty-nine football fields or fifteen city blocks. The ritual of reading the names of the dead was added to the 1988 Quilt display in Washington, D.C. At the October 1996 display, the names of the 70,000 dead represented in the panels—more than on the Vietnam War memorial—were read.

Each of the quilt panels, made to remember the life of a person lost to AIDS, is the size of a human grave. Quilts are made of a wide array of materials, from photographs, love letters, and condoms to stuffed animals and wedding rings. As the AIDS epidemic grows, so does the Quilt; over fifty new memorial panels are added each week [55].

The Names Project conducts a number of display programs with the Quilt. These include community-based, academic, high school, interfaith, and corporate programs, as well as World AIDS Day and international displays. By October 1996, the AIDS Quilt had been visited by over seven million people and had raised over $1,700,000 for AIDS organizations [55]. It includes the participation of some forty countries, including Australia, Hong Kong, Poland, Zambia, Thailand, Russia, France, Guatemala, and Puerto Rico. The AIDS Quilt has helped to broaden international awareness and action about the AIDS epidemic. Nominated for a Nobel Peace Prize in 1989, the Quilt is perhaps the world's most effective AIDS educator to date.

A GROWING BODY OF
HEALTH EDUCATION PRACTICE

While the AIDS Quilt is the premiere example of using a cultural form for health education, it is among a growing body of experience using the arts and literature in health promotion around the world.

Some of these efforts have been systematically evaluated. In a program of AIDS prevention in Ghana, dramas with AIDS themes were written and performed as a means of educating people about the disease [56]. Focus groups were conducted to evaluate the impact of plays and songs about AIDS in changing people's attitudes and behavior. Besides clearing up misconceptions about the disease, the plays affected focus group participants by making them more aware and causing them to change some of their behaviors. As one participant put it, "I've changed because I'm young and wouldn't like to shorten my life by chasing many women. I used to have three girlfriends but now I stick to my wife only" [56, p. 306]. When asked about the effectiveness of the play as a means of educating about AIDS, a participant commented, "When I watch [the play] it looks so real to me that I think they are talking to me" [56, p. 308]. The researcher concluded that ". . . the importance of drama and songs as vehicles for AIDS education cannot be understated. . . . Drama and songs have been found to have a strong potential for changing sexual behavior in both urban and rural Ghana" [56, p. 317].

Plays were also used in an AIDS prevention program in Sri Lanka [57]. Short plays with AIDS themes were performed by volunteers on the West Coast of the island nation. The plays' impact on knowledge, attitudes, and behaviors was evaluated by means of a pretest and posttest given to those who attended the play. While there were numerous difficulties encountered in conducting the study, including very limited participation by women, the study found that the plays increased knowledge and promoted attitudinal changes, such as an increased perception of susceptibility to HIV infection [57].

Health education interventions like these which have been evaluated are the exception, however, as more and more health educators seek to broaden their tools for change. The growing use of the arts and literature was reflected in the program of the XVI World Conference on Health Promotion and Health Education held in San Juan, Puerto Rico in June 1998 [58]. In what is among the first efforts to include cultural vehicles for health education in a major international health promotion conference, the XVI World Conference offered a full, distinct festival of health education programs using the arts [59]. Entitled the "Art and Health Festival," the program offered ten different sessions with presenters from Puerto Rico, Chile, Australia, and New Caledonia [59]. In addition, parallel special, oral, video, and poster presentations included a session entitled "The Arts in Health Promotion and Health Education" [59, p. 48] and sessions which examined the use of marionettes, puppets, and plays [59, p. 66] in health education. Conference planners correctly read the pulse of innovative health education efforts worldwide and sparked valuable reflection on this growing area of health education practice through their successful inclusion of diverse offerings demonstrating the effectiveness of arts and literature in health promotion.

ARTS AND LITERATURE IN URBAN
HEALTH EDUCATION

The arts and literature play a particularly important role in urban health education, because of the very nature of cities. The physical environment of cities provides unique public places that serve as sites where people can express themselves—sidewalks, buildings, subways, and parks. Additionally, the population density of cities brings people into contact with one another constantly, creating endless opportunities for common experiences and communication. For many people living in the city, popular culture is their only possible exposure to noncommercial art forms.

Weaving Unity in Diversity

A number of forms of art and literature have been used in cities to give voice to communities. These include community murals, guerilla theatre, poetry slams, dance brigades, and even graffiti [34, 60]. The forms used are as diverse as communities themselves.

A reality of most major urban areas today is diversity of culture, language, and ethnicity. The arts and literature can give voice to the diversity of urban populations, breaking down barriers in the process. Ethnic, racial, and linguistic diversity exist in urban areas alongside diversity of age, gender, economic status, and sexual orientation. When developing community health programs in urban areas, health educators need to address diversity directly, rather than ignore or downplay it [61]. The arts and literature can be effectively used to express and respect diversity, in a process that can weave unity among the community's different threads.

The Arts in Urban Health Education: An Example from Urban Louisiana

The belief that the arts and literature can play a role in health education became the basis for the Summer Arts Discovery Program in Kenner, Louisiana, in 1996. The program was the first stage of a community health education plan developed by the Latino Health Outreach Project (LHOP), a collaboration of students and faculty at Tulane's School of Public Health and Tropical Medicine in New Orleans.

At the invitation of local Latino community educators, LHOP members began their work at a housing development in the summer, donating their labor and art supplies. The predominantly Latino (87 percent) Redwoods subsidized housing development, home to some 500 families, is located in Kenner, a city in the greater New Orleans metropolitan area. A local community organizer assisted with initial contacts and provided LHOP with rent-free space in the after-school tutoring center he had started in the housing complex.

The objectives of the Summer Arts Discovery Program were threefold: to gain entry into the community, to begin community assessment, and to offer something of value to the community. Through door-to-door outreach visits to the 500 housing units, distribution of bilingual fliers announcing the free workshops and preregistration of children, LHOP members established recognition and familiarity in the community.

The second objective involved community assessment and asset mapping. This included gathering as much information as possible about the organization, family life, community dynamics, and health education concerns of the Redwoods community. In implementing the Summer Arts Discovery Program, the LHOP team hoped to learn from the outreach process, from the children's artwork and interactions, and from the contact with the parents. Art activities were designed around the themes of community, family, and school to elicit the children's perceptions of their community.

The response to the arts workshops was positive. An average of twenty-five children participated in each session, with about eighteen to twenty return participants. The group was able to establish a rapport with the children as well as the mothers who dropped the children off and picked them up. Interaction with mothers led to input for topics, such as cancer prevention and nutrition, for future health education activities in the community. This resulted in a series of *charlas* (talks) conducted in the following months.

The process of carrying out the Summer Arts Discovery Program allowed the LHOP team to make a number of useful observations. These concerned language preferences (the children preferred to use English in the workshop setting), family unity, gender roles, and recurrent themes. These insights helped in the planning of future activities and gave LHOP a realistic understanding of important community dynamics. As the initial stage of a community health education project now in its third year, the Summer Arts Discovery Program accomplished the objectives of introducing LHOP to the community and providing valuable data and insights for future health education efforts. Several women in the community became involved in community health education activities as a direct result of the summer art workshops. The use of art and the interaction with children greatly enhanced the group's ties to the community.

CONCLUSION

Health education and promotion can be defined and described in many ways. Most agree that health education is a process of change in which new attitudes, understandings, or practices come about. The authors hope to open a discussion about why and how the arts and literature can assist in that change process. Given the many challenges that confront health education in the coming decades, new ways to awaken and empower ourselves and our communities are needed [18, 50]. The arts and literature can be among our most effective tools.

REFERENCES

1. A. Lorde, *Sister Outsider,* The Crossing Press, Freedom, California, 1984.
2. W. Guthrie, *California to the New York Islands,* The Guthrie Children's Trust Fund, New York, 1958.
3. D. Kunzle, *The Murals of Revolutionary Nicaragua,* University of California Press, Berkeley, 1995.
4. G. Black, *Triumph of the People: The Sandinista Revolution in Nicaragua,* Zed Press, London, 1981.
5. T. Borge, *Los Primeros Pasos,* Siglo Veintiuno, Mexico, 1981.
6. E. Cardenal, Defendiendo la cultura, el hombre, y el planeta, *Nicarauac, 3,* pp. 149-152, 1982.
7. E. Cardenal, *Tocar el cielo,* Editorial Nueva Nicaragua, Managua, 1982.
8. L. Ferlinghetti, *Seven Days in Nicaragua Libre,* City Lights, San Francisco, 1984.
9. C. M. Godoy, *La Misa campesina nicaragüense.* Managua, Colección Popular, Numero 6, Minsterio de Cultura, 1981.
10. S. Meiselas, *Nicaragua,* Pantheon, New York, 1981.
11. M. Randall, *Risking a Somersault in the Air: Conversations with Nicaraguan Writers,* Solidarity, San Francisco, 1984.

12. P. Rosset and J. Vandermeer (eds.), *Nicaragua. Unfinished Revolution,* Grove, New York, 1986.
13. J. Collom and S. Noethe, *Poetry Everywhere. Teaching Poetry Writing in School and in the Community,* Teachers and Writers Collaborative, New York, 1997.
14. K. Calman and R. Downie, Why Arts Courses for Medical Curricula, *Lancet, 347,* pp. 1499-1500, 1996.
15. M. G. Winkler, The Visual Arts in Medical Education, *Second Opinion, 19,* pp. 60-70, 1993.
16. R. Longman, Creating Art: Your RX for Health, *American Artist, 58,* pp. 68-73, 1994.
17. M. Smith, Community Outreach Art Program for Hospitalized Children, *School Arts, 94,* pp. 21-22, 1995.
18. N. M. Clark and K. McElroy, Creating Capacity Through Health Education: What We Know and What We Don't, *Health Education Quarterly, 22,* pp. 273-289, 1995.
19. O. Ordones and H. Vanolli (eds.), *Violence and Health: Memoirs of the Inter-American Conference on Society, Violence and Health,* Pan American Health Organization, Washington, D.C., 1995.
20. A. Cabral, The Role of Culture in the Liberation Struggle, in *Communication and Class Struggle,* A. Matterlart and S. Siegelaub (eds.), International General, New York, pp. 205-212, 1979.
21. M. Randall, *Walking to the Edge. Essays of Resistance,* South End Press, Boston, 1991.
22. J. Cheney, M. Deihl, and D. Silverstein, *All Our Lives: A Women's Songbook,* Diana Press, Baltimore, 1976.
23. A. Rich, *What is Found There. Notebooks on Poetry and Politics,* W. W. Norton, New York, 1993.
24. J. Chicago, *The Birth Project,* Doubleday and Company, New York, 1985.
25. B. Hooks, *Outlaw Culture. Resisting Representations,* Routledge, New York, 1994.
26. K. Whitehead, *The Feminist Poetry Movement,* University Press of Mississippi, Jackson, 1996.
27. T. Olsen, *Silences,* Delta, New York, 1978.
28. N. Mairs, *Voice Lessons,* Beacon, Boston, 1994.
29. M. Rukeyser, *The Life of Poetry,* Paris Press, Ashfield, Massachusetts, 1996.
30. P. Freire, *Pedagogy of the Oppressed,* Continuum, New York, 1990.
31. P. Freire, *Education for Critical Consciousness,* Continuum, New York, 1990.
32. P. Freire, Cultural Action and Conscientization, *Harvard Educational Review, 40:*3, August 1970.
33. A. Boal, *Categories de Teatro Popular,* Ediciones Cepe, Buenos Aires, Argentina, 1972.
34. A. Boal, *Theater of the Oppressed,* Urizen Books, New York, 1979.
35. M. Minkler and K. Cox, Creating Critical Consciousness in Health. Applications of Freire's Philosophy and Methods to a Health Care Setting, *International Journal of Health Services, 10,* pp. 311-321, 1980.
36. N. Wallerstein and E. Bernstein, Empowerment Education: Freire's Ideas Adapted to Health Education, *Health Education Quarterly, 15,* pp. 379-394, 1988.

37. M. Weinger and N. Wallerstein, Education for Action: An Innovative Approach to Training Hospital Employees, in *Essentials of Modern Hospital Safety,* W. Charney and J. Schirmer (eds.), Lewis Publishers, 1990.

38. M. Horton and P. Freire, *We Make the Road by Walking. Conversations on Education and Social Change,* Temple University Press, Philadelphia, 1990.

39. D. Werner and B. Bower, *Helping Health Workers Learn,* Hesperian Foundation, Palo Alto, 1982.

40. C. Wang and M. A. Burris, Empowerment through Photo Novella: Portraits of Participation, *Health Education Quarterly, 21,* pp. 171-186, 1994.

41. S. Laver, B. Van den Borne, and G. Kok, Using Theory to Design an Intervention for HIV/AIDS Prevention for Farm Workers in Rural Zimbabwe, in *Progress in Preventing AIDS? Dogma, Dissent, and Innovation, Global Perspectives,* D. Buchanan and G. Cernada (eds.), Baywood Publishing, Amityville, New York, 1998.

42. S. Laver, B. Van den Borne, G. Kok, and G. Woelk, Was the Intervention Implemented as Intended?: A Process Evaluation of an AIDS Prevention Intervention in Rural Zimbabwe, *International Quarterly of Community Health Education, 16,* pp. 25-46, 1996-1997.

43. C. Wang and M. A. Burris, Photovoice: Concept, Methodology, and Use for Participatory Needs Assessment, *Health Education & Behavior, 24,* pp. 369-387, 1997.

44. I. Rosenstock, The Health Belief Model: Explaining Health Behavior Through Expectancies, in *Health Behavior and Health Education,* K. Glanz, F. M. Lewis, and B. K. Rimer (eds.), Jossey-Bass, San Francisco, 1990.

45. C. Perry, T. Baranowski, and G. Parcel, How Individuals, Environments, and Health Behavior Intersect: Social Learning Theory, in *Health Behavior and Health Education,* K. Glanz, F. M. Lewis, and B. K. Rimer (eds.), Jossey-Bass, San Francisco, pp. 161-186, 1990.

46. B. Israel and S. Schurman, Social Support, Control, and the Stress Process, in *Health Behavior and Health Education,* K. Glanz, F. M. Lewis, and B. K. Rimer (eds.), Jossey-Bass, San Francisco, pp. 187-215, 1990.

47. M. Minkler, Improving Health Through Community Organization, in *Health Behavior and Health Education,* K. Glanz, F. M. Lewis, and B. K. Rimer (eds.), Jossey-Bass, San Francisco, pp. 257-287, 1990.

48. Children Put Peace to Paper in Contest, *Times Picayune,* Section B, page 1, May 16, 1996.

49. J. Kretzman and J. McKnight, *Building Communities from the Inside Out. A Path Toward Finding and Mobilizing A Community's Assets,* ACTA, Chicago, 1993.

50. A. Steckler, J. Allegrante, D. Altman, R. Brown, J. Burdine, R. Goodman, and C. Jorgenson, Health Education Intervention Strategies: Recommendations for Future Research, *Health Education Quarterly, 22,* pp. 307-328, 1995.

51. National Latino Communications Center, *The Struggle in the Fields. Episode 2: Chicano! History of the Mexican American Civil Rights Movement,* LCC Educational Media, Los Angeles, video, 1996.

52. The Clothesline Project: Bearing Witness to Violence Against Women, Clothesline Project Brochure, East Dennis, Massachusetts.

53. The Many Faces of Feminism, *Ms*, p. 5, July/August 1994.
54. C. Walter, Community Building Practice: A Conceptual Framework, in *Community Organization and Community Building for Health*, M. Minkler (ed.), Rutgers University Press, New Brunswick, New Jersey, 1997.
55. NAMES Project Foundation: The AIDS Memorial Quilt, The Names Project Foundation, San Francisco, 1996.
56. K. Bosompra, The Potential of Drama and Songs as Channels for AIDS Education in Africa: A Report on Focus Group Findings from Ghana, in *Progress in Preventing AIDS? Dogma, Dissent, and Innovation. Global Perspectives*, D. Buchanan and G. Cernada (eds.), Baywood Publishing, Amityville, New York, 1998.
57. D. McGill and W. D. Joseph, An HIV/AIDS Awareness Prevention Project in Sri Lanka: Evaluation of Drama and Flyer Distribution Interventions, *International Quarterly of Community Health Education, 16*, pp. 237-255, 1996-97.
58. Comité Organizador de la XVI Conferencia Mundial de Promoción de la Salud y Educación para la Salud: *New Horizons in Health: From Vision to Practice. Book of Abstracts*, Graduate School of Public Health, Medical Sciences Campus, University of Puerto Rico, San Juan, 1998.
59. Comité Organizador de la XVI Conferencia Mundial de Promoción de la Salud y Educación para la Salud: *New Horizons in Health: From Vision to Practice. Conference Program*, Graduate School of Public Health, Medical Sciences Campus, University of Puerto Rico, San Juan, 1998.
60. A. W. Barnett, *Community Murals: The People's Art*, The Art Alliance Press, Cornwall, 1984.
61. C. O. Airhihenbuwa, Health Promotion and the Discourse on Culture: Implications for Empowerment, *Health Education Quarterly, 21*, pp. 345-353, 1994.

CHAPTER 10

Street Theater as a Tool to Reduce Family Planning Misinformation

Thomas W. Valente
Patricia R. Poppe
Maria Elena Alva
Rosario Vera De Briceño
Danielle Cases

Mass media campaigns can be effective at communicating health information to a mass audience rather inexpensively by reaching large numbers of people simultaneously. Critics of mass media campaigns, however, often contend that interpersonal communication is more effective at changing behavior. They acknowledge that mass media may be effective at reaching many people at low per capita cost and at making people aware of health information, but these critics argue that mass media campaigns do not bring about behavior change. Only person-to-person, face-to-face communication, it is argued, is effective in changing behavior [1].

Many have argued that the mass media are effective at bringing about changes in awareness and knowledge but that subsequent interpersonal communication too is necessary for changing behavior [2-6]. The different functions of mass and interpersonal communication date from early voting studies [7, 8] and brought about the two-step flow model [9-11]. More recent studies have compared the effectiveness of each of these channels in bringing about health behavior change [12, 13]. It is now felt that the media can have powerful effects on behavior only under certain historical and/or cultural circumstances [1].

Face-to-face or interpersonal communication may be effective at changing behavior because the persuasion process is immediate, providing opportunity for feedback. The persuader and subject can exchange information and doubts about a health practice, which can thus be clarified immediately. As practiced in many programs, however, interpersonal communication also has limitations. Interpersonal communication can be: 1) expensive, 2) private, and 3) may provide nonstandardized information. First, it is expensive to train personnel to visit households and provide high-quality information. Outreach activities must often recruit master trainers and train them before they, in turn can conduct training workshops among volunteers or low-paid workers.

Second, interviews are conducted in private rooms or residences which facilitate discussion of intimate topics. The private nature of these discussions, however, does not help create public awareness of existing social norms, attitudes, and beliefs. Also, these interviews might not occur in natural settings, that is, the interviewer would not normally be at the respondent's door, or the patient is not usually at a hospital or clinic. Third, since personnel may be trained by trainers, the information they impart to clients may vary. While these disadvantages do not make outreach activities worthless, they do decrease their effectiveness.

STREET THEATER

Given the advantages and limitations inherent in both mass media and interpersonal channels for promoting behavior change, it seems helpful to develop "meso-level" (intermediate between micro- and macro-level) programs and theories that draw on the advantages of both. Dramatic public performances, in the form of street theater, represent one meso-level form of communication that is both mass and interpersonal.[1] Street theater is a form of mass communication, in that it consists of communication from a single source to an audience of many people and at the same time a form of interpersonal communication in that it enables immediate feedback and dialogue between source and receiver(s).

The advantages of the street theater format are its: 1) low cost, 2) pubic nature, and 3) entertainment value. Street theater is relatively inexpensive because each performance attracts a crowd. Thus, five street theater actors can easily reach crowds of 50 to 500 people at a time rather than just reaching people one-on-one.

Second, the street performance is a public event and thus reinforces public support for a message. By contrast, in a face-to-face interview, the private nature of the interaction allows a respondent to say to him or herself, "Well I might support this behavior (family planning in this example), but my neighbors or community leaders might be opposed, and so I had better not go against the grain and risk alienation."

---

[1] Street theater is broadly defined as any performance conducted in public places to inform or entertain, most often with the solicitation of payment [14]. Other meso-level forms of communication might include public speaking in town squares, electronic mail broadcasts to groups or organizations, or conference presentations.

The public nature of street theater sends a different signal: "I might support this behavior, and, since this behavior is being presented in public, it must be socially acceptable." Furthermore, if the performance is good and the audience laughs and claps it adds to the social support necessary to reinforce adoption decisions.[2] Also, some members of the audience will be less hesitant to ask sensitive questions in public and will raise issues that others would be afraid or too inhibited to ask even in a private setting.

Third, street theater is entertaining. The entertainment value insures that the audience becomes involved and pays attention to the message. Door-to-door recruitment, in contrast, may be intrusive and interrupt people, causing them to resist messages or recruitment. When entertained, in natural settings (e.g., markets or plazas), an audience is more inclined to attend to the message.

Entertainment strategies such as music videos and television and radio soap operas have been used extensively in Latin America [17] and elsewhere [18-21]. Many of these programs have been linked to attitude and behavioral changes among target audiences (e.g., [21]). But these effects may be limited by the "mediated" nature of entertainment. That is, most entertainment strategies are broadcast in some form, whereas live drama is direct and therefore may make a greater impression on the audience.

Street theater is thus a cost-effective, public, entertaining and engaging strategy that may be an effective way to communicate health information. The format of street theater provides the opportunity to impart considerable information about family planning and deal substantially with barriers to family planning. A further benefit of street theater performances is that they are mobile and so can be repeated in different locales (e.g., urban and rural locations, or among language subgroups). Also, it can be videotaped (live or in a studio) and broadcast. Finally, street theater is current and interactive and so can respond to feedback and be adapted to changing circumstances.

Street theater is a traditional medium that has existed since humans banded into communities. Community performances communicate stories and lessons from generation to generation and create a sense of community. Street theater has a venerable history in Latin America [22, 23], particularly in Perú [24].

Public stages, both established and makeshift, dot the capital city of Lima, and on Sunday afternoons many street performers can be seen plying his or her trade. The street theater format provides a novel means to put family planning on the public agenda. It was hypothesized that street theater would be effective at improving family knowledge and attitudes.

---

[2] Public displays of support such as clapping, laughing, and interacting with the drama help to deflate pluralistic ignorance [15, 16] by reassuring audience members that many people publicly support or approve of a position that might be thought controversial.

In South Africa a street theater puppet performance was used to inform audiences about HIV/AIDS behavioral risks [25]. The evaluation found that the performance increased knowledge and intention to adopt safer behaviors. The long-term impact of that intervention was questioned, however, since it was a "stand alone" event. In the Peruvian street theater project, we integrated the street theater with other activities to reinforce the impact of the messages. The other activities included posters, flyers, and radio and television spots. Mass media activities also included getting family planning on the media agenda through appearances on talk shows.

"MS. RUMORS"

"Ms. Rumors" was created, designed, rehearsed, and pre-tested over a four-month period. Each performance lasted about twenty minutes and was followed by a group question-and-answer counseling session. The "Ms. Rumors" cast portrayed four characters: Ms. Rumors, Don Victor, a pharmacist, and a young couple in love. The couple was sexually active and faced the question of contraceptive use. Ms. Rumors tried to sabotage the couple's attempt to gain credible correct information by whispering misinformation about family planning methods to the couple and tried to convince them that using contraceptives was bad.

The misinformation statements consisted of knowledge and attitude statements found in previous research to be barriers to adoption of family planning methods in Perú. Examples of misinformation statements are: the pill produces cancer, the pill affects the fetus, or the IUD produces abortions. The purpose of the drama was to show how Ms. Rumors promotes misconceptions, or negative attitudes, and then to show how Don Victor, the local pharmacist, dispels these myths, or at least alleviates people's fears with simple explanations.

The play was performed in parks and squares and, like much folk art of this type, was designed to attract audiences made up of passersby. The play was also performed outside hospitals and clinics to entertain people waiting for services. An estimate of the number of people who saw the play was obtained by counselors who were present at most of the dramas for follow-up discussions. From April 1992 to July 1994, the play was performed about 200 times to an estimated total audience of about 61,000 (with an estimated 4,500 face-to-face counseling sessions).

Did the drama change people's knowledge and/or attitudes concerning modern family planning models? If it did change them, how effectively did it change them, and for whom? Finally, what are the implications of this research for future street theater productions and other communication activities?

METHODOLOGY

To answer these questions a study was conducted by interviewing people before and after they saw the drama. Since people decided to watch the play based on whether they passed by and on their desire to learn about family planning, there is some self-selection bias to the survey. Interviewers had to catch the same individuals before and after the drama, and so a limited number of interviews were conducted at each performance.[3]

Approximately four selected members of the audience at each performance were recruited to be interviewed. Interviewers reported almost no refusals, yet the number of completed interviews varied from one to seven per performance. Data were collected at seventeen different performances, yielding a total of 102 respondents of which eighty-five contained complete information. While the drama was performed in public places throughout Lima, interviews were conducted primarily during performances outside health centers.

The experimental design for this research is referred to as a "one-group pretest-posttest design" [26]. This design was chosen because of logistical constraints. Still, this is the appropriate research design for this setting, because the drawbacks to the one-group pretest-posttest design are eliminated in the present study. For example, one-group research designs do not control for 1) history, 2) maturation, 3) statistical regression, or 4) instrumentation [26, pp. 99-102].

The present research does not suffer from these effects due to the short time interval between pre- and post-test surveys. Hence, in the present case, the one-group pretest-posttest design is ideal. Specifically, we asked audience members to state whether they agreed or disagreed with eleven knowledge and attitude statements before and after the drama to determine whether viewing the drama decreased the level of misinformation.

RESULTS

The counselors present at the performances provided information to approximately thirty people per performance. Approximately 80 percent of the questions asked of the counselors concerned topics covered by the play, that is, the most common misinformation items associated with specific modern contraceptives. It seems that the play created an opportunity for people to confront their own fears and misconceptions without the embarrassment of showing ignorance or lack of complete information.

Apart from the counseling sessions, interviews were conducted with the study population described above. Change in misinformation as a result of the play was measured quantitatively with the eleven misinformation statements reported in Table 1. For each statement, the respondent was asked to state the degree of agreement or disagreement on a 5-point Likert scale in which 1 equaled strongly disagree and 5 equaled strongly agree. Table 1 reports the average scores on the

---

[3] Interviewers were recruited from the Psychology Department of the University of Ricardo Palma in Lima and trained in questionnaire administration.

Table 1. Misinformation Item Scores, Changes, and
T-Test Results ($N = 85$)

Misinformation items	Pre-test Ave.	Decrease	t-Value	Sign.
1. The pill produces cancer.	2.18	.41	3.44	.001
2. The pill affects the fetus.	2.72	.78	5.08	.001
3. The pill affects the nerves.	3.59	.71	4.35	.001
4. The pill is easy to use (reversed).	1.89	.21	1.41	NS
5. The pill produces abortions.	2.34	.20	1.61	NS
6. The IUD produces cancer.	2.60	.35	2.66	.01
7. The IUD sticks into the fetus.	2.76	.23	2.04	.05
8. The IUD produces abortions.	2.49	.36	2.84	.01
9. The condom is uncomfortable.	3.10	.42	3.13	.01
10. The condom inhibits sexual pleasure.	2.98	.26	2.28	.05
11. The condom is easy to use (reversed).	1.94	.06	0.47	NS
Total	28.7	4.0	6.51	.001

pre-test and the decrease in item scores between the pre- and post-test measures. For example, the statement one "the pill produces cancer," had a pre-test average of 2.18 that decreased an average of .41, indicating that respondents slightly disagreed with the statement and that disagreement decreased still further .41 points. (The .41 can be divided by 4, the item range, to get an estimate of the percentage change, e.g., .41/4 = 10.2 percent decrease.)

As Table 1 shows, all the item scores decreased between pre- and post-test measures indicating that exposure to the drama reduced misinformation. Knowledge statements such as 1, 2, 3, and 9 ("The pill produces cancer," "The pill affects the fetus," "The pill affects the nerves," and "The condom is uncomfortable") changed the most. Attitudinal statements such as 4, 5, and 11 ("The pill is easy to use," "The pill produces abortions," and "The condom is easy to use") changed very little. Thus, the goal of the drama, to reduce misinformation, seems to have been met according to these data.[4]

Table 2 reports factor analysis of the 11 items to determine if the misinformation items represented one overall construct or whether they clustered into discernable groups. For example, did responses vary according to the method

---

[4] The overall scale average was 2.58. In a survey among lower-middle income Peruvians (in Lima and elsewhere) conducted in March 1995 the overall average for this scale was considerably higher at 3.26. Thus, sampling from health center sites has yielded a sample with a lower initial level of misinformation.

Table 2. Factor Analysis Results for Misinformation
Items (N = 85)

Misinformation item	Factor loading	Factor loading
1. The pill produces cancer.	.58	.58
2. The pill affects the fetus.	.59	.59
3. The pill affects the nerves.	.29	
4. The pill is easy to use.	−.09	
5. The pill produces abortions.	.54	.53
6. The IUD produces cancer.	.51	.48
7. The IUD sticks into the fetus.	.54	.53
8. The IUD produces abortions.	.55	.55
9. The condom is uncomfortable.	.54	.55
10. The condom inhibits sexual pleasure.	.38	.38
11. The condom is easy to use.	.20	
Eigenvalue	2.40	2.24
Cronbach's alpha	.71	.75

that the item asked about—pills, IUDs, and condoms? Or did responses vary according to statements about the effects of methods on the individual? The factor analysis showed that most statements clustered on one dimension, however, three statements did not vary with the others.

Table 2 shows that statements 3, 4, and 11 did not load on the factor and hence do not vary with the other knowledge and attitude statements. Inspection of the statements shows why 3, 4, and 11 are different: Statements 4 and 11 represent positive and statement 3 represents a negative *attitude* about a contraceptive method. These attitude statements do not vary with the more knowledge-based questions in the rest of the scale. It is surprising, however, that statements 9 and 10 cluster with the rest of the scale as these two statements are attitude statements as well.

Statements 3, 4, and 11 were dropped, and an overall misinformation scale was created using the eight remaining statements. The misinformation scale had a high reliability, Cronbach's alpha equals .75. The misinformation scale then consisted of 8 Likert-type items with an average score of 21.1 in the pretest and a range of 8 to 34. A *t*-test was then conducted to compare the average scores between pre- and post-test conditions. The results indicate that family planning misinformation decreased significantly from before the drama to after the drama (Table 3). The average score on the scale before the drama was 21.1, and the average score after the drama decreased to 18.1, representing an average decrease of 3.0 points ($p < .001$) or 9.4 percent $(((3.0/8)/4) = .375/4 = .094)$.

Table 3. *T*-Test Results for Misinformation Scale by Gender, Education,
Past Family Planning Use, and Marital Status

Characteristic	*N*	Pre-test	Post-test	Decrease	*t*-Value	Sign.
Overall	85	21.1	18.1	3.0	5.88	.001
Married						
No	48	21.1	17.8	3.3	4.62	.001
Yes	32	22.2	19.1	3.1	3.90	.001
Past Use						
No	34	21.0	17.4	3.6	4.39	.001
Yes	50	21.1	18.7	2.4	3.78	.001
Gender						
Men	18	22.6	20.6	2.0	1.66	NS
Women	67	20.8	17.5	3.3	5.82	.001
Education						
Primary	8	26.6	23.9	2.7	1.21	NS
Junior High	20	21.5	19.7	1.7	1.82	NS
High School	22	21.3	18.8	2.5	2.20	.05
Some College	33	19.5	15.4	4.1	5.70	.001

MISINFORMATION CHANGE AMONG SUBGROUPS

Did the increase in misinformation about family planning decrease uniformly among everyone who say the drama? To answer this question, we conducted *t*-tests separately for various subgroups in the study. The results showed that the drama was equally effective among married and unmarried respondents, and among past and never users of modern contraceptives. We found, however, that women, rather than men, and those with higher education, had greater decreases in misinformation scores.

Table 3 reports the *t*-test scores for women and men separately. For women, misinformation decreased an average of 3.3 points ($p < .001$), whereas for men, misinformation only decreased 2.0 ($p = $ NS). For education levels, Table 3 shows that misinformation decreased the least for those with only a primary school education, but decreased the most (and significantly) for those with the most education.

DISCUSSION

This field study has demonstrated two important ideas. First, a street theater drama can decrease misinformation about family planning. Between pre- and post-tests, overall scale scores decreased significantly. The short time interval between the two measures insures that no other factors were likely to be responsible for the change recorded.

Also, the street theater particularly tried to dispel three specific misinformation items: 1) the pill produces cancer, 2) the pill affects the fetus, and 3) the pill affects the nerves. Two of these three individual misinformation items decreased most between pre- and post-tests, and represented the most statistically significant decreases. This indicates that the drama message was directly influencing the respondents. Other misinformation items not addressed in this specific play can be themes for later street theater dramas.

It is important to note that the drama had less effect on changing attitudes. Of the five attitudinal statements in the scale, three did not change significantly as a result of the drama, whereas all the knowledge statements decreased. Perhaps attitudes will change more slowly as more accurate information about modern contraceptive methods circulates among Peruvians.

Second, the drama had some selectivity in its impact. Specifically, the drama may have been more effective among more educated women. While the misinformation score decreased among all subgroups, it decreased more significantly among women rather men, and among educated respondents rather than less educated respondents.[5]

Street theater offers a novel medium which has the advantage of publicly communicating information to an audience, thus providing public support for behavioral change. At the same time street theater provides the opportunity for feedback and discussion, thus providing more information to the public. Street theater may be used to great advantage in other applications as its potential is more fully realized.

ACKNOWLEDGMENT

This project was supported by USAID cooperative agreement # DPE-3052-A-00-0014 Johns Hopkins University, Population Communication Services.

REFERENCES

1. D. J. McQuail, *Mass Communication Theory: An Introduction* (2nd Edition), Sage, Newbury Park, California, 1987.

---

[5] Analysis of variance showed that there was no interaction effect between education and gender, indicating that they have separate influences. In other words, the effects were not stronger among educated women than among educated men.

2. S. H. Chaffee, Mass Media and Interpersonal Channels: Competitive, Convergent, or Complementary?, in *Inter/Media: Interpersonal Communication in a Media World*, G. Gumpert and R. Cathart (eds.), Oxford University Press, New York, 1982.

3. W. J. McGuire, Theoretical Foundations of Campaigns, in *Public Communication Campaigns*, R. E. Rice and C. K. Atkin (eds.), Sage, Newbury Park, California, 1989.

4. K. K. Reardon and E. M. Rogers, Interpersonal versus Mass Media Communication: A False Dichotomy?, *Human Communication Research, 15*:2, pp. 284-303, 1988.

5. E. M. Rogers, *Diffusion of Innovations* (4th Edition), The Free Press, New York, 1995.

6. T. W. Valente, *Network Models of the Diffusion of Innovations*, Hampton Press, Cresskill, New Jersey, 1995.

7. B. Berelson, P. F. Lazarsfeld, and W. McPhee, *Voting*, University of Chicago Press, Chicago, 1954.

8. P. F. Lazarsfeld, B. Berelson, and H. Gaudet, *The People's Choice* (2nd Edition), Columbia University Press, New York, 1948.

9. E. Katz and P. F. Lazarsfeld, *Personal Influence: The Part Played by People in the Flow of Mass Communications*, The Free Press, New York, 1955.

10. E. Katz, The Two-Step Flow of Communication: An Up-to-Date Report on a Hypothesis, *Public Opinion Quarterly 21*, pp. 61-78, 1957.

11. E. Katz, Communications Research since Lazarsfeld, *Public Opinion Quarterly, 51*, pp. S25-S45, 1987.

12. R. C. Hornik, Channel Effectiveness in Development Communication Programs, in *Public Communication Campaigns*, R. E. Rice and C. K. Atkin (eds.), Sage, Newbury Park, California, 1989.

13. L. B. Snyder, Channel Effectiveness Over Time and Knowledge and Behavior Gaps, *Journalism Quarterly, 67*, pp. 875-887, 1990.

14. B. Mason, *Street Theatre and Other Outdoor Performance*, Rutledge, New York, 1992.

15. H. O'Gorman and S. Garry, Pluralistic Ignorance: A Replication and Extension, *Public Opinion Quarterly, 40*, pp. 449-458, 1976.

16. H. J. O'Gorman, The Discovery of Pluralistic Ignorance: An Ironic Lesson, *Journal of the History of the Behavioral Sciences, 22*, pp. 333-347, 1986.

17. E. M. Rogers and L. Antola, Telenovelas: A Latin American Success Story, *Journal of Communication, 35*, pp. 24-35, 1985.

18. Food and Agriculture Organization (FAO), *Education through Entertainment: The British Radio Drama Series "The Archers—An Everyday Story of Country Folk."* Food and Agriculture Organization of the United Nations, Rome, Italy, 1987.

19. D. L. Kincaid, J. G. Rimon, P. T. Piotrow, and P. Coleman, *The Enter-Educate Approach: Using Entertainment to Change Health Behavior*, paper presented at the annual meeting of the Population Association of America, 1992.

20. A. Singhal and E. M. Rogers, Prosocial Television for Development in India, in *Public Communication Campaigns*, R. E. Price and C. K. Atkin (eds.), Sage, Newbury Park, California, 1989.

21. T. W. Valente, Y. M. Kim, C. Lettenmaier, W. Glass, and Y. Dibba, Radio and the Promotion of Family Planning in The Gambia, *International Family Perspectives Planning, 20*:3, pp. 96-100, 1994.

22. G. Luzuriaga (ed.), *Popular Theater for Social Change in America* (2nd Edition), UCLA Latin American Center for Publications, Los Angeles, California, 1978.
23. J. A. Weiss, *Latin American Popular Theater: The First Five Centuries*, University of New Mexico Press, Albuquerque, New Mexico, 1993.
24. A. Boal, Teatro del Opimido: Una Experiencia de Teatro Popular Educativo el Perú, in *Popular Theater for Social Change in Latin America*, G. Luzuriaga (ed.), UCLA Latin American Center for Publications, Los Angeles, California, 1978.
25. D. Skinner, C. A. Metcalf, J. R. Seager, J. S. DeSwardt, and J. A. Laubscher, An Evaluation of an Education Programme on HIV Infection using Puppetry and Street Theater, *AIDS Care, 3*:3, pp. 317-329, 1991.
26. T. D. Cook and D. T. Campbell, *Quasi-Experimentation: Design & Analysis Issues for Field Settings*, Houghton Mifflin, Boston, 1979.

CHAPTER 11

Developing and Evaluating a Radio-Linked Telephone Helpline for Hispanics

D. Michael Anderson
Elmer E. Huerta

Estimates show that, on average, people are faced with a symptom or medical problem one out of every three days [1]. Studies have also shown that up to 85 percent of health and medical care is handled by the person affected or by their guardian [2, 3]. Knowledge and skills play major roles in increasing an individual's ability to handle self-care more effectively, and making them better consumers of health care [4, 5]. The issue for health education is how to increase knowledge and skills. Mass media are often seen as a magic bullet but, while mass media can be effective, how they work is unclear [6]. What is intuitively clear, however, is that what applies to the "mass" may not apply to the individual. This project combined mass media (radio) with one-on-one counseling (a telephone helpline) into what we hypothesized as a more comprehensive, and effective approach.

The long-term goal of this research was to develop and evaluate a culturally specific combined radio and telephone helpline, staffed by bi-lingual nurses with physician supervision, to assist Spanish-speaking people make knowledgeable, skill-based health and medical care decisions. Based on our own pilot study findings that strongly demonstrated Spanish language radio to be both the most effective and most economical caller recruitment medium, the helpline was enhanced by directly linking it to educational vignettes broadcast on Spanish language radio. Radio broadcasts and the helpline were coordinated to focus on a single topic per day, although general health and medical information based on caller requests were also available.

The radio program and helpline provided four main services to listeners and callers: 1) advice on routine medical concerns; 2) guidance and behavioral suggestions on cancer and chronic disease prevention; 3) information about cancer screening and treatment; and 4) references to local Spanish-speaking health care services.

METHODS

Toll-free telephone helplines were staffed by physician-supervised R.N.s, in the Washington-Baltimore and the San Francisco-Oakland metropolitan areas. The service was pilot tested (Phase I) for three, two-hour call-in periods per week for three months. Callers were recruited through radio ads, print ads, and flyers in Hispanic neighborhoods. Main Phase I findings include:

1. Radio was by far the number one medium for learning about this service (91.9 percent of calls).
2. Most callers called about their own health (77.8 percent) rather than that of a spouse, relative, or friend.
3. Most callers were female (69.7 percent).
4. Most calls were about chronic problems of greater than six months duration (53.5 percent).

Based on these findings, we established an expanded Spanish language telephone call-in helpline (Phase II) and called it *La Linea de la Salud* ("The Health Line"). The primary differences between Phases I and II is that in Phase II we linked our call-in service to a daily radio health information radio program, and intensified our intervention to a three-hour call-in period, five evenings per week for one year. We also eliminated all print ad efforts. Our principal intervention approaches were to: 1) provide information on medical and self care options, including the benefits, risks, and (if known) costs of options; and 2) provide assertiveness training to enhance skills to help users overcome emotional, situational, or cultural barriers affecting choices. Data were collected by nurse-counselors through a Call Record Form and through a separate call follow-up study. This chapter reports on the Call Record Form data.

We broadcast one year's worth of five-minute educational radio programs, called *Cuidando Su Salud* ("Taking Care of Your Health") three times per day—morning, noon, and late afternoon—each weekday on Spanish language radio in the greater Washington, D.C.–Baltimore, Maryland and San Francisco–Oakland, California, metropolitan areas. The programs dealt extensively with cancer and other chronic disease prevention, control, diagnosis, and treatment. They addressed specific risk behaviors, screening issues, topics important to subpopulations such as women and children, and other subjects of ongoing or current interest. There was also an emphasis on producing several programs throughout the year that provided information on self care issues and on medical care utilization.

Caller Recruitment

Callers were recruited through announcements by Dr. Huerta on *Cuidando Su Salud*. The program reached an estimated 58 percent of those 20 years of age and older out of approximately 500,000 Hispanic people in the Washington, D.C., Baltimore, suburban Maryland, and Northern Virginia metropolitan areas, and approximately the same number of listeners in the San Francisco Bay area [7]. Listeners heard the educational program and were told about the availability of the telephone service, that it was for personalized counseling and further information on that day's topic or any other topic, and that it was free. They were also informed that by calling they would also take part in a study on the usefulness of the telephone service, and that some anonymous demographic and call-related information would be requested. The toll-free phone number and hours of the helpline were repeated in each broadcast.

Take Calls and Collect Data

Nurses staffed the helpline telephones week nights (except major holidays) from 7:00 to 10:00 PM (Eastern Time), the period found in Phase I to have the highest call volume. Data from each call was collected on the Call Record Form—a forced choice and short response format instrument developed and field-tested in Phase I. The Call Record Form consisted of: 1) the nurse-counselor's self introduction and the verbatim reading of a legal disclaimer and a confidentiality statement; 2) background information consisting of sex (estimated from voice), level of education, age (in decade), country of origin, city and state of residence; 3) the chief complaint or the subject of inquiry; 4) the referral or behavioral suggestion provided; and 5) other information such as date, counselor, length of call, and counselor's notes.

RESULTS

The call-in—or intervention—portion of this study yielded 1,569 subjects. Of these, 300 or 19 percent, called more than once, although each non-first time call was for a different question. Most callers (77.9 percent) were from the Washington, D.C. metropolitan area. This is almost undoubtedly due to the great local popularity of Dr. Huerta's radio program. Most subjects had a high school education or greater (63.8 percent), but over a third (36.2 percent) had not completed high school. Most callers were in their 30s or 40s. The mean age was 42.2 years and the range was from 8 to 88 years. Not surprisingly, most callers (64 percent) were female. This is about the same as for similar studies we and others have done using the National Cancer Institute's Cancer Information Service telephone helpline data [8-16].

Since many of our callers were immigrants, we asked them what country they came from. The largest percentage (21.8 percent) came from El Salvador, and the next largest group (14.9 percent) came from Peru. Since Dr. Huerta is from Peru, we expected many callers from there. After that, 13.5 percent of callers came from Mexico and 10.5 percent came from Bolivia. Since Mexicans are the most common Hispanic group in the San Francisco Bay area, and Central Americans are the most common Hispanic nationality in the Washington/Baltimore area, this may account for some of these results.

Once subjects called in and reached a nurse-counselor, they were read a disclaimer statement and asked if they understood the disclaimer, and if confirmed, they were read a confidentiality statement. This was also confirmed in order to continue. They were then asked their chief complaint and if it was associated with a known diagnosis. For about a third of all callers it was, and there were a wide variety of responses, some of the most common being diabetes, high blood pressure, cancers, gastritis, allergies, and back problems.

If the caller's diagnosis was not known, the nurse-counselor would solicit comments on the nature of the caller's problem. These responses were categorized by body system. Among the most common inquiries (> 30 calls) were 152 calls about headache, 101 calls about abdominal pain, 93 calls about back or lower back pain, 67 calls about anxiety ("nervousness"), 62 calls for cough, 46 calls about ovarian pain, 45 calls about joint pain, 43 calls about skin rash, 34 calls about pain on urination, 33 calls for nausea, and 31 calls each for eye pain and depression. Callers were also asked how long they had their chief complaint. Over 75 percent reported a chronic problem of greater than one month's duration. They were also asked how they felt before their chief complaint, or if they had any recent changes in their health. Callers were also asked if they had secondary symptoms related to the chief complaint. These were also recorded by body system. Headache was again very common with 109 calls, as was abdominal pain with 104 calls.

By far, most callers (69.7 percent) contacted us about a chronic problem of greater than one-month duration. Only six callers gave less than one hour for the duration of their problem. Nevertheless, nine callers were told to go to an emergency room immediately. Of the rest, 18.9 percent of calls were considered urgent (go see a provider in the next three days) and 75.5 percent were routine (take care of the problem at home or see a provider in the next few weeks).

Whether the caller's diagnosis was known or not known, the nurse-counselor would make recommendations for further action. For most callers (65.2 percent), nurse-counselors recommended a physician visit or general home-care recommendations (31.8 percent). Other recommendations are shown in Table 1.

Because so many callers were recent immigrants, we also asked about their health insurance status. Fortunately, about 60 percent had some type of coverage: 27.2 percent had an HMO, 23.2 percent had other insurance, and 9.2 percent

Table 1. Primary Recommendation

	Frequency	Percent	Valid percent	Cumulative percent
Valid				
Consult MD	962	61.3	65.2	65.2
Go to ER	18	1.1	1.2	66.4
Stop smoking	2	.1	.1	66.5
Reduce alcohol	6	.4	.4	66.9
General consultation	470	30.0	31.8	98.8
See mental health	1	.1	.1	98.8
Go to a clinic	2	.1	.1	99.0
Get a check-up	6	.4	.4	99.4
Go on a diet	3	.2	.2	99.6
Vaccination	1	.1	.1	99.7
Get a second opinion	2	.1	.1	99.8
Find more information	1	.1	.1	99.9
Exercise	1	.1	.1	99.9
Get AIDS check-up	1	.1	.1	100.0
Total	1476	94.1	100.0	
Missing				
System missing	93	5.9		
Total	93	5.9		
Total	1569	100.0		

had Medicare, Medicaid, or Medical Assistance. Unfortunately, this leaves about 40 percent of our subjects who either did not have any medical insurance or did not know whether or not they were covered.

DISCUSSION

Firstly, we were happy to have served the 1,569 callers who took advantage of the helpline. They expressed great appreciation to our nurses, and many expressed much disappointment to the staff of *La Linea de la Salud* and to Dr. Huerta when they learned that the service would end. We continued to receive calls for months after the shut-down.

Main findings are that Hispanic people: 1) do listen to health messages and medical information on the radio; and 2) that they will use a toll-free telephone to speak to a health professional for personal information. A secondary finding is that, at least for subject recruitment, and by extension, attracting other health information seekers, print ads pale in significance to radio ads. At least this is true for a well-regarded radio program. Anecdotally [10], we and others [16], have found that Dr. Huerta's radio program, *Cuidando Su Salud,* is held in high esteem in the Hispanic community, and that listeners have a great deal of respect for his advice as a physician.

This project took advantage of two mature technologies that have much in common: both radio and telephones are easy to use; they are both very low cost on a per-use basis; and they are both nearly ubiquitous. Even in low income areas, as is the case with many Hispanics in the United States, there is probably near universal radio ownership and almost 90 percent level of homes with telephones [10]. And for those without a home phone, virtually everyone has access to and can afford a pay telephone. Both radio and telephones have been used individually to educate people about health, and they have also been used in combination for health related call-in radio programs.

Our combination radio and telephone helpline offered a communication model of enormous potential for the dissemination of health information. As a mass medium, radio offers blanket exposure at virtually no cost to the listener after initial purchase. Also as a type of mass medium, telephone combines the convenience of time and place with anonymity, very low cost on a per-use basis, and one-on-one attention. Communication research posits that people seek information to reduce uncertainty and interpret reality. Those seeking health information may see the anonymity of radio and telephone as non-threatening, and as a way to maintain some control in an unfamiliar area of knowledge [8, 17, 18]. In terms of our radio-telephone service, those seeking information were able to access it at or near the time they were considering the health problem or issue. Studies have shown that people want access to information at the time they are considering action rather than get information to be applied at a later date [5].

From a public health viewpoint, radio used in combination with a telephone helpline has the potential to cause a large effect because of the sheer volume of potential contacts with people. There are other advantages as well. Health professionals serving as helpline counselors are able to follow-up radio information that might not have been initially contemplated by the caller and may be unrelated to their original subject of inquiry. Helpline counselors also have the ability to follow-up an educational radio vignette with a reinforcement message [19, 20]. This is particularly attractive with certain behaviors such as smoking, because cessation is a cyclical and dynamic process of quitting and relapse that benefits from ongoing support [21–23].

In spite of their popularity, a review of the literature reveals little real evaluation of the effects of health related radio programs, whether they are the call-in type or not. This could be a reflection of the difficulty in statistically establishing causation. Health related telephone helplines have been evaluated, however. The literature reveals two basic types of helplines: those with prerecorded messages and those with interactive services where trained counselors respond directly to each caller's inquiries [24].

Interactive helplines are particularly attractive from a health education perspective because they have the flexibility to shape each message into a uniquely personal intervention [25, 26]. Interactive telephone helplines, at least for medical and health matters, deal with two basic categories of information requests. The first is counseling patients on the meaning and outcomes of medical diagnosis and treatment. Use of the telephone for patient counseling and management, especially for certain acute, self-limiting conditions is very common [9]. For instance, in some medical practices up to 70 percent of problems are dealt with solely by telephone [27]. The second basic type of call involves questions about the prevention of disease and promotion of healthy lifestyles. Help may include advice on weight loss or a more nutritious diet, or steps to take to quit smoking, or where to find local resources or support groups [10]. An interactive helpline can facilitate inclusion of each caller in planning his or her own unique course of action [28]. Counselors, working directly with callers, can set measurable objectives with practical criteria, and can exploit what works best for each individual's health improvement efforts. This is crucial since people are more likely to change their behaviors and maintain changes if they have taken an active part in planning their behavioral goals [29, 30].

Studies have shown that knowledgeable consumers usually choose less risky and less expensive options than do the uninformed [31]. In a Harvard study of nurse advice telephone services, 82 percent of insured callers and 92 percent of Medicaid callers who were about to visit an emergency room chose a lower level of care. More than 20 percent of them learned how to treat their problems at home without further assistance. Of those callers who were planning to see a physician for their problem, 89 percent of insured callers and 75 percent of Medicaid callers chose less costly alternatives [32]. And while, as stated, medical costs and their reduction is not an outcome of this study, it is useful to note the striking findings other investigators have found with medical self care programs. One, *Take Care of Yourself,* using written material, audio and video tapes, and group sessions, found that for each $1.00 spent, there was a savings of $2.41 to $3.43 [33]. Another evaluation of the same program found a savings of $4.90 for every $1.00 spent [34]. In the *Healthwise* program, using the same intervention materials, for every $1.00 spent there was an estimated savings of $4.22 [5]. In *Options and Choices,* a telephone counseling service supplemented with written materials, program implementation for employees in three companies resulted in one-year reductions in medical claims of 5.5 percent, 8.0 percent, and 14.0 percent respectively. Three years of data from one of the companies showed a 34.7 percent reduction in short-term disability claims and a 30.5 percent reduction in length of disability. Over a one year period, workers' compensation costs were reduced by 46 percent compared to non-participants [5].

A radio-telephone helpline combination has the potential to function as a laboratory for communications research and hypothesis testing, in addition to providing an important service to specific communities and target groups [35-37].

A communications research component may, in the long term, be one of the most important strategies for maximizing mass media's impact, particularly for under-served and linguistically isolated populations such as Hispanics [11, 38]. It is important to investigate these effects since the future holds so many opportunities for the use of combined mass media sources for health education messages [12, 36, 39]. It is possible that in the near future telephones will cease being restricted to audio and FAX uses, and will become part of a visual medium as well [13, 40]. Many efforts will continue to develop Web-based applications, or the transmission of televison images over the Internet for medical uses, particularly in the fields of radiology, dermatology, and pathology [38, 39]. The future also holds potential on-line applications of nurse advice services as well.

ACKNOWLEDGMENT

This work was supported by grants from the National Cancer Institute (R43/R44CA66496).

REFERENCES

1. D. C. Morrell, Symptoms Perceived and Recorded, *Journal of the Royal College of General Practitioners, 26,* pp. 410-413, 1976.
2. K. L. White, R. F. Williams, and B. C. Greenberg, The Ecology of Medical Care, *New England Journal of Medicine, 268,* pp. 885-888, 1961.
3. J. D. Williamson and H. Danaher, *Self-Care in Health,* Croom Helm, Ltd., London, 1978.
4. J. Rudd and K. Glanz, How Individuals Use Information for Health Action: Consumer Information Processing, in *Health Behavior and Health Education,* K. Glanz, F. M. Lewis, and B. K. Rimer (eds.), Jossey-Bass Publishers, San Francisco, pp. 15-139, 1990.
5. D. M. Vickery and D. C. Iverson, Medical Self-Care and Use of the Medical Care System, in *Health Promotion in the Workplace* (2nd Edition), M. P. O'Donnell and J. S. Harris (eds.), Delmar Publishers, Inc., Albany, New York, pp. 367-389, 1994.
6. L. Wallack, Media Advocacy: Promoting Health Through Mass Communication, in *Health Behavior and Health Education,* K. Glanz, F. M. Lewis, and B. K. Rimer (eds.), Jossey-Bass Publishers, San Francisco, pp. 370-386, 1990.
7. E. E. Huerta, *Use of Radio as a Tool for Public Health in the Latino Community in the Washington, D.C., Metropolitan Area,* American Society of Preventive Oncology, 18th Annual Meeting, Washington, D.C., 1994.
8. V. Freimuth, J. Stein, and T. Kean, *Search for Health Information: The Cancer Information Service Model,* University of Pennsylvania Press, Philadelphia, 1989.
9. S. E. Radecki, M. A. Nelille, and R. A. Girard, Telephone Patient Management by Primary Care Physicians, *Medical Care, 27*:8, pp. 817-822, August 1989.
10. D. M. Anderson, H. I. Meissner, and B. Portnoy, Media Use and the Health Information Acquisition Process: How Callers Learned about the NCI's Cancer Information Service, *Health Education Research, 4*:4, pp. 419-427, 1989.

11. J. A. Ward, D. M. Anderson, C. G. Pundik, A. Redrick, and R. Kaufman, Cancer Information Service Utilization by Selected U.S. Ethnic Groups, *Journal of the National Cancer Institute Monographs, 14,* pp. 147-156, 1993.

12. H. I. Meissner, D. M. Anderson, and J. O. Odenkirchen, Meeting Information Needs of Significant Others: Use of the Cancer Information Service, *The Journal of Patient Education and Counseling, 15,* pp. 171-179, 1990.

13. J. P. Pierce, D. M. Anderson, R. M. Romano, H. I. Meissner, and J. C. Odenkirchen, Promoting Smoking Cessation in the United States: Effect of Public Service Announcements on the Cancer Information Service Telephone Line, *Journal of the National Cancer Institute, 84*:9, pp. 677-683, May 6, 1992.

14. A. C. Marcus, M. A. Woodworth, and C. J. Strickland, The Cancer Information Service as a Laboratory for Research: The First 15 Years, *Journal of the National Cancer Institute Monographs, 14,* pp. 67-79, 1993.

15. From analysis of National Cancer Institute, Cancer Information Service data conducted by Principal Investigator in his former role at NCI.

16. P. Constable, Health-Conscious Latinos Tune in to Voice of Authority: Doctor's Radio Show Opens Community to World of Medical Advice, *The Washington Post,* pp. 1, 6, January 26, 1995.

17. E. B. Arkin, R. M. Romano, J. P. Van Nevel, and J. W. McKenna, Effects of the Mass Media in Promoting Calls to the Cancer Information Service, *Journal of the National Cancer Institute Monographs, 14,* pp. 35-43, 1993.

18. L. Siegal, In Touch: Telephone Message System for Teenagers, *American Journal of Public Health, 79*:1, p. 100, 1989.

19. S. L. Hammond, V. S. Freimuth, and W. Morrison, The Gatekeeping Funnel: Tracking a Major PSA Campaign from Distribution through Gatekeepers to Target Audience, *Health Education Quarterly, 14*:2, pp. 153-166, 1987.

20. K. M. Cummings, S. L. Emont, C. Jaen, and R. Sciandra, Format and Quitting Instructions as Factors Influencing the Impact of a Self-Administered Quit Smoking Program, *Health Education Quarterly, 15*:2, pp. 199-216, Summer 1988.

21. J. O. Prochaska, C. C. DiClemente, W. F. Velicer, S. Ginpil, and J. C. Norcross, Predicting Change in Smoking Status for Self-Changers, *Addictive Behavior, 10*:4, pp. 395-406, 1985.

22. S. Cohen, E. Lichtenstein, J. O. Prochaska, J. S. Rossi, et al., Debunking Myths about Self-Quitting: Evidence from 10 Prospective Studies of Persons Who Attempt to Quit Smoking by Themselves, *American Psychologist, 44*:11, pp. 1355-1365, November 1989.

23. N. S. Wilcox, J. O Prochaska, W. F. Velicer, and C. C. DiClemente, Subject Characteristics as Predictors of Self-Change in Smoking, *Addictive Behavior, 10*:4, pp. 407-412, 1985.

24. J. P. Pierce, T. Dwyer, G. Frape, S. Chapman, A. Chamberlain, and N. Burke, Evaluation of The Sydney "Quit for Life" Anti-Smoking Campaign: Part 1. Achievement of Intermediate Goals, *The Medical Journal of Australia, 144,* pp. 341-344, 1986.

25. K. E. Bauman, C. A. Padgett, and G. G. Koch, A Media-Based Campaign to Encourage Personal Communication among Adolescents about Not Smoking Cigarettes: Participation, Selection and Consequences, *Health Education Research, 4*:1, pp. 35-44, 1989.

26. D. M. Anderson, K. Duffy, C. D. Hallett, and A. C. Marcus, Cancer Prevention Counseling on Telephone Helplines, *Public Health Reports, 107,* pp. 278-283, 1992.

27. P. Curtis and A. Talbot, The Telephone in Primary Care, *Journal of Community Health, 6*, p. 194, 1981.
28. E. E. Bartlett, Eight Principles from Patient Education Research, *Preventive Medicine, 14*, pp. 667-669, 1985.
29. L. W. Green, Modifying and Developing Health Behavior, *Annual Review of Public Health, 5*, pp. 215-236, 1984.
30. I. Ajzen and J. T. Madden, Prediction of Goal-Directed Behavior: Attitudes, Intentions, and Perceived Behavioral Control, *Journal of Experimental Social Psychology, 22*, pp. 435-474, 1986.
31. F. L. Kritz and J. Novack, Patient, Educate Thyself, *Forbes*, pp. 505-506, September 14, 1992.
32. G. Levenworth, Preventive Medicine: Informed Employees Make Better Health Consumers, *Business and Health, 13*:3(Supp. A), pp. 6-10, 1995.
33. D. M. Vickery, H. Kalmer, D. Lowry, M. Constantine, E. Wright, and C. N. Loren, Effect of a Self-Care Education Program on Medical Visits, *Journal of the American Medical Association, 250*, pp. 2952-2956, 1983.
34. T. Golaszewski, D. Snow, W. Lynch, and D. Sosomita, A Benefit-to-Cost Analysis of a Work-Site Health Promotion Program, *Journal of Occupational Health, 34*:12, pp. 1164-1172, 1992.
35. J. Ward, K. Duffy, R. Sciandra, and S. Karlins, What the Public Wants to Know about Cancer: The Cancer Information Service, *The Cancer Bulletin, 40*:6, pp. 384-389, 1988.
36. A. C. Marcus, R. Bastani, K. Reardon, S. Karlis, Das I. Prabhu, M. P. Van Herle, M. W. McClatchey, and L. A. Crane, Proactive Screening Mammography Counseling within the Cancer Information Service: Results from a Randomized Trial, *Journal of the National Cancer Institute Monographs, 14*, pp. 119-129, 1993.
37. B. Thompson, S. Kinne, F. M. Lewis, and J. A. Wooldridge, Randomized Telephone Smoking-Intervention Trial Initially Directed at Blue-Collar Workers, *Journal of the National Cancer Institute Monographs, 14*, pp. 105-112, 1993.
38. R. Denniston and R. Romano, *Determination of Hispanic Knowledge, Attitudes, and Practices Related to Cancer for the Purposes of Educational Program Development*, National Cancer Institute, Office of Cancer Communications, Bethesda, Maryland, 1979.
39. L. J. Perlman, *School's Out: Hyperlearning, the New Technology, and the End of Education*, William Morrow and Co., Inc., New York, 1992.
40. M. L. Carnevale, US West Will Overhaul Network, Enabling it to Carry Video Signals, *The Wall Street Journal*, Section B, February 5, 1993.
41. J. Preston, F. W. Brown, and B. Hartley, Using Telemedicine to Improve Health Care in Distant Areas, *Hospital and Community Psychiatry, 43*:1, pp. 25-31, 1991.
42. R. S. Weinstein, K. J. Bloom, and L. S. Rozek, Telepathology: Long Distance Diagnosis, *American Journal of Community Psychology, 91*:4(Supp.1), pp. S39-S42, 1989.

CHAPTER 12

Spanish Language Television News Portrayals of Youth and Violence in California

Vivian Chávez
Lori Dorfman

The innovative use of mass media as a strategy to promote public health has received considerable attention in recent years [1]. This exploratory study introduces Spanish language media into the larger discussion on the agenda setting theory of news media, which suggests that the content of news will affect policy decisions [2, 3]. The data presented here are the Spanish subset of a study on how youth and violence are portrayed on local television news in California. The purpose of the overall study was to establish an empirical base for how youth and violence are portrayed on local television news in California, with the intent that the study findings be applied to violence prevention efforts. Including non-English media in this discussion expands the frame of reference to the multicultural, multilingual realities of California.

Our study departs from the usual exploration of whether that televised violence has direct behavioral effects on viewers to examine a different aspect of how mediated violence may influence public health. The authors were interested in finding out if the premise that television news stories on violence will influence policy-makers responses applies to Spanish language television news. In examining this concern, this chapter will describe the intersection of three areas: Latinos, violence, and Spanish language television news media. It will describe portrayals of youth and violence on Spanish news and compare Spanish and English portrayals where appropriate. Finally, it will draw conclusions based on the context of Spanish language television news and application to violence prevention efforts (see Figure 1).

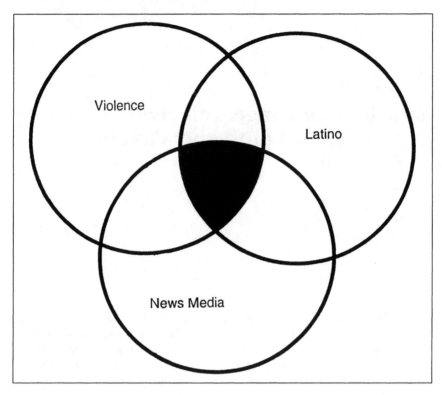

Figure 1. Context for research.

VIOLENCE IN LATINO COMMUNITIES

The structural arrangement of American society together with norms favoring the use of violence to solve problems is thought to produce a high rate of family violence. In fact, violence is often an adaptation to stress produced by structural inequalities [4]. There are many contributing factors related to violence including economic injustice, power and resource inequalities, family problems, lack of jobs, as well as the availability of alcohol, drugs, firearms, and the prevalence of violence in the media [5]. In California, people under the age of twenty are nearly ten times more likely to be victims of crime than persons over the age of sixty-five [6].

Increasingly, Latino activists and researchers are interested in describing and clarifying differences in world view, values, psychosocial responses, and familial organization of people conventionally clustered together as Latinos [7]. In the United States, the census numbers Latinos at 22,752,000, close to eight million of whom are California residents [8]. This number is highly contested by some demographers who estimate the actual number to be several millions higher, given that many are missed because of inadequate census counts and their undocumented status (i.e., no immigration documents) [9], as well as unreliable ethnic categorization. Latinos residing in the United States are also one of the youngest ethnic/racial groups. Given Latino's average age, high fertility, and migration patterns, Latino youth represent the fastest growing segment of the U.S. population [10].

As with other aspects of Latino health, research in the area of violence or violent injuries among Latinos is limited [11]. Nevertheless, the research available indicates that violence is an increasingly significant problem given that Latino communities bear a disproportionate share of violence-related morbidity and mortality when compared to the general population [12]. Additionally, Latinas contend with being female in a sexist society. Although some studies indicate that as a whole Latinas do not differ significantly from Anglo-American women in their odds of assaults when norms regarding violence approval, age and economic stressors are held constant [13], some studies have reported a higher incidence of physical and/or mental abuse in Latino homes [14]. This may be explained by the growing number of Latinos in poverty, and the disproportionately high number of Latino female headed households [15].

SPANISH TELEVISION NEWS

Spanish language media has broad reach and audience [16]. It constitutes an important part of the Latino social environment in which the selection, presentation, definition, and discussion of public issues occur. In California, of the vast network of broadcast outlets directed at the Latino populations, there are eleven television stations with full-time Spanish language programs. Nine of these stations are affiliated with the Univision network, the other two with the Telemundo network. Local Spanish-language news media carry out three major functions: to provide Latin American news in greater detail than does mainstream media, to provide extensive coverage of local Latino communities, and, in some cases, to serve an advocacy function for Latino issues such as immigration, bilingual education, and housing [16, 17]. Industry observers note that Spanish-language media will continue to grow because language is central to the culture [17].

TELEVISION NEWS IN GENERAL

Shanto Iyengar, in his studies of English language network news [3], has operationalized television news frames as either predominantly "episodic" (focused on events) or "thematic" (focused on context). He found that most television news stories on crime (89 percent) were framed episodically, without much attention to the context of those events. Iyengar also found that after watching episodic stories, audiences tend to place responsibility for the cause and solution of the problem on the person with the problem, in effect "blaming the victim." However, when exposed to alternate news stories that place incidents in a larger social context, audiences will be more likely to identify social institutions and governments as responsible for treating the problem. Thematic frames are issue-oriented, general, and abstract. They use data, reports, and "talking heads" to tell long complicated social stories. The effect is to focus attention on social responsibility, which leads to solutions focused on the policy level [3]. This suggests that how violence is portrayed on the news will influence the types of responses the public will support [18]. It is likely, then, that local television news can have a large influence on the issues to which policy makers and the public turn their attention, including violence among youth. Is this the case for Spanish language media? Can the ways in which Spanish television news frames the issue influence the solutions considered by policy makers and the public?

Methods

This study posed three basic research questions. First, how are youth and violence portrayed on local Spanish language television news? This basic accounting of the content is important because there is very little known about local Spanish television news. Second, the authors were interested in the scope of violence portrayals. In particular, do local television news stories explore a public health perspective on violence? That is, does coverage of violence among youth on Spanish language local television news discuss prevention or include the social, economic, and community context in which violent events occur? Finally, the study is interested in whether there were key differences between how Spanish language news and English news portray youth and violence.

To answer these questions an ethnographic content analysis of local television news aired on Spanish language stations in California was conducted [19]. The authors came to the study with many preliminary questions and categories determined ahead of time and revised those categories as themes emerged in the data. The content analysis was ethnographic insofar as questions and categories were reformulated after gaining new knowledge from preliminary assessments of the news stories, after discussion with Spanish speaking journalists, and after conversations with Spanish language television viewers. The reflexive research design and the exploratory nature of the study allowed the authors to discover emerging patterns, emphases, and themes in the analysis.

The research was organized into four primary categories: *Youth and Violence; Violence, No Youth; Youth, No violence*; and *"related reports."* This last category was created to capture stories that fell outside the coding manual definitions of violence or youth, but related to the root causes or exacerbators of violence among youth, such as racism, alcohol, drugs, prisons, guns, etc.

Sample

The sample of news collected was professionally videotaped with complete local broadcasts from twenty-six stations throughout California [20]. Five of the broadcasts were Spanish language news, twenty-one were in English. The media markets were: San Francisco, Los Angeles, Sacramento, San Jose, and San Diego-Baja California. Our objective was to collect a sample of local television news that would include the maximum number of stories that might involve youth in any way. Therefore, one week broadcast September 19-25, 1993, after school had begun, augmented with the weekend of Halloween and "Day of the Dead" (October 29-November 2, 1993) was sampled. ("Day of the Dead," is a Chicano/Latino cultural-heritage day of remembrance of family and friends who have died.)

Coding

Each tape was logged by the primary researcher who noted the time each new story or commercial began and indicated when a story concerned youth and/or violence. Stories concerning youth and/or violence were then coded in more detail, including format, length, or placement in the broadcast, and variables that assessed the degree to which the context of violence was reported. The first few sentences of each story were transcribed verbatim and translated into English. Narrative description and comments were translated into English to enable the authors to draw comparisons with the English sample of local news in California.

Pre-structured, consistent strategies for youth and/or violence were defined as follows: a story was coded as being about youth if it portrayed, described, or involved any person appearing to be age twenty-four or younger (if no age given); any mention of gangs; or any mention of schools. Our inclusion of all gang stories in the youth category was intended to reflect the assumption that gangs are largely composed of people under twenty-four.

A story was coded as being about violence if it portrayed, described or involved: any deliberate act of physical force or use of weapon in an attempt to achieve a goal, further a cause, stop the action of another, act out an angry impulse, defend oneself from attack, secure some material gain or to intimidate others; any deliberate use of the threat of such physical force; any armed crime, regardless of whether injury resulted; or any individual, community or organizational response to such crimes, including law enforcement [21]. Included in the violence categories are reported actions by individuals, groups, or communities to prevent youth violence.

Stories on youth and/or violence were coded further for measures of context, modeled after Iyengar's categories "episodic" and "thematic" [3]. Episodic stories were defined as those in which the majority of the story focused on specific events or incidents, with minimal attention to the context or broader implications of the event. Thematic stories were defined as those in which the majority of the story focused on context, themes, trends, or root causes of problems (as specified by the reporter or people interviewed), as opposed to a specific event.

After this initial coding, the stories were viewed several times for further coding and analysis to refine exploration and comparison. Topical categories emerged from the four primary categories. At least two members of the research team coded and reviewed a select sample of stories. Further, to facilitate data triangulation, accuracy in categorization, and cultural interpretation, a second bilingual, bicultural researcher was included. Intercoder reliability for variables reported here ranged from 81 to 97 percent, depending on the variable reported. Decisions on story topics were highly correlated (97 percent) while more complicated decisions about the degree of context were less highly correlated (81-85 percent).

FINDINGS

Sample Description

The broadcasts from Spanish language stations yielded thirty-six complete broadcasts, for a total of twenty-one hours, two minutes, and forty-three seconds of tape. News stories accounted for 60 percent of the total time on tape, while commercials were 23 percent, sports 10 percent, weather 5 percent, and teasers for upcoming stories 2 percent of the time (see Figure 2).

In Spanish language news the overwhelming number of stories (86 percent) did not concern youth or violence (see Table 1). However, in the first three segments of the broadcasts, more time was devoted to stories about violent crime than to any other single topic, with the exception of health care reform (see Table 2). Health care reform dominated coverage in our sample because the first week of taping coincided with President Clinton's first major speech to Congress announcing his health care reform plan.[1] Along with violent crimes and health care reform, the major stories covered during this time were: the Los Angeles fires, the North American Free Trade Agreement (NAFTA), the Mexican economy, and Latin American news.

A total of 124 stories about youth and/or violence were identified, for a total of two hours, thirty-nine minutes and fifty seconds of news (see Figure 3). Of those 124 stories, thirty-eight were about violent crimes, and thirty-one were about root causes/broader aspects of violence, including stories about gun policy, law enforcement, alcohol and other drugs, social conditions, and discrimination.

---

[1] Separate analyses of health care reform coverage in the English language television news sample were reported in S. Dorfman et al., Local Television News Coverage of President Clinton's Introduction of the Health Security Act, *Journal of the American Medical Association, 275*:15, pp. 1201-1205, 1996.

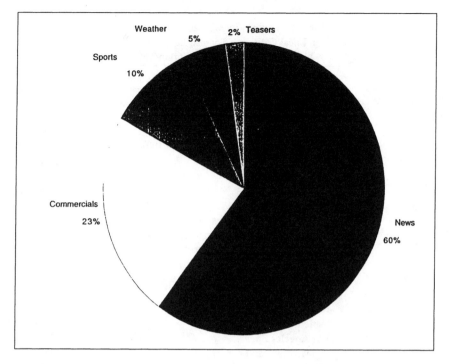

Figure 2. Spanish language sample distribution.

Sixteen stories were about school issues, eleven about community events, nine about gangs, eight about violence prevention programs, six about trials, and five stories about unintentional injuries. The following is a presentation of the story content for the four categories in the study.

Youth and Violence

There were fifty-one stories that included both youth and violence, totaling 8 percent of news time, or one hour, two minutes, and two seconds of news. Sixteen stories focused on specific crimes, including shootings, gang activity, abductions, child abuse, and neglect. Four stories were on trials, dominated by two prominent murder cases: the Menendez brothers, who were accused of shooting their parents, and Ellie Nesler, who shot her son's alleged molester. Nine stories mentioned gangs (see Table 3).

Eight stories were about youth violence prevention and community responses to violence, including three stories about a new Latino police officer-sponsored violence and drug prevention program, a Latino domestic violence theater called "Love and Pain"; a story which was part of a five-day special series on family

Table 1. Youth, Violence, and Other Topics
on Local California Spanish Language TV
News, by Percentage of Program Time

	Youth	No youth
Violence	6%	3%
No Violence	4%	86%

Note: These numbers do not sum to 100% due to rounding error.

Table 2. Major Topics Covered on Local
California Spanish Language TV News,
1st-3rd Segments, Sept. 19-25 and
Oct. 29-Nov. 3, 1995, by Time

Topic	Time
Health Care Reform	1:03:51
Violent Crime	0:46:09
Los Angeles Fires	0:44:23
Salinas/Mexican Economy	0:42:56
NAFTA	0:39:25
Election News	0:36:02
Halloween/Dia de los Muertos	0:29:59
News from Latin America	0:29:43
Immigration/INS	0:25:33
Hurricane Gert	0:10:39
Environmental Issues	0:10:13

violence called "Pesadilla Familiar" (Family Nightmare) which focused on a range of issues including child abuse, domestic violence, gangs, and breaking the cycle of violence; two stories about neighborhoods coming together to fight drug problems; and one story about a conference on violence in Mexico. Four stories were about school issues including a school bomb threat, two about dress codes at schools used as a violence deterrence, and one on a school board candidate who mentions violence prevention in his remarks.

Four of the *youth and violence* stories, which varied from the violent crimes category, were about citizens holding institutions accountable for violence, one of which reported on a mother who received a $75,000 settlement from a lawsuit against a police department for her son's death. Shortly after his interrogation, her ten-year-old son was shot and killed outside the police department door. Another

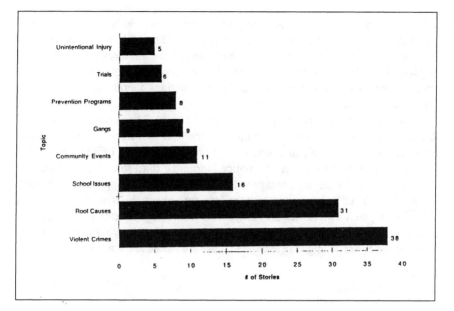

Figure 3. Story Topics for Youth and/or Violence Stories on
Local California Spanish Language TV News,
Sept. 19-25 and Oct. 29-Nov. 2, 1993 ($n = 124$).

Table 3. Story Topics for Youth and
Violence Category on Local California
Spanish Language TV News,
Sept. 19-25 and Oct. 29-Nov. 2, 1993

Topic	No. Stories
Violent Crimes	16
Gangs	9
Prevention Programs	8
Institutional Accounts	4
School Issues	4
Trials	4
Youth Incarceration	2
Other	4
TOTAL	51

of these stories reports on the family of a fifteen-year-old boy filing a formal complaint with his school district for negligence. The child was shot while in school. The remaining two stories were about the mothers of abused and neglected children, who have had their children removed from their homes and were protesting the department of social service actions blaming them for "taking away their children."

Four *youth and violence* stories were labeled "other" because they concerned broader miscellaneous issues of youth violence. One discussed armed youth and reported on gun control; in another story law enforcement officials asked the public to increase the sales tax for police funding; a third story reported on how San Diego included paying homage to "homeboys killed in gang warfare" in their "Day of the Dead" celebrations; and the last story about children under ten years old planning their own funerals. Finally, there were two *youth and violence* stories about youth incarceration. In general, story topics for the youth and violence category on Spanish language television news are varied and contextual in nature.

Violence, No Youth

The twenty-nine stories, totaling thirty-seven minutes and one second, about violence that did not involve youth were predominantly (79 percent) on violent crime (see Table 4). These included stories on drive-by shootings, sexual assaults, car chases resulting in death, a family violence massacre, a hate crime resulting in murder, a vigilante check cashier and others involved in shoot-outs, border patrol violence, and armed robbery. Three *violence, no youth* stories were about incarceration, including one which compared the Pelican Bay maximum security prison to a Nazi concentration camp, another about violence in jails and a "South of the Border" story about jail visitation rights for inmates being limited. There were two *violence, no youth* stories about gun policy regarding the

Table 4. Story Topics for Violence,
No Youth Category on Local California
Spanish Language TV News,
Sept. 19-25 and Oct. 29-Nov. 2, 1993

Topic	No. Stories
Violent Crimes	21
Incarceration	3
Guns	2
Trials	2
Law Enforcement	1
TOTAL	29

Brady Bill passage, and one about a new police auditor who will be reviewing citizen complaints against law enforcement.

Stories in this category appeared sensationalized, such as the story on a child molester who was asking to be castrated, or the one on a man who killed his son "in God's name." There were no stories on prevention or community responses to violence in this category.

Youth, No Violence

There were thirty stories, for a total of thirty minutes and fifteen seconds, that concerned youth but not violence (see Table 5). One-third of the *youth, no violence* stories involved school policy issues, such as public school funding, school board members running for office and protests about the denial of bilingual education rights. Another third of the *youth, no violence* stories focused on community events such as festivals, fairs, and celebrations where youth were present. The last third includes topics ranging from unintentional injury to discrimination and social conditions. Included here were four stories focused on traffic-related injuries among youth. Two stories reported on discrimination against Latino youth. The first one focused on California Governor Pete Wilson's anti-immigrant proposed policy of no education for undocumented children; the other was about Latino children dying of encephalitis due to their parents' working conditions and exposure to pesticides. The last two *youth, no violence* stories reported on social conditions such as the increase in teen pregnancy and a report card on youth services from a coalition interested in child and family issues. In general, when Spanish-language television news reported on youth the emphasis was placed on the community context where young people live and carry out activities.

Table 5. Story Topics for Youth,
No Violence Category on Local California
Spanish Language TV News,
Sept. 19-25 and Oct. 29-Nov. 2, 1993

Topic	No. Stories
School Issues	11
Community Events	10
Unintentional Injury	4
Discrimination	2
Social Conditions	2
Drugs	1
TOTAL	30

Related Reports

Fourteen stories from the remainder of the sample were related to violence, though they fell outside the strict definition of violence or youth previously described (see Table 6). These stories related to the root causes of violence, violence prevention, or violence-related policy. They included three stories related to drug busts, including the Mexico-U.S.A. police partnership against drug trade, three stories about administrative and budget issues within law enforcement, three stories on racism and anti-immigrant sentiment fostered by California policy makers, and one story about African Americans discriminated against within law enforcement. Two stories reported on social issues including funding for housing and the number of people living below the poverty line. One story described unintentional injury, and one, which will be discussed in detail below, on prison policy.

The Context of the News

Each story concerning youth and/or violence was examined for whether it focused primarily on an event (episodic), or whether the news event was connected to other issues in the larger social context (thematic). Approximately 61 percent of the Spanish language news stories were thematic. That is, they included substantial reference to factors outside the news event. This contrasts with findings from the English language sample where only 17 percent of the stories were thematic (see Figure 4) [20].

The following example helps to illustrate the difference between episodic and thematic stories, as well as between the English and Spanish language local television news frames (see Figure 5). During the time our sample was collected, there were stories on both Spanish and English television news about controversy at Pelican Bay, a maximum security prison in Northern California. The

Table 6. Story Topics for Related Stories
of Interest on Local California
Spanish Language TV News,
Sept. 19-25 and Oct. 29-Nov. 2, 1993

Topic	No. Stories
Discrimination	4
Drugs	3
Law Enforcement	3
Social Conditions	2
Unintentional Injury	1
Incarceration	1
TOTAL	14

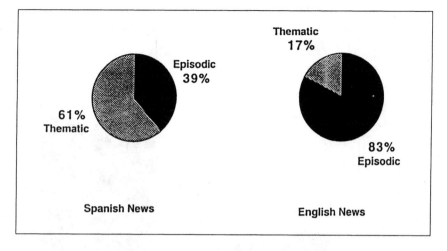

Figure 4. Context of Youth and/or Violence Stories on Local California
TV News, Sept. 19-25 and Oct. 29-Nov. 3, 1993.

stories in English emphasized allegations of brutality and torture of a specific inmate who was scalded with boiling water; the stories were coded as episodic because they focused on a specific incident and not broader issues. By contrast, the lead of the Spanish language story focused on the Little Hoover Commission's investigation and policy-related issues at Pelican Bay and in the prison system generally; the Spanish story was coded as thematic. Translated verbatim the story's lead was:

> In State news yesterday, in a meeting regarding prisons, the Little Hoover State Commission questioned whether the union that represents peace officers has too much power over political decisions which affect state prisons. This is the most feared union at the State capital.

The Spanish-language story was thematically framed because it focused on issues about the prison system and prison policy as opposed to the treatment of an individual prisoner.

Although Spanish language local television news stories are framed thematically more often than stories from the English sample, when violence stories did not involve youth the news frame tended to be strictly episodic. Violence stories in the category *Youth and Violence* included community responses to violence. Violence stories in the *Violence, No Youth* category focused on the violent incident with minimal reference to the social, economic, and environmental context of violence. Episodic frames tend to reinforce individual responsibility and lead audiences to support solutions focused on the personal level.

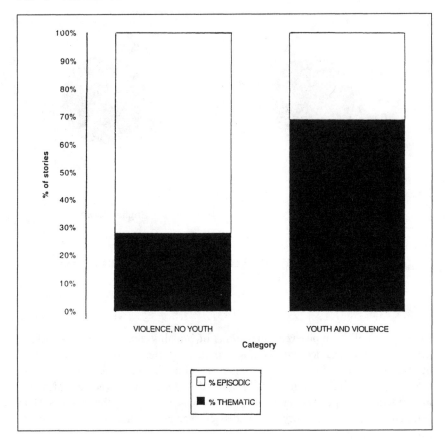

Figure 5. Measures of context: episodic and thematic news frames for
violence stories on local California Spanish language TV News,
Sept. 19-25 and Oct. 29-Nov. 2, 1993.

As a result, politicians and public institutions are insulated from responsibility
for the problem [3].

DISCUSSION

Study Limitations

The findings from this study must be viewed in light of several limitations.
First, only twenty-two hours of Spanish-language news were available to analyze
from the larger sample that included 192 hours of English news. Due in part
to the exploratory nature of the study, sample size requirements were not

predetermined. This subsample may be too small to draw conclusions from. In addition, the sample was not random, it was designed to collect news when the most stories about youth might be present.

We need much more information about the Spanish language media, as most research has been done on English language media. From this preliminary study, we were unable to ascertain if the agenda setting function of the news media applies to Spanish language television. It is difficult to assess whether Spanish news portray youth in a more negative or a positive light than that of the English language media. An important first step and recommendation are to reconceptualize this study, inquiring specifically about television news in Spanish without the limitations that arise from being a sub-sample of a larger study.

Portrayals of Youth and Violence in a Cultural Perspective

As measured by the large number of thematic news frames employed, Spanish language television news broadcasters are more likely to be reporting issues contextually rather than treating them as singular events. As such, Spanish language news may provide a promising opportunity for health practitioners to advocate for the prevention of violence and other health outcomes.

In general, local Spanish language television news journalists and others in radio and the press often see themselves as advocates with a social responsibility. Kaniss notes that "the specialized press have in common the objective of providing detailed information to their communities concerning local, national, or intentional events that affect the community, written from the perspective of the community's interests" [18]. Spanish-speaking media advocates have the opportunity to promote violence prevention policy and programs in an environment more receptive to framing issues thematically. Although Spanish language news has not played a powerful role in influencing which solutions to problems are considered by policy makers and the public, it can nevertheless be an essential partner in promoting effective prevention, public information, and community organizing campaigns.

Prevention Not Addressed

Our research indicates that thirty-eight out of the one hundred and twenty-four stories (31 percent) in this sample reported on violent crimes. Although Spanish language media is most likely to report thematically, when attention comes only after a reported incident of violence, too often prevention is left out of the equation. Prevention advocates can assist Spanish-speaking journalists in producing more accurate reports by giving them access to data and helping them understand specific epidemiological factors related to violence among youth. Reporters who know about the context in which violence occurs can ask questions related to factors such as whether the incident involved people known to each other; whether alcohol or other drugs were involved, and if so, where they were obtained; what the weapon was, how it was obtained, and whether it had been used in violence before; what the income level and employment status of victims and perpetrators were and whether those involved in the incident had histories of child abuse or battering. Violent crime reports can discuss what preventive action is being taken by law enforcement, public health agencies, and community organizations [22].

Where there are Latino communities, it is likely that there is Spanish mass media. Although seldom studied, Spanish mass media communication of health information seems to be a very important issue in future health promotion [23]. *Throughout the United States, there are communities where speaking Spanish is the norm rather than the exception. Spanish is probably the main language of family communication for the majority of the temporary or long-term immigrants and many other first-generation Latinos. Given the demographic reality of the growing Latino population in California, a study on how local television portrays youth and violence needed to include Spanish language news. This study highlights the importance of engaging the Spanish media, sharing information with them related to the multiple factors associated with violence, and outlining the policy and programmatic solutions we, as public health advocates, seek. Spanish-speaking journalists potential contribution to violence prevention and participation in mass media cannot be neglected. In the words of news anchor Aracely Martinez of the San Francisco Univision affiliate, "Many Spanish speaking journalists have strong political and social objectives, as well as a high degree of credibility with Latino audiences" [24].

ACKNOWLEDGMENT

This study was supported by The California Wellness Foundation and the California Department of Health Services, Emergency Preparedness and Injury Control Branch, as part of a statewide initiative to prevent youth violence in California.

REFERENCES

1. L. Wallack, L. Dorfman, D. Jernigan, and M. Themba, *Media Advocacy and Public Health: Power for Prevention*, Sage Publications, Newbury Park, California, 1993.
2. M. McCombs and D. Shaw, The Agenda Setting Function of Mass Media, *Public Opinion Quarterly, 36*, pp. 176-187, 1972.
3. S. Iyengar, *Is Anyone Responsible?* Chicago, 1991.
4. R. J. Gelles and M. A. Strauss, Determinants of Violence in the Family: Towards a Theoretical Integration, in *Contemporary Theories about the Family*, W. R. Burr, R. Hill, F. I. Nye, and I. L. Reiss, New York Free Press, pp. 549-581, 1979.

5. Pacific Center for Violence Prevention, *Preventing Youth Violence in California: Reinvesting Our Resources*, San Francisco, California, 1993.
6. Legislative Analyst's Office, *Crime in California*, Sacramento, California, p. 10, 1994.
7. A. Magan and N. Clark, Examining a Paradox: Does Religiosity Contribute to Positive Birth Outcomes in Mexican American Populations? *Health Education Quarterly, 22*, pp. 96-109, February 1995.
8. *Statistical Abstract of the US Bureau of the Census*, U.S. Government Printing Office, Washington, D.C., 1995.
9. C. W. Molina and M. Aguirre-Molina, *Latino Health in the US: A Growing Challenge*, American Public Health Association, pp. 3-22, 1994.
10. RAND Institute on Education and Training, *RAND Issue Paper*, September 1995.
11. M. Rodriguez and C. Brindis, Violence and Latino Youth: Prevention and Methodological Issues, *Public Health Reports*, pp. 37-47, May/June 1995.
12. P. Sorlie, E. Backlundm, N. Johnson, and E. Rogot, Mortality by Hispanic Status in the United States, *Journal of the American Medical Association, 270*, pp. 2464-2468, November 26, 1993.
13. K. Kaufman, J. Jasinski, and E. Aldarondo, Sociocultural Status and Incidence of Marital Violence in Hispanic Families, *Violence and Victims, 9*:3, 1994.
14. G. Maisonet and A. Luz, Maternal/Perinatal Health, Chapter 6, *Latino Health in the US: A Growing Challenge*, American Public Health Association, pp. 135-187, 1994.
15. W. Vega and K. Barnett, *Community-Based Health Promotion/Disease Prevention Programs for Latina/Latino Youth in California: Comparative Analysis and Policy Recommendations*, Chicano/Latino Policy Project Working Paper, Volume 3, Number 2, University of California at Berkeley, January 1996.
16. F. A. Subervi-Velez, M. Denney, A. Ozuna, and C. Quintero, *Communicating with California's Spanish Speaking Populations*, California Policy Seminar Publication, pp. 1-8, 1992.
17. A. Veciana-Suarez, *Hispanic Media, USA: A Narrative Guide to Print and Electronic Hispanic News Media in the United States*, The Media Institute, p. 3, 1987.
18. P. Kaniss, *Making Local News*, The University of Chicago Press, 1991.
19. D. Altheide, Ethnographic Content Analysis, *Qualitative Sociology, 10*:1, pp. 65-77, Spring 1987.
20. L. Dorfman, K. Woodruff, V. Chavez, and L. Wallack, *Youth and Violence on Local Television News*, under review. (The stories described here constitute 10% this larger study.)
21. Definition of Violence Modified from S. R. Lichter and D. Amundson, *A Day of TV Violence 1992 vs. 1994*, Center for Media and Public Affairs, 1994.
22. J. E. Stevens, Treating Violence as an Epidemic: An Expanded Role for Public-Health Techniques, *Technology Review*, Massachusetts Institute of Technology, pp. 22-31, August/September 1994.
23. B. Noguerol, M. Follana, A. Sicilia, and M. Sanz, Analysis of Oral Health Information in the Spanish Mass Media, *Community Dent Oral Epidemiology, 20*, pp. 15-19, 1992.
24. A. Martinez, personal communication, October 1994.

SECTION THREE

Ensuring Participation of the Community in Program Planning, Implementation, and Evaluation

The seven chapters in this section are examples of methodologies to ensure the participation of community members in the planning, implementation and evaluation of community health education programming intended to address specific sexual and reproductive health problems in Latin American and U.S. Latino communities. Chapters are organized by intervention methodologies.

Training the trainers or lay health workers is one of the community health education methodologies highlighted in several chapters, but more specifically addressed by our collaborators in the first two. The first, Chapter 13, presents an evaluation of a training program for TBAs in Guatemala that suggests the need for an additional cultural component designed to disseminate, through social marketing methodologies, the health risks of oxytocin administration to women during the birthing process. The next, Chapter 14, describes another training program for women identified as opinion leaders who were recruited to plan and implement a breast cancer prevention and education project for Latinas in California. Using a community organizing approach, the project involved Latina opinion leaders at all stages of the project development: in the process of developing a BSE film and curriculum for breast self-examination as a strategy to prevent breast cancer as well as in the actual facilitation of education sessions in their communities.

Cultural training for health providers also emerged as one of the recommendations provided in Chapter 15 after the Latina Women's Health Project from San Francisco researched strategies to increase prenatal care outreach. The establishment of social support groups and self-help networks also were recommended to conduct effective outreach and in-reach activities in the Latino community to address negative pregnancy outcomes.

The next three chapters feature participation of community residents in early phases of HIV prevention and education program planning. Chapters 16 and 17 are situated in two neighboring urban Puerto Rican communities in Western Massachusetts. Chapter 16 is based on formative ethnographic research with Puerto Rican and African American women. Designed to study the experience of sexual decision making using a 30-day trial of the female condom, this project involved women's networks and organizations in the planning and implementation phases as well as in the examination of the data collected. Data reports of this study were utilized by a group of Puerto Rican women who participated in the project to establish an HIV prevention program in 1999. Chapter 17 explains a participatory planning model for a community-based HIV education program, with emphasis on successes and challenges experienced by the planners. Using a community development framework informed by the critical thinking methodologies of the Freirian approach to community education, the authors acknowledge the push and pull of the power distribution in decision making associated with the direction of the project that often emerged in partnerships between professionals and community residents. Chapter 18 takes us to the other side of the border for an account of the politics of HIV prevention in Mexico since the early 1980s. As in other countries, community advocacy by activists and NGOs plays a significant role in the Mexican experience with HIV prevention and education.

Finally, our last contribution, Chapter 19, provides three examples of culturally-based successful interventions strategies to promote the health of Latino families in California. Designed to address the intercepts of culture, health and community systems, the three intervention models are *promotoras* (lay health promoters) as outreach workers, a neighborhood resource center called *El Centro Familiar,* and a parent safety patrol named *Padres y Madres para Seguridad.* These community health education interventions rely on the participation of community residents to serve their own information and social support needs, promote health, and protect the community. As a closing note we encourage programs to have strong community participation that supports capacity building of community members individually and collectively.

CHAPTER 13

Maternal Exhaustion as an Obstetric Complication: Implications of TBA Training

Kathleen O'Rourke

In Guatemala, the majority of births occur in homes with care provided by traditional birth attendants (TBAs). Typically, TBAs are older women who have minimal formal training, are often illiterate, and may be the only providers of maternal and child care in rural areas [1, 2]. TBAs are able to manage normal pregnancy and childbirth, but they often do not have the skills or equipment to manage high-risk obstetrical and neonatal conditions. Training of TBAs has been promoted as a means of improving maternal and neonatal outcomes, particularly in areas where there is a shortage of trained medical personnel [3].

A program to train TBAs to identify and transfer patients with specific obstetric complications was implemented in Quetzaltenango, Guatemala. This is a rural area with high rates of infant mortality in which 80 percent of deliveries are attended by TBAs. The Quetzaltenango TBA training program, conducted from March 1992 to May 1992, focused on training TBAs to identify and transfer women with high risk obstetrical situations to a referral hospital. TBAs also were trained not to administer the labor inducing drug, oxytocin, during labor and to have the mother initiate active bearing down only when she felt the urge rather than early in labor. A detailed description of the TBA training program and obstetric practices are available [4, 5].

Every culture has developed a set of birthing practices which reflect that culture's beliefs and traditions. The majority of practices by Guatemalan TBAs are either harmless or beneficial, such as delivery in a kneeling position, keeping the mother warm, abdominal massage, and inclusion of other women as support

217

during active labor. However, some practices such as the administration of oxytocin during labor and encouraging the patient to begin actively bearing down early in labor may be harmful.

TBAs administer oxytocin by injection. This method of administration can cause uterine hyperstimulation which can lead to maternal exhaustion, uterine rupture, and perinatal or maternal mortality [6]. It has been noted that increased neonatal death is associated with TBA administration of oxytocin [7]. In addition, TBAs often have women actively bearing down (pushing) from very early in labor before the cervix is fully dilated. This practice can result in increased pain and exhaustion [8].

Maternal exhaustion in the United States is seen as a result of prolonged labor and may also be associated with dehydration [9]. One study evaluated the energy expenditure of labor patients and found that normal labor did not impose high energy demands, but that prolonged labor resulted in increased energy input and maternal metabolic disturbances [10]. However, there have been limited studies identifying the cause of maternal exhaustion with different childbearing practices.

The purpose of this study was 1) to examine the relationship between maternal exhaustion with prolonged labor, oxytocin administration by TBAs, and extended bearing down; and 2) to determine if the TBA training program was effective in changing specific TBA practices.

METHODOLOGY

Selection of Communities

The department of Quetzaltenango is divided into ten health districts of which four were selected for participation in the TBA training project. Non-intervention districts were located within the same department and served as comparison groups. Selection of intervention communities was predominantly determined by location, with both intervention and non-intervention communities within four hours of the referral hospital, *Hospital General de Occidente San Juan de Dios.*

Data Collection and Analyses

Data were collected on all TBA referred women from September 1990 through April 1993. Information was obtained through medical record review and the administration of questionnaires to the women during their hospital stay. Data were collected on sociodemographic variables, obstetrical history, prenatal events, and obstetrical complications. Additional data included a description of the reason for the referral, the timeframe in which the TBA decided to refer the mother, the time the mother arrived at the hospital, treatment given to the mother by the TBA and at the hospital, and maternal and neonatal outcomes. Data collection were taken during three periods corresponding to TBA training: pre-training ($n = 225$), during training ($n = 64$), and post-training ($n = 556$). The overall study design utilized two groups, intervention and non-intervention communities, to evaluate the effect of the training program on TBA practices. Evaluation of the effect of the TBA training program on TBA practices was limited to pre- to post-training periods, with data during the training period excluded ($n = 781$).

Statistical Tests

Two types of statistical tests were used: univariate to identify associations and differences between groups and multivariate to determine program effect controlling for other variables. Univariate analyses were performed in SAS and multivariate analyses in STATA [11].

Chi-square tests were performed on univariate analyses of associations; odds ratios were calculated separately for intervention and non-intervention communities for comparisons between communities. The Breslow-Day test of homogeneity of odds ratios [12] was performed to determine if there were significant differences in odds ratio obtained for the two communities.

Logistic regression modeling was used to determine the effect of the TBA training program on changes in TBA practices. Model assessment was performed using the Hosmer-Lemeshow goodness-of-fit testing and plots of diagnostic statistics [13]. Four diagnostic statistics were utilized: leverage, change in Pearson chi square, change in Deviance chi-square, and standardized change in Delta Beta.

RESULTS

Identification of Obstetrical Complications in Referred Women

Table 1 presents the frequency and percentage of hospital diagnoses of patients referred by TBAs. These diagnoses were not mutually exclusive, and one patient may have had several assigned. In approximately 25 percent of the cases, no complications were identified and the diagnosis of normal delivery was assigned. The most common prenatal diagnoses were prolonged labor (22.8 percent) and malposition (20 percent) and the most common postpartum diagnosis was retained placenta (13.6 percent). Irregular labor, which resulted in a normal delivery about half of the time, occurred in 10.6 percent of the women, while preterm labor was less common and diagnosed in only 8.3 percent of the women (Table 1).

Reasons for TBA Referrals

TBA reasons for referrals to the hospital (TBA diagnosis) were identified through maternal interviews. Most women who identified a specific reason for

Table 1. Most Common Hospital Diagnoses of
Women Referred to Quetzaltenango
Hospital by TBAs ($n = 845$)

Diagnosis	Number	Percent
Normal delivery	215	25.4
Prolonged labor (>12 hrs)	204	24.1
Malpresentation		
Breech	80	9.5
Transverse	87	10.3
Compound	2	0.2
Retained placenta	115	13.59
Preterm labor	70	8.3
Irregular labor	90	10.6

the referral indicated that they had a good understanding of the reason. Only 1.7 percent of the women indicated they were unaware of the reason for the referral, while 7.2 percent only knew that the TBA felt the infant could not be delivered safely at home but not the specific reason (Table 2).

The most common TBA diagnoses were malpresentation (19.0 percent), maternal exhaustion (16.2 percent), and retained placenta (13.7 percent). TBA reasons were not mutually exclusive, and women could be referred for more than one reason.

Maternal exhaustion is a relatively common diagnosis which may be the result of birthing practices as opposed to a pre-existing condition. In this study, TBAs identified 137 women as having maternal exhaustion and eighty-five with prolonged labor (Table 2). Twenty-six of these women were identified by TBAs as having both maternal exhaustion and prolonged labor (data not shown).

In the univariate analysis, maternal exhaustion was significantly associated with three factors: prolonged labor, extended bearing down, and oxytocin administration (Table 3). Diagnosis of prolonged labor was based on time (> 12 hours) before the onset of labor and delivery and was not dependent on the TBA diagnosis. Active pushing for an extended period of time (> 2 hours) is very common. Most women (93.28 percent) with maternal exhaustion pushed > 2 hours as compared with 55.83 percent of women without this condition. TBA oxytocin administration was also more likely in women with maternal exhaustion, 30.37 percent as compared to 16.98 percent. In addition, women with maternal exhaustion were more likely to have prolonged labor, 40.44 percent versus 21.05 percent.

To determine the significance of each individual factor on maternal exhaustion, a multivariate analysis was conducted (Table 4). Since number of pregnancies

Table 2. Most Common TBA Reasons for
Women Referred to Quetzaltenango
Hospital by TBAs ($n = 845$)

Reason	Number	Percent
Malpresentation		
Breech	82	9.7
Transverse	79	9.3
Maternal exhaustion	137	16.2
Retained placenta	116	13.7
Prolonged labor (>12 hrs)	85	10.0
Mother did not know	14	1.7
Could not deliver at home	61	7.2

Table 3. Percent Women with Maternal Exhaustion and
Three Associated Risk Conditions ($n = 845$)

Variable	Maternal exhaustion ($n = 137$) n (%)	No material exhaustion ($n = 708$) n (%)	p-Value
Push >2 hrs[a]	125 (93.28)	388 (55.83)	<0.001
TBA oxytocin use[b]	41 (30.37)	119 (16.98)	<0.001
Labor >12 hrs	55 (40.44)	149 (21.05)	<0.001

[a]$n = 829$
[b]$n = 836$

Table 4. Statistics for the Fitted Logistic Regression
Analysis of Maternal Exhaustion

Parameter	Estimate	Std. error	p-Value	Odds ratio	95% CI
Intercept	3.28	0.56	<0.001		
Pushing >2 hrs	2.27	0.36	<0.001	9.66	4.8, 19.5
Oxytocin	−0.21	0.22	0.356	0.813	0.5, 1.2
Prolonged labor	0.70	0.21	<0.001	2.02	1.3, 3.0

Note: Log likelihood = −318.04, Chi-square p-value = <0.001; 2[LL(N)-LL(0)] = 93.735, 2df; Hosmer-Lemeshow Goodness of Fit = 5.42, 8df, p = 0.7122.

was a potential confounder, this variable was included in the initial analysis, but it was not statistically significant so it was removed.

Pushing for > 2 hours was the strongest predictor of maternal exhaustion. Oxytocin administration was no longer significant and prolonged labor remained a significant factor. The Hosmer-Lemeshow test indicated good fit of the model and no extreme observations were identified with diagnostic statistics.

Effect of TBA Training on TBA Practices

To identify if the TBA training program had an impact on TBA practices of oxytocin administration and encouraging extended pushing, the frequency of these practices were evaluated before and after the training program. Comparisons were conducted separately for both intervention and non-intervention communities (Tables 5 and 6).

Table 5. Oxytocin Administration by TBAs for Women in
Intervention and Non-Intervention Communities during
Pre- and Post-Training Periods ($n = 772$)

Community	Pre-training n (%)	Post-training n (%)	Odds ratio	p-Value
Intervention ($n = 291$)	58 (73.42)	178 (83.96)	1.896	0.041
Non-intervention ($n = 481$)	114 (78.08)	273 (81.49)	1.236	0.386

Note: Breslow-Day test for Homogeneity of Odds Ratios between Communities, Chi-square = 1.148, 1df; p-value = 0.284.

Table 6. Extended Pushing for Women in
Intervention and Non-Intervention Communities during
Pre- and Post-Training Periods ($n = 765$)

Community	Pre-training n (%)	Post-training n (%)	Odds ratio	p-Value
Intervention ($n = 189$)	54 (70.13)	135 (63.38)	0.737	0.287
Non-intervention ($n = 475$)	83 (59.29)	200 (59.70)	1.017	0.933

Note: Breslow-Day test for Homogeneity of Odds Ratios between Communities, Chi-square = 0.837, 1df; p-value = 0.360.

The TBA training program had no impact on the above TBA practices as indicated by the Breslow-Day tests (Tables 5 and 6). In fact, oxytocin administration increased significantly for trained TBAs during the post-intervention period but there were no significant differences between the communities (Table 5). The incidence of extended pushing remained fairly stable in both intervention and non-intervention communities (Table 6). Consequently, the program was not effective in changing TBA practices.

DISCUSSION

Childbirth is affected by the cultural system of a society and may best be understood within a bio-social framework as identified by Jordan [8]. Although the physiology of birth is relatively uniform throughout the world, the act of childbearing varies greatly from one culture to another. TBAs are members of a given culture and their childbirth practices reflect their culture. In addition, women within a given community expect TBAs to participate in specific practices which they feel are culturally important. If TBAs deviate from the culturally accepted practices, women may seek other practitioners who are more in line with their expectations.

This chapter examined the diagnosis of maternal exhaustion as a reason for TBA referral of women to a hospital. In the United States, maternal exhaustion is generally viewed as a result of prolonged labor, possibly the result of underlying dysfunctional labor [6]. Although there is limited information about obstetrical practices of Guatemala TBAs, birthing practices in a similar cultural group in southern Mexico have been studied [8]. It was found that Mayan women were instructed by TBAs to initiate bearing down early in labor because it is believed that labor is hard work and that women should play an active role.

In this study, while maternal exhaustion is strongly associated with prolonged labor, there is an even stronger association with prolonged bearing down. It is possible that some other factor, such as dysfunctional labor, contributed to maternal exhaustion and that factor led TBAs to encourage extended bearing down. However, this does not appear to be the sole cause as it was clear that extended bearing down was occurring even when labor was not prolonged and in these cases dysfunctional labor was not likely.

Oxytocin administration by TBAs has been associated with increased rates of perinatal mortality [7]. In this study there was no association between oxytocin administration and perinatal mortality (data not shown), possibly because the sample consisted of women with a higher risk of other complications. However, based on previous associations, it was recommended in the training program that TBAs not administer oxytocin to their patients.

The fact that the TBA training program was not effective in changing specific TBA practices may be due to community expectations. A survey conducted in Sacatepequez, Guatemala, found that women expected TBAs to administer oxytocin and that oxytocin administration often occurred at the request of mothers [14]. Thus, TBAs were providing the obstetrical care which their patients expected and was in accordance with their own beliefs. Consequently, TBA training programs alone may not be sufficient to change such deeply held beliefs.

An alternative method may be to develop a social marketing approach in which the dangers of oxytocin administration are explained to both TBAs and mothers. Social marketing focuses on implementation and control of programs seeking to increase the acceptability of a social idea or practice [15]. Social marketing has been used successfully for a variety of health programs, including condom use to prevent HIV, oral rehydration therapy, and anti-malarial drugs [16-18]. This type of approach may be more effective because not only the TBAs but also the mothers will be more aware of potential birthing complications, and cultural norms may be more amenable to change.

However, it is essential that such a program be developed within the cultural framework of the communities. For example, if mothers feel that their contractions need greater force, this need should be recognized. Other culturally appropriate methodologies should be encouraged, such as massage or upright birthing positions, depending upon current community practices.

ACKNOWLEDGMENTS

This study was supported by a grant from MotherCare/John Snow, Inc., under USAID Contract #DPE 5966-Z-00-8030-00, and INCAP/PAHO. The contents of this chapter do not necessarily reflect the views or policies of the U.S. Agency for International Development or of MotherCare/JSI.

REFERENCES

1. B. E. Kwast, Midwives: Key Rural Health Workers in Maternity Care, *International Journal of Gynaecology and Obstetrics, 38*(Suppl), pp. S9-S15, 1992.
2. E. Leedam, Traditional Birth Attendants, *International Journal of Gynaecology and Obstetrics, 23*:4, pp. 249-274, 1985.
3. A. Mangay-Maglacas, Traditional Birth Attendants, in *Health Care of Women and Children in Developing Countries,* H. Wallace and K. Giri (eds.), The Third Party Publishing Co., Oakland, pp. 229-241, 1990.
4. B. Schieber et al., Risk Factor Analysis of Peri-Neonatal Mortality in Rural Guatemala, *Bulletin of Pan American Health Organization, 28*:3, pp. 229-238, 1994.
5. K. O'Rourke, An Evaluation of a TBA Training Program: Its Effect on TBA Practices and Perinatal Mortality, *Bol Oficina Sanit Panam,* 1995.
6. H. Oxorn, *Human Labor and Birth,* Appleton-Century-Crofts, E. Norwalk, Connecticut, 1986.
7. A. Bartlett and M. P. deBocaletti, Intrapartum and Neonatal Mortality in a Traditional Indigenous Community in Rural Guatemala, *Acta Paediatric Scandinavica, 80*:3, pp. 288-296, 1991.

8. B. Jordan, *Birth in Four Cultures* (4th Edition), Waveland Press, Inc., Prospect Heights, p. 235, 1993.
9. J. Huey, Monitoring of Uterine Activity, *Clinics in Obstetrics and Gynaecology, 6*:2, pp. 315-324, 1979.
10. M. Katz et al., Energy Expenditure in Normal Labor, *Israel Journal of Medical Sciences, 26*:5, pp. 254-257, 1990.
11. R. Cody and J. Smith, *Applied Statistics and the SAS Programming Language* (3rd Edition), North-Holland, New York, 1991.
12. K. Rothman, *Modern Epidemiology,* Little, Brown and Co., Boston, 1986.
13. D. Hosmer and S. Lemeshow, *Applied Logistic Regression,* John Wiley & Sons, New York, 1989.
14. A. Bartlett, M. deBocaletti, and M. P. deBocaletti, Use of Oxytocin and Other Injections during Labor in Rural Municipalities of Guatemala: Results of a Randomized Survey, *Working Paper #22,* MotherCare Project, Arlington, 1993.
15. P. Kotler and G. Zaltman, Social Marketing: An Approach to Planned Social Change, *Journal of Marketing, 35,* pp. 3-12, 1971.
16. P. Koul et al., Evaluation of Social Marketing of Oral Rehydration Therapy, *Indian Pediatrics, 28*:9, pp. 1013-1016, 1991.
17. N. Soderlund et al., The Costs of HIV Prevention Strategies in Developing Countries, *Bulletin of the World Health Organization, 71*:5, pp. 595-604, 1993.
18. S. Foster, Pricing, Distribution, and Use of Antimalarial Drugs, *Bulletin of the World Health Organization, 69*:3, pp. 349-363, 1991.

CHAPTER 14

Cuidaremos: The HECO Approach to Breast Self-Examination

Kate Lorig
Esperanza Garcia Walters

This chapter is the outcome of the work of two nurse health educators who combined the skills of their two professions to develop, implement, and evaluate a health education, community organization program model aimed at facilitating behavior change in a hard-to-reach minority population. Their project, entitled Cuidaremos (we will care for ourselves), was an attempt to get Spanish speaking women to practice breast self-examination. The program utilizes the acronym HECO for Health Education-Community Organization.

BACKGROUND

In 1975, the Santa Clara Unit of the American Cancer Society (ACS) formed a Special Populations Committee of ethnic minority women and others to function as an advisory committee to a cervical cancer screening project for minority populations operated by the Santa Clara County Health Department. The county is approximately fifty miles south of San Francisco and encompasses twenty separate cities including Palo Alto and San Jose. Nearly 20 percent of the county's 1.2 million population is Spanish speaking, Spanish surnamed.

The committee, largely selected by one ACS staff member, was composed mainly of Chicana[1] women who held various professional and semi-professional positions with such diverse organizations as migrant education, neighborhood

---

[1] A term in common use in the United States for women of Mexican descent.

health centers, community colleges, and agricultural extension nutrition programs. What is important to note is that most of these women had a long history of
working with each other on various health and social service projects in the
county. Quite literally, they had professionally grown up together since the early
days of the War on Poverty.

After meeting for almost a year, the committee began to discuss ways in which
it could have an impact on the breast screening procedures of Chicana women.
This interest was further stimulated as two of the committee members had had
mastectomies. During the ensuing discussions, the lack of acceptable Spanish
health education materials was pin-pointed as a problem. While some materials
did exist, they were, and continue to be, translations from English and dubbed
films which had little cultural relevance to the Chicana population. In a rather
wishful way, the women talked of producing their own film.

From this inauspicious beginning, the Cuidaremos project and the HECO
approach were born. Through a series of circumstances, the committee applied
for and received Macomber Legacy funds from the California Division of the
American Cancer Society. The funds were to be used to create a film and
implement a county wide health education project with broad-based community
support. The following is a detailed description of the model which was
developed and implemented to accomplish these objectives.

THE HECO APPROACH

HECO, pronounced echo, is a seven-step program model which can be
utilized with many groups in the United States and in other countries (see
Figure 1). Drawing in part upon standard health education planning guidelines,
it incorporates additional elements believed to increase its utility in gaining
health behavior changes in hard to reach populations. It should be noted that
this approach is designed specifically to reach late accepters of new health
behaviors. To use it on populations which will easily change behaviors would
be an over-kill.

Step 1: Identification of a Problem

Ideally, problem identification is achieved through a community-wide needs
assessment utilizing the delphi or similar needs assessment technique [1-3].
However, all too often, the problem is identified by special interest agencies such
as the American Cancer Society or by the availability of federal funds. It should
be noted that funding is sometimes, but not always, based on need. Consequently,
many programs in health education are based largely on the needs of the funding
agencies not on the needs of the population to be educated.

In Santa Clara County, the Cuidaremos project was based on the felt needs
of a small group of community women. The authors do not believe that breast

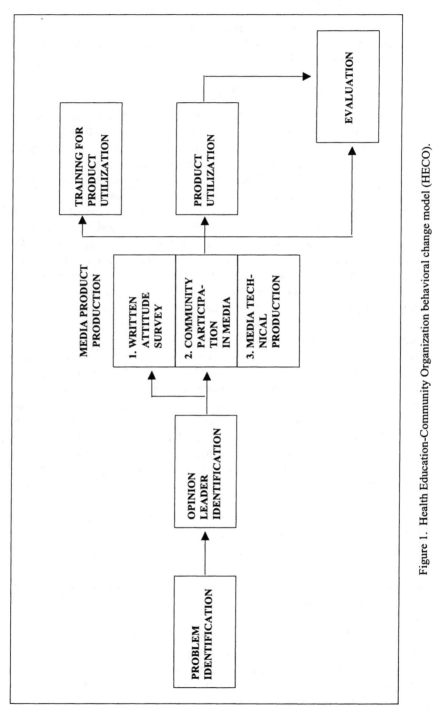

Figure 1. Health Education-Community Organization behavioral change model (HECO).

self-examination would be the first health priority of Chicana women. However, it seemed to serve the needs of the Special Populations Committee, the local ACS unit and finally was fundable.

Step 2: Opinion Leader Identification

The HECO approach is based on the concept of gatekeepers or opinion leaders and their importance in influencing the acceptance of new health practices [4]. Rogers suggests a method for identifying opinion leaders which was used by the Cuidaremos staff [5]. Each Chicana on the Special Populations Committee was asked to name five to ten other Chicanas whom they felt might be health opinion leaders. Each of the women named was then contacted and asked to name two or three persons from whom she sought advice regarding health problems. All the women named were then contacted and asked the same question. A total of more than three hundred women were contacted either in person or by phone over a period of three weeks. From those contacted, approximately eighty women were named two or more times. These women were then designated as opinion leaders. It should be noted that only two members of the Special Populations Committee, both community health workers were designated as opinion leaders. This is important as all too often leaders of minority communities serve on committees as representatives of their communities and their work is taken as representative of that community. From the Cuidaremos experience, it can be seen that it is important to distinguish between what Merton calls local and cosmopolitan influentials [6]. Local influentials are those who are interested in knowing as many people as possible and tend to join groups as a means of extending their personal relationships. On the other hand, cosmopolitan influentials are those who see themselves in the light of the greater society. They are concerned with the quality of their relationships and tend to join organizations because of their activities. The HECO approach depends on the use of both types of influentials. The planners, if possible, should be cosmopolitan influentials while the opinion leaders/trainers should be local influentials.

Step 3: Community Survey

To build an effective health education program, it is necessary to first identify a problem of felt need as outlined in step one. Then it is necessary to determine the prevailing community attitudes, beliefs, and practices around the health issue. In family planning this is often referred to as a KAP (knowledge, attitudes, and practice) survey.

Thus, the third step of the Cuidaremos project was the development, implementation, and analysis of a survey. Opinion leaders assisted first in devising a survey instrument and secondly in administering the instrument to nearly three hundred households randomly selected in five census tracts with a high percentage of Spanish speaking, Spanish surname population. These census tracts were representative of the varying geographic areas of the county. This survey dealt with such issues as the respondents beliefs about cancer, their practice of breast self-examination and frequency of pap smears, their attitudes toward male and female physicians, their attitude toward non-Spanish-speaking physicians, their use of alternate health care providers, and finally demographic data such as age, place of birth, level of education, etc.

While it will not be possible to report all of the findings from this survey, some are of special interest. Not surprisingly, the women showed a strong preference for female physicians. More surprisingly, there was no indication of a high trust level of folk practitioners such as curanderos, although there are several curanderos in the areas. Rather, the primary, non-physician source of health care was the pharmacist. This latter has implication in health education campaigns and should be explored further.

Finally, the opinions of the women did not vary with age. Thus, younger and older women seemed to have very similar opinions. The major variance was place of birth. Those women born outside of the United States, mainly in Mexico, tended to be more traditional than those women born in the United States, regardless of age. Further details of this survey are reported elsewhere [7].

Step 4: Media Production

The centerfold of the HECO approach is the production of a media product which reflects the community norms and values. This can be as simple as the production of a pamphlet. However, because of the community involvement, it is suggested that the media product be a slide tape show, a video tape, or a 16 mm film.

As adequate funding had been obtained, the Cuidaremos project produced a videocassette which was later transferred in both 8 mm and 16 mm film. Days were spent with a mobile video unit in taping Chicana women in the community. Special attempts were made to recruit women from varying socioeconomic levels and geographic areas. Again, opinion leaders assisted staff in developing the interview questions and recruiting women to be interviewed for the film. Women were interviewed in migrant labor camps, clinics, and neighborhood parks. The interview questions were very similar to those of the survey.

The results of the household survey were then utilized in editing the thirteen hours of videotape to seventeen minutes. Scenes were selected which portrayed attitudes and values reflective of the survey results.

It is important to understand the purpose of the film and how it differs from traditional health education films. The objective of most health films is to give information. They teach how to drive safely, why one should eat a balanced diet, or how to examine one's breasts. The film in the HECO approach is developed to reflect community norms about an issue. There is no attempt to give instruction. It is important that both sides of controversial issues are discussed, in accordance with the work of Hovland, Janis, and Kelley [8]. Thus, only thirty seconds of the Cuidaremos film is devoted to a woman examining her breasts. During the rest of the film, women talk about health, health care providers, cancer, their fears, and experiences. One woman says cancer means death, another says it is a disease that can be triumphed over, etc.

Another unusual feature of the film is that it is both Spanish and English. Thus, some interviews are in Spanish with English subtitles and others are in English with Spanish subtitles. This is in keeping with the realities of the community where some women are more comfortable in one language and others in the other. In fact, there is one interview which starts in English, switches to Spanish, and then switches back to English, reflecting a common street phenomena.

In review, the purpose of the media piece is to reflect the attitudes of the community and most importantly, to serve as the basis for group discussion. At no time was it conceived that the film would "stand alone." This has since caused some problems as many groups wish to use the film without a trained facilitator. When this is done, the purpose of the whole project is lost and the film is subject to criticism. This was best shown when it was entered in a national nursing media contest. The critique from the judges was that it received low rating because it wasted too much time on talking and not enough on teaching people how to examine their breasts. This again reflects the common mistake of nursing which seems to emphasize giving information.

Step 5: Training of Community Facilitators

Forty Spanish-speaking women completed between twelve and eighteen hours of training to conduct breast self-examination classes in the community. Many of these women had previously been identified as opinion leaders. In addition, several women were friends of opinion leaders and others were enrolled in the community health work program at a local community college.

The training consisted of four main content areas:

1. Information about cancer and specifically about breast cancer and breast self-examination. This information was kept at a very simple level. A great deal of time was spent talking about the myths and realities associated with the word cancer.
2. The facilitators received specific instructions about how to conduct a community class including format, leading a discussion, and the use of audio-visual equipment. In addition, they all had an opportunity to practice teaching in a class setting.
3. Time was devoted to identifying and discussing community resources which deal with cancer such as the American Cancer Society, the local health department, and neighborhood clinics where free or low cost Pap tests were available.

4. Instructions and discussions were presented on how to form a breast self-examination class.

One of the more unique aspects of this program is that each facilitator was responsible for finding her own group to teach. Many women invited friends and neighbors into their homes. Other women gave their classes at church meetings, adult education classes, and Head Start parent meetings. Of the forty leaders trained, only one failed to organize and give at least one class. These classes ranged in size from four or five to over fifty women. In all, more than fifteen hundred women were reached within six months of the completion of the film.

Step 6: Giving Community Classes

As mentioned, the facilitators were responsible for forming and giving their own classes. These classes all followed the same format, based on getting maximum adoption of the new practice. With very little introduction, the film was shown. Following this, the leaders asked one or two open-ended questions such as "with what in the film did you agree or disagree?" It was not unusual for this one question to elicit twenty to forty minutes of discussion about cancer, what cancer meant to the women attending, personal experiences, etc. In short, it provided the base for conducting an attitude forum. No leader ever reported having to use more than three questions to elicit this type of a discussion.

Almost always at some point in the discussion the women in the class asked how to do a breast self-examination. If the question did not come up, the group leader was instructed to ask after about twenty minutes of discussion if the group would like to learn. The facilitator then demonstrated breast self-examination on herself through her clothing. By being an opinion leader, filling a group-expressed need, and by modeling the desired behavior, she became a very powerful change agent. She also sanctioned the touching of the breasts which is often not considered to be an acceptable behavior among Chicanas.

Following the demonstration, the leader asked all the women present to stand and to examine their own breasts with her. Thus, she provided the trial which Beal and Bohlen find so important in accomplishing behavior change [9]. It is interesting to note that those facilitators who had a problem getting women to take part in a return demonstration were those who themselves showed hesitance. In this case, at least, it was true that the action met the expectation. The class ended by giving information about free and low cost cervical screening clinics and answering questions.

At the inception of the program, many of the trainers who had seen a traditional breast self-examination class, wanted to use another film to demonstrate breast self-examination. Others wanted to use the "Betsy" breast model. While this was not prohibited, it was highly discouraged, because it has been shown that self-modeling brings about more behavior change than the use of artificial models [10]. We found that for the first class, additional aides were often checked out.

These were seldom used and rarely mentioned again. Only two of the facilitators continued to ask for another film or the "Betsy" breast models.

Step 7: Evaluation

The project had a strong commitment to the evaluation of its educational programs. Not only is this the only way of knowing if one is having any effect, but it is also necessary to justify continuing and expanding funding. In the HECO approach, as with most health education programs, the item to be evaluated is the adoption of the desired behavior. According to Sackett and Haynes [11] one of the best ways to determine compliance is to ask the people who are supposed to be doing the complying. There are many faults with this method including a possible high aquiescent response rate. However, possibly it is all that can be hoped for when dealing with a behavior as personal as breast examination.

Before the Cuidaremos classes, women were asked to complete a card for the purpose of obtaining base line data regarding their practice of breast self-examination, cervical screening, etc. Six weeks after having attended a class, these same women were contacted by phone and asked questions to determine if they had practiced breast self-examination, taught the technique to anyone else, or had a Pap smear during the six-week period.

The short-term follow-up of the results tended to be very encouraging. At the beginning of the classes, 30 percent of the women indicated that they were examining their breasts. This was raised to 76 percent six weeks later. Ware reports a 10 percent acquiescent response set in lower socioeconomic groups [12]. Even if this figure were doubled, it can be seen that the HECO approach seemed to have a substantial effect on the eighty-six women who were included in the evaluation. These conclusions gain more significance when it is considered that we were dealing with a hard-to-reach segment of the population.

The HECO approach, thus far, has been used in only one major trial. We are encouraged by the community response and our preliminary evaluation. The authors would be most interested in hearing from others who are trying to utilize this or similar methodologies.

ACKNOWLEDGMENTS

Work conducted at the Santa Clara County American Cancer Society; funding by the Macomber Legacy, California Division, American Cancer Society.

REFERENCES

1. A Van de Ven and A. Delbecq, The Nominal Group as a Research Instrument for Exploratory Health Studies, *American Journal of Public Health*, pp. 337-342, March 1972.

2. K. Lorig, An Overview of Needs Assessment Tools for Continuing Education, *Nurse Educator, 2*:2, pp. 12-16, 1977.
3. N. Dalkey, Use of the Delphi Technique in Educational Planning, *Educational Resources Agency Herold, 4*:2, 1970.
4. K. Lewin and P. Grabbe, Conduct, Knowledge and Acceptance of New Values, *Journal of Social Issues, 1,* pp. 53-64, 1945.
5. E. Rogers and F. Shoemaker, *Communication of Innovations,* The Free Press, New York, 1971.
6. K. Merton, *Social Theory and Social Structures,* The Free Press, New York, 1968.
7. H. Garcia-Manzanedo, E. Walters, and K. Lorig, Health and Illness Perceptions of the Chicana, M. Melville (ed.), *Twice a Minority,* C. V. Mosby Company, St. Louis, 1980.
8. C. Hovland, I. Janis, and H. Kelley, *Communication and Persuasion,* Yale University Press, New Haven, Connecticut, 1953.
9. G. Beal and J. Bohlen, *The Diffusion Process: Special Report No. 18,* Agricultural Extension Service, Iowa State College, Ames, Iowa, 1957.
10. A. Bandura, E. Blanchard, and B. Ritter, Relative Efficiency of Desensitization and Modeling Therapeutic Approaches for Inducing Behavioral, Affective and Attitude Changes, *Journal of Personality and Social Psychology, 13,* pp. 173-179, 1969.
11. D. Sackett and R. B. Haynes, *Compliance with Therapeutic Regimes,* The Johns Hopkins University Press, Baltimore, 1976.
12. J. Ware, Effects of Acquiescent Response Set on Patient Satisfaction Ratings, *Medical Care, 16*:4, pp. 327-336, 1978.

CHAPTER 15

Improving Access to Prenatal Care for Latina Immigrants in California: Outreach and Inreach Strategies

Sylvia Guendelman
Sandra Witt

Prenatal care is widely recognized as a cost effective intervention that is associated with improved pregnancy outcomes [1]. The Institute of Medicine recently completed a thorough analysis of the major deterrents to early prenatal care in the United States. It concluded that expanding access to prenatal care among underserved populations generally depends on the removal of financial and legal barriers to care, increased health systems capacity, improved institutional attitudes and effective outreach programs [2].

Prenatal outreach is particularly necessary for difficult-to-reach women in areas with high concentrations of multi-ethnic populations and indigent immigrant groups such as San Francisco. In the city and county of San Francisco 75 percent of births in 1987 were to members of racial/ethnic minority groups. Nineteen percent of these births were to Latina (i.e. Hispanic) women and 77 percent of Latino infants had foreign-born mothers. Among the foreign-born, a large proportion are newcomers from Mexico seeking economic opportunity or Central American refugees fleeing political unrest. Many immigrants tend to receive little or no prenatal care. For instance, of all births to Latina women in 1987, 21.5 percent had no early prenatal care (first trimester) and over 5 percent had third trimester onset or no prenatal care whatsoever [3]. Because currently one of every four births in San Francisco and one of every three births in California is to a Latina woman, improving access to prenatal care through outreach programs can have pervasive implications [3, 4].

There is a paucity of data on prenatal care outreach to the Latino population. Several studies show an underutilization of prenatal care and other health services by Latinos, indicating that structural, cultural and socio-demographic factors are important barriers to care. Major obstacles include the lack of health insurance, poverty, language barriers, a cultural orientation that views pregnancy as a natural rather than a medical event, lack of bicultural health providers, low education and an undocumented status [5-8].

To assess outreach strategies which could ensure early prenatal care for low income immigrants in San Francisco, the Latina Women's Prenatal Care Project was undertaken in 1990 [9]. The project sought the views and perceptions concerning barriers to early prenatal care of both the health care providers to Latina women in the county as well as the Latina consumers of health care. Additionally, both groups were asked to suggest improvements to prenatal health outreach programs. Outreach was defined to include "various ways of identifying pregnant women and linking them to prenatal care (case finding) and services that offer support and assistance to help women remain in care once enrolled (social support)" [2].

This chapter focuses on the results of the Latina Women's Project. It examines outreach strategies that can reduce barriers to prenatal care. In addition to recommending strategies that reach out to the community, this review suggests that complementary "inreach" strategies which modify provider attitudes and organizational practices can be effective in reducing barriers and ensuring improved usage of prenatal care in the immigrant Latino population.

METHODOLOGY

A case study method using focus groups was adopted for this project. Focus group interviewing is a qualitative technique aimed at uncovering the feelings, opinions and perceptions of target populations concerning a specific problem, experience, service or product [10-12]. Participants are encouraged to express their beliefs in small, homogeneous groups, following a semi-structured interview guideline.

Twelve focus group sessions were conducted with sixty-seven participants between April and September, 1990. Initially, providers of prenatal care and health promoters in each of the five main institutions serving pregnant Latina women in San Francisco were contacted. The participating institutions were The Mission Neighborhood Health Center, San Francisco General Hospital, St. Luke's Hospital, St. Mary's Hospital and the Good Samaritan Center. Each institution was requested to invite to the discussion sessions those providers who are most involved in delivering care to Latina pregnant women. A purposive sample of twenty-three providers, 87 percent of which were female and 57 percent of Latino origin, including seven lay health providers, four nurses, four social workers, three health educators and two nutritionists attended the discussion sessions. Each session lasted approximately one hour and included from three to eight participants.

Separate sessions were held with Latina consumers of prenatal care. With the assistance of the providers from the main institutions, thirty-four women were recruited and were paid an $18 incentive for a two-hour session. Women were selected if they 1) identified themselves as Latinas, 2) had San Francisco residency, 3) had delivered a baby within the last eighteen months, 4) were at least seventeen years old, and, 5) had valid information on timing and quantity of prenatal care available through participating agency records. Separate sessions were conducted with thirteen documented and twenty-one undocumented women, and, whenever, possible, women who had started prenatal care early (i.e. first four months) were invited to join separate groups from women who had delayed (fifth month or later) or no care. A total of seventeen "early care" and seventeen "late care" starters were interviewed. These groups were selected because for the most part they typified the women utilizing maternity services. Demographic characteristics of the consumers of care are presented in Table 1. The data were obtained from a brief survey administered prior to each session.

The focus group sessions were led by three bilingual, female health professionals highly experienced with the interviewing technique. Both providers and consumers of prenatal care were systematically requested to identify and explain perceived barriers to effective usage of care by Latina women. Additionally, both groups were invited to suggest recommendations for improvements. Content analysis was used to analyze the transcribed tape recorded responses and to compare providers and consumers' perception of barriers and recommendations for action.

RESULTS

The mean age of the participants in the consumer focus groups was 26.3 (S.D. 5.4). On average, they had 9.6 (S.D. 3.5) years of education and had lived in the Bay Area for 4.9 years (S.D. 4.4). Most were married housewives and almost half were primigravidas. Although 54.4 percent had obtained some health insurance during pregnancy, only 24.4 percent kept it after the infant was born. Most identified public hospitals and community clinics as their regular sources of care.

Perceptions of Barriers to Prenatal Care

While specific expression varied in and among focus groups, the principal barriers to effective utilization of prenatal care identified by the consumers closely resembled those identified by the providers. As Figure 1 indicates, low socio-economic status, and immigrant status, cultural attitudes and beliefs and

Table 1. Socio-Demographic Characteristics of Consumer
Focus Group Participants

Characteristics	$N = 33$	Mean (S.D.) or %
Age (in years)	33	26.3 (5.4)
Education (in years)	33	9.6 (3.5)
Length of time in Bay Area (in years)	30	4.9 (4.4)
Marital status	31	
Single, never married		12.9%
Married		77.4%
Free union		3.2%
Separated or divorced		6.5%
In the labor force	33	0.0%
Number of pregnancies	33	
1		48.5%
2		18.2%
3 or more		33.3%
With insurance last 12 months	33	24.2%
Public		87.5%
Private		12.5%
With insurance during pregnancy		54,5%
Public		94.4%
Private		5.6%
Regular source of care for mother	33	
Public hospital		54.5%
Community clinic		24.2%
Private hospital		3.0%
Private physician		—
Self care		18.2%
Regular source of care for child	32	
Public hospital		40.6%
Community clinic		34.4%
Private hospital		12.5%
Private physician		9.4%
Home care		3.1%
Has a confidant in the area	33	78.8%
Primary confidant	25	
Spouse		72.0%
Relative		12.0%
Friend		12.0%
Therapist		4.0%

institutional constraints were perceived as the main deterrents. These similarities notwithstanding, providers were more likely than consumers to focus on a low education, fear of deportation and feelings of isolation among newcomers as factors that delay the use of prenatal care. Providers also tended to identify personality and cultural attributes, such as female modesty, passivity and low self esteem, as more severe or frequent barriers to care.

1. Socio-Economic Barriers

Both consumers and providers agreed that lower incomes and lack of health insurance compounded by the absence of legal documentation constitute important barriers to seeking early prenatal care. People just cannot afford care. As one provider commented "Money is the initial concern. Women think that if they wait until the last minute it is going to be cheaper." Latina patients are generally conscientious about paying their bills. Yet when huge bills start accumulating they get scared and respond by delaying or dropping out of care. Several participants mentioned that women are afraid of ignoring the hospital financial statements and waiting for Medicaid because of the possibility of detection by Immigration and Naturalization Services. The fear of running into problems with Immigration and jeopardizing their chances of legalizing their status is also sometimes reinforced by immigration lawyers. Attorneys counsel families against obtaining public assistance to "keep their records clean." Yet this discourse clearly contradicts that of health professionals which urges women to apply for Medicaid. Such conflicting messages may help to explain why, despite changes in the California law which now provides Medicaid coverage of prenatal care for the undocumented, this group still seems to avoid public insurance. Lack of health insurance is common among Latina patients and many who don't want to rely on public assistance have no recourse but to pay for expenses out of pocket.

Low educational levels are perceived as another deterrent to prenatal care utilization by many providers. Some suggest that Latina women are neither trained nor accustomed to ask questions about their health or bodies. This helps to explain why women frequently fail to recognize early signs of pregnancy, thereby delaying onset of prenatal care. Nor do they understand the emphasis US culture places on medical care as a means of averting risks and ensuring favorable birth outcomes.

2. Newcomer Status

New immigrants, most of whom are undocumented, are most likely to be very poor according to providers. They often migrate from small towns where they knew everyone to large, impersonal cities where they feel lonely and isolated. Newcomers lack information and understanding of available community resources for health and social assistance. Language barriers also impose

PERCEPTIONS OF BARRIER

Category	Providers of Care Dimensions	Consumers of Care Dimensions
1. Socio-economic	• Low income • Unemployment spouse • Lack of health insurance or underinsurance • Low education	• Lack of money • Unemployed spouse • Lack of health insurance
2. Immigrant	• Undocumented status • Language barriers • Isolation • Fear of deportation • Unfamiliarity with community resources • Misinformation on Medicaid	• Undocumented status • Language barriers • Unfamiliarity with community resources • Care is very different from what they were used to back home • Misinformation and fear of Medicaid
3. Attitudes and Beliefs	• Machismo • Female modesty • Fear of pelvic exams, medical treatments • Low self-esteem (timid, insecure, passive) • Communication gap between providers and consumers	• Machismo • Husband or boyfriend refuses to support pregnant woman • Female modesty • Mother died in child birth back home • Fear of poor care obtained from provider • Care too medicalized • Communication gap between providers and consumers

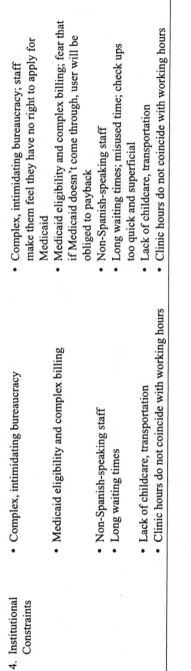

4. Institutional Constraints	• Complex, intimidating bureaucracy	• Complex, intimidating bureaucracy; staff make them feel they have no right to apply for Medicaid
	• Medicaid eligibility and complex billing	• Medicaid eligibility and complex billing; fear that if Medicaid doesn't come through, user will be obliged to payback
	• Non-Spanish-speaking staff	• Non-Spanish-speaking staff
	• Long waiting times	• Long waiting times; misused time; check ups too quick and superficial
	• Lack of childcare, transportation	• Lack of childcare, transportation
	• Clinic hours do not coincide with working hours	• Clinic hours do not coincide with working hours

Figure 1. Perceptions of barriers to prenatal care among providers and consumers of care.

obstacles to care. Combined, these factors tend to increase feelings of isolation and stress. Isolation also seems to reinforce misconceptions and fears among immigrant populations such as "if you apply for Medicaid, the baby becomes the property of the state, will never be allowed to leave and will have to repay the money owed to the state when he grows up."

3. Cultural Beliefs and Attitudes

"Machismo" was identified by providers and consumers as an obstacle to seeking care. Some Latino men are possessive of their wives and do not want them examined by male physicians. As one participant expressed: "My husband did not want to join me for the appointments. When the baby was born he was out with his friends . . . He had watched a delivery on T.V. and didn't want to see it again. He kept asking me, who introduced his fingers into your vagina?" Participants also commented that female modesty is a strong factor influencing delayed care. Latina women often feel uncomfortable exposing their "private parts" to male providers. As one woman commented: "I would hide my face when men would examine me. I felt better with women." Providers believe that Latina women may fear pelvic exams since many have never had gynecologic checkups prior to pregnancy and are reluctant to accept an exam. In addition many Latinas view pregnancy as a normal, healthy state which does not require special medical care.

The communication gap between patients and providers is another cultural factor inhibiting the use of prenatal care. Unlike Latin America, U.S. doctors and nurses dress less formally. As one consumer observed, "Doctors and nurses come dressed in jeans . . . in our countries they always wear uniforms." Providers are also more direct and expedient, asking far more personal questions rather than taking time to build a trusting relationship with patients. This intimidates many patients who frequently adopt passive and submissive behaviors in response to medical authorities. As stated by one consumer, "The doctor kept asking me all these questions . . . and I would answer yes or no but I did not understand what he was saying and I kept wondering how all this was going to turn out."

4. Institutional Constraints

Providers and consumers agreed that problems with a complex, intimidating bureaucracy and billing system, lack of bilingual staff, long waiting periods during appointments, lack of child care or transportation and inflexible clinic hours all constituted constraints to seeking and continuing prenatal care.

The Medicaid application process is complex, takes a long time and the Medicaid eligibility workers are often seen as harsh, overburdened and burned out. Undocumented women note that they feel stigmatized by Medicaid workers who make them feel that they have no right to apply for financial assistance.

According to one consumer "The worker told me that she couldn't give me Medicaid, that I had the money. In a very impolite way she said that I shouldn't have any more children." Latina women are not used to filling out forms and the eligibility workers are unresponsive to the special needs and language limitations that Latinas face. The consumers often saw the cumbersome paperwork and the detailed personal information required every three months as impossible to meet.

The billing system is also seen as a complex process that exerts too much pressure. Regardless of the financial arrangements made with the health facility, bills continue to be mailed to patients. Women often have difficulty reading and understanding the billing statements and fail to understand who is responsible for paying for which services. Since applicants are uncertain as to whether Medicaid will come through and cover the costs of prenatal care, cumulative bills will escalate their anxiety because they know that they cannot afford to pay. Several women mentioned that when their anxiety levels rose too high they would cancel prenatal appointments in an attempt to lower costs.

There is also a lack of bilingual/bicultural professional staff particularly female physicians in the clinics which increases distance in patient-doctor relationships. While consumers felt that the quality of professional care provided is good, usually exceeding what is available to them in their countries of origin, the treatment they receive from non-professional staff, i.e., nurses's aids, receptionists, and eligibility workers, is often demeaning. Insensitive treatment, particularly by the Latino staff was emphasized. For instance, consumers claimed that "Receptionists do shocking things. They think that because they are Latinas they know it all." or ". . . they treat you like despots. One complained because I had come a day ahead of my appointment." According to consumers Latino staff treat them badly because of their need to show off to other immigrants their successes in securing jobs and becoming acculturated to mainstream society. Women with delayed care were more likely to express feelings of dissatisfaction about harsh treatment than early prenatal care starters.

Furthermore, providers and consumers felt that waiting periods of two to three hours at the time of prenatal care appointments were too long. Whereas providers acknowledged that their clinics are understaffed and overbooked, users of care claimed that quick and superficial medical check-ups do not warrant long waiting periods. Moreover, many consumers could not afford long waiting periods because of childcare expenses and accompanying spouses could no afford lost wages. On the other hand they did not see that bringing their children along was a solution due to the lack of childcare facilities.

Finally, prenatal care users were particularly concerned that clinic hours did not coincide with their work hours or those of their spouses. Low security of employment and jobs in the informal sector discourage absence from work for health reasons.

PARTICIPANTS' RECOMMENDATIONS FOR IMPROVING EARLY PRENATAL CARE

In an attempt to overcome the perceived barriers to early and sustained use of prenatal care, participants were asked to suggest recommendations for improving outreach to the Latino community. The recommendations were classified according to their purpose, namely, to improve casefinding and recruitment of pregnant women or expand social supports that increase motivation for health care utilization. Providers and users' suggestions are reported in Figure 2.

I. To Increase Casefindings

According to the participants, the strategies to improve casefinding include.

1. Provide Health Education and Information

Both providers and users of care agreed that improved information and health education were needed in two areas, one stressing the importance of prenatal care and preventing risks in pregnancy, another providing information on the medical and ancillary support services available in the community and how to access these services. Providers and users of care recommended that radio and television spots as well as talk shows on health be considered as outreach tools. Flyers, posters, regular health campaigns and school-based health promotion programs should be used for community outreach. These informational and advertising outreaches should be in Spanish and be provided in suitable locations for the community such as churches, public transportation stations, supermarkets, hair salons, Latino restaurants, adult education programs and schools. Elementary schools were preferred by multiparous mothers because they serve as resource facilities where newcomer families learn about community programs, norms and expectations.

2. Increase Interagency Coordination of Services

Providers noted that effective casefinding relies on existing social services such as immigration support services and other legal services, food distribution programs, adult education programs and religious charities. By extending interagency coordination efforts which link health providers with service workers in other community programs, referrals and mutually beneficial cross-referrals of hard to reach pregnant women or of patients with multiple health and social needs can be more readily achieved.

Whereas providers recommended an increased coordination with grassroots programs as well as training of community leaders to facilitate casefinding and influence peers to seek early care, consumers of care emphasized the need for more self help networks. Several women recommended that "neighbor to neighbor" campaigns be developed to teach immigrants about health risks, the value of prenatal care and women's rights.

OUTREACH STRATEGIES

Purpose and Strategic Area	Providers of Care Activity or Intervention	Consumers of Care Activity or Intervention
I. To Increase Casefinding:		
1. Health information and education	• Encourage Spanish mass media • Conduct health campaigns • Provide information at appropriate community locations	• Encourage Spanish mass media • Conduct health campaigns • Provide information at appropriate community locations
2. Coordinated community resources	• Ensure cross-agency referrals • Identify community leaders and train them as casefinders	• Encourage self-help networks; neighbor to neighbor campaigns
II. To Improve Motivation Toward Early and Continuous Use of Care:		
1. Expanded pregnancy test		• Formalize first contact with agency • Provide information on care and help • Offer family planning information
2. Women's support groups	• Offer in hospitals, community, and local agencies • Strive to involve male participation in the community	• Offer in hospitals, community, and local agencies
3. Transportation, child care services	• Provide services	• Provide services

Figure 2. Participants' recommendations for improved early prenatal care.

II. Improving Motivation Toward Use of Care

To improve motivation to seek early and continuous prenatal care, the following recommendations for action were suggested.

1. Expand Pregnancy Test

Consumers of care strongly felt that women would be more likely to start early care if pregnancy tests were made amply available in the community and if social, nutritional and family planning services were offered at the time of the test. The cost of an individual pregnancy test is high for low income women, making the offer of a free, or low-cost test attractive. Furthermore, women are open to exploring resources during this initial phase in which options are being considered. Currently, women have to wait until their first prenatal clinic visit to obtain counselling. Because of the long waiting periods for receiving first appointments, the advice and counsel may come too late.

2. Promote Women's Groups

Women's groups especially designed for Latina women, and held prior, during and after pregnancy, were perceived by providers and consumers as effective means of obtaining emotional and instrumental support. Such groups can assist women in overcoming doubts and fears regarding medical care and birth in the United States. Support groups may also help to decrease feelings of isolation among newcomers and to learn about sexuality and family planning in a safe environment.

Providers seemed more insistent than consumers about the need to design programs that involve male partners in prenatal care.

3. Provide Transportation Services

Pregnancy passes for public transportation facilities would reduce transportation costs associated with prenatal visits. As well, mobile health units might be employed in providing services to the community.

With respect to social supports, we observed that documented women reported more self seeking of prenatal care resources than undocumented women. The latter seemed to be more reliant on their networks, particularly on their spouses, relatives or friends to encourage them to seek care. Undocumented immigrants who reported that their spouse opposed the pregnancy or their use of health services, were particularly at risk of delayed care. These findings suggest that undocumented women may be especially responsive to improved outreach strategies.

Besides these behavioral differences, there were few discrepancies in the recommendations for outreach offered by documented and undocumented women nor between those who had used early prenatal care and those who had delayed their entry into the prenatal care system.

III. Inreach

A range of recommendations were advanced in the focus groups that addressed improvements not specific to reaching out to the community, but rather aimed at improving health clinics' attitudes and practices. These recommendations, illustrated in Figure 3, could be considered "inreach" in that they imply altering provider attitudes and negative elements in the clinic or hospital organization to ensure adequate care.

1. Reduce Bureaucratic Effects by Adding a Personal Touch

Both providers and consumers noted that often a Latina woman's first experience with the clinic is with a cold, unfriendly bureaucracy and a barrage of information and repetitive questions which overwhelm the client. Latina women are usually not familiar with completing applications and forms. Instead consumers felt that some basic staff training in friendly interpersonal relations would expedite the care and that bilingual and bicultural trained eligibility staff (a high burnout position) would make a substantial difference. The personal touch seems to be valued in these initial procedural contacts.

Providers on the other hand, suggested that clients should first see a triage nurse not an eligibility worker and that the extensive form filling and eligibility questioning could be done later in the visit. The woman's first visit should not overwhelm them, but rather stimulate clients to come back for followup visits. Providers frequently mentioned that the multiple needs of immigrant patients requires "knowing how to prioritize needs" and knowing when to intervene. Consumers agreed that their psycho-social needs, which extend far beyond medical care, cannot be dealt with all at once.

2. Increase Providers' Responsiveness to Long Waiting Periods

Consumers strongly recommended that long waiting periods be reduced or at least filled with health education classes and health videos in Spanish. This could help them learn about aspects of pregnancy and childcare that are important to them. As well, if child care could be provided during these visits it would reduce patient-incurred costs and therefore allow longer waiting at the clinic.

3. Facilitate Financing and Billing of Health Services

Widespread dissatisfaction with the billing system was expressed by providers and consumers of care. Both groups argued for the need to cut down and simplify billing forms to reduce the need for assistance in completing the forms and avoid recurrent errors. Consumers in particular, urged that bills only be sent periodically rather than after each visit or on a monthly basis, since they escalate the anxiety about payment and often pressure women to drop out of care. The detailed billing for Medicaid requires simplification because it is a pervasive source of

INREACH STRATEGIES

Purpose and Strategic Area	Providers of Care Activity or Intervention	Consumers of Care Activity or Intervention
I. To Improve Organizational Attitudes and Practices:		
1. Increase the personal touch	• Hire bilingual staff • Decrease personnel turnover • Prioritize needs	• Hire bilingual staff • Train eligibility staff in public relations • Prioritize needs
2. Increase responsiveness to long waiting periods	• Reduce waiting time	• Provide in agency health education and health videos • Provide childcare • Reduce waiting time
3. Facilitate billing of health services	• Cut down and simplify billing forms • Familiarize users with billing procedures • Reduce fears and misconceptions regarding public assistance	• Cut down and simplify billing forms • Familiarize users with billing procedures • Reduce fears and misconceptions regarding public assistance

Figure 3. Participants' recommendations for improved early prenatal care.

misunderstanding and fear for Latino families. Furthermore, the long waiting period between application and confirmation of Medicaid eligibility leaves many indigent families uncertain about their financial obligations and future repercussions should third party payment fall through. Insensitive treatment by eligibility workers often compounds the anxiety surrounding health care financing and reinforces the stigma, that poor women, particularly the undocumented, are not worthy of public assistance. In light of these constraints, participants noted that if women are to be effectively linked to the Medicaid program, they must be prepared for the application process. Learning what to expect when they apply, what documentation to bring and which are the most current eligibility regulations, were seen as valuable preparatory tools.

DISCUSSION

The results of this project indicate a high concordance between providers and consumers of care in their perceptions of barriers to prenatal care that affect the Latino community in San Francisco. Both groups readily identified structural factors such as low socio-economic status, lack of health insurance and documentation as strong deterrents of care. Attitudes and beliefs proper of the culture, language barriers, unfamiliarity with community norms and resources and communication gaps between providers and consumers were frequently identified as cultural obstacles to full utilization of care. In addition, participants recognized that numerous institutional constraints influenced women's motivation and perceived accessibility to care.

While there was consensus among providers and consumers in the frequency and severity with which structural and institutional constraints affect utilization of care, providers were more likely to identify personal attributes and cultural beliefs of the consumer as likely risk factors discouraging use of prenatal care. The extent to which personal and cultural barriers to care independently influence utilization of prenatal care among Latinas or whether they are products of pervasive structural and institutional barriers to care is an area requiring further research. An understanding of the relative effects of different types of barriers to care may prevent victim or culture blaming while promoting effective social change.

The findings also suggest practical recommendations for decreasing structural and cultural obstacles to care through improved outreach strategies. Enrollment into early prenatal care services can be achieved with improved information and health education, preferably in Spanish, widely disseminated in the community. Casefinding can also be increased by establishing linkages, either through self-help networks or through inter-agency coordination. Whereas several consumers suggested the need to develop grassroot efforts that mobilize women's support for outreach and information, providers were more likely to indicate the need for improved cross-referrals among community agencies. Perhaps the two recommendations can be blended into one program. For example, the Better

Babies Project of Washington D.C. successfully combined these two approaches in their efforts to recruit low income, black pregnant women into their program designed to reduce risks of low birthweight [13].

Recommendations for improving outreach through increased motivation to seek early and sustained prenatal care, could also result in the removal of structural and cultural barriers. The most important suggestion offered by the consumers in this regard was the need for the health system to provide free or low-cost pregnancy tests. It was suggested that this test should be the occasion of making contact and providing counseling on prenatal care requirements, general health and nutrition and family planning services. Additionally, both consumers and providers recognized the need for promoting women's support groups that could inform as well as reduce the isolation of immigrant women in the community.

The above recommendations suggest ways of reaching out to the community by informing people of the value of prenatal care, of the availability of services and of ways in which early and continuous care can be sustained through supportive interventions. The findings of this study suggest however, that these outreach strategies alone may not be effective in breaking down the institutional barriers to care. Inreach strategies that alter certain negative elements within the organization, smooth communication between patients and providers and attain better follow through, may be required to better address institutional barriers. Specific recommendations for improving inreach suggested by the focus group participants were: the need for adding a personal touch to bureaucratic interactions; train eligibility workers and support staff in interpersonal relations; develop protocols and triage systems that prioritize needs of multi-problem families; convert waiting periods into productive opportunities for health education and simplify billing procedures.

While the Latina Women's Project was initiated to assess strategies for improving outreach programs to Latina women which would ensure early prenatal care, the results of the project suggest that outreach cannot be treated separately from "inreach" activities that improve policies, modify behaviors and management tools at the prenatal care site. Both types of strategies may have to act in concert to exert effects on the structural, cultural and institutional barriers to care. This finding closely parallels the Institute of Medicine assertion that outreach should only be one component of a well-designed, well-functioning system [2].

Outreach which depends solely on increased numbers of health promoters to do case finding in the community can become a costly proposition [14, 15]. Furthermore, legislation can be put in place to overcome some of the socio-economic, legal and immigration status barriers to adequate prenatal care. However, these alone might not change provider and consumer behaviors and cultural attitudes concerning health. The effective application of inreach and outreach strategies in designing prenatal care programs for the Latino population is an exciting area of planning for health promotion. Future implementation and further evaluation will help us determine its potential success in improving timely access to prenatal care.

ACKNOWLEDGMENT

This study was funded by the San Francisco Department of Health under an independent consultant agreement.

REFERENCES

1. Institute of Medicine, *Preventing Low Birthweight*, National Academy Press, Washington, D.C., 1985.
2. Institute of Medicine, *Prenatal Care: Reaching Mothers, Reaching Infants*, National Academy Press, Washington, D.C., 1988.
3. Health of Uninsured and Underinsured Project, *Perinatal Health in San Francisco: A Report on Community Needs (Initial Report)*, University of California at San Francisco, Department of Family and Community Medicine and San Francisco Department of Public Health, Family Health Bureau, July 1989.
4. State of California, Department of Health Services, *Vital Statistics Birth Records, 1988*, State of California, Sacramento, 1988.
5. L. Chavez, Mexican Immigrants and the Utilization of U.S. Health Services: The Case of San Diego, *Social Science and Medicine, 21*, pp. 93-102, 1985.
6. R. Alcalay, Perinatal Care Services for Hispanic Women: A Study of Provider-Receiver Communication, *International Quarterly of Community Health Education, 2*:3, pp. 199-214, 1981-82.
7. A. Medina, Hispanic Maternity Care: A Study of Deficiencies and Recommended Policies, *Public Affairs Report, 21*:2, 1980.
8. A. Estrada, F. Trevino, and L. Ray, Health Care Utilization Barriers among Mexican Americans: Evidence from HHANES, 1982-1984, *American Journal of Public Health, 80*, supplement, pp. 27-31, 1990.
9. S. Guendelman, *The Latina Women's Project: Improving Outreach for Prenatal Care*, Report submitted to the San Francisco Department of Health, Family Health Bureau, October, 1990.
10. D. Glik, A. Gordon, W. Ward, L. Koume and S. Guessan, Focus Group Methods for Formative Research in Child Survival: An Ivorian Example, *International Quarterly of Community Health Education, 8*:4, pp. 297-316, 1987-88.
11. E. Folch-Lyon and J. F. Trost, Conducting Focus Group Sessions, *Studies in Family Planning, 12*, pp. 443-449, 1981.
12. C. E. Basch, Focus Group Interview: An Underutilized Research Technique for Improving Theory and Practice in Health Education, *Health Education Quarterly, 14*, pp. 411-448, 1987.
13. D. L. Coates and J. M. Maxwell, *Lessons Learned from the Better Babies Project*, March of Dimes, April 1990.
14. M. C. McCormick, J. Brooks-Gunn, T. Shorten, J. Holmes, et al., Outreach as Case Finding: Its Effect on Enrollment in Prenatal Care, *Medical Care, 27*, pp. 103-111, February 1989.
15. J. Brooks-Gunn, McCormick, R. Gunn, T. Shorten, et al., Outreach as Case Finding: The Process of Locating Low-Income Pregnant Women, *Medical Care, 27*, pp. 95-102, February 1989.

CHAPTER 16

Focused Female Condom Education and Trial: Comparison of Young African American and Puerto Rican Women's Assessments

M. Idalí Torres
Robert Tuthill
Sarah Lyon-Callo
C. Mercedes Hernández
Paul Epkind

OVERVIEW OF THE PROJECT

This chapter presents data from a CDC funded project undertaken to understand better the social and cultural contexts within which young urban African-American and Latina women make decisions and act to protect themselves from sexually transmitted infections, including HIV. Of particular interest are strategies used by women who were successful in negotiating the adoption of the female condom for vaginal sex with their male sexual partners. The project's transdisciplinary orientation includes 1) health education's focus on promoting protective behaviors, and 2) anthropology's holistic perspective to study the sociocultural environment in which behavior happens, with focused ethnographic methodologies.

Our work reflects the body of literature on the urban experience synthesized in health education [1] and anthropology [2] within the past year. Key to our analysis are the reciprocal transactions between African-American and Puerto Rican women and resources that effect sexual health protective behaviors at the community level. We use the concept of sociocultural templates to represent the urban complexity involved in the interaction of multiple psychosocial, economic, political, and sociohistorical factors outside the control of the individual and group circles that influence new cultural constructions and segmentation in urban communities. In what are often dialectical and interdependent transactions between people and their multicultural mix (ethnic cultural identities, gender identities, social classes, religions; and the language and transnational networks that immigrants bring), the layers of the evolving sociocultural template restructure to effect in diverse ways cultural scripts and behaviors within segments of the same community. These sociocultural complexities shape the organization of community resources—information channels, natural and institutional support, cultural capital, social norms and expectations—for health protection. It is within this sociocultural context that urban African-American and Puerto Rican women view their bodies, make sexual decisions, and develop strategies for protecting themselves against HIV, other sexually transmitted infections (STIs) and unplanned pregnancy. In turn, they consider new technologies such as the female condom to enhance their resources for minimizing exposure to the negative consequences of unprotected sexual encounters.

THE FEMALE CONDOM

The female condom has been well described in the health literature [3-12]. It has been found to be "an effective mechanical barrier to viruses, including HIV" [3] with a typical success rate in first year of 79 percent for typical users and 95 percent for perfect users [4]. Studies on its acceptability from several countries have produced qualitative and quantitative data from women who are HIV-infected, engaged in drug use, active in the sex trade, practicing unprotected sex, involved in other behaviors considered risk factors for HIV, and other sexually transmitted infections [5-7], or just segments of the general population [8-12].

In the above range of studies, the most frequently mentioned advantages of the female condom were: more control over protection, more safety than with the male condom, and good mechanical performance. Perceived disadvantages included large size, messiness produced by the lubricant, and inconvenience caused by rings. There is consensus about women's willingness to recommend the female condom to other women regardless of their personal experiences with the device, and reports about male partners' mixed reaction to its use. The experience of Latina and African-American women who have participated in some of these studies has been combined with no examination of potential inter-group differences [7-10] or has been examined as single group [11-12]. As a result, there is no culture-specific information to guide the design and implementation of female condom focused education in transcultural urban communities.

METHODOLOGY

Population and Community Setting

Participation for the current study centered on African-American and Latina women eighteen to twenty-nine years of age who met the following criteria: had a connection with one of two participating neighborhood-based health centers either directly or through family members; had vaginal intercourse at least twice in the past month; had no history of HIV infection, substance abuse or sex trade; and were not pregnant, or thinking about getting pregnant within six months of the time of the recruitment. In addition, women who were interested in the trial had to be free from ulcerative STIs in order to be eligible to participate. A total of twenty-eight African-American women and twenty-four Puerto Ricans started the thirty-day trial of the female condom. Of those, four African Americans and four Puerto Ricans were lost to follow-up, or became ineligible because of genital ulcerative or a positive result on the test for pregnancy, for HIV, or for other STIs performed as part of the STI assessment. This chapter presents data from the remaining twenty-four African Americans and twenty Latinas of Puerto Rican origin.

We followed the social science tradition in defining "ethnic group" as a group with a similar cultural tradition and identity, that exists as a segment of the larger community. Grouping was based on ethnic self-identification during screening for eligibility criteria, and on a concerted effort to maintain participation circumscribed to the neighborhood constellation recognized as the main enclaves for African American and Puerto Ricans. These six neighborhoods that form the core inner-center have the highest proportion of African-American and Puerto Rican women (ages 15 to 44) in the city of Springfield, Massachusetts.

The city is included in the standardized metropolitan statistical area (SMSA) that ranks as the twenty-fifth area in the country in number of AIDS cases per 100,000 residents (33.5). Of the fifty-one female cases in the age group eighteen to twenty-nine years reported in the city through 1995 (the year in which our data were collected), the highest percentage were Hispanic (61), followed by African American (27), and White (12).

The two participating community health centers were the main primary health care source for these multi-ethnic neighborhoods at the time of the study. Neighborhood Health Center (NHC) serves the highest proportion of African-American residents of four neighborhoods in an area with a population of 23,173. Brightwood/Riverview Health Center (BRHC) serves the two neighborhoods with the highest concentration of Puerto Ricans in an area with 10,366 residents. In addition to the traditional primary care services, these health centers provide family planning, prenatal care, and other OB/Gyn clinics and HIV/AIDS related services to women. A state-funded STD clinic serves both health centers.

Focused-Education Component

The health education component of this project focused on the use of the female condom as a method of protection against HIV infection, other STIs, and unplanned pregnancies. It was implemented in collaboration with the state-funded STD clinics at the health centers. The female condom was introduced during an initial focused session with a videotape, pictures, and samples of the device inserted in a female pelvic model. Participants had an opportunity to touch and manipulate the device. At the end of the session a specialized STD nurse answered questions which emerged from the presentation and discussion.

Women who expressed an interest in the thirty-day trial of the female condom were provided with an appointment for a STI assessment and physical exam followed by a half-hour individual educational session with the STD nurse. The educational session focused on learning how to use the female condom, and how to keep a calendar with notes on experiences using the female condom. Participants had an opportunity to practice insertion with the female pelvic model and privately themselves. The nurse suggested strategies for negotiating use of the female condom with male partners.

Women were provided with a number of female condoms to take home according to self-reported need. Packages of female condoms were accompanied by a packet of written educational materials. Participating women were told to contact the RN or clinic Women Health Outreach Workers (WHOWs) for more information, more female condoms, questions, or support. A card with the telephone numbers of the RN and the WHOWs was provided to participants. Participants were given an appointment to come back for two follow-up visits. The first return visit was scheduled at two weeks past start date for further education and support, and the second visit was scheduled at four weeks for a post-trial exit interview.

Focused-Ethnographic Data Collection

We applied a focused ethnographic methodology that integrates data obtained through observations and in-depth interviews similar to the approach described by Pelto and Pelto [13]. In this study, observations recorded throughout the life of the project focused on the community context in which women considered 1) the female condom as a technological device for sexual health protection, and 2) the opportunity to participate in the trial. Emphasis was given to community structures that facilitate communication of information and access to social supports for sexual health protection, and how they affected the socio-cultural shared views and actions of participants.

The in-depth interviews conducted at the end of the trial focused on the experience of participants with the female condom. These post-trial interviews combined unstructured, semi-structured, and structured questions to obtain both qualitative and quantitative data about women's experiences introducing, negotiating and using the female condom. This combined approach to data collection increased our ability to gather information on African-American and Latina women's assessment of the female condom. Areas of interest included the experience of practicing insertion, how the female condom was introduced to male partner, and the partner's initial reaction, opinions transferred to members of women's social networks such as friends, and suggestions for future female condom focused education.

Interviews were conducted by the lead author and two research assistants who were female graduate students from the School of Public Health. Length of time for the interviews varied from one to two hours. Participants were provided with gift certificates for $10 in merchandise at local stores as an incentive and as a symbol of appreciation for the time spent sharing their experiences with the project. Throughout the entire data collection process the interviews were tape-recorded, except in the few cases where the participants preferred otherwise. To maintain the emic perspective and voice of participants, interviews and transcriptions were done by staff members from similar cultural and linguistic backgrounds as the participants. Latina women were interviewed in their language of preference.

Data Management and Analysis

Qualitative data analysis for this chapter focused on the systematic discovery and examination of themes embedded within situation-specific observations and topic-specific exit interviews that followed the female condom trial. Situational observations were synthesized by emerging themes. Text from topical interview transcriptions was organized in topical question-specific matrices for grouping responses describing the same idea. These matrices included text segments (e.g., word, phrase or sentence) that best described the content of the partici- pant's thoughts in response to an interviewer's question or intervention. After examining the resulting topical matrices for each participant, we constructed thematic matrices for each ethnic group. Using these group-based matrices, we compared emerging themes within and across groups to discover connections, similarities and differences in idea systems and behavioral domains. Results of these analyses are presented in narrative form. Selective text segments illustrating analytical themes represent emic constructions that are shared by large segments of each or both groups.

Responses to structured questions were entered into the computer and validated. Quantitative analysis for this chapter includes descriptive statistics and examination of data in contingency tables using both chi square test of significance and Mantel-Haenszel analysis stratified by cultural groupings to assess both confounding and interaction.

SYNTHESIS OF PARTICIPANT OBSERVATIONS

Women's Organization and Advocacy

A group of African-American women, who were infected with HIV and/or affected by a family member's positive HIV status and were providing AIDS information and support for protection against HIV, organized a community meeting to advocate for distribution of the female condoms to all women, regardless of participation criteria. The comments of one woman summarized the general assessment of the group. She felt that by focusing on eighteen to twenty-nine year old healthy, sexually active women, "the project excluded women who most needed the protection provided by the female condom: teenagers vulnerable to STIs, women who were themselves HIV positive or had HIV positive partners, IV drug users, and commercial sex workers." The women's group negotiated their support for the project in exchange for access to female condoms for "at risk" populations not included in the study. Although similar concerns were expressed by a few Puerto Rican health practitioners, there was no observed organized advocacy efforts in their community that matched the demonstration of the African-American women volunteer community educators.

Communication Channels

Another illustration of inter-community differences in social structures of support for sexual health protection emerged from observations of the role of African-American community health practitioners. In programs aimed at the prevention of teenage unplanned pregnancy, HIV and other sexually transmitted infections the practitioners succeed in transferring information to informal women networks in the community. Word-of-mouth within service and natural networks, including some churches, proved to be our best recruitment strategy for two-thirds of the African-American women who completed the project in the last two cycles of implementation. In contrast, we observed that Puerto Rican women who participated in the final cycle learned about the project from other women in their own networks who participated in earlier cycles, not always linked to the organized systems of service provision as experienced by African-American women.

Ethnic Culture and Language

We found greater support among practitioners and the general community for our project in the Puerto Rican community when it was promoted as a general "women's health project," while in the African-American community our project was promoted most effectively as a "sexual health project." These names for the project were used when approaching and initially talking to women about the project. Most African-American women asked to participate in the project responded directly, even if they refused to participate, while Puerto Rican women responded more indirectly and often postponed a final decision about participation for several days.

Felt Need for New Technologies and Prior Knowledge at the Community Level

Both health practitioners and women in the African-American community were more likely than in the Puerto Rican community to share with project staff how much they knew about the existence of the female condom. This difference was further documented in the difference in level of interest in trying other barrier methods against unplanned pregnancy and STIs than those they were presently using or had tried in the past, and in the difference in the level of knowledge about the female condom reported by participants before the trial.

FINDINGS FROM IN-DEPTH INTERVIEWS

Trial Female Condom Alone Privately and With Male Partner

Among the twenty-four African-American women who entered the trial 91.7 percent used the female condom with a male partner at least once, while 90 percent of the twenty Latina women reported similar use. Of those who entered the trial, 54.2 percent of the African-American women and 60 percent of the Puerto Rican women had tried the female condom privately one or more times. Except for one African-American woman and two Puerto Ricans who inserted it only privately, the rest used the female condom at least once with their male partners for vaginal sex during the trial period (30 days). A comparison of the average number of uses for each ethnic group shows that Latina women tried the female condom with their partner on average one additional time (5.7) more frequently than the African-American women (4.6). Both groups tried the female condom a median of four times.

In the case of one African American, she had tried it by herself successfully, but while trying with male partner she "couldn't get it to go right" even though her partner "was excited about using it." The two Latina women who tried the female condom by themselves but not with their partner reported reasons for non-use associated with their male partners. One told the interviewer that "he was not interested at all." The other reported that the man had said that "I didn't have to use it if I really trusted him."

The seven women who used the device only once with their partners shared reasons why they stopped trying. Reasons given by African Americans could be classified into two theme categories: 1) not liking the female condom because they "like it real natural" or "it was uncomfortable," and 2) no sex because "he went away." Reasons given by Latina women included mechanical problems experienced by male partners. For example, in one case, the participant reported that "the ring, when he inserted it, bumped into him, . . . he is not used to it." The second woman reported that in addition to having found it uncomfortable, "the ring part it was rubbing on him too, . . . he was burning a lot."

Getting Male Partner's Agreement for Trying the Female Condom

Strategies the women used for negotiating with their male partner the use of the female condom for vaginal sex are presented in Table 1. The most frequently used strategy for introducing female condom to male partners for the first time in both groups was verbal communication. Other strategies reported, such as giving reading materials and showing the female condom to their partners, were non-verbal and were used either independently or in combinations with verbal communication. Table 2 illustrates that women began their conversations with partners about the female condom in a variety of ways: 1) describing our project and its connection with the health centers or known staff members before or at the time they took home the female condoms, 2) presenting it as a method of protection against pregnancy and STIs, a "new thing" available for protection or an alternative to the male condom, 3) sharing what they have seen in the video shown at the focus group, and 4) directly telling their male partner their intentions to try the female condom.

Both groups used similar strategies to introduce the female condom to their male partner. While African-American women waited until they received the female condoms from the nurse to raise the topic with their male partners, Puerto Rican women introduced it gradually as exposure to education activities increased. One explained that she started by "telling him that I was coming to this project, . . . when I would come home he'd say 'how was it?'. That day I just told him . . . babe look . . . look at the condoms . . . he looked at them, we made jokes out of them and he goes well then go and try it. So I went to the bathroom I tried it and then we tried." An African-American participant said (I) 'just told him that (I) was going to this women's project before I even got them (*female condoms*)."

Reactions from male partners to the initial introduction of the female condom by women can be divided in three groups: initial enthusiastic support, initial reluctance accompanied by gradual acceptance, and unwillingness to cooperate. Some thirteen African Americans and ten Puerto Ricans indicated that their partners were agreeable to the trial after their initial introduction to the idea. According to African-American participants, male partners who reacted enthusiastically "had seen it before (*in*) low security prison," "wanted to help," and did "anything to have sex." While sharing similar reactions, Puerto Ricans said their

Table 1. Strategies Used to Introduce Female Condom
to Male Partners

Strategy	African Americans	Puerto Ricans
Verbal Communication		
• connected the use of the female condom to the health centers	+	+
• raised within the context of sexual protection beyond pregnancy prevention	+	−
• introduced it as an alternative to the male condom or other methods	+	+
• communicated their intentions to try the female condom directly	+	+
Non-Verbal Communication		
• gave him reading materials to enhance verbal communication or without verbal communication	+	+
• shown the female condom to illustrate verbal message or without verbal message (i.e., left box in the table; inserted it before sex)	+	+
Context of Communication		
• started to talk to partner about the project before taking condoms home	+	+
• waited after she got the condoms to show them	+	+
• raised topic just before sex	+	+
• proposed it as a device that could be used to have sex during the menstrual period	+	−

+ = present in the interview transcription text.
− = absent from the interview transcription text.

male partners were "curious," "willing to give it a try," "thought it was a good idea" and "like(d) to experiment."

Nine African-American women and ten Puerto Rican women explained that although their partners were initially reluctant and expressed negative and mixed reactions, gradual exposure to the device and/or insistence from women resulted in later acceptance. Among this segment, there were reports that some partners had laughed and made jokes about the female condom in both ethnic groups. African-American participants reported that their initially reluctant partners had found the female condom "weird, funny-looking, "was a little bit shocked," asked a lot of questions or "wanted to know what it was," "acted like men . . . grouchy and fidgety." Puerto Ricans' male partners thought that the device was "too

Table 2. Frequency of Use of the Female Condom by Who Inserted
the Condom and by Cultural Group

Who Inserted the Condom	African-Americans times used					Puerto Ricans* times used				
	n	1-2	3-4	5+	Total	n	1-2	3-4	5+	Total
Woman only	15	40.3	33.0	26.7	100.0	12	41.7	8.3	50.0	100.0
Man only/both	7	14.3	28.6	57.1	100.0	5	0	60.0	40.0	100.0

*Missing value = 1 (10.0)

big" and were "fearful" (*temeroso*) of using it. One Latina woman reported that her male partner argued and said that she "didn't have to use it because he was always with me."

Women presented their own theories about what they thought had finally persuaded their reluctant partners to try the female condom. Several African-American women told the interviewers, "I told him that if he doesn't try it, he can't get any (*sex*)." Others believe that after asking their partners, they decided to "show consideration for me," and "helped me with the program." One Latina women who introduced the female condom to her male partner as "a tampon" reported that her partner thought the device "would (*produce*) the same discomfort in women as male condoms (*produce*) for men." Another Latina woman believe that the support of a male friend made the difference. She described that her partner shared the reading materials about the female condom with a male friend who told him "women need their own protection too, it is not only us." Other reasons included preventing pregnancy.

First Time Use of Female Condom with Partner

Most women experienced difficulties with the insertion process, mechanics, and physical experience on their first trial with their partners. The value of the experience of having used other technologies that require penetration such as tampons and diaphragm was raised by some participants. Describing their experiences, two African Americans said "it was just like putting (*in*) a tampon" and "it felt like a diaphragm. You could feel the head of it." A third woman said that "I never really use the ummm, diaphragm . . . I really didn't know how to insert it all that well because my body was kind of tight, but other than (*that*) no (*problem*)." Even though there was no mention of other technologies among Puerto Ricans, one woman said that "it was hard because I never tried to do (*meaning inserting*) anything like that before." While some African-American women described having spent sometimes more than an hour inserting the female condom, one Latina woman reported having tried three times with no problem.

First time use mechanical problems were related to the ring, lubrication, and ability to maintain the female condom inside. Interestingly while two African Americans found the outer ring uncomfortable, one Latina found that the inner ring "pushed and hurt." One African American mentioned that "he said that it rubbed against him, that ring. . . ." The Latina woman said that "he didn't like it that he could feel the inside ring . . . and I took it out." Only African-American women mentioned problems with lubrication such as "wasn't too lubricated," "it was kinda slippery," "I had to use a lot of lubricant." In both groups there were difficulties in keeping the device in place. Three African-Americans reported that the female condom "came out twice," "came out in the middle of the motions" and "ended up on him." One Latina explained that "the semen comes down when you are in the top position."

In describing their first experience with the device once inside the vagina, African-Americans mentioned "uncomfortable," "slightly uncomfortable but not massive pain," "not a natural feeling like having sex without a condom," "it hurt—didn't push it up far enough," "you do not feel real with it," "it doesn't feel like a man's (condom)," and "a little hard to use it during sex." Puerto Ricans experienced "discomfort," "felt funny to have it inside" and "strange."

Women's persistence in addressing the aforementioned challenges in their first try is reflected in their successful strategies in succeeding tries. For example, an African-American woman whose partner found the device to be physically uncomfortable because the outer ring rubbed against his testicles reported that "I didn't think that I had it up there right and then I fixed it and it was comfortable." Others said "it kept slipping off my fingers as I was putting it on . . . after three hours I get it right." A Latina woman described that on her first try she felt "strange and had a hard time following what the book said, this was like this until I get used to it."

Male Partner's Participation in Inserting the Female Condom

Regardless of the number of tries with male partners, women were primarily the ones who inserted the female condom (Table 2). In both groups, over two-thirds of the participants reported that they had inserted the device themselves. However, the insertion pattern for the other third reflects inter-group differences. Reports that *only* the male partner participated in the insertion of the female condom were given by slightly over 18 percent of the African Americans and approximately 6 percent of Puerto Ricans. In contrast, over 20 percent of Puerto Ricans reported that both—women participants and their male partners—had participated in the insertion of the female condom, compared to approximately 14 percent of African Americans. The percentage of women who were assisted by their male partner during the insertion of the female condom increased with the number of times it was tried. This increase was more significant among Latina women as illustrated by the probability value shown in Table 2.

Opinions about Information and Education Materials

Table 3 summarizes participants' opinions in terms of helpfulness (very helpful, somewhat helpful, or not particularly helpful) of the video film shown at the focus group session and six different pamphlets and single-page handouts provided at the end of the educational session to take home with the female condom for trial. More Puerto Ricans than African Americans found the video at least somewhat helpful.

When the percentage of women who found pamphlets at least somewhat helpful are ranked in descending order, we see 100 percent inter-group consensus

Table 3. Opinions about Education Materials

Education Materials	African Americans (n = 24)		Puerto Ricans (n = 20)	
	At least somewhat helpful % [Rank]	Would recom- mend to friends %	At least somewhat helpful % [Rank]	Would recom- mend to friends %
Video				
Film on the Female Condom[a]	78.0	12.5	90.0	35.0
Pamphlets Spanish and English Versions				
Instructions for the F.C.[a]	100.0 [1]	37.5	100.0 [1]	0
Sexually Transmitted Diseases[b]	96.0 [2]	37.5	85.0 [3]	45.0
How to Talk to a Man about the F.C.[a]	69.0 [3]	12.5	90.0 [2]	5.0
What You Should Know about STDs[c]	4.0 [4]	0	80.0 [4]	15.0

[a]Female Condom Company, Division of Wisconsin Pharmacal Co., Inc., Chicago, Illinois
[b]Massachusetts Department of Public Health, Boston, Massachusetts
[c]Burroughs Wellcome Company, Research Triangle, North Carolina

about *Instructions for the Female Condom*. Ranked percentages for the other three titles show differences. The most marked difference was found in the written materials focused on communication about condoms. While *How to Talk To a Man about Female Condoms* ranked second in the percentage of Puerto Ricans (90 percent) who found it at least somewhat helpful, it ranked third in the percentage of African Americans (69 percent) who felt similarly. In addition, different inter-group opinions were found in women's reaction to materials related to STDs. The pamphlet *Sexually Transmitted Diseases* produced by the State Department of Public Health ranked second and third among African Americans (96 percent) and Puerto Ricans (85 percent) respectively. The pamphlet *What You Should Know about STDs* was mentioned as being helpful by 80 percent of Puerto Ricans but only 4 percent of African-American participants.

Only one woman in each group reported having not had their questions about the female condom completely answered by the nurse during the education session prior to having tried the condom. The African-American woman wanted to ask if any of the staff members "have tried (*the female condom*) or not and what was their experience like." The Latina women wanted more information about what would happen "if you feel the inner ring, . . . was it because it was inserted wrong." However, the number of women who reported unanswered questions *after* having tried the female condom increased to three African Americans (12.6 percent) and four Puerto Ricans (20.0 percent). The only African Americans who shared her questions with the interviewer said that she wanted to know "what (*happen*) if it get stuck." For the two Latina women who discussed the topics, their questions were: "was it normal that it came out when he was pulling out" and "how does it feel in certain positions?"

Suggestions for Female Condom-Focused Education

Women also shared their thoughts about the most important information that a woman should know before using the female condom. African-American and Latina women agreed in five main general areas of knowledge: 1) general information, 2) mechanics of use, 3) its protective function and effectiveness, 4) ability to increase women's own protection, and 5) negotiation with partner.

General information referred to a basic description of the device expressed by women with questions such as "what is it?," "what does it look like?" and "how can it protect us?" Two mechanical aspects of female condom use were represented in the comments made by women in both ethnic groups: insertion and extraction, and practice before having sex with a partner. In addition, one African-American woman identified the appropriate number of times one female condom can be used as information a potential user should know. In addition to learning about the protective function of the female condom, participants advocated for a balanced perspective on the protective effectiveness versus risks involved. This is clearly illustrated in the words of an African-American participant who told the interviewer that a woman "should know how effective the female condom is . . . you know the pros and cons . . . you can get an infection, a rash or allergic reaction . . . so I think you should cover all."

A composite of text from an interview from each group illustrates participants' feelings about the female condoms' potential for increasing women's ability to protect their sexual health. "[W]omen should know about the female condom, because it is something for us, we no longer have to depend on the man, we can depend on ourselves for own protection," and "it helps to protect women and gives you more control over the sex life." Raising the importance of male partner's acceptance of the device as something a woman should know before using the female condom, a Spanish speaking Puerto Rican woman indicated that it would be best if she can ensure [her] partner's acceptability before using. A suggested strategy given by an African-American woman was to "give the brochure about how to talk to the male about the condom . . . she'll feel easier . . . using it."

Sharing Information about the Female Condom with Friends

All participants in both groups indicated that they would recommend that their friend try the female condom. The most frequently mentioned reasons included protection against pregnancy, HIV/AIDS, and other STIs, as well as women's own protection and uncertainty about men's behavior and the role of the male partner in insertion of the female condom. In both groups, women said they would recommend the female condom to their friends because they see it as protection from HIV/AIDS. A Latina woman reported that, "most of my friends are dying of AIDS I'd rather go through the pain for a little bit than (*losing my*) life." Her concern was supported by an African-American woman who said she has told her friends that "if you had a choice between living and dying, and the man won't put that condom on, what are you gonna do? You can use the female condom." Participants in both groups will recommend it as a method to ensure women's own protection. In the words of a Latina "something that they can do for themselves, and they do not have to worry about men." And in the event that men "try to act like they forgot their condom, women can just go get it (*female condom*) out" according to an African-American woman. Furthermore, in their recommendations to friends, participants will address uncertainty about men's behavior ("you do not know about him. [T]he women have to realize that a lot of men like being with men").

It is interesting that 82 percent (23) of the twenty-eight African-American trial participants would not recommend any of the education materials (Table 3) to a friend who is interested in learning about the female condom. The other five would recommend three pamphlets: *How to Talk about Condoms, Instructions for the Female Condom,* and *Most Often Asked Questions about the Female*

Condom. In contrast, 62 percent (14) of the Latina participants would suggest to their friends watching the video film on the female condom and reading *What You Should Know about STDs, How to Talk to a Man about the Female Condom,* and *Instructions for the Female Condom.*

DISCUSSION

Our data validate findings of previous studies, adds knowledge about intergroup diversity in the experience of African-American and Puerto Rican women with the female condom, and suggests further research on the effects of community supports in the local cultural context for sexual health protection behaviors.

Supporting previous studies, our data show that segments of the general African-American and Latino communities tried the female condom when made available free-of-charge (like the male condom) and accompanied by focused-education in STD clinics based at community health centers. Similar proportions of the two cultural groups reported feelings of discomfort caused by mechanical aspects of the device during first time insertion and subsequent successful trials, intention to continue using the female condom and to recommend it to other women, and reasons why they would recommend it to their friends.

In contrast to previous research on the female condom, our ethnographic study provided an opportunity to compare similarities and differences in the experience of African-American and Puerto Rican women with the female condom. Our data showed considerable thematic consensus among participants of both groups, accompanied by variation in the context in which shared ideas appeared and in the magnitude and range of expressed ideas and actions. Intergroup diversity was best illustrated in the women's patterns of communication, descriptions of their male partner's reactions to the device and trial activities, and suggestions for health education focused on the female condom.

Reflecting patterns of general communication about sex in our society, there was intergroup consensus in the adoption of non-verbal and verbal strategies of communication for introducing the female condom to male partners for the first time. Although similar in action(s), content and situations, adopted strategies were executed differently. The majority of Puerto Ricans used indirect statements and progressive exposure to information in communicating about the female condom with partners throughout the pre-trial period, which contrasted with the more open and direct introductions reported by African-American participants. In general, African Americans provided more details about their thoughts, behaviors and personal experiences related to the female condom in contrast to the Puerto Rican women. African-American women's style of communicating information about sexual health protection was further observed in their willing-ness to promote the project in the community as "sexual health protection." They were more successful in recruiting additional study participants through established women's networks (i.e., churches) with the same message, reflecting the cultural norms that underlie communication about sexual health protection in the local community.

Consistent with reports of women's experiences in negotiating male condom use in previous studies [12, 14, 15], the majority of participants in both cultural groups reported not being able to obtain the collaboration of their male partners in the process of inserting the female condom. Among those who reported participation of male partners, the majority of African-Americans stated that only their male partners inserted the female condom, while the majority of Puerto Ricans reported that *both* partners had contributed to the insertion. In addition, the association between the increase of male participation and of smooth management by couples with an increase in the number of tries was stronger among Puerto Rican than among African-American women. Variation in these experiences may result from cultural constructions of gender-role patterns in the local cultural template that facilitates a greater level of autonomy for African-American women in their relationship with men and a stronger orientation toward mutuality for Puerto Rican women, which in the arena of sexual decision making often translates into less self-reliance.

Different assumptions that shape women's experiences in the two cultural groups may explain why Puerto Rican women who did not try the female condom at all or tried it only once reported reasons associated with partner's negative feelings about the device's mechanics of insertion and keeping it in place after insertion. By contrast African-Americans emphasized their own negative experience with the device and sex cessation during the trial period.

Contextual diversity continued to emerge in women's recommendations for education focused on the female condom. Much of the suggested content of information that a woman should have before using the female condom was consistent with previous studies [7, 8, 12]. However, the emphasis on the device's potential for enhancing women sexual health protection and on facilitating negotiation of protection with partner and on insertion strategies reflected situational diversity that further illustrated Puerto Rican women's value of gender interdependency and the African-American women's reliance on effective communication and advocacy within their own community. For example, the importance of male partner's acceptability of the device was raised by Puerto Rican women as a desired pre-trial condition and by African-American women as a consideration for education strategies to enhance women's capacity to communicate about the female condom. In assessing the potential for equality in protection provided by the female condom, women in the Puerto Rican group spoke of it as an equilibrium in condom availability for men and women while the African-American group discussed it as an increase in women's flexibility and responsibility in the use of "condom" technologies, particularly among women they considered "high risk" for HIV. Implicit in this concern was the advocacy for distribution of the female condom to segments not included in our participation criteria observed in the African-American community at different points during the implementation of our project.

Inter-group differences in focus of sexual health protection and previous experience with use of other protective technologies appear to influence the experiences with the female condom for segments of our study participants. Among women who knew about the device prior to their participation in the education session, Puerto Ricans were more likely to associate its protective function with pregnancy while African-American women emphasized HIV and other STIs. African-American women preferred pamphlets with information about how to communicate to a resistant partner about *male* condoms, and compared their experiences with the *female* condom with other insertive technologies (i.e., tampons and diaphragm). In contrast Puerto Rican women focused on communication with male partners about *female* condoms and made no references to the *male* condom.

While formative in nature, this ethnographic local case study suggests that Puerto Rican and African-American women have different patterns in communicating their very similar experiences to others, in addressing equivalent gender roles in negotiating a sexual health protection device with their male partners and in meeting their needs for information and access to protective technologies. The implications of these findings for future health education practice and research lies in understanding differences in the socio-historical dimensions of the local sociocultural template's gender dynamics interacting with ethnic traditions and community structures to create support for sexual health protection strategies such as the use of the female condom.

Health education efforts to promote sexual health among African-American women should build on community supports that form the core of their collective cultural capital: 1) an oral tradition to transfer information with personal meaning combined with a seemingly more progressive attitude toward human sexuality, that facilitates communication about sexual protection between women and men, and through community network channels, 2) familiarity with other protective barrier and insertive methods, 3) a central role for women's self-reliance in family and community spheres, and 4) strong bridges between natural support systems and institutionalized community health networks.

In contrast, program planners of sexual health education for Puerto Rican women should consider the development of community structures that address two seemingly contradictory but reciprocal conditions of the migration experience. First, Puerto Rican women have limited access to local institutionalized networks due to the complexity and the multiplicity of factors in the sociocultural urban template of the host community. Second, and the result of the first condition, Puerto Rican women have continued their ties with natural support systems of family, friends, and social networks ("al otro lado del charco") on the island of Puerto Rico. While these transnational relationships represent opportunities for Puerto Rican women to access the best resources of home and host communities for themselves and their families, they do *not* appear to increase women's ability to transform gender roles [16].

The context described above is fertile soil for the reproduction of cultural vestiges such as prudishness and reticence rooted in the *interaction* of Spanish colonialism, Catholicism and patriarchal systems that has been used to explain patterns of indirect communication about sexual matters and sexual roles in the literature [15, 17, 18], the preference for female sterilization surgery [19], and decisions against insertive technologies [17]. Yet, there are also indications that urban sociocultural templates present opportunities for redefining these socio-historical legacies and constructing new cultural blueprints that promote adoption of strategies for sexual health protection among segments of Puerto Rican women. Examples are found in studies from New York City describing changes in contraceptive behavior among those born in the United States [20] and efforts undertaken by sterilized women to redefine their sterilization as a strategy to create necessary social space that can influence non-reproductive areas of their lives [21].

We believe that in our study the basis for equivalency in thematic consensus on narratives about sexual health protection between urban young Puerto Rican and African-American women comes from segments of Puerto Rican women who in the midst of the competing challenges are successfully adopting new protective behaviors, such as the use of the female condom, and in the process, they are charting new cultural roads to promote direct open communication and negotiation of sexual health protection methods in their urban transcultural communities.

ACKNOWLEDGMENTS

Research for this chapter was funded by an ASPH/CDC Cooperative Agreement and the Massachusetts Department of Public Health STD Program. Technical guidance provided to the entire project by Carolyn Beeker, Katherine Stone, Carolyn Guenther-Grey is acknowledged. Some data in this chapter were presented at the 1996 Meetings of APHA and SfAA. Comments on early versions by Margaret Weeks and anonymous reviewers are also acknowledged.

REFERENCES

1. N. Freudenberg, Community-Based Health Education for Urban Populations: An Overview, *Health Education and Behavior, 25*:1, pp. 11-23, 1998.
2. N. Garcia Canclini, Urban Cultures at the End of the Century: The Anthropological Perspective, *International Social Science Journal, 49*:3, pp. 345-356, 1997.
3. CDC MMWR, Update: Barrier Protection against HIV Infection and Other Sexually Transmitted Diseases, *42*:30, pp. 589-591, 1993.

4. R. Hatcher, F. Stewat, J. Trussell, D. Kowal, F. Guest, G. Steward, W. Cates, and M. Policar, *Contraceptive Technology* (16th Edition), Irvinton Publishers, Inc., New York, 1994.
5. P. Campbell, Efficacy of the Female Condom, *Lancet, 341*:8853, p. 1155, 1993.
6. C. Sakondhavat, The Female Condom, *American Journal of Public Health, 80*:4, p. 498, 1990.
7. R. F. Schilling, N. El-Bassel, M. A. Leeper, and L. Freeman, Acceptance of the Female Condom by Latin and African American Women, *American Journal of Public Health, 81*:10, pp. 1345-1346, 1991.
8. R. S. Ashery, R. Carlson, R. Falck, H. Siegal, and J. Wang, Female Condom Use among Injection Drug and Crack Cocaine-Using Women, *American Journal of Public Health, 85*:5, pp. 736-737, 1995.
9. G. Farr, H. Gabelnick, K. Sturgen, and L. Dorflinger, Contraceptive Efficacy and Acceptability of the Female Condom, *American Journal of Public Health, 84*:12, pp. 1960-1964, 1994.
10. E. L. Gollub, Z. Stein, and W. El-Sadr, Short-Term Acceptability of the Female Condom among Staff and Patients at a New York City Hospital, *Family Planning Perspectives, 27*:4, pp. 155-158, 1994.
11. D. Shervington, The Acceptability of the Female Condom among Low Income African American Women, *Journal of the National Medical Association, 85*, pp. 341-347, 1995.
12. V. Gil, The New Female Condom: Attitudes and Opinions of Low Income Puerto Rican Women at Risk for HIV, *Qualitative Health Research, 5*, pp. 178-203, 1995.
13. P. Pelto and G. Pelto, Studying Culture, Knowledge and Behavior in Applied Medical Anthropology, *Medical Anthropology Quarterly, 11*:2, pp. 252-255, 1997.
14. J. Moore, J. S. Harrison, K. L. Kay, S. Deren, and L. Doll, Factors Associated with Hispanic Women's HIV-Related Communication and Condom Use with Male Partners, *AIDS Care, 7*:4, pp. 415-427, 1995.
15. M. Weeks, J. Schensul, S. Williams, M. Singer, and M. Grier, AIDS Prevention for African American and Latina Women: Building Culturally and Gender-Appropriate Intervention, *AIDS Education and Prevention, 7*:3, pp. 251-263, 1995.
16. M. Alicea, "A CHAMBERED NAUTILUS": The Contradictory Nature of Puerto Rican Women's Role in the Social Construction of a Transnational Community, *Gender and Society, 11*:5, pp. 597-626, 1997.
17. E. Acuña-Lillo, The Reproductive Health of Latinas in New York City: Making a Difference at the Individual Level, *Centro de Estudios Puertorriqueno, Bulletin, 2*:4, pp. 29-38, 1988.
18. E. Sotot, Sex-Role Traditionalism and Assertiveness in Puerto Rican Women Living in the United States, *Journal of Community Psychology, 11*, pp. 346-354, 1983.
19. A. Ramírez-de-Arrellano, *Colonialism, Catholicism and Contraception*, University of North Carolina Press, Chapel Hill, 1980.
20. J. Salvo, M. Powers, and R. Santan-Cooney, Contraception Use and Sterilization among Puerto Rican Women, *Family Planning Perspectives, 24*:5, pp. 119-223, 1992.
21. López, Agency and Constraint: Sterilization and Reproductive Freedom among Women in New York City, *Urban Anthropology, 22*:3-4, pp. 299-323, 1993.

CHAPTER 17

The CEPA Project: A New Model for Community-Based Program Planning

David Buchanan
Edna Apostol
Dalila Balfour
Carmen Claudio
Joani Marinoff
Nancy O'Hare
Maria Rodriguez
Carlos Santiago

In recent years, there has been a growing interest in "community-based" approaches to health promotion and disease prevention. A number of authors [1-4] have made a distinction between community-based strategies and what could be termed "social planning" approaches, borrowing from the classic typology by Rothman [5]. In the social planning model, the goals, objectives, and implementation activities are identified by public health professionals who design the programs based on their own training and expertise. The pioneering heart disease prevention programs, such as the Stanford three- and five-community studies, the North Karelia project, the Minnesota Heart Health plan and the Pawtucket (RI) project, are well-known examples of the social planning approach to community interventions. But, for a variety of reasons, many people have become disenchanted with expert-driven interventions and have called for new approaches in which lay citizens play a central decision-making role.

There are many reasons supporting a shift from expert-led to citizen-led interventions. First, there is a growing recognition that expert models have been, at best, only modestly successful and not with all populations. Also, there is a sense that, if many public health problems are rooted in community disintegration and anomie (e.g., alcohol and drug abuse, suicide, violence, unsafe sexual behavior, etc.), then a rekindling of community *civitas* [6] may be necessary to alleviate these problems. This kind of communal rejuvenation is not something that can be imposed by outsiders. Similarly, if a sense of powerlessness contributes to health problems, then a reliance on outside experts may foster or exacerbate feelings of dependency and incompetence.

In the larger picture, many people think government-run programs benefit middle-class program managers more than the populations in need. Some authors have gone even further to suggest that bureaucratic programs do more harm than good [4, 7]. Furthermore, there is a growing disillusionment with the ability of positivist social science methods to determine truths about the human condition, and hence, there have been renewed calls for moving away from the idea of a scientifically-guided" society and toward a "self-guiding" society [8]. Within the field of health education there have long been injunctions to "start where the people are" [9]. Finally, a powerful democratic impulse provides a moral imperative to open up any processes that might allow people to control the conditions that affect their lives.

Based on the foregoing, the call for community-based health promotion programs is well justified. In this chapter, we present a case study of a new program that has developed an innovative approach to community-based public health programming. The Centro de Educacion, Prevencion y Accion (CEPA) project is designed to break down the barriers between program developers and program recipients to the greatest degree possible. The program described here illustrates both the possibilities and the limitations of intensive citizen involvement. The case study presents some of the lessons learned in the process in hopes that they may be of value to others trying to develop community-based approaches to health promotion.

BACKGROUND

The Centro de Educacion, Prevencion y Accion (CEPA) project is a collaborative endeavor between the Holyoke Latino Community Coalition and the University of Massachusetts School of Public Health. The CEPA program is one part of a larger project funded under the "Community-Based Public Health" initiative of the W. K. Kellogg Foundation. To set the context for the discussion, a brief description of the overall initiative is in order.

The Community-Based Public Health initiative grew out of the recommendations contained in the Institute of Medicine's *Future of Public Health* (1988) report, the "Faculty-Agency Forum" meetings and original thinking from within the W. K. Kellogg Foundation. The initial "request for proposals" was released in March 1991. The Community-Based Public Health initiative was unique in at least two respects. Where both the IOM report and the

Faculty-Agency Forum focused on building stronger ties between academic programs and public health agencies (health departments), the Kellogg Foundation thought it essential to include community groups as well in any new efforts to revitalize the field of public health (for many of the reasons cited previously). Hence, they required a tripartite relationship: academics, professional practitioners, and community-based organizations.

Second, realizing that the creation of viable linkages among these three major partners was going to be an unprecedented and undoubtedly difficult process, the Foundation established a two-stage proposal process. The Request For Proposals (RFP) called for the submission of brief concept papers. From over 100 submissions, the Foundation selected fifteen semi-finalist consortia from across the country to participate in a year-long "Leadership and Model Development" phase. The LMD phase was unfunded (except for travel expenses) and, over the course of five national meetings, culminated in the development of full proposals. The full proposals were submitted in April 1992; seven consortia were awarded funding in September.

The Massachusetts Community-Based Public Health Consortium is composed of five major member organizations: the University of Massachusetts School of Public Health; the Massachusetts Area Health Education Centers (AHEC); the Massachusetts Association of Health Boards; the University of Massachusetts (Worcester) Medical School; and, four communities located in central and western Massachusetts. The project is located in semi-rural New England, with two distinct population groups participating: rural, white, working class communities, and rural Latinos (predominantly Puerto Ricans) now living in urban centers.

The initial contact that led to the creation of the Consortium was between the School of Public Health and the Massachusetts AHEC. At that time, the MAHEC had initiated and was staffing three conmmunity coalitions. In addition, the Executive Director of one of the local AHEC offices was also the co-chair of the Holyoke Latino Community Coalition. Thus, collaboration with the MAHEC was instrumental in initiating contacts between the university and the community coalitions.

The CEPA program is based in the city of Holyoke, a small city (pop. 42,463) in the throes of industrial decline. Holyoke has experienced large demographic shifts over the last two decades, with a major influx of Puerto Rican migrants who now compose over one-third of the population. Holyoke has among the highest rates in the state for infant mortality, teen pregnancy, children living in poverty, Latinos living in poverty, substance abuse problems, and people with HIV and AIDS. In a recent report, the Massachusetts Civil Rights Commission cited Holyoke as one of five cities in the Commonwealth likely to experience widespread civil disturbances in the next five years. A summary of select demographic and public health indicators comparing Holyoke with statewide averages is presented in Figures 1-3. By any measure, the health status indicators for Holyoke are grim.

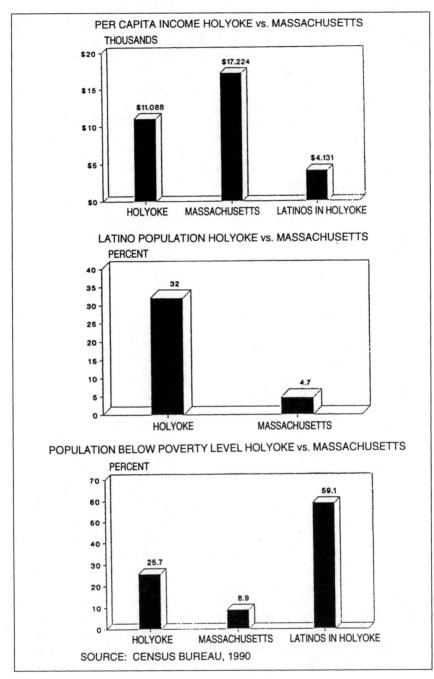

Figure 1. Select demographic indicators.

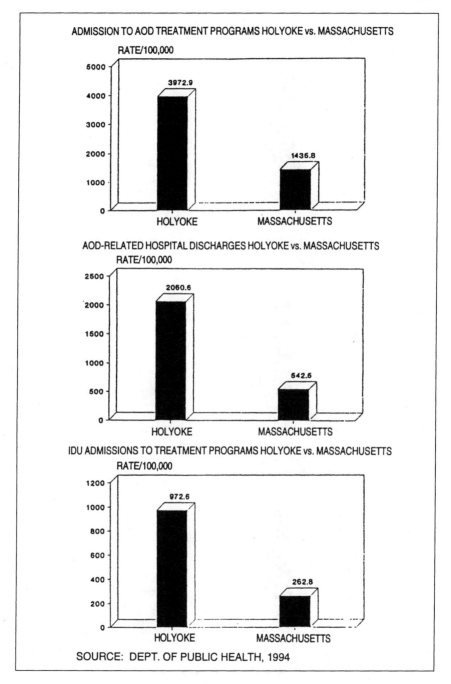

Figure 2. Select health indicators.

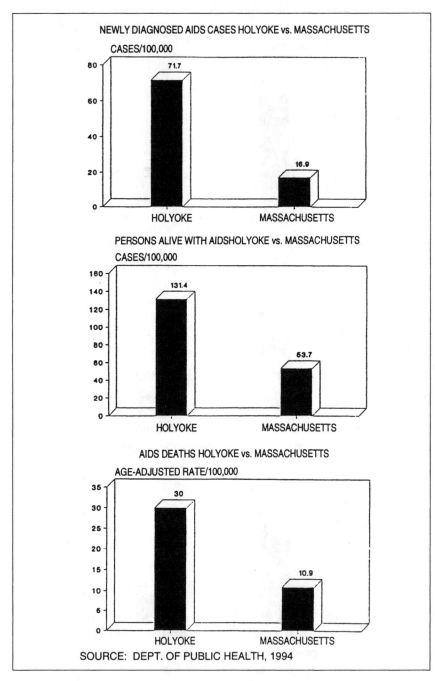

Figure 3. Select HIV/AIDS indicators.

This report describes the first two phases of the CEPA program, the planning and initial implementation phases, which occurred during the first two years of the project.

THE CEPA PROGRAM: PLANNING STAGE

During the Leadership and Model Development stage of the Community-Based Public Health initiative, an extensive needs assessment process was undertaken in each of the participating communities. One of the major advantages of this initiative is that there were no pre-conceived notions about the types of public health problems to be addressed. This opportunity enabled the Consortium to conduct a true community needs assessment, with free rein to pursue whichever connnunity priorities emerged, rather than—as is more commonly the case—responding to funding agency's mandates.

In Holyoke, a faculty member began working with the Health Promotion group of the Holyoke Latino Community Coalition (HLCC). The HLCC was founded in 1984 and is now the longest standing independent community organization serving the health needs of the Holyoke Latino community. The Health Promotion group is one of four action subgroups of the HLCC; the group ranges in size from six to ten members. The Health Promotion group is made up of Latinos who are Holyoke residents or health and human service providers working in Holyoke.

In the planning stage, the Health Promotion group used three methods to gather needs assessment information: focus groups with residents, personal and telephone interviews with providers, and a community forum. The basic protocol for the focus groups, interviews, and community forum is shown in Table 1. Information was collected in Spanish or English, whichever language was more comfortable for the participants.

A total of six focus groups were conducted by members of the Health Promotion group. Focus groups were held with: teenagers (two groups), residents in a public housing project, elders, and residents recruited on street corners (two groups). The responses gathered in the focus group interviews are notable for their insight into the health needs of the community. They also serve to illustrate the differences between a community-based approach and standardized needs assessment protocols (such as the CDC's Behavioral Risk Factor Survey).

For example, focus group participants were asked "¿Que cosas necesitan las personas/comunidades para ser saludables?" (What do people/communities need to be healthy?). Among the residents' responses were: "a person you can trust," "leaders who care," and "role models." While these answers may not fit into the response categories of standardized instruments (e.g., seat belt use, low-fat diets, and the like), they do offer insight into the limits of current epidemiological thinking.

Table 1. Focus Group and Interview Protocol

1. Que cosas necesitan las personas/comunidades para ser saludables?
   [What things do communities/persons need to be healthy?]

2. Que problemas de salud existen en Holyoke?
   [What are the health problems in Holyoke?]

3. Cuales de estos problems son los tres mas importante?
   [Which of these health problems are the three most important?]

4. Que tipo de programas tu puedes sugerir para ayudar a resolved algunos de estos problemas?
   [How can these problems be addressed?]

5. Que tipo de ayuda puede proveer la Escuela de Salud Publica en Holyoke?
   [How can the UMass School of Public Health help with some of these problems?]

In addition to the focus groups, the Health Promotion group conducted personal and telephone interviews ($N = 25$) with representatives from virtually all health agencies located in Holyoke. The use of a community-driven interview protocol, developed and implemented by members of the Holyoke community, again elicited remarkably perceptive responses. For example, in reply to questions about what people need to be healthy, providers answered: "purpose in life," "a sense of moral coherence," "good relationships," "a good basis for spiritual growth," as well as more conventional answers such as non-smoking and exercise.

Finally, the Holyoke Latino Community Coalition organized a community forum to allow other community members the opportunity to provide input into determining priority health needs. The forum was advertised through coalition mailings, the community newspaper, phone calls, and flyers distributed in the community. The community forum resulted in a lively discussion about current social conditions in Holyoke. Many pointed questions were directed at the academics regarding their motives for pursuing the project in the Holyoke community. The community forum was tape-recorded, transcribed, and analyzed by a consultant to the coalition.

The focus groups, telephone interviews, and the community forum resulted in the identification of four priority issues: 1) HIV/AIDS, 2) substance abuse, 3) domestic violence, and 4) medical interpreting services. Since the first three problems are closely related, the Health Promotion group decided to focus on HIV/AIDS prevention, with the expectation that any program that could have an impact on reducing the risk of HIV infection would also necessarily have to have an impact on issues like substance abuse and domestic violence. The needs assessment results were bolstered by Department of Public Health data that show that Holyoke suffers a vastly disproportionate share of the AIDS epidemic (see Figure 3).

In summary, in using a community-based approach, the CEPA project called on community members to identify their own questions and to collect information from other community members on their own terms. The academic partners played a minor secondary role. The results of this process were not only robust but in many respects more thought-provoking than standardized needs assessment protocols.

INITIAL IMPLEMENTATION STAGE

From the community needs assessment, the HLCC Health Promotion group proposed to initiate an innovative, community-based HIV/AIDS prevention program. The HP group (now joined by a faculty member and a graduate student) re-constituted itself as an Advisory Board for the CEPA project. Because of the history of Puerto Rico's colonial status, gross inequalities in economic status, and extensive personal experiences with discrimination, the HP group decided that the CEPA program should be based on a participatory, critical thinking and empowerment model.

The basic philosophy of the CEPA program is that people in high risk environments know better than anyone else what will be effective in preventing HIV infection given their circumstances. Therefore, the fundamental strategy of CEPA is to reduce the gap between program developers and program recipients to the greatest extent possible. This strategy ensures that program activities will be the most relevant, culturally appropriate, and well-suited to meet the needs of those at risk.

To put this strategy into practice, the CEPA program has developed a three-stage process: 1) Conciencization/Education, 2) Planning, and 3) Action (C-E-P-A). The stages are dynamic, not sequential; they overlap and inform one another.

Conciencizacion/Education

In stage one, the CEPA staff (a project coordinator and an outreach worker) participated in an intensive self-led educational process with the Advisory Board. The conciencization/education process [10, 11] focused on community development, community organizing, community empowerment, critical consciousness, and participatory education. The Advisory Board thought these topics were essential because of their experiences with discrimination and social and economic disenfranchisement in Holyoke. Particular readings were also identified by the Advisory Board. Sessions were conducted as a process of mutual self-education and consciousness-raising, with weekly meetings extending over a three-month period.

Growing out of the praxis of conciencization, the Advisory Board and CEPA staff developed an eleven-session training program to carry out with community residents. Even though the Advisory Board is composed of community residents and community providers, they felt they needed to get even closer to the population at risk, and hence, work directly with local neighborhood residents.

Like the staff development experience, the resident training program is based on models of empowerment and participatory education. Based on the work of Paulo Freire, the empowerment process has been described by Wallerstein [12]; it consists of listening, dialoguing, problem-posing, and action. As the Advisory Board discovered, the respective models (empowerment and participatory) are not entirely compatible, with an inherent bias toward examining the "root causes" of health problems in the empowerment model and a more open self-directed approach in the participatory education model [13-16]. The challenges in balancing these approaches will be examined in greater detail in the discussion section.

Planning

In stage two planning, the CEPA staff set out going door-to-door in a neighborhood selected because of its high level of risk factors (i.e., poor, rundown housing stock, high unemployment rates, high numbers of school drop-outs, presence of sex industry workers, and presence of drug dealers and shooting galleries). The staff also met with community agencies, social organizations, church representatives, tenants groups, and so on. They introduced themselves and the program and invited community residents to participate in planning the program.

The objective at this stage was to recruit a small group of eight to twelve neighborhood residents to form a Residents Planning Board. After lengthy discussions, the Advisory Board decided to enlist a planning group as diverse as possible, rather than seek out specific subgroups (e.g., sex workers, adolescents, etc.). Board members were opposed to the idea of recruiting community members according to pre-selected categories. In contrast to expert planning models, they thought that such a process would further fragment the community by stressing differences over more significant shared commonalities.

Based on a successful outreach effort, a highly diverse group was recruited in the initial round. The ten participants ranged in age from thirteen to fifty-five. There were two men and eight women, two people with AIDS, and one family unit (father, mother, and daughter). They work in a variety of occupations, from insurance, to homemaker, teacher, counselor, unemployed, and student. All are Puerto Rican.

All sessions were planned originally to be conducted in Spanish. As the group evolved, however, they decided to encourage people to speak in whichever language they felt most comfortable, as virtually everyone was bilingual. The residents were stipended for their participation. The stipends are not motivational incentives, but due compensation for the time, knowledge, and labor supplied by the residents.

The community residents then met once a week for two hours in the evening to participate in a series of structured discussions designed by the Advisory Board. At the heart of the community-based approach, these sessions are designed to have people living in high risk environments identify the needs, barriers, and resources they personally experience in trying to respond effectively to the threat of AIDS. The purpose of these discussions is to have those at highest risk decide for themselves the types of services, support, and actions that will best address the causes of their susceptibility.

(To recall the overlapping nature of the three identified stages, these sessions are also clearly a part of the community conciencizacion and education process and a part of the Action of the CEPA project.)

An outline of the objectives for the eleven sessions is shown in Table 2. The planning process took three months to complete. Each session was tape-recorded and each concluded with time for immediate feedback, so the process could be replicated and modified as needed. The end result of these sessions was the identification of the types of services needed for effective community-based HIV prevention. The desired program characteristics were framed in terms of a simple user-friendly "request for proposals."

Growing out of the planning process, the Residents Planning Board decided that community programs should focus on work with the teenage population. They identified four major goals for community programming. To prevent HIV infection, they said programs should: 1) promote self-esteem, both individually and collectively; 2) promote life-enhancing family values; 3) create a public space for the Puerto Rican community; and 4) promote effective communication skills.

The goals identified deserve a couple of comments. First, it is important to note that the community residents did not think that clinical information about modes of HIV transmission was essential. In contrast to many conventional programs, they understood well that the problem of AIDS was due to more than a simple lack of information. As one member put it, "You have to feel pretty good about yourself to want to protect yourself from HIV."

Second, the goal of promoting life-enhancing family values is a distinct reflection of Puerto Rican cultural values. In contrast to the high value placed on individualism in the United States, Puerto Rican community members situated the issue in the social context of inherent familial relationships. Echoing this priority, participants noted that the name of the project, "cepa," can be translated as "core" or "root," as in family roots of genealogical trees.

Table 2. Outline of Resident Training Sessions

Session	Objectives
1	To get to know group members To understand project expectations To understand individual/collective commitment and responsibilities To develop a schedule of next five meetings
2	To continue developing group cohesiveness To review project expectations To review schedule of meetings To introduce the topic of HIV
3	To share personal migration stories To share personal understanding of Holyoke To compare/contrast stories to connect collective experiences
4	To increase knowledge of HIV/AIDS To explore and begin to understand root causes of HIV infection To become more aware about why Latinos, specifically Puerto Ricans, are vulnerable to HIV To understand the social, psychological, and medical impact of HIV
5	To discuss further the root causes of HIV infection among Latinos To establish linkages among causes To illustrate with case studies how these linkages are interrelated
6	To continue discussing the root causes of HIV infection among Latinos To identify and discuss factors contributing to low self-esteem
7	To identify ways by which individuals can take individual and/or collective action to impact systems To identify individual/collective strengths that protect communities from low self-esteem and lack of well-being
8	To facilitate a process by which participants identify effective HIV prevention strategies To emphasize the individual's role as an impetus for change To connect the ideas that will be identified by this process with the resources that are available through the mini-grants
9	To continue the process of identifying the criteria for programs To prioritize the program proposals and ideas
10	To identify a process for announcing, selecting, reviewing, and evaluating the program proposals To identify participants who would like to continue as voluntary members of the advisory board To evaluate the residents' training program
11	To establish a timetable for the RFP and projects To recognize the efforts of the participants To celebrate the planning process

The Residents Planning Board identified seven additional characteristics or criteria that would make programs more effective: 1) peer (teen) involvement in programming and outreach activities; 2) Persons With AIDS (PWA) involvement in all levels of programming; 3) the appropriation of leadership and guidance roles by program participants; 4) a focus on the strengths within the community; 5) well trained staff; 6) an ongoing evaluation process; and 7) guarantees of confidentiality for participants. They advised that programs should focus on self-esteem, self-determination, community development, and the promotion of peer interaction. Typical activities might include after-school activities, summer programs, sports and other team activities, peer support groups, and drop-in neighborhood centers.

Action

In stage three, a call for community action was issued through the requests for proposals, providing funding for grants up to $5,000. The proposal was widely circulated in the community through flyers, radio programs and announcements, newspaper articles, outreach, handbills, mailings, community parties, presentations in agencies, a press conference, an open house, and word of mouth through informal interpersonal networks.

Members of the Residents Planning Board, Advisory Board, and CEPA staff jointly participated in reviewing the proposals and determining which groups received funding. In line with the project's philosophy, the reviewers decided from the outset to give preference in funding to non-traditional groups or agencies. Residents involved in the planning stage eagerly volunteered for a monitoring role in reviewing the progress of the community grants too.

In the first round, the reviewers decided to fund three proposals. One proposal was to lend partial support to a Latino teen theater troupe focusing on adolescent themes, one proposal was to set up a summer teen drop-in center (submitted and run by teenagers), and third was to fund a mother's group to start dance, music, and basketball lessons for neighborhood teens. As a condition of funding, the CEPA project requested that each group participate in a shortened version of the residents critical thinking process.

At this point, the CEPA project has successfully engaged community members in a substantive role in a community-based program planning process. Whether or not this process will result in more effective HIV prevention efforts is unknown at this time. In collaboration with community members, the Advisory Board will be monitoring the progress of the community grants over the next three years. CEPA is also in the process of replicating the program in two other neighborhoods. Based on the CEPA experience, there are several points for discussion about the prospects for community-based program planning.

DISCUSSION

At this point in the CEPA program, the Advisory Board members are deeply impressed both with the difficulties in creating a fully participatory model (and not slipping into a "banking" mode of education that presumes people need to be filled with the experts' information) and with the benefits of such an approach. The dilemma of reconciling a commitment to a participatory, community-based approach with the aspirations and expectations of the program initiators has become a central theme in ongoing discussions of the CEPA project. Several examples will serve to illustrate this point.

From the outset, the Advisory Board has wrestled with questions about how to define the project. Members were committed to a *process* of involving community members in designing the project. But we also recognized that funding agencies usually require quite specific delineation of the proposed program activities before extending their support. How, then, could CEPA specify the program activities before it had engaged the very people who were to decide which activities were most appropriate?

In the original grant proposal, the Health Promotion group compromised by describing the planned process and listing a number of *potential* activities. The W. K. Kellogg Foundation accepted the idea. But, when CEPA has sought additional funding, other foundations have responded as expected in demanding to know exactly what they were going to be getting for their money. The idea that program activities would emerge from the process and could take many unforeseeable forms has been difficult to sell (even to some of the other partners in the larger Kellogg CBPH project).

Then, the Advisory Board had to decide how to structure the residents training program. Again, we wrestled with the trade-offs. If the Advisory Board designed the training, then we would be assuming control, telling the participants what we expect them to do, and inevitably reproducing our own assumptions, interests, and biases. But if we did not provide any structure to the discussions, we feared people would think we were unprepared and did not know what we were doing. Again, a delicate, carefully considered compromise emerged as the process proceeded.

In the event, we decided to plan all of the sessions in advance (see Table 2). But during the training, we tried—largely unsuccessfully—to encourage the residents to take over and lead the sessions. We struggled too over revealing the full plan of the sessions. Some of us thought that presenting a completed plan would discourage the residents from realizing they could re-direct the sessions; others thought that failing to tell them what was planned was even more manipulative.

So, as the process was underway, we decided to share plans for the next immediate session and ask the residents for their suggestions and approval. Few changes were made. The feedback from the residents was that they were generally comfortable with the direction of the sessions. But they also expressed concerns—on more than one occasion—that they did not fully understand why we were doing a few particular activities and that they wanted to move more quickly into designing the HIV prevention program.

Two further examples: In planning the sessions, the Advisory Board decided to dedicate one session to a discussion of the historical relationship between Puerto Rico and the United States. Here, the tensions between a critical empowerment model and a participatory model became most apparent. On the one hand, Advisory Board members thought it was important to make clear the connection between the history of U.S. imperialist domination and the present disproportionate share of health burdens borne by the Puerto Rican peoples. On the other hand, Board members wanted just to hear and share personal migration stories and believed that collectively these stories would make the same point. So the CEPA project was again faced with questions about how to proceed.

In the session at hand, the Advisory Board tried to prepare a concise history of Puerto Rico's colonial status. It was of course impossible to cover a complete history in such a short period of time. So, a member of the Advisory Board ended up presenting a long lecture that took up almost the entire time that evening. The community voices were left out, the residents reduced to a passive role of being fed information. More to the point, the session jarred us into thinking about the seductiveness of power and control and about how we too had internalized the banking system of education.

Similarly, we felt obligated to present the clinical perspective about HIV transmission in another session. We invited a guest speaker, but we knew we needed to prepare her for the CEPA mutual teacher-learner educational process. We also thought the standard medical model needed to be balanced with a broader sociopolitical perspective that we could present. But despite the best laid plans, the guest speaker wound up dominating the session and the residents were again treated as empty vessels waiting to be filled.

As was the case after each session, the Advisory Board and staff took time immediately afterwards to process these sessions and reflect self-critically on the experience. Like at many other points in the project, we came face-to-face with the possibilities and limits of community-based program planning. The experience brought home how difficult it is to set up a process that enables people to take control of the conditions that affect their lives and how difficult it is not to assume a powerful, controlling role in telling people what we think they need to know.

We shared our concerns with the residents at the next meeting. Collectively, we decided to repeat the AIDS 101 session, this time, however, listening to the knowledge each of us already had. The candor of the Advisory Board, admitting our mistakes, dropping any pretensions as experts with answers about how people should live their lives, changed the tone and dynamic of the meetings. The distance between program developers and program recipients was narrowed. Community members and board members came a little closer in understanding that answers to questions about how to live in the face of the threat of AIDS could not be dictated, but must be generated through a process of mutual discussion, reflection and dialogue about the kind of community we want to live in together.

The Advisory Board was struck by the possibilities and benefits of this project as well. The most moving experience for everyone involved was a rekindling of pride in our Puerto Rican identity. The sense of confusion and ambivalence around having "dual identities"—and its relationship to a sense of low self-esteem—was openly discussed for the first time for many of us. Discussions about the influence of cultural roles and how they shape perceptions, both positively and negatively, of possible choices and subsequent decisions were frank, deeply personal, and collectively liberating. The experience reconnected each of us with the bonds of community.

In conclusion, the CEPA experience shows how program initiators inevitably make decisions that shape the direction of any resulting community programs. The idea that program developers can totally bracket their assumptions is difficult to maintain. The extent to which a program might be called "community-based" will always be a matter of degree. Hence, rather than presuming they have the best interests of the people at heart, public health professionals might better approach community development work by self-critically examining their own interests and biases first.

But these constraints are not insurmountable. As long as feedback is openly and continuously solicited and incorporated, the gap between program developers and recipients can continue to be narrowed. The CEPA project thus provides a powerful model for maximizing community involvement in issues vital to the health and well-being of community residents.

REFERENCES

1. D. Chavis and P. Florin, *Community Development, Community Participation, and Substance Abuse Prevention,* Bureau of Drug Abuse Services, Department of Health, Santa Clara County, California, 1990.
2. S. Fawcett, A. Paine, V. Francisco, and M. Vliet, Promoting Health through Community Development, in *Promoting Health and Mental Health: Behavioral Approaches to Prevention,* D. Glenwick and L. Jason (eds.), Haworth Press, New York.
3. H. Grace, Building Community: A Conceptual Perspective, *International Journal of the W. K. Kellogg Foundation,* W. K. Kellogg Foundation, Battle Creek, Michigan, Spring 1990.
4. J. McKnight, Regenerating Community, *Social Policy,* pp. 54-58, Winter 1987.
5. J. Rothman, Three Models of Community Organization Practice, Their Mixing and Phasing, in *Strategies of Community Organization: A Book of Readings* (3rd Edition), F. M. Cox, J. Erlich, and J. Rothman (eds.), F. E. Peacock, Itasca, Illinois, 1979.
6. D. Bell, *The Cultural Contradictions of Capitalism,* Basic Books, New York, 1976.
7. C. Murray, *Losing Ground,* Basic Books, New York, 1984.

8. C. Lindblom, *Inquiry and Change: The Troubled Attempt to Understand and Shape Society,* Yale University Press, New Haven, 1990.

9. D. Nyswander, The Open Society: Its Implications for Health Educators, *Health Education Monographs, 1,* pp. 3-13, 1967.

10. P. Freire, *Pedagogy of the Oppressed,* The Seabury Press, New York, 1968.

11. P. Freire, *Education for Critical Consciousness,* The Seabury Press, New York, 1973.

12. N. Wallerstein, Powerlessness, Empowerment and Health: Implications for Health Promotion Programs, *American Journal of Health Promotion, 6*:3, pp. 197-205, 1992.

13. CUSO, *Basic and Tools: A Collection of Popular Education Resources and Activities,* CUSO Education Department, Ottawa, 1985.

14. B. L. Hall and J. Kidd (eds.), *Adult Learning: A Design for Action,* Pergamon Press, Toronto, 1978.

15. M. Knowles, *The Adult Learner: A Neglected Species,* Gulf Publishing, Houston, 1978.

16. J. Mezirow, A Critical Theory of Self-Directed Learning, in *Self-Directed Learning: From Theory to Practice,* S. Brookfield (ed.), Jossey-Bass, San Francisco, 1985.

CHAPTER 18

The Intersections of Culture, Health, and Systems in California Latino Communities

Zoe Cardoza Clayson
Xóchitl Casteñada
Emma Sanchez
Claire Brindis

Strategies adopted within California *Latino* neighborhoods to improve community health provide important lessons for practitioners shaping health promotion programs, particularly with populations migrating across national boundaries. First, programs serving these *Latino* communities need to be crafted with a global perspective. Patterns of migration between Mexico, Central and South America, the Caribbean, and the United States require health-related community interventions to be culturally grounded in practices from the countries of origin and the United States. Second, a contextual analysis of the economic, political, and social conditions shaping the lives of these group members provides important insight for program developers. Because migration in and out of California is expected to grow, the characteristics of communities will continue to change, and, thus, health promotion strategies will need to remain flexible and receptive to modification. In addition, it is important for community members to understand how public and private systems function to access resources for long-term, sustainable development.

Creating effective health programs by those working in the service delivery and policy arenas, e.g., health and social service providers, coalitions focusing on legislative reform, and grassroots organizers, requires an understanding of the interrelationships of cultural and contextual factors. The analyses presented in this chapter are based on the authors' experiences over the past five years evaluating community health and economic development initiatives located in multi-ethnic, low-income California communities. The lessons learned from these initiatives may provide insight to practitioners in other countries working with diverse ethnic and socio-economic groups migrating across national boundaries. These factors will become more important as economic and political constructs become increasingly globalized.

A MODEL INTEGRATING CULTURE, HEALTH, AND CONTEXT

Developing culturally[1] grounded models built on *Latino* family concerns for health are important for providers, advocates and community members alike. While considerable research has focused on the influence of cultural factors on individual health seeking behaviors and health outcomes, very little has related to the intersection of culture and health with system-wide issue[2] [3, 4]. The community health interventions discussed in this chapter demonstrate how culture and health issues intersect with larger system-wide factors. Further, each intervention relates to three common factors important to California's *Latino* communities: language as a common symbol, the youthfulness of the population, and the importance of family. These models, a *promotora* health outreach effort, a neighborhood family resource center, and a school-based parent safety patrol, illustrate the strengths and challenges inherent to these types of efforts. The interrelationships between culture, health, and the larger environmental context are depicted in Figure 1, and each of the interventions will be discussed from the viewpoint of this multi-layered contextual analysis.

In this figure, the outer square with the broken line depicts the larger U.S. and cross-border context (the larger political, social, and economic constructs) while the inner square with the solid line represents the system in which the intervention is occurring, such as the publicly funded Medicaid health insurance system (Medi-Cal in California). Circle 1 represents cultural aspects of the community and Circle 2 represents the health issues of the population. The striped area

---

[1] Culture, as used in this context, can be viewed from the perspective of symbolic interactionism. That is, it is created over time through social interaction as people validate the past, construct the present and look toward the future. It is because people share perspectives and interact that the continuity of a social group is possible. "The beliefs, values, and prescribed behaviors of a culture are learned through traditions and transmitted from generation to generation" [1].

[2] In this chapter, the use of the term "system" is grounded in the work of Foucault who defines the social apparatus as "a system of relations that can be established between a heterogeneous ensemble of elements consisting of institutions, laws, administrative measures, scientific statements, and philosophical propositions . . . a social apparatus is grounded in a particular historical period and responds to an urgent need . . . thus the apparatus has a strategic function which is related to power" [2]. Navigating the system specifically refers to the ability of individuals and groups to interact with U.S. public and private institutions to obtain resources.

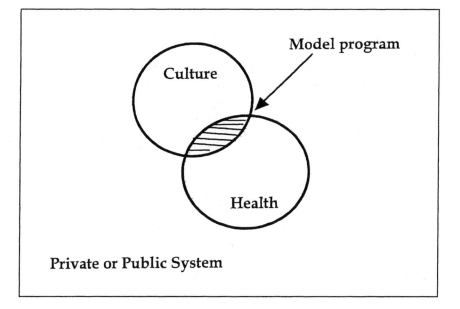

Figure 1. Social, political, and economic landscape.

where the circles overlap is the particular health promotion intervention. If this figure is viewed on three planes, then cutting through the striped section blends the imperatives of the *Latino* culture (e.g., the centrality of *la familia*), the health promotion intervention (e.g., children's health insurance), interacting with a particular system (e.g., Medi-Cal), and the larger environmental contexts such as U.S. migration policies and economic conditions in Mexico. Shaping and understanding the outcomes of these interventions while incorporating a contextual analysis with the goals of the health-related program are crucial. Prior to the discussion of the individual programs, the characteristics of California's *Latino* population and their common factors are described.

LATINOS IN CALIFORNIA

"Latinos" is a political term used to designate a heterogeneous Caribbean and Latin American population sharing a historical background and cultural perspectives. In California by 2015, *Latinos* will comprise the largest single ethnic/racial group living in California, representing between 15 and 20 million persons [4]. In California[3], Mexicans comprise the largest *Latino* group. A shared

[3] Mexicans represent about 63 percent of the *Latino* population (approximately 14 million people) in the United States. The Hispanic Population in the U.S.: March 1990. Current Population Reports. Series P-20 No. 449. Washington, D.C.: U.S. Bureau of Census, 1991.

border, agro-business expansion, and a sustained political, economic, and social crisis in Mexico all contribute to the growing representation of Mexicans in California. In the early 1980s, many Central Americans migrated to the United States, primarily from El Salvador and Guatemala [5], and, by 1990, nearly one out of every five *Latinos* was of Central American origin [4].

Previous studies have discussed the complexities in typifying the *Latino* identity [6–8]. First, *Latinos* come from various countries and are the heirs to *mestizaje* or hybrid cultures. In each country, multiple levels of development, wealth, and racial mixtures coexist and media, tourism, migration, and translocal and transnational networks play a major role in the configuration of *Latinos* identity(ies). Second, to define settings as purely urban or rural is difficult because of the multiple, overlapping relationships people establish. Through the use of technology, mass media, and oral histories, urban dimensions are increasingly brought to remote places, thus diminishing the isolation of rural communities. Finally, patterns of settlement and migration are important to understanding and working with *Latino* communities. There are significant differences between *Latinos* who were born in the United States, other who migrated 20 years ago, and those who recently crossed the border and may follow a pendulum pattern of migration[4]

THREE COMMON FACTORS: LANGUAGE, YOUTHFULNESS, AND FAMILY

In providing a framework for this chapter, three common factors have been identified which are relevant to a discussion of community health issues within major sectors of the *Latino* population: language as a common symbol, the growing proportion of the population that are children and youth, and the importance of the family.

Language as a Common Symbol

Although there are many differences in terms of words stemming from place of origin, class, and education, language is probably the main common symbol among *Latinos* living in California. Hertzler states that "the key and basic symbolism of human beings is language. Language is a culturally constructed and socially established system, in a given society" [9, p. 29]. Every conceptualization

---

[4] Using Rouse's formulation, the term "migrants" rather than "immigrants" will be used throughout this chapter. The term immigrants suggests an unidirectional movement, which does not portray the reality of millions of *Latinos* going back and forth between their countries of origin and the United States, as well as between geographical locations within the United States. Instead, the term migrant implies a continuum in the migration process of individuals who spend varying amounts of time in multiple communities across borders, often following seasonal growing patterns and economic cycles [8].

of health or illness (experienced, observed, or perceived) is accomplished through language. Eighty percent of *Latino* households are Spanish-speaking [4]. This linguistic homogeneity has contributed to the emergence of numerous Spanish communication networks, including hundreds of newspapers and magazines, several television channels, as well as local and national radio stations.

Youthfulness of the Population

With a median age of 26.2 years, *Latinos* are one of the youngest population groups in the United States. Thirty-two percent of the *Latino* population in the country is children 18 years of age and under. One of every three children in California is *Latino*; and, of every two newborns, one is Latino [4]. Poverty is the primary challenge to the health of many *Latino* children. In 1994, 40 percent of Latino children under six years of age were living in poverty. These are the children whose health status is most likely to be affected by family socio-economic status [10]. For *Latino* adolescents and young adults, many risk behaviors are linked to the complex social and psychobiological factors that condition their lives. Behaviors associated with drug use, alcohol consumption, smoking, sexual activity, physical inactivity, and lack of entertainment affect not only the individual's health, but also her or his family and social network [11, 12].

The Importance of the Family

Latino families in California tend to be configured in nuclear and interdependent extended kinship structures, with multiple and mobile networks. "Familism" is considered to be one of the most important cultural values of *Latinos* [13]. This term implies an attachment and interdependence of individuals with their nuclear and extended families and strong feelings of loyalty, reciprocity, and solidarity among members [14]. The *Latino* family has been characterized as being highly emotionally and materially supportive of its members [13]. It has been well documented that the *Latino* family, even in highly acculturated circumstances, is perceived by its members as the single most important institution protecting people against external problems [15-17]. High levels of support and trust perceived from the family include *"compadres"* (godparents) and adopted *"tios and tias"* (uncles and aunts) who play an important role in family life. These factors may have direct and indirect relationships to individual, family, and community health.

Strategies for building healthy *Latino* communities require developing interventions that are grounded in these cultural strengths and at the same time take into consideration the challenges of the larger political and economic context. California communities are diversifying rapidly on many dimensions and these changes require flexibility and innovative approaches to crafting health promotion interventions.

CHANGE COMMUNITIES REQUIRE
FLEXIBLE APPROACHES

As California's population expands and diversifies, strongholds of strictly homogenous neighborhoods are becoming scarce, and communities that thrive are those able to deal effectively with changing demographic patterns. Communities in which neighbors know each other well, take care of each other's children, and implicitly trust one another rarely exist today. Just as technology has altered modern life, the demands of an advanced industrial society have changed the time and intensity required for work, and thus reduced the time available for family interaction, recreational pursuits, and participation in civic affairs. Over the past decade, the polarization of wealth within the United States has increased significantly [18–21]. The least affluent are required to work longer and harder to meet their basic needs, a fact particularly relevant in low-income migrant communities.

Assets and deficits co-exist in these neighborhoods. For example, the lives of California's migrant farmworkers are shaped by historical racism, current anti-migrant sentiment, and the globalization of capital across the U.S.–Mexico border. While many families have strong ties, spiritual connections, and cohesive cultural practices, they may suffer from the effects of poverty, violence, and chemical dependency. In some California new-migrant communities, neighborhood in- and out-migration reaches 50 percent per year. Yet, existing within these mobile neighborhoods are structures, sometime invisible to outsiders, spoken, unspoken, formal and informal rules, and culture- and gender-specific imperatives. For those developing strategies to build healthy communities, understanding these co-existing micro and macro contexts are important.

METHODOLOGY

Guided by a critical theory social science perspective, the authors' evaluations have utilized constructivist methods extensively described by others [22, 23]. A theory of change approach is utilized along with a variety of qualitative and quantitative measures, e.g., grantee surveys, in-depth interviews, focus groups, and participant observation. The analyses presented in this chapter are based on the authors' evaluations of three California community initiatives conducted between 1993 and 2000: the Communities 2000 Initiative, the Lifeline Initiative, and the National Economic Development and Law Center's Family Supportive Initiative. The David and Lucile Packard Foundation's Communities 2000 Initiative, a 4-year, $3 million community-building effort, implemented in three California counties, provided small grants to over 100 neighborhood groups. The Initiative focused on building a sense of community, strengthening leadership, and enhancing civic engagement at the grassroots level. Over half the rural neighborhoods were *Latino,* primarily Mexican-American. Lifeline, a 5-year,

$3 million San Francisco Foundation Initiative, encouraged systemic change in programs serving low-income children and their families in the greater San Francisco Bay Area. Twenty-two collaboratives were funded, including 157 organizations within all the major ethnic urban communities of the area, including Spanish-speaking organizations serving those of Mexican and Central American origin in urban communities. Finally, the continuing, statewide-focused National Economic Development and Law Center's Family Support Initiative is crafted to assist community-based family support organizations to identify and adopt economic development strategies appropriate for their agencies. This Initiative included agencies from both urban and rural *Latino* communities.

In the following sections three models illustrating the interrelationships between culture, health, and systems in California low-income *Latino* communities are presented: 1) the *promotora* health outreach model; 2) El Centro Familiar: a neighborhood family resources center; and 3) Padres and Madres Para Sante: a school-based parent safety patrol.

A CROSS-BORDER PERSPECTIVE: THE PROMOTORA HEALTH OUTREACH MODEL

For decades, the *promotora* model for community health outreach has been successfully implemented in many Latin American countries [24]. This model, replicated and adapted in the United States, is based on a holistic conception of health, placing personal health within an economic, cultural, and political context. It focuses on a person-to-person approach: home visits or community events are conducted by *promotoras,* who share with their peers similar socio-economic characteristics and cultural norms. It has been well-documented that *Latinos* prefer personal contacts rather than impersonal interaction [25]. Thus, effective clinical interactions are guided by *personalismo,* which means "the trust and rapport that is established with others by developing warm, friendly and personal relationships . . . (these interactions) influence relations between individuals and with the health care system" [3, p. 25]. Among the U.S. *Latino* population, *promotora* projects have been identified as a particularly effective outreach method in rural areas [26].

In a sense, *promotoras* are community health advocates, as well as community health outreach workers (CHOW's). Some are volunteers and others are the paid staff of clinics, public programs, or community-based organizations. However, despite adopting this culturally grounded approach to community outreach, there remain significant system barriers that *promotora* efforts cannot address alone [27, 28]. For example, fear and lack of understanding of the requirements for eligibility to perceive publically funded services and the relationship of these services to U.S. migration policies are widespread in *Latino* communities. As one *promotora* reported, "In our Latino community, the two greatest barriers to enrolling children in Medi-Cal are parents' negative attitudes toward Medi-Cal and their fear that enrolling in Medi-Cal will be considered a 'public charge' and cause them to be deported or denied citizenship" [28, p. 19]. Public charge refers to portions of the U.S. immigration law that forbid those who are dependent on public resources from becoming naturalized citizens.

In addition, the Medi-Cal system is fraught with bureaucratic barriers. For example, to enroll in the publicly-funded Healthy Families, which is a children's health insurance program, children must have legal residential status. Therefore, all the children in one family may not be eligible for health insurance or to receive health services. Providing services to one child and not to another within the same family violates a major cultural value in *Latino* communities, the centrality of *toda la familia*. These kinds of cultural factors have been reported as important issues related to the low enrollment of *Latino* families in California's Healthy Families program [16, 29, 30]. Thus, for effective outreach to enroll families in an insurance program or screen for diabetes, *promotoras* as a single strategy are insufficient. In addition, systems barriers should be identified and public policies advocated to reduce or eliminate them. For example, in the California First Things First Initiative, a California Healthcare Foundation sponsored effort to enroll families in the Healthy Families, a children's health insurance program, alliances were forged in one county between Spanish-speaking *promotora* outreach workers and staff from the local Department of Social Services. These linkages eventually led to system-level modifications to simplify the paperwork necessary for family enrollment and follow-up [31]. In some communities, *promotoras* operate from neighborhood family resources centers like El Centro Familiar, the second example of a culturally grounded model designed to support the health and well-being of *Latino* families.

CULTURAL PRACTICES INTERSECT ECONOMIC AND POLITICAL REALITIES: THE CASE OF EL CENTRO FAMILIAR

Located in a multi-ethnic, urban, *Latino* community, El Centro Familiar (a pseudonym) has existed for many decades. In recent times, 400-500 families per year were engaged in events and services through El Centro, including participating in traditional community celebrations (Posadas), case management and referral services, and soccer teams for youth. Some of the powerful ways traditional celebrations directly intersected with health promotion activities are illustrated by the flower-making classes and El Centro-sponsored soccer clubs. In Mexico and Central America, women create paper flowers for a variety of purposes including gifts and decorations for special events and holiday celebrations. El Centro had several well-attended flower-making classes where women made flowers, visited with one another, and received information about breast self-exams and diabetes screening. Sometimes health screenings were conducted during the classes. Soccer, a sports activity valued in all Latin American societies, also had good participation by neighborhood youth and parents from the neighborhood.

Despite this culturally grounded format, broader system issues permeated the life of El Centro. One example related to the enormous basic material needs of low-income families, and the other involved the growing anti-migrant sentiment in California. Staff tried to involve volunteers, primarily women, from the neighborhood in organizing events at El Centro. However, as in other communities, competing demands prevented neighbors from participating. Often they were required to hold several jobs and work long hours to meet their basic needs. Case managers expressed frustration regarding the overwhelming level of material needs of families coming to El Centro. For example, it was common for 10 or more people to live in one apartment sublet from an absentee landlord. As gentrification accelerated in this urban community, housing costs escalated exacerbating an already desperate situation for some families. Employment for family members was also problematic where English-speaking abilities, resident documentation status, and job skills presented significant barriers.

The unfolding story of California's Proposition 187 demonstrated the added ingredient of anti-migrant sentiment in the state. A California ballot initiative designed to prevent undocumented residents from receiving any health, education, or social public services was voted on in the November 1994 general election (Proposition 187). Latino communities particularly feared this anti-migrant initiative because many residents were undocumented. While El Centro served a large number of undocumented families, no preparations were made or systematic discussions held with families as Election Day approached. The day after the initiative was passed by a large majority of voters, attendance at El Centro fell to almost zero. This incident illustrates two points. First, El Centro management had become isolated from the issues that most directly affected the community; and second, the Executive Director was afraid to do anything that might be perceived as advocacy by the Internal Revenue Services (IRS). Regarding this second issue, IRS policies limit the amount of advocacy non-profit organizations can conduct and still maintain their non-profit status (501c3). Usually, the IRS does not enforce these regulations unless complaints are received or the issue involved becomes very politicized, such as in the case of migration reform. Although El Centro management feared that any discussion might have been considered advocacy, clearly there was a role to play in providing basic information and education regarding the initiative and the potential implications of its passage, including the basic rights that would continue to exist.

After this incident, El Centro management needed to reflect on their priorities and services to better learn how to adapt as a result of these events. What had been most lacking was a strategic vision that linked the political and economic context with the priorities of El Centro. Management acknowledged that their approach to volunteerism needed to be more realistic; case managers had to prioritize their workloads to match the actual resources of El Centro more appropriately with the needs of the community; and finally, a strategy linking El Centro to public policy advocates was required.

These examples demonstrate that a comprehensive approach to strengthening community health is embedded in a broader context, where variables like migratory status, housing availability, and language proficiency intersect with culturally grounded health concerns. In some instances, the starting point for neighbors is a challenge that already exists in the community, like ensuring children's safety around schools.

SCHOOL-BASED PARENT SAFETY PATROLS LINK PARENTS WITH PUBLIC SYSTEMS: PADRES AND MADRES PARA SANTE

In Padres and Madres Para Sante (a pseudonym), a dozen parents organized within one public elementary school in a neighborhood that was approximately 98 percent of Mexican origin. The majority of these families were first generation migrants, with limited English-speaking ability, and had very little experience with U.S. public systems. The school is located in a rural suburban community where agro-business has dominated the economy for almost a century, along with discrimination toward people of Mexican origin in housing and employment. Although in recent times this situation has improved, the remnants of these past practices still exist in public and private institutions. In addition, the neighborhood where the school was located experienced a high rate of in- and out-migration, particularly from the Michocan Province of Mexico.

Each morning as parents brought their children to school, they began to discuss their concerns for their children's safety, including cars driving too fast past the school and gang activity in the neighborhood. In time, these parents met with the Principal of the school and with staff from a local non-profit organization involved in community violence prevention to express their concerns. Particularly Ms. Martinez (pseudonym), a Spanish-speaking staff member with a local non-profit organization, was very helpful in assisting the parents in thinking about how they could act on their concerns. Finally, with support from the Principal and Ms. Martinez, the mothers and fathers implemented a school-based parent patrol program. Intersecting with the area's police department, they received training from police officers on pedestrian and school traffic rules. On a volunteer basis, parents ensured that cars stopped within the marked areas to drop children off at the school. Within a year and a half, the parent patrol was functioning well. They had obtained attractive jackets for all the members, with their group's name on the back, with funds provided by a local community foundation.

Leaders from this successful group met with and trained parents from several nearby schools. At one of the other schools, parents attempted a similar effort but were unsuccessful. The basic reason was resistance from the Principal. While this individual espoused interest in parental involvement, he wanted parents involved only in certain activities, e.g., holiday celebrations. Also, his lack of Spanish-language ability presented barriers to communicating effectively with parents. Traditionally in this community, parents had little influence on school policies and some school officials were reluctant to change this balance of power.

The school-based parent safety patrol illustrates how a community effort supporting health and safety can build on the cultural strengths of the *Latino* community, e.g., concern for *la familia,* educating parents about public institutions, and structuring mentoring opportunities and leadership development among parents. At least one of the group leaders was required to speak English to negotiate with the police department trainers and school system officials. As the parents built school to community linkages, they became educated about the functioning of an important U.S. public institution. Though this neighborhood had high in- and out-migration rates, most of the families originated from one area of Mexico and the relationships established with the local school system extended to the next group of arriving families. Presently, parent patrols create school-wide awareness about traffic and safety issues, build and expand parent involvement, and generate a presence in their community. These visibility factors were cited by parents as an important element in reducing gang activities around their school. For the future, they will continue to build capacity in the neighborhood to use their cultural assets, leadership, and systems knowledge to strengthen their community.

TOWARD THE FUTURE

The above examples demonstrate the importance of linking cultural perspectives and community health strategies to contextual analyses. Further, the growing migration of groups across national borders and the globalization of economic and political constructs, point to the importance of structuring a global perspective into these interventions. Particularly for *Latino* communities in the United States, the recognition of language as a common symbol, the growing proportion of the population who are children and youth, and the importance of the family also should be included in framing interventions.

Recognizing the central importance of language, efforts should be conducted in a linguistically appropriate manner including attending to the nuances of the Spanish language used among different ethnic, socio-economic, age groups, and geographic configuration. The growing proportion of the children and youth in California's *Latino* population implies that health promotion and advocacy strategies should incorporate youth perspectives. This could be achieved by using engaging cultural formats while recognizing that, especially in low-income communities, economic investments in childcare, recreational facilities, and jobs are also needed by youth.

Family is perceived as the most important social institution among the *Latinos*. In this sense, family-focused interventions can impact *Latino* community health and well being positively. Use of *promotoras* is one family-oriented, holistic model that expands beyond direct traditional health-related concerns to assist family members with a wide range of issues including housing and employment. Neighborhood-based family resource centers, offering a comprehensive array of services and cultural celebrations, are another strengths-based approach for supporting *Latino* families. In addition, parental involvement in their children's schools can strengthen the links between children and their parents and public institutions, reinforce positive cultural values, and decrease the later need to focus on anti-social behaviors, e.g., violence prevention.

All of these efforts to involve *Latino* families in improving community health are vibrant and exciting, at the same time their social, economic, and cultural challenges should be recognized. Those having limited English-speaking ability or who are from cultures where business is conducted differently than in the United States, have additional barriers to overcome, whether accessing health care or negotiating with a school principal. Many systems like Medi-Cal (Medicaid in California) have limited low-income people's access to public resources regardless of their ethnic group. In addition, past and present treatment of *Latinos* in California, including migration restrictions and employment and housing discrimination, speak to concerns that those involved in building healthy communities will be required to address.

Finally, the active involvement of community members in the implementation of health promotion and advocacy efforts is the essence of community health. Migration patterns of *Latinos* in and out of California suggest that the characteristics of communities will continue to change, and thus health promotion strategies should remain flexible. Understanding how public and private systems function and building bridges between them and communities to access resources will remain crucial for creating healthy and sustainable communities.

REFERENCES

1. M. Kagawa-Singer, Today's Reality: Research Issues in Underserved Populations, *Journal of the American Cancer Society*, pp. 1-17, 1994.
2. M. Foucault, *Power/Knowledge: Selected Writing*, Pantheon Books, New York, 1980.
3. M. Aguirre-Molina and C. Molina, Latino Populations: Who Are They? in *Latino Health in the US: A Growing Challenge*, C. Molina and M. Aguirre-Molina (eds.), American Public Health Association, Washington, D.C., 1994.
4. D. Hayes-Bautista, *The Health Status of Latinos in California. California*, The California Endowment and California HealthCare Foundation, 1997.
5. N. Hamilton and N. Chinchilla-Stolz, Central America Migration: A Framework for Analysis, *Latin American Research Review*, 6:1, pp. 75-110, 1991.

6. M. Kearney, Borders and Boundaries of the State and Self at the End of the Empire, in *Migrants, Regional Identities and Latin American Cities,* T. Altamirano and L. Ryo-Hirabayashi (eds.), American Anthropological Association, Arlington, Virginia, pp. 151-168, 1995.

7. M. Kearney and C. Nagensgast, *Anthropological Perspectives on Transnational Communities in Rural California,* California Institute for Rural Studies, Davis, California, 1989.

8. R. Rouse, Questions of Identity. Personhood and Collectivity in Transnational Migration to the US, *Critique of Anthropology, 15*:4, pp. 351-380, 1995.

9. J. Hertzler, *Sociology of Language,* Random House, New York, 1965.

10. H. Rodriguez-Trias and A. Ramirez-de Arellano, The Health of Children and Youth, in *Latino Health in the US: A Growing Challenge,* C. Molina and M. Aguirre-Molina (eds.), American Public Health Association, Washington, D.C., 1994.

11. R. DiClemente, C. Boyer, and E. Morales, Minorities and AIDS: Knowledge, Attitudes, and Misconceptions among Black and Latino Adolescents, *Public Health Briefs, 78*:1, pp. 55-57, 1988.

12. Control Centers for Disease Control, Vigorous Physical Activity among High School Students, *Morbidity and Mortality Weekly Report, 41,* pp. 33-35, 1992.

13. J. Moore, *Mexican-American,* Prentice-Hall, Englewood Cliffs, New Jersey, 1970.

14. F. Sabogal, G. Marin, and R. Otero-Sabogal, Hispanic Familism and Acculturation: What Changes and What Doesn't? *Hispanic Journal of Behavioral Sciences, 9*:4, pp. 397-412, 1987.

15. S. Cobb, Social Support as a Moderator of Life Stress, *Psychosomatic Medicine,* pp. 300-314, 1976.

16. L. Cohen, *Culture, Disease and Stress among Latino Immigrants,* Smithsonian Institute, Washington, D.C., 1979.

17. S. Keefe, A. Padilla, and M. Carlos, The Mexican-American Extended Family as an Emotional Support System, *Human Organization, 1979.*

18. D. Coburn, Income Inequality, Social Cohesion and the Health Status of Populations: The Role of Neo-Liberalism, *Social Science and Medicine, 51,* pp. 135-146, 2000.

19. I. Kawachi, B. Kennedy, et al., *The Society and Population Health, Reader: Income Inequality and Health,* The New Press, New York, 1999.

20. D. Feenbeerg, *Income Inequality and the Incomes of Very-High Income Taxpayers: Working Paper, 4229,* National Bureau of Economic Research, Cambridge, 1992.

21. N. Alder, T. Boyce, et al. Socioeconomic Status and Health: The Challenge of the Gradient, *American Psychologist, 49,* pp. 15-24, 1994.

22. K. Charmaz, Grounded Theory: Objectivist and Constructivist Methods, in *Handbook of Qualitative Research* (2nd Edition), Y. Denzin NaL (ed.), Sage Publication, Inc., Thousand Oaks, California, 2000.

23. E. G. Guba and Y. S. Lincoln, *Competing Paradigms in Qualitative Research,* Sage, Thousand Oaks, California, 1994.

24. J. Meister, *Community Outreach and Community Mobilization: Options for Health at the US Mexico Border,* Department of Health Services, Phoenix, 1996.

25. T. Raven BaL-A, Interpersonal Influence and Social Power in Health Promotion, *Advances in Health Education and Promotion, 1,* pp. 181-209, 1986.

26. L. Rundall TW, et al. *Lessons Learned about Outreach: Findings from Ten First Things First Community Coalitions Created to Enroll Eligible Children in MediCal,* California Health Care Foundation, Oakland, pp. 1-35, 1999.

27. E. Perry MS, *Barriers to Medi-Cal Enrollment and Ideas for Improving Enrollment: Findings from Eight Focus Groups in California with Parents of Potentially Eligible Children,* The Henry J. Kaiser Foundation, Menlo Park, 1998.

28. The 100% Campaign, *Health Insurance for Every Child. Community Voices: Findings from the Children's Health Insurance Feedback Loop on Efforts to Enroll Children in Medi-Cal and Healthy Families,* The 100% Campaign, Los Angeles, 1998.

29. D. Horner, W. Lazarus, et al., *How to Enroll Large Groups of Eligible Children in Medicaid and CHIP,* The Henry J. Kaiser Family Foundation, Menlo Park, 1999.

30. M. Ellwood, *The Medicaid Eligibility Maze: Coverage Expands, but Enrollment Problems Persist: Findings from a Five-State Study,* The Urban Institute, New York, 1999.

31. T. Rundall, *The Final Evaluation Report: Findings from the First Things First Initiative,* The California Health Care Foundation, Oakland, California, 2000.

CHAPTER 19

Another Crack in the Mirror: The Politics of AIDS Prevention in Mexico

Héctor Carrillo

Since 1983, when the first case of AIDS in Mexico was identified in a Mexico City hospital, thousands of Mexicans have been diagnosed with the syndrome (called "SIDA" in Spanish) and thousands more have been infected with HIV. To attempt to stop the epidemic, a variety of groups have responded: the Mexican government, nongovernmental groups, and individuals interested in the prevention of HIV transmission. Although the general response to AIDS in Mexico resembles, at least in principle, the efforts developed in other countries like the United States, it is flavored by the particular characteristics of the local culture, social organization, economics and politics.

This chapter presents a broad analysis of the social context in which AIDS prevention takes place in Mexico. The premise is that, to understand the role of prevention, to analyze the feasibility of its methods, and to project the possibilities of its success, public health practitioners must consider broader social forces in the formulation of their strategies. The distinctive epidemiological characteristics of AIDS in Mexico, the relationship between common people and the state, the role of civil society in the resolution of social problems, attitudes toward difference and social diversity, and the availability of funding are all factors that may influence the success or failure of public health interventions.

In more general terms, the case of AIDS prevention in Mexico exemplifies the importance of politics, society and culture in the design of educational interventions. As a result, the case should also illustrate the fact that prevention efforts cannot be planned without contact with the community, but rather must be shaped and molded according to the social conditions of the people whom they intend to serve.

THE NATURE AND SCOPE OF THE AIDS
EPIDEMIC IN MEXICO

As of January 1993, Mexico had reported to the World Health Organization (WHO) 12,540 cumulative AIDS cases [1].[1] This figure put Mexico in eleventh place worldwide in terms of the number of AIDS cases, and third place in the American continent (after the United States and Brazil). The official number of cases, however, is considered to be but a fraction of the actual total. The Secretariat of Health (SSA), the agency that compiles epidemiological data in Mexico, has estimated a rate of underreporting of more than 50 percent that would yield a more realistic figure of about 19,000 cases. Other studies have projected a total of around 25,000 cases by the end of 1993 [2].

Based on the number of yearly cases since 1983, the SSA has stated that the increase in number of cases was slow between 1983 and 1986, exponential between 1987 and 1990, and moderate since 1991, tending to stabilization. Yet, although it is true that the number of cases reported in 1992 (3,219) was just slightly higher than that reported in 1991 (3,166), it is too early to predict that the epidemic is stabilizing. In fact, before 1991, the number of yearly cases reported had been 2,400 or less, so any figure above 3,000 is considerable.

The majority of AIDS cases in Mexico have been reported in large urban areas and tourist resorts. The number of cases per million is highest in Guadalajara (523), Veracruz (488), Mexico City (462), Cuernavaca (448), and Mérida (379). The total number of cases is highest in Mexico City (33 percent of all cases) and the states of Jalisco (22.6 percent), Mexico (which borders Mexico City) (4.8 percent), and San Luis Potosí, Michoacán and Yucatán (4.0 percent each). Most of the cases have affected middle class people; however, the proportion of cases among lower income groups is growing [3]. There is increasing concern about the potential for an epidemic in rural areas, particularly in towns that have a large number of seasonal agricultural migrants to the United States.[2] In fact, officials have detected what appears to be a shift in regional patterns: the increase in the number of cases in large cities appears to be slowing down, while smaller cities and towns with fewer cases have increasingly higher rates.

In urban areas, as in most other countries, some social groups have been affected disproportionately. Following an epidemiological pattern similar to that in the United States, the first cases were detected among homosexual men. Currently, of 10,425 adult men with AIDS, 87.7 percent acquired HIV sexually: 40 percent have been homosexual, 27.7 percent bisexual, and 20 percent heterosexual. The transmission mode of the remaining cases is thought to be blood

---

[1] All statistics related to the number of AIDS cases in Mexico in this section are provided by INDRE [1].

[2] In Michoacán, one of the states with largest migration to U.S., of 323 cases reported, 110 are among people returning from the United States [4].

transfusions (6.2 percent), professional blood donation (2.7 percent), hemophilia (1.3 percent), and IV drug use (0.8 percent). No risk information is available for 15.3 percent of the men, while 1.3 percent are categorized as both homosexual and IV drug users.

Among adult women, the distribution is very different. In general, it is thought that most women with AIDS have acquired HIV from blood transfusions (57.9 percent of 1,726 women), or through heterosexual sex (38.8 percent). Other risk factors are donating blood (2.6 percent), and IV drug use (0.5 percent). No risk information is available for 14.2 percent of the cases among women. Contrary to popular perceptions, as of 1991 there were more cases of AIDS among housewives than among female prostitutes [5]. Studies of HIV seroprevalence among Mexican female prostitutes have yielded results of between 0 and 5 percent [3, 6].

In terms of age, a majority of cases have affected men and women between twenty-five and thirty-four years old (40.6 percent). The number of pediatric cases is 389, of which 51.7 percent acquired HIV from their mothers, 28 percent from blood transfusions, 18.3 percent due to products to treat hemophilia, and 2.0 percent from sexual abuse.

The picture that emerges from these data is one of an epidemic with characteristics different from those of the AIDS epidemic in the United States. Not unlike the United States, homosexual and bisexual men in Mexico are the group most affected by the disease (57 percent of all cases in the United States, and 67.7 percent in Mexico) [7].[3] However, while in the United States almost 23 percent of the cases are among IV drug users, in Mexico IV drug use accounts for only 0.7 percent.[4] As in the United States, AIDS in Mexico has affected more men than women. However, compared to the United States, the role of heterosexual transmission in Mexico appears to be greater (22.7 percent of all cases in Mexico versus 6.4 percent in the United States). As time passes, an increasingly larger number of women are being diagnosed with AIDS in Mexico, in comparison to men. In 1984, there were twenty-five new cases among men for every new case affecting a woman. By 1992, the ratio had dropped to only 5:1.

The consensus among officials and AIDS activists is that bisexual behavior is a "bridge" that has brought HIV from homosexual men to women. As a result, Mexican officials have been careful to distinguish between homosexual *and* bisexual men in their statistics. Yet, no studies have fully demonstrated that "bridge." And a comparison with the United States is difficult, given that U.S.

---

[3] All statistics about the number of AIDS cases in the United States are provided by the Centers for Disease Control and Prevention [7].

[4] Recently, there has been an increase in the number of people with AIDS who acquired the infection through IV drug use, particularly in border cities such as Tijuana and Mexicali and in the three largest cities: Mexico City, Guadalajara, and Monterrey [8].

epidemiological statistics lump together homosexual and bisexual men in one single category.

Another interesting comparison is the number of women with AIDS who acquired HIV from blood transfusions in Mexico. Not only is blood transfusion the main cause of infection among women with AIDS, but there are many more women infected in this way than men with AIDS (894 versus 611). Mexican officials explain this disparity as caused by the high number of women who receive blood transfusions during labor. However, in the United States the relationship is the opposite: 3,036 men versus 1,994 women with AIDS who acquired HIV from a blood transfusion. Although it is possible that, proportionally speaking, more women receive transfusions during labor in Mexico, one could speculate that an additional factor could be medical reluctance to diagnose risk as sexual among women, given the level of stigma attached to women's sexuality in Mexico. However, only a study could determine the cause of this disparity.

A common perception is that blood transfusions have been responsible for a greater problem in Mexico than in the United States. However, the number of transfusion AIDS cases per million in Mexico is 16.7 compared to 21.3 in the United States. Nevertheless, the perception of higher risk in Mexico might be related to the existence of less stringent and consistent procedures to protect the blood supply from contamination with HIV.

Also in relation to blood, there has been an unusual form of HIV transmission in Mexico that was not present in the United States. A large number of Mexican professional blood donors acquired HIV in the blood banks. This happened because many commercial blood banks reutilized syringes when they collected blood samples. As a result, in places such as Nezahualcóyotl, a working class suburb of Mexico City, entire families of paid blood donors became HIV-positive [9]. Some studies have found HIV-infection of up to 20 and 30 percent in samples of blood donors [10, 11]. However, due to the closing of all commercial blood banks in 1987, the number of new infections through blood donation has been greatly reduced.

All the statistics quoted above are based on the total number of diagnosed AIDS cases. Few studies in Mexico have been conducted about the number of people who are infected with HIV. Thus, there are no accurate estimates of the number of asymptomatic HIV-positive persons in Mexico. In 1988, the SSA estimated a 24:1 ratio between diagnosed cases and asymptomatic infection. For that year, the use of this ratio yielded 115,000 cases of HIV infection. Around the same time, Gonzalez Block estimated the number of HIV-positive people to be anywhere between 35,000 and 70,000 [12]. Other officials at SSA used similar figures (between 31,600 and 97,700) [13]. If the rate is applied today, using the official number of cases, the number of HIV-positive people would be 300,960. If we account for underreporting, that number would jump to 457,440. Some activists have used the WHO ratios of 1:50 to 1:100 in estimating between

660,400 to 1,320,800 HIV-positive people [14]. However, none of these figures can be scientifically substantiated.

A few seroprevalence studies with homosexual and bisexual men have yielded high proportions of HIV infection in that population. Valdespino and García report that the findings vary from 2 percent to 35 percent in Mexico City, 36 percent and more in Puebla, and lower in other cities [3]. Hernández et al. found a seroprevalence rate of 34 percent among homosexual men and 21 percent among bisexual men in a sample of 2,314 homosexual and bisexual men in Mexico City, between 1988 and 1989 [15]. A recent study in Monterrey found 93 percent seroprevalence in a sample of 100 homosexual men. However, this is the only study that has yielded such high seroprevalence levels [16].[5]

These data on AIDS cases suggest the broad contours of the epidemic in Mexico. However, to understand how to prevent the further spread of HIV, we need to analyze the social and political environment in which the AIDS epidemic has unfolded.

THE FIRST RESPONSE TO AIDS

Although the first news about AIDS in the United States arrived in Mexico early in the 1980s, few people had heard of the disease until 1985. The announcement of Rock Hudson's diagnosis, and the subsequent series of newspaper articles about the existence of AIDS cases in Mexico, brought the disease out of the closet. As Mejía points out, the first attempts by Mexican reporters to cover AIDS were tainted by moralism and by a condemnation of sex and particularly of homosexual practices [12]. These early articles also openly blamed people with HIV for acquiring the disease.

Between 1983 and 1985 there were no statements about AIDS made by Mexican government officials. However, as a result of the publicity that AIDS received in 1985, and the rumors about an epidemic that was out of control, public health officials were forced to break their silence about AIDS in 1986. A report by the Secretary of Health read:

> Mexicans have *no reason to be alarmed* by the acquired immunodeficiency syndrome that has reached high incidence in other countries because, of 63 detected cases, only 17 have been confirmed (quoted in [12], p. 31, my emphasis and translation).

The official view was that the disease did not represent a problem for Mexicans, and the commentary aimed to justify the lack of state response to confront it.

---

[5] This study does not report how the subjects were selected. Other studies have recruited homosexual and bisexual men who seek HIV testing.

This view was confirmed by the opinions of other prominent physicians and public health officials, who stated that most Mexicans were not at risk because "the population of Mexico does not belong to the risk groups."[6] Given that there were few cases, "it makes no sense to distract large amounts of economic and human resources . . . to combat the malady when there are other diseases [to attend to]."[7]

Also in response to the news about AIDS, a wave of anti-homosexual rhetoric and actions took shape. Stereotypical views of homosexuals, combined with ignorance about the disease, promoted a discourse of condemnation of people with AIDS [12]. Fear of the disease resulted in discrimination against people with AIDS. In fact, these fears have later resulted in the systematic violation of the human rights of people with HIV in hospitals, clinics and their work places. There are multiple reports and testimonials about doctors and nurses who would refuse to come close to a person with AIDS, would deny treatment and care, and, in extreme cases, would leave patients without any sanitary care or food for days for fear of catching HIV [17, 18, 19].[8] There have also been many cases of people who were fired from their jobs after being tested for HIV antibodies, many times without having given consent for the test. These cases have occurred in banks, private corporations, and state companies such as PEMEX, the state's petroleum company. In one legal case involving PEMEX, after months of legal battles, a federal court ordered that the worker be reinstated in his job, establishing an important legal precedent [21, 22].

In September of 1985, the attention to AIDS was displaced by another unexpected disaster. An earthquake measuring 8.5 in the Richter scale shook about half of the country's territory causing major damage in Mexico City and killing several thousand people.

The earthquake was a pivotal event in Mexico that influenced many spheres, including AIDS. Many analysts see it as the trigger for the real earthquake that was still about to happen [23]. Governmental confusion and lack of preparedness for the event, and the repression of thousands who sought to help in the rescue efforts, made many Mexicans aware of the limited participation of civil society in political decision making. Many potential volunteers felt indignation when the military prevented them from reaching collapsed buildings due to the federal government's fear of a popular uprising. However, despite the controls, extensive popular organizing took place during the months after the earthquake, which taught many Mexicans the value of civil participation in issues normally controlled by the state [23].

---

[6] Dr. Martha Céspedes, quoted in [12], p. 31, my translation.

[7] Dr. Guillermo Ruiz Palacios, quoted in [12], p. 31, my translation.

[8] For reports of human rights violations in AIDS see [20] and *Sociedad y SIDA,* a monthly supplement of the Mexico City newspaper *El Nacional* where many cases have been documented.

Politically speaking, the consequences were many. Calls for democratization and for an end to the unquestioned sixty-year-old power of the official party gained renewed popularity [23].[9] Another example is the government's recent acknowledgment of human rights violations in Mexico. This development, which was partly a result of community organizing and political pressure, has stimulated and validated the involvement of nongovernmental groups in the investigation of cases, including those cases affecting people with AIDS.[10] From the perspective of AIDS prevention, what seems most important about the earthquake is the emergence of a new consciousness about the role of civil organizations in public life. The earthquake provided the leeway for the formation of new nongovernmental organizations (NGOs) attending to a variety of social problems, including AIDS [24, 25]. The politics of AIDS prevention in Mexico have been greatly influenced by the relationship between the state and NGOs, and the NGOs' demands for government accountability.

CONASIDA AND THE NON-GOVERNMENTAL AIDS GROUPS

After the initial denial about AIDS in the Mexican government waned, international pressure from the World Health Organization resulted in the first official effort to combat the spread of the disease. In 1986, the Mexican government created CONASIDA—the National Council of AIDS—which was made official by presidential decree the following year [12]. WHO had asked that governments establish national AIDS councils, which would administer international prevention funds channeled through its AIDS program [26]. CONASIDA was to become the recipient and administrator of the bulk of the international money for AIDS prevention that flowed to Mexico.

Parallel to the creation of CONASIDA, a number of existing groups around the country (labelled *grupos civiles*), and some newly created ones, began independent efforts to fight AIDS in their own communities. The development of these NGOs had three stages:

1. The first civil groups to respond were those of homosexuals who had been actively fighting for their rights since the late 1970s. *GHOL* (Homosexual Liberation Group), Colectivo Sol (Collective of the Sun), *Círculo Cultural Gay* (Gay Cultural Circle), *FHAR* (Homosexual Revolutionary Action Front), and *Guerrilla Gay*, among other groups, had organized political rallies, marches, cultural events in support of homosexual liberation. Because

---

[9] In the 1988 presidential elections, Carlos Salinas de Gortari received merely 52 percent of the popular vote and won through actions that many analysts classified as the most complicated fraud in Mexican electoral politics [23].

[10] As a result the government created a National Human Rights Commission that includes a number of prominent intellectuals and activists to officially conduct the investigations [23].

AIDS was mostly affecting homosexual men, most of these groups initiated prevention activities and advocacy for the rights of people with AIDS.

2. Other new community-based groups were formed with an exclusive focus on AIDS. Most of these NGOs were run by homosexuals and lesbians, prostitutes, blood donors, or people with HIV and their relatives [24]. As in other countries, the people responding to AIDS were those already affected or those who could see the threat of the disease close at hand. Several of these groups grew as a result of the renewed emphasis on nongovernmental action after the 1985 earthquake, and some, like *Brigadistas Contra el SIDA* (Rescue Workers Against AIDS), had originated from the homosexual participation in the post-earthquake rescue efforts [24]. Among the AIDS NGOs were the *Fundación Mexicana para la Lucha contra el SIDA* (Mexican Foundation for the Fight Against AIDS), *CHECCOS* (Humanitarian Committee of Shared Efforts Against AIDS in Guadalajara), *Azomalli, Ave de México* (Mexican Volunteer Educators/Friends), *GIS-SIDA* (Social Investigation Groups for AIDS and Human Rights), and *Organización SIDA Tijuana* (Tijuana AIDS Organization).

3. Soon after the initiation of civil efforts against AIDS, many groups realized that there were two fronts: On the one hand, CONASIDA was emerging as a large organization with resources to fund programs. On the other, the NGOs were small, independent and with no coordination in their efforts. Leaders of some of the groups began thinking about the need for consolidation that would create a stronger NGO front. Several efforts were undertaken to create networks of NGOs, including the formation of *Mexicanos contra el SIDA* (Mexicans Against AIDS), which had 22 member groups nationally in 1992 [27] and the *Red Nacional de Comunicación y Solidaridad Contra el SIDA* (National Network of Communication and Solidarity Against AIDS) with three member groups [28]. Consolidation has proven to be very difficult, however, due to several barriers. One is ideological differences among the groups. Galván et al. identify the political persuasions of the NGOs as ranging from the far left and anarchism to center-left and democratic liberalism [29]. A second problem that these authors note is that many of the groups to be consolidated have very poor organizational structures and programs. In the absence of performing effective AIDS prevention work, each group's legitimacy becomes peculiarly dependent upon the public perception that they are in the vanguard of the struggle.[11] To consolidate, then, is to surrender their identity and

---

[11]This issue is not made explicit in most of the writings about AIDS in Mexico, because the writers tend to be sympathetic to NGOs and to present them as a front that opposes the government. However, the reality of leadership conflicts has emerged repeatedly in conversations with the heads of different groups both in Mexico City and Guadalajara, who furiously claim their leadership and minimize the importance of the work of other NGOs.

popular appeal. Furthermore, when groups actually have joined together to create umbrella structures, the result is merely a new name while the weaknesses in programs remain [29].

THE POLITICS OF FUNDING

Underlying all the programmatic difficulties of NGOs is the problem of financing that most of them face. This is in striking contrast with the strength and level of funding available to CONASIDA. As mentioned before, WHO channels its own and other international funds for AIDS prevention to CONASIDA. Until recently, these funds were CONASIDA's only source of support, and the agency has the power to decide either to administer them or to use them to fund other projects. The agency, however, has mostly used the funds to support its own programs.

Overall, most NGOs have survived on the little money provided by their members and from small donations collected at events. Generally speaking, few of these groups have any significant experience in grant writing and development, and, until recently, they had been able to attract only small international donations and in-kind donations of condoms and brochures for their outreach. As a result, their programs have been very limited and in some cases almost nonexistent. As Galván Díaz et al. point out, only some of these groups (the ones they call "mature organizations") have been capable of establishing effective programs, while others have been mostly fancy labels for good intentions with no practical results [29].

Some of the NGOs, however, have begun to be the recipients of larger sums of international money. *Colectivo Sol*, for instance, has received several grants from renowned foundations, including Ford and MacArthur, that amount to almost half a million dollars in less than three years. Among its programs are the publication of *Acción en SIDA*, an AIDS newsletter for Latin American NGOs; a Latin American networking program for human rights and advocacy; an education program to promote sexual health; a clearinghouse for AIDS related materials, annotated bibliographies, reference lists, and technical assistance for bibliographical consultation; and the publication of *Del Otro Lado*, a magazine for homosexual men and women. Colectivo Sol currently has a staff of twelve and six volunteers.[12]

Juan Jacobo Hernández, the group's director, explains their success as resulting from a recognition of the need for professionalization. He emphasizes that most NGOs in Mexico focus on political activism to the exclusion of organizational planning, and this prevents them from accessing international funding. In his opinion, the international funds of the kind received by *Colectivo Sol* have always

[12]Personal communication with Juan Jacobo Hernández, director of *Colectivo Sol,* on July 29, 1993.

been available, but the NGOs have not had the grantwriting expertise, and have not adequately followed the guidelines established by foundations for grant proposals. In the case of *Colectivo Sol*, an initial grant that was offered to them during a site visit served as a springboard for additional fundraising to ensure continuation and expansion of their efforts. Today, the group writes its own grants and has built up a resumé that ensures a name for itself among new potential funders.

Yet, although this success story represents the future directions available to NGOs in Mexico, it is atypical. Even today, the contrast between the more common experience of Mexican AIDS NGOs and their counterparts in the United States is striking. In the United States, the NGOs created to fight AIDS have been capable of attracting private funding, first from middle class gay donors, and later from the community at large and private foundations. In Mexico, there has been no tradition of giving among the middle class. This has prevented any systematic efforts to capture individual donations. In addition, the conservative character of most large local foundations has prevented access to large private donations. And, third, the NGOs themselves have had little access to learning the skills needed to organize fundraising from private sources [25]. In the United States, for instance, fundraising courses for non-profit organizations are readily available, and AIDS groups have effectively organized major fundraising events such as the AIDS Walk and the AIDS Dance-a-Thon in San Francisco that, together, raise almost three million dollars every year. But, ultimately, the main barrier that Mexican NGOs face is the overall financial crisis of the country as a whole, which makes fundraising events like those in San Francisco nothing but a dream.

Another major difference in funding patterns is the role that the U.S. government plays in the allocation of funds to NGOs. Unlike CONASIDA in Mexico, most U.S. government agencies involved in AIDS prevention have assumed the role of coordinating and directing civil efforts through the distribution of federal and local funds [30]. While the Mexican government was more aggressive and direct in establishing AIDS prevention programs, the U.S. government has distributed more funds to community-based groups. The funding role of government has been even stronger at the local level in U.S. cities. Cities that were heavily impacted by AIDS, such as San Francisco, have taken a strong role in developing funding programs for local nonprofit organizations.

In Mexico, no such tradition exists. In fact, the power of the Mexican state since the revolution of 1910 has been characterized by the centralization and administration of all public funds by the government, which is seen as the ultimate provider of services [23]. Having access to services is not, however, an automatic right. The state has created a complex system of patronage by which groups, usually clustered by occupation, must organize and demand services to receive them, and in turn offer their political support to the regime. This system has been labelled "corporatism" by political analysts [23]. In practical terms, this means that the state controls the bulk of funds for social services, and their distribution has a very strong political undertone: the funds are overtly used to extract votes and to pacify oppositional forces. A second consequence is the pervasive dependency of civil society on the state and the resulting absence of strong nongovernmental institutions created by common people.

CONASIDA is a somewhat anomalous case in that it explicitly tried to move away from assuming a role as the dispenser of funds. In an interview in 1991, CONASIDA's director declared that "CONASIDA does not distribute funds for people to implement their ideas" [31, p. 5]. He added that the organization was considering the possibility of funding new projects, but he did not clarify whether any of those projects would take place outside of CONASIDA. This lack of funding, combined with what many NGOs perceived as the inability of CONASIDA to serve their particular communities, created confrontational relationships between the agency and community-based groups. Although the agency had effectively avoided establishing a paternalistic relationship with the NGOs, by monopolizing international funds CONASIDA had also limited their channels to seek international funding independently.

The NGOs, on the other hand, have been split in their opinion about what to do about CONASIDA's funds. Some openly advocated for the governmental agency to dispense money to civil groups [32]. Some others insisted that CONASIDA should use the available funds in its own programs but should also be held accountable for that use [29]. While both approaches involve some risk, the latter seems particularly problematic in so far as it reinforces the subordination of civil society to the state.

This tension between NGOs and the state was evident not only at the federal level, but also at the state and local levels. In Guadalajara, for instance:

> the NGOs . . . asked that the director of COESIDA [the State AIDS Council] resign arguing that the prevention campaigns are poor and that COESIDA spends only 20% of its budget on prevention. The rest, they say, is spent in administration or to improve the director's image . . . Without denying the work performed by NGOs, [COESIDA's director] Díaz Santana says that those organizations are sometimes more worried about financial support than about concrete work. Although he did not provide names, he stated that more than one [NGO] is looking for a solution for its financial problems rather than doing true educational campaigns [32, p. 3, my translation].

From this quote, it is evident that although the problems between the state and the NGOs were strongly motivated by the distribution of financial resources, they extended to the level of the programs themselves. While the NGOs perceived that the government was not being effective with the money that it spent on AIDS prevention, the government charged that by demanding funds, NGOs were oriented to self-benefit rather than service. In Díaz Santana's comment there is the assumption that an NGO does not need to have a comfortable financial situation to do its work, let alone pay a salary to its full time members.

Beginning in 1992, with a new administration in CONASIDA, the working relationship between the organization and the NGOs appears to be becoming closer. Some of the groups have begun to receive "seed funding" to initiate their efforts. In one instance, the organization has worked closely with one of the NGOs in the development of an educational video for bisexual men.[13] The Mexico City AIDS hotline, TelSIDA, has also coordinated efforts with an NGO, *Voz Humana* (Human Voice), which provides telephone information during evenings.[14] These examples may indicate a greater willingness of all parties involved to work together toward common goals. However, because of the differences in funding and organization that remain, CONASIDA's ability to implement prevention efforts still contrasts sharply with that of the NGOs. The characteristics of the educational programs for AIDS in Mexico is the topic of the next section.

INTERVENTIONS TO PROMOTE SAFE SEX

CONASIDA has conducted mass media campaigns that include billboards, posters, brochures, radio and TV commercials. The campaigns are tied to a hotline in Mexico City where volunteers answer 3,000 calls monthly. CONASIDA also coordinates information centers and anonymous testing, and maintains CRIDIS (Regional Center for Exchange, Documentation, and AIDS Information), a library of academic and educational AIDS related materials.

Except for family planning campaigns, the Mexican government has no previous experience promoting behaviors in areas directly related to sexuality. In fact, when the government began to speak up about AIDS, its first actions were devoid of references to sexuality: the emphasis was on control of the blood supply. However, soon after its inception, CONASIDA began addressing openly condom use and safe sex. Around 1988, condoms were visible in billboards and TV ads and became a common household word for the first time in Mexican history. CONASIDA embraced condom use as the center piece of its educational message. In a fashion similar to the AIDS education that was taking place in the United States and Europe, its model was strongly influenced by social marketing techniques and by theories about dissemination of information. Interestingly, in direct contrast to the U.S. government response during the Reagan and Bush administrations, CONASIDA's efforts have been

---

[13] Personal communication with Dr. José Antonio Izazola, Conasida's Research Director, on June 10, 1993.

[14] Personal communication with Ms. Elvira Carrillo, Director of TelSIDA, on July 15, 1993.

bolder and less conservative, and have successfully shattered the taboo against condom advertising in television and the mass media in Mexico. In fact, perhaps motivated by the precedent set by CONASIDA, Mexican television now accepts advertising by condom manufacturers (which U.S. television networks do not).

With far fewer resources, the efforts of the NGOs concentrated on grassroots approaches for the dissemination of information. Outreach, for most groups, consists of distributing donated brochures and condoms, giving safe sex talks, and providing one-on-one safe sex counseling. In some instances, the NGOs have specialized in performing outreach in specific places and with specific populations, and have been adventurous enough to do AIDS prevention in places like the public baths where many men go to have sex.

Street outreach, however, has not been without its problems. There are reports of police repression against AIDS activists for what the police perceive as an attack on morality. In one instance in Zapopan, a suburb of Guadalajara, AIDS educators were harassed by policemen, who threatened to arrest them for passing out brochures and condoms in the main plaza and proceeded to escort them to the town limits. AIDS activists have strongly protested these actions as a violation of the constitution and of their rights. However, no official action was taken against the police [33].

The NGOs have also attempted to gain some access to the media. Most commonly, they have ensured their participation in talk shows and interviews. However, their efforts have also included the development of a *"radio novela,"* an AIDS soap opera written by a member of *"Mexicanos Contra el SIDA"* who successfully gained the support of a radio station in Mexico City and the collaboration of a famous TV soap opera actress [34, 35]. Another example is the publication of a monthly AIDS supplement, called *Sociedad y SIDA*, in one of the major newspapers in Mexico City. *GIS-SIDA*, an NGO that works mostly in the area of human rights, compiles and supplies the articles, and the newspaper publishes and distributes the supplement. The NGOs have also begun printing some educational materials and, as I indicated above, are beginning to success- fully tie together homosexual liberation and AIDS prevention in the publication of magazines targeting homosexual men and women.

Similar to CONASIDA, the NGOs operate under the assumption that condom use should be the central focus of prevention and that behavior change can be achieved through the dissemination of information. However, not all in Mexico agree with these assumptions. From the viewpoint of the political right, for instance, there should be no dissemination of information about condoms at all. Behavior change, for them, consists of a return to traditional values and sexual abstinence. For AIDS activists who are more oriented toward popular education and community organizing, the issue is whether dissemination of information is enough to ensure behavior change. AIDS activists are also concerned with the selection of target populations and the exclusion of homo- sexual men in mass media campaigns. In the following two sections, I will address the perspectives of the political right and AIDS activists' concerns about methods of prevention.

OPPOSITION FROM THE POLITICAL RIGHT

As in other countries, the political right in Mexico has reacted vehemently against AIDS education messages that speak openly about sex and that promote condom use. Immediately after the release of the first safe sex campaigns, the Catholic church, the National Action Party (whose Spanish acronym is PAN), and a group that opposes family planning called Provida (Pro-life, mocked as "ProSIDA" by AIDS activists) strongly condemned the governmental AIDS program as promoting homosexuality, promiscuity and social degeneration. As an alternative, they offered abstinence, strengthening of the traditional family, the good influence of parents to prevent the development of homosexuality in their children, and the need to praise the sanctity and moral soundess of the monogamous heterosexual marriage.

This reaction is not different from the opposition of U.S. fundamentalist groups toward AIDS prevention. However, what is different is the force with which the Mexican government counteracted this opposition and disregarded the right as being out of touch with Mexican reality. While in the United States the position of right wing groups was used to justify government inaction, in Mexico the right was much less effective in opposing more liberal educational efforts. Mexico has not had a Jesse Helms or a William Dannemeyer with enough power or political clout to actually prevent the federal government from spending funds on the promotion of condom use and safe sex.

There are several possible reasons for this phenomenon. The main one might be the historical separation between church and state in Mexico instituted in the 1850s by president Benito Juárez, who broke official relations with the Vatican, and took away the church's right to own property, and the priests' right to preach in public places or run for public office [23]. After the Mexican revolution of 1910, the relations between the church and the state became even more fully severed, resulting in the revolt of the "Cristeros"[15] in the 1920s and the emergence of civil conservative organizations that survive even today [38]. These groups and the Catholic church, however, remained somewhat marginal to the mainstream political life of Mexico in subsequent decades. Their only organized political party, the PAN, was considered until recently to be a minor force in opposition against the PRI, the party in power.

---

[15]The "Cristeros" were a guerrilla movement of ultraconservative Catholics who organized several revolts in central Mexico during the 1920s. Their efforts were repressed by the federal government and ultimately controlled. Recently, 26 Cristero leaders were beatified by Pope John Paul II, an event that caused controversy in Mexico [36, 37].

Yet, the efforts of the political right in Mexico cannot be ignored, especially as their power grows. President Salinas de Gortari has recently introduced changes in policy that have given the right greater power and new impetus for organizing. One of such changes was the restoration of diplomatic relations with the Vatican, and the reinstallation of the Church's rights to preach in public places, to rally, and to own property [23, 36, 39, 40]. The PAN has also emerged as a strong political force that has claimed the government of two Northern states (an unprecedented phenomenon given that the official party, the PRI, had held power in all the states for the last sixty years).

The question is whether the political right will be instrumental in preventing any significant progression in the development of AIDS prevention efforts. Although the work of CONASIDA and the NGOs has managed to reduce the constant misinformation of sensationalist media, the potential for new waves of intolerance should always be considered. When the opposition to the condom campaigns occurred, CONASIDA struck back, defending its approach and lashing out against tolerance and "backward" ideas. AIDS activists claim, however, that CONASIDA has suffered from the pressure of the right and has given in by shying away from the bold messages that it used in the past [12, 29].

An example of this change is the shifting tone of CONASIDA's campaigns. A series of TV spots in 1989 used the popular drawings and cards of the Mexican lottery (bingo). A group of people dressed in costumes similar to characters in the cards sits around a table playing. (In the game, the cards are drawn one by one and their names are read aloud.) In the TV spot, the reader gets to the card that represents death (a skull), and the group shivers. The card that follows is a new one in the game, labeled by CONASIDA "The Lifesaver," which portrays an unrolled condom. The metaphor suggested that playing lottery cards was similar to taking chances in life, and that the only safe chance to take against death was the condom. The characters, men and women, represented a diversity of ages, social classes, and ethnicities, using symbols embedded in the original game cards themselves. The result was a very culturally specific message that was charged with implicit sexuality and a clear promotion of condoms.

In contrast, a more recent campaign was much more subtle. In 1992 CONASIDA's TV ads showed a child asking questions about AIDS while a parent reads a newspaper (his face hidden behind the newspaper). When the parent puts the newspaper down, the viewer sees that his eyes are covered by a blindfold. The slogan that follows reads "take off the blindfold" meaning "open your eyes" and suggesting that parents should call TelSIDA, the national AIDS hotline in Mexico City for information. The message was that it was a responsibility of parents to become informed in order to answer their children's questions. The message, however, said nothing about condoms or safe sex.

Some writers argue that CONASIDA' efforts have been co-opted by the influence of the political right [41]. They see the change as a symptom that CONASIDA is not willing to put out bold messages anymore, and as a sign of a return to conservative family values. Furthermore, they criticize CONASIDA for the absence of positive references to homosexuality in their campaigns. However, from a different perspective this campaign has been one of the most successful ones, because it has made AIDS a relevant topic for a great number of families by using a challenging and visually striking message. In fact, the campaign has generated great interest that has translated into a large number of calls to TelSIDA, where the callers' concerns may be discussed openly and with explicit reference to condoms and safe sex. However, examples such as this one fail to indicate a consensus about what type of messages should be disseminated: For whom should the information be intended? What are the methods that should be used? This brings us to a discussion about the design of AIDS prevention messages.

WHAT TYPES OF AIDS PREVENTION?

Throughout the last decade, AIDS educators in the United States faced the dilemma of whether to acknowledge that some population groups have a higher risk for HIV, and thus to risk their stigmatization, or whether to emphasize that everyone is at risk if they practice certain behaviors. The advantage of the second approach is that it softens the perception of "risk groups" and focuses on risky behavior. The first approach, however, allows for specific communities to be alerted about the problem and to claim the need for targeted education.

AIDS activists in cities like San Francisco and New York, strongly advocated for the de-homosexualization of AIDS as a way to create awareness in the general community that would reduce the stigma attached to the disease [42]. However, after successfully getting across the message that everyone is at risk, activists discovered that funds for education of gay men began to wane. It seemed easier for many foundations and for the government to give funds to educate families, for instance, than to educate gay men. AIDS groups then began to emphasize that, although it is true that everyone is at risk, gay men are at a specially higher risk and have more educational needs regarding AIDS prevention [42].

These issues have been present in Mexico as well. After 1985, the media published multiple articles about the "pink pest" and attributed the disease to homosexuals and degenerates, proclaiming that social avoidance of such people would prevent the disease and calling for mandatory testing of people who were known to be homosexual. In fact, some cities in Mexico conducted raids of homosexuals and prostitutes [43], and in a town in Veracruz the local government went to the extreme of shaving the heads of gay men to ensure that everyone could recognize them and avoid them [12]. The president of CONASIDA at the time, Jaime Sepúlveda Amor, declared:

> The Secretariat of Health strongly condemns the persecution that homosexuals are suffering due to AIDS. We have utmost respect for the sexual preference

of every person. Ignorance about the causes of the disease and its transmission have resulted in the false notion that AIDS is caused by homosexuality, which creates the potential for exacerbation of antihomosexual attitudes [12, p. 45, my translation].

His voice was joined by those of intellectuals, defenders of human rights, and by one of the more progressive political parties.

After the popular perception that AIDS is connected to homosexuality was softened, if not eliminated, the official messages in mass media campaigns began to address the general population: first, by moving away from the concept of risk groups and emphasizing behavior, and second, by conveying the sense that anyone could get AIDS. In fact, although AIDS has affected homosexual and bisexual men disproportionately, CONASIDA has never launched a mass media campaign addressing that population or printed materials that show two men together in their graphics. And, because they lacked the funds, NGOs had also not been able to do it. In practical terms, what this has meant is a lack of educational materials for one of the groups at highest risk for HIV. There are indications, however, that this might be changing: CONASIDA has recently produced safe sex videos for homosexual men and for bisexual men, one of them in collaboration with an NGO in Mexico City, a type of project that would be unimaginable for the U.S. federal government to undertake or fund.

On a more general level, although there have been posters and materials targeted at other groups such as women, students, and prostitutes, it is unclear whether using those media is effective in achieving behavior changes in those populations. Many U.S. AIDS activists have recognized that the dissemination of information by itself does not guarantee a change in behavior. Several barriers that may strongly interfere with intentions to assume healthy behaviors have been identified, particularly among educators working with people of color [44-49]. The effects of poverty, inequality in sexual relations, and the oppression of women and homosexuals, among others, are social problems that may come in the way of AIDS prevention. Common examples of the effects of these problems are the inability of many Latinas—given their relative powerlessness in relationships with men—to convince their male partners to use condoms, the agreement of male hustlers to not use a condom when their clients offer to pay them more that way, and the coercive exchange of sex for crack between sellers and female users.

In Mexico, some officials and health educators have recognized similar local barriers to safe behavior. However, little has been done to find alternative AIDS education methods that address such social barriers. In an interview in 1988, Gloria Ornelas, executive director of CONASIDA at the time, declared: "it is not enough to provide information. That does not guarantee a change in conduct. We have launched mass media campaigns, but unfortunately they lack the credibility that we wish they had" [26, p. 309]. But the alternative that she offers is the provision of information in face-to-face interaction—a solution that fails to address those problems of power and inequality.

Rosas comes closer to the recognition of the social barriers for AIDS prevention [50]. He bases his analysis on his experience teaching condom use in places where men go to have public sex. He describes an appalling lack of knowledge about sexuality: people who learn about sex through trial and error and with no previous exposure to any sex education. He also addresses the effects of homophobia, and the difficulties of being an AIDS educator in an erotophobic environment. These two factors are not only barriers to effective AIDS prevention in Mexico but can even make the work of AIDS educators potentially dangerous. Last year, a prominent AIDS activist was murdered with two other homosexual men in his apartment in Mexico City. Since then, there have been more than 30 unexplained murders of homosexuals throughout Mexico, including the slaying of a transvestite leader in Chiapas [51-55].

Rosas's article concludes with a series of recommendations for the future of AIDS education in Mexico: First, he argues that AIDS educators in Mexico must stop using foreign educational models that ignore cultural differences. Second, he criticizes the tendency to use Freirian educational methods in a superficial way, and insists upon a true commitment to social change [56]. Third, he points out that no studies have assessed the efficacy of mass media campaigns in Mexico. Fourth, he calls for the integration of methods of community education in AIDS prevention. Finally, he emphasizes the difficulties faced by middle class educators doing AIDS prevention with working class communities that may operate with different cultural codes, and he notes how difficult it is to gain entry into those communities.

As this summary illustrates, questioning the indiscriminate use of U.S. AIDS prevention methods is an essential task in Mexico. A more in-depth analysis of the social and cultural conditions of AIDS in Mexico, in contrast to those of the United States, might provide a path to adapt and modify the methods. Furthermore, because many of the barriers to AIDS prevention in Mexico are probably influenced by broader social problems such as poverty, discrimination, and social inequality, a consideration of popular education, community organizing, and other methods for social change might prove to be useful in developing new AIDS prevention methods.

The need for the connection between AIDS prevention and social change is stated even more clearly by those who acknowledge that many Mexicans assign a low priority to AIDS in the list of everyday problems that they face:

> Street children are more concerned with having something to eat; sex workers are most preoccupied with having work to support themselves and their children; for young people, exploring sex takes precedence over any concerns about disease [57, p. 6, my translation].

However, even these authors fail to recognize the far-reaching implications of their statement and end up recommending that community organizing be used to disseminate more information about the disease. What is missing is the link between the broad political and social problems and the effects of those problems on the lives of individuals and communities. Rather than using community organizing solely to disseminate information, prevention aimed at behavior change could be integrated into larger efforts to achieve cultural and social changes that are badly needed. What this requires, among other possible strategies, is an effort to coalesce with broader political causes and to question Mexican society and culture at a deeper level: to promote open discussion about sexuality, homosexuality, and women's rights, even if the results are controversial; to confront rightist ideology and question the anti-AIDS prevention policies of the Catholic church; and to encourage street activism as a way to raise a voice that reaches the society at large.

CONCLUSION: THE CHALLENGES AHEAD

In this chapter, I have touched upon a number of broad social issues and epidemiological patterns that affect both the development of effective AIDS prevention and the individuals' potential for implementing behavior changes. In my opinion, the key to the success of AIDS prevention in Mexico lies in the fulfillment of two large social and political projects: 1) a greater participation of the civil society accompanied by a greater intersection of AIDS prevention with other struggles for social change, and 2) the careful evaluation of current methods and the creation of new ones that are more responsive to Mexican society, in two senses—avoiding the simple importation of methods developed for other cultures; and transcending the current narrow focus on the provision of information.

Preventing AIDS in Mexico appears to be much more complex than what the simple dissemination of information about condoms can achieve. I have tried here to identify some of the issues to be considered, but there are many unanswered questions about the specific changes that would make AIDS prevention more effective.

In the area of civil participation, for instance, there seems to be a clear need for actions that improve the conditions of the NGOs, including their level of funding, stability, and programmatic quality. However, the possibilities for such actions are wide open. What can CONASIDA and the NGOs do to increase available funding for AIDS educational programs? CONASIDA might decide to be a catalyst to ensure funding for NGOs, aid them in developing grant-writing skills, and encourage them to bid directly to international foundations. Conceivably, the NGOs themselves might decide to pursue the development of a culture of funding from the state and other private sources from in and outside Mexico, including the organization of fundraising events.

Another set of questions pertains to the development of administrative and programmatic skills in the NGOs. How can the groups focus their attention on the development of new educational strategies and longer term planning for their activities? How can they begin to address the barriers to behavior change and develop new educational methods? And, on an even broader political level, how can the survival of a progressive approach to AIDS prevention be ensured? The boom of political rightist ideology, and the recent violations of the human rights of homosexuals, people with AIDS, and AIDS activists, indicate the possibility of greater repressive actions against AIDS prevention. The question is whether the NGOs and CONASIDA will be able to defend against conservative forces if there is a larger wave of anti-AIDS education attacks. Most importantly, can stronger NGOs have a better chance of organizing and forming coalitions to combat homophobia, repression of prostitutes, inequality of women, and violations of human rights, among other political goals?

The evaluation of AIDS methods implies a fundamental research task. First, the increasing awareness of the problems with importing foreign methods could be used as a departure point for the development of research about sexuality, gender relations, the effects of poverty on AIDS, and other topics in the Mexican context. Second, the experience of popular organizations in Mexico can provide a foundation for research about the expansion of AIDS education methods. Ultimately, the goal would be to include community empowerment and social mobilization as vehicles for behavioral change, rather than relying simply on the provision of information. A research agenda in these two broad areas might provide much needed data for the reformulation of AIDS education strategies.

Despite all the challenges described in this chapter, Mexico might be better equipped than other countries to develop innovative AIDS prevention methods. The robust governmental response to AIDS, the experience that the NGOs are gaining in community work, the incipient collaboration between CONASIDA and the NGOs, and the long tradition of popular education that exists in Mexico, for instance, might be a strong starting point to reevaluate existing programs and define new ones. For innovation to happen, however, AIDS educators and researchers must unleash their creativity and be willing to allow the fight against larger social maladies to take its part in their work.

AIDS prevention has already created a small crack in the political mirror of Mexico. A close inspection of the social factors that currently limit educational efforts may prove to be crucial in ensuring that future interventions achieve a greater impact in the control of the epidemic and the betterment of the Mexican population.

REFERENCES

1. INDRE—Instituto Nacional de Diagnóstico y Referencia Epidemiológicos, *Boletín Mensual de SIDA/ETS*, México, 7:2, pp. 2356-2373, February 1993.

2. S. Ruiz Velasco and F. Aranda Ordaz, Short-Term Projections of AIDS Cases in Mexico, *Human Biology, 64*:5, pp. 741-755, 1992.

3. J. L. Valdespino y M. de L. García, Epidemiología del SIDA en México. Logros y Nuevos Retos [AIDS Epidemiology in México. Accomplishments and New Challenges], *Sociedad y SIDA, 14*, pp. 8-9, November 1991.

4. AIDS: Growing Problems and a Search for More Effective Answers, *Notimex*, April 21, 1992.

5. AIDS Detected in 2,200 Mexican Women by 1991, *Notimex*, January 26, 1992.

6. A. Pérez López et al. Prevalencia de la Infección por Virus de la Inmunodeficiencia Humana (VIH) y Relación con Otras Enfermedades Transmitidas Sexualmente en un Grupo de Prostitutas en Huixtla, Chiapas [HIV Prevalence and Relationship With Other Sexually Transmitted Diseases in a Group of Prostitutes in Huixtla, Chiapas], *Revista de Investigación Clínica, 43*, pp. 45-47, 1991.

7. Centers for Disease Control and Prevention (CDC), *HIV/AIDS Surveillance Report*, February 1993.

8. R. Morales, Migración y VIH. Algunos Factores Explicativos [Migration and HIV. Some Explanatory Factors], *Sociedad y SIDA, 28*, p. 5, January 1993.

9. Health Minister Compares Mexican AIDS Problems With Those of Africa, *Notimex*, May 16, 1992.

10. E. Vázquez-Valls et al. Efecto de la Legislación Sanitaria Contra el VIH en la Donación de Sangre en Guadalajara, México [Effects of Sanitary Legislation Against HIV in Blood Donation in Guadalajara, Mexico], *Salud Pública de México, 32*:1, pp. 38-42, 1990.

11. C. Avila et al., The Epidemiology of HIV Transmission among Plasma Donors, Mexico City, Mexico, *AIDS, 3*, pp. 631-633, 1989.

12. M. Mejía, SIDA: Historias Extraordinarias del Siglo XX [AIDS: Extraordinary Stories of the 20th Century], in *El SIDA en México: Los Efectos Sociales*, F. Galván Díaz (ed.), Universidad Autónoma Metropolitana, México, D.F., pp. 17-57, 1988.

13. J. L. Valdespino Gómez, et al., Patrones y Predicciones Epidemiológicas del SIDA en México [AIDS Epidemiological Patterns and Predictions in Mexico], *Salud Pública de México, 30*:4, July-August 1988.

14. R. Morales, Sexo con Plenitud a Pesar del VIH/SIDA [Sex With Fulfillment Despite HIV/AIDS], *Sociedad y SIDA, 13*, pp. 1-3, October 1991.

15. M. Hernández et al. Sexual Behavior and Status for Human Immunodeficiency Virus Type 1 among Homosexual and Bisexual Males in Mexico City, *American Journal of Epidemiology, 135*:8, pp. 883-894, 1992.

16. M. S. Flores-Castañeda et al., Anticuerpos Anti-virus Linfotróficos de Células T Humanas en Sujetos de Alto Riesgo Para la Infección por VIH en Monterrey [HTLV-1 Antibodies in Subjects with High Risk for HIV Infection in Monterrey], *Revista de Investigación Clínica, 44*, pp. 37-42, 1992.

17. R. Alvarez, Pacientes y Médicos. Entrevistas [Patients and Physicians. Interviews], in *El Sida en México: Los Efectos Sociales*, F. Galván Díaz (ed.), Universidad Autónoma Metropolitana, México, D.F. pp. 161-169, 1988.

18. L. Cárdenas, Dramatismo, Esperanza y Frustración. Dos enfermos de SIDA. Entrevistas [Drama, Hope and Frustration. Two People with AIDS. Interviews], in *El Sida*

en *México: Los Efectos Sociales*, F. Galván Díaz (ed.), Universidad Autónoma Metropolitana, México, D.F. pp. 173-179, 1988.

19. Robledo Valencia, Luz Adriana, Para Mi Fue un Poco Morir, Casi el Fin. Testimonio [For Me It Was Like Dying. Almost the End. Testimony], in *El Sida en México: Los Efectos Sociales*, F. Galván Díaz (ed.), Universidad Autónoma Metropolitana, México, D.F., pp. 183-190, 1988.

20. F. Galván Díaz (ed.), *El Sida en México: Los Efectos Sociales* [*AIDS in Mexico: The Social Effects*], Universidad Autónoma Metropolitana, México, D.F., 1988.

21. F. Galván Díaz y F. Luna Millán, Walter Vs. PEMEX ¿Prevalecerá el Derecho? [Walter versus PEMEX: Will the Law Prevail?], in *Sociedad y SIDA, 24*:1, September 1992.

22. G. Pereyra, Caso PEMEX. SIDA y Derechos Humanos [PEMEX Case: AIDS and Human Rights], in *Sociedad y SIDA, 27*:1, December 1992.

23. T. Barry (ed.), *Mexico. A Country Guide*, The Inter-Hemispheric Resource Center, Albuquerque, New Mexico, 1992.

24. A. Díaz Betacourt, De la Lucha Contra el SIDA: Ser y Quehacer de las ONGs en Mexico [About the Fight Against AIDS: Identity and Tasks of the NGOs in Mexico], in *Sociedad y SIDA, 6*:5, March 1991.

25. P. Preciado, ONG's contra el SIDA a Debate [For Debate: NGOs Against AIDS], in *Sociedad y SIDA, 4*:7, January 1991.

26. L. Pérez Franco, El Centro Nacional de Información de CONASIDA: Entrevista con Gloria Ornelas [CONASIDA's National Information Center: Interview With Gloria Ornelas], in Galván Díaz, Francisco (ed.), *El SIDA en México: Los Efectos Sociales*, Universidad Autónoma Metropolitana, México, D.F., pp. 309-325, 1988.

27. *Mexicanos Por La Vida Contra el SIDA Newsletter*, July 1, 1992.

28. Red Nacional de Comunicación y Solidaridad Contra el SIDA, in *Sociedad y SIDA, 6*:8, March 1991.

29. F. Galván Díaz, R. González Villarreal, y R. Morales, Del SIDA en México. Aspectos de Gobierno y Sociedad [Of AIDS in Mexico. Aspects of Government and Society], Appendix in Lumsden, Ian, *Homosexualidad, Sociedad y Estado en México* [*Homosexuality, Society and State in Mexico*], Solediciones, México, D.F., 1991.

30. D. Altman, *AIDS in the Mind of America*, Anchor Press, Doubleday, Garden City, New York, 1986.

31. D. A. Murillo, Dr. Manuel Ponce De León (interview), in *Amigos Contra el SIDA, 1*:1, pp. 5-7, September 1991.

32. A. Y. Reyes, EL VIH en Jalisco. ONG's y COESIDA [HIV in Jalisco. NGOs and COESIDA], in *Sociedad y SIDA, 29*:3, February 1993.

33. Policia de Zapopan: Luchar Contra el SIDA es Atentar a la Moral [Zapopan's Police: To Fight Against AIDS is to Attempt Against Morality], Sociedad y SIDA, 4:15, January 1991.

34. M. Palet, La Radio y el SIDA [Radio and AIDS], in *Sociedad y SIDA, 8*:6, May 1991.

35. A. Sánchez, Radio Novela [Radio Soap Opera], in *Sociedad y SIDA, 10*:3 , July 1991.

36. Mexican Church-State Relations Modified in 1992, *Notimex*, December 28, 1992.

37. Catholics Celebrate Beatification of Cristero `Martyrs', *Notimex*, November 22, 1992.

38. F. Barbosa Guzmán, *La Iglesia y el Gobierno Civil* [*The Church and the Civil Government*], Series "Jalisco desde la Revolución" Vol. VI, Universidad de Guadalajara, Guadalajara, 1988.
39. Mexican Clergy React Positively to Salinas' Address to Nation, *Notimex,* November 2, 1992.
40. Mexico's Renewed Relations With Vatican Meet With General Approval, *Notimex,* September 21, 1992.
41. Taller Documentación Visual, Jueces, Acusados y Abogados. SIDA y Culpabilidad [The Judges, the Accused, and the Attorneys: AIDS and Guilt], in *Sociedad y SIDA, 24*:1, September 1992.
42. R. Bayer, *Private Acts, Social Consequences. AIDS and the Politics of Public Health,* The Free Press, New York, 1989.
43. C. Monsiváis, SIDA y Homofobia: Furia Represiva [AIDS and Homophobia: Repressive Fury], in *Sociedad y SIDA, 5*:1, February 1991.
44. E. Guerrero Pavich, A Chicana Perspective on Mexican Culture and Sexuality, *Journal of Social Work and Human Sexuality, 4*, pp. 47-65, 1986.
45. H. Amaro, Considerations for Prevention of HIV Infection among Hispanic Women, *Psychology of Women Quarterly, 12*, pp. 429-443, 1988.
46. A. Carballo-Diéguez, Hispanic Culture, Gay Male Culture, and AIDS: Counseling Implications, *Journal of Counseling and Development, 68*, pp. 26-30, September 1989.
47. V. M. Mays, and S. D. Cochran, Issues in the Perception of AIDS Risk and Risk Reduction Activities by Black and Hispanic/Latina Women, *American Psychologist, 43*:11, pp. 949-957, November 1988.
48. C. Texidor de Portillo, Poverty, Self-Concept and Health: Experience of Latinas, *Women and Health, 12*:3-4, pp. 229-242, 1988.
49. V. De la Cancela, Minority AIDS Prevention: Moving Beyond Cultural Perspectives Towards Sociopolitical Empowerment, *AIDS Education and Prevention, 1*:2, pp. 141-153, 1989.
50. F. Rosas, Lecciones de Trabajo Comunitario [The Lessons of Community Work], *Sociedad y SIDA, 27*:10, December 1992.
51. U.S. Researchers Report Murders of Gays in Latin America, *Notimex,* March 10, 1993.
52. New Gay Killing Reported in Chiapas, *Notimex,* November 5, 1992.
53. Chiapas Governor Promises Investigation on Killings of Gays, *Notimex,* September 15, 1992.
54. Human Rights Groups Protest Wave of Gay Killings, *Notimex,* September 10, 1992.
55. Recent Murders Alarm Mexico's Gay Community, *Notimex,* September 4, 1992.
56. P. Freire, *Pedagogía del Oprimido* [*Pedagogy of the Oppressed*], Siglo XXI, México, 1970.
57. F. Rosas and J. J. Hernández, El SIDA y Nuestra Comunidad [AIDS And Our Community], in *Sociedad y SIDA, 24*:6, September 1992.

Contributors

The authors' affiliations coincide with the time the original chapters were written.

MARGARITA ALEGRÍA, University of Puerto Rico

MARIA ELENA ALVA, LIC, Apoyo a Programas de Población, Lima, Peru

D. MICHAEL ANDERSON, Ph.D., MPH, Health Media Lab, Washington, D.C.

GIOVANNI ANTUNEZ, MD, MPH, School of Public Health and Tropical Medicine, Tulane University

EDNA APOSTOL, Centro de Educacion, Prevencion, y Accion, Holyoke, Massachusetts

ELVA M. ARREDONDO, Duke University, Durham, North Carolina

DALILA BALFOUR, Centro de Educacion, Prevencion, y Accion, Holyoke

ROSARIO BARTOLINI, Instituto de Investigacion Nutricional, Lima-Peru

JANE T. BERTRAND, Tulane University, New Orleans

CLAIRE BRINDIS, Dr.P.H., University of California, San Francisco

DAVID BUCHANAN, Dr.P.H., University of Massachusetts, Amherst

MARGARITA BURGOS, Ph.D., South Carolina Department of Education, Columbia

HÉCTOR CARRILLO, MCP, MPH, School of Public Health, University of California, Berkeley

DANIELLE CASES, LIC, Apoyo a Programas de Población, Lima, Peru

XÓCHITL CASTEÑADA, MA, University of California

GEORGE P. CERNADA, Dr.P.H., University of Massachusets, Amherst

VIVIAN CHÁVEZ, MPH, Berkeley Media Studies Group, Berkeley, California

CARMEN CLAUDIO, Centro de Educacion, Prevencion, y Accion, Holyoke

ZOE CARDOZA CLAYSON, Sc.D., San Francisco State University

ANN L. COKER, University of South Carolina, Columbia

WILLIAM A. DARITY, Ph.D., Professor/Dean Emeritus, School of Public Health and Health Sciences, University of Massachusetts, Amherst

ROSARIO VERA DE BRICEÑO, MA, Apoyo a Programas de Población, Lima, Peru

LORI DORFMAN, Dr.P.H., Berkeley Media Studies Group, Berkeley, California

PAUL EPKIND, Dr.P.H., STD Program, Massachusetts Department of Public Health

PAMELA I. ERICKSON, Dr.P.H., Ph.D., University of Connecticut, Storrs

VINCENT E. GIL, Southern California College, Vanguard University, Costa Mesa

LISA K. GILBERT, Ph.D., American Social Health Association, Research Triangle Park, North Carolina

MEGAN GOTTEMOELLER, MPH, School of Public Health and Tropical Medicine, Tulane University

SYLVIA GUENDELMAN, DSW, University of California, Berkeley

C. MERCEDES HERNÁNDEZ, MPH, University of Massachusetts, Amherst

ELMER E. HUERTA, MD, MPH, Washington Cancer Institute at Washington Hospital Center, Washington, D.C.

KATE LORIG, RN, Dr.P.H., Stanford Arthritis Center, California

SARAH LYON-CALLO, MS, University of Massachusetts, Amherst

JOANI MARINOFF, Centro de Educacion, Prevencion, y Accion, Holyoke

GRACE MARQUIS, Ph.D., University of Alabama, Birmingham

MARIAN McDONALD, Dr.P.H., School of Public Health and Tropical Medicine, Tulane University

NANCY O'HARE, Centro de Educacion, Prevencion, y Accion, Holyoke

CATHERINE OLIVEROS, MPH, Loma Linda University, California

GAIL ORMSBY, MPH, Loma Linda University, California

KATHLEEN O'ROURKE, Ph.D., School of Public Health, University of Texas Houston, El Paso

FRANCISCO PAUC (formerly) DataPro S.A., Guatemala City, Guatemala

PATRICIA R. POPPE, MA, MS, Population Communication Services, The Johns Hopkins University, Baltimore, Maryland

BELINDA REININGER, Dr.P.H., University of South Carolina, Columbia

MARILYN RICE, Office of Substance Abuse Prevention, Rockville, Maryland

DONNA L. RICHTER, Ed.D., University of South Carolina, Columbia

MARIA RODRIGUEZ, Centro de Educacion, Prevencion, y Accion, Holyoke

NANCY ROMERO-DAZA, Ph.D., University of South Florida, Tampa

EMMANUEL RUDATSIKIRA, MD, MPH, Loma Linda University, California

EMMA SANCHEZ, MPH, Harvard University

CARLOS SANTIAGO, Centro de Educacion, Prevencion, y Accion, Holyoke

RUTH SAUNDERS, University of South Carolina, Columbia

CARA S. SIANO, MPH, Latino Health Institute, Springfield, Massachusetts

MERRILL SINGER, Ph.D., Hispanic Health Council, Hartford, Connecticut

M. IDALÍ TORRES, MSPH, Ph.D., University of Massachusetts, Amherst

ROBERT TUTHILL, Ph.D., University of Massachusetts, Amherst

THOMAS W. VALENTE, Ph.D., Population Communication Services, The Johns Hopkins University, Baltimore, Maryland

MILDRED VERA, University of Puerto Rico

ESPERANZA GARCIA WALTERS, RN, MPH, Santa Clara County Health Systems Agency, California

VICTORIA WARD, Columbia University, New York

MARGARET WEEKS, Ph.D., Institute for Community Research, Hartford, Connecticut

ROSE A. WILCHER, American Social Health Association, Research Triangle Park, North Carolina

SANDRA WITT, MPH, University of California, Berkeley

Index